BIG PICTURE PERSPECTIVES ON PLANETARY FLOURISHING

This book, split across two volumes, is a follow-up and companion to *Metatheory for the Twenty-First Century* (Routledge, 2016). All three of these volumes are the dialogical outcome of a multi-year symposia series wherein critical realists and integral theorists deeply engaged each other and their distinct but complementary approaches to integrative metatheory. Whereas *Metatheory for the Twenty-First Century* is primarily theoretical in its focus, *Big Picture Perspectives on Planetary Flourishing: Metatheory for the Anthropocene* aims to more concretely and practically address the complex planetary crises of a new era that many scholars now refer to as 'the Anthropocene'.

In this first of two new volumes, participants of the symposia series articulate a variety of 'big picture perspectives' and transformative interventions in the domains of society and economics, social psychology, and education. Together, these chapters demonstrate how integrative metatheory and its application can make powerful contributions to planetary flourishing in the Anthropocene.

With one of the defining characteristics of the Anthropocene being the sheer complexity and multi-valent nature of our interconnected global challenges, these volumes crucially present new forms of scholarship that can adequately weave together insights from multiple disciplines into new forms of metapraxis. As such, this book will be of interest to students, scholars, and practitioners in the areas of philosophy, social theory, critical realism, integral studies, metamodernism, and current affairs generally.

Nicholas Hedlund is a visionary philosopher working at the nexus of philosophy of science, worldviews, and socioecological transformation. He obtained his PhD in philosophy and social sciences from University College London, studying under the philosopher Roy Bhaskar. Nicholas also holds a master's degree in philosophy and religion, as well as one in psychology. He is director of the Eudaimonia Institute, an emerging social innovations lab for planetary flourishing. Nicholas was an exchange scholar at Yale University, executive director of the Integral Research Center, and organizer of the CR-IT symposia series. His work has appeared in numerous anthologies and peer-reviewed journals. He is co-editor of *Metatheory for the Twenty-First Century: Critical Realism and Integral Theory in Dialogue* (Routledge, 2016). Nicholas has received several academic honors including the Jacob Van Ek Scholar Award, the Honors Graduating Senior Scholarship Award, Best Paper Award at the Integral Theory Conference, and the Yale–UCL Bursary Award. He currently teaches at the California Institute of Human Science.

Sean Esbjörn-Hargens is Dean of Integral Education at the California Institute of Human Science. In 2011 he founded the MetaIntegral Foundation, a social impact network that supports change leaders around the world in applying integrative principles to projects and organizations. In 2018 he founded the Exo Studies Institute through which he is pioneering an integral approach to anomalous phenomena including UFOs/ETs. Sean combines a strong academic background in the philosophy of science and integrative metatheories with an open-hearted exploration of the mystery and multi-layered nature of reality. He has published and edited numerous articles, chapters, and books. He is the co-editor of both *Metatheory for the Twenty-First Century* (Routledge, 2016) and *Dancing with Sophia: Integral Philosophy on the Verge* (2019).

Routledge Studies in Critical Realism

Critical realism is a broad movement within philosophy and social science. It is a movement that began in British philosophy and sociology following the founding work of Roy Bhaskar, Margaret Archer and others. Critical realism emerged from the desire to realize an adequate realist philosophy of science, social science, and of critique. Against empiricism, positivism and various idealisms (interpretivism, radical social constructionism), critical realism argues for the necessity of ontology. The pursuit of ontology is the attempt to understand and say something about 'the things themselves' and not simply about our beliefs, experiences, or our current knowledge and understanding of those things. Critical realism also argues against the implicit ontology of the empiricists and idealists of events and regularities, reducing reality to thought, language, belief, custom, or experience. Instead critical realism advocates a structural realist and causal powers approach to natural and social ontology, with a focus upon social relations and process of social transformation.

Important movements within critical realism include the morphogenetic approach developed by Margaret Archer; critical realist economics developed by Tony Lawson; as well as dialectical critical realism (embracing being, becoming, and absence) and the philosophy of metaReality (emphasizing priority of the non-dual) developed by Roy Bhaskar.

For over 30 years, Routledge has been closely associated with critical realism and, in particular, the work of Roy Bhaskar, publishing well over 50 works in, or informed by, critical realism (in series including Critical Realism: Interventions; Ontological Explorations; New Studies in Critical Realism and Education). These have all now been brought together under one series dedicated to critical realism.

The Centre for Critical Realism is the advisory editorial board for the series. If you would like to know more about the Centre for Critical Realism, or to submit a book proposal, please visit www.centreforcriticalrealism.com.

Metatheory for the Twenty-First Century
Critical Realism and Integral Theory in Dialogue
Edited by Roy Bhaskar, Sean Esbjörn-Hargens, Nicholas Hedlund and Mervyn Hartwig

Critical Realism, Feminism, and Gender: A Reader
Edited by Michiel van Ingen, Steph Grohmann, and Lena Gunnarsson

The Morphogenesis of the Norwegian Educational System
Emergence and Development from a Critical Realist Perspective
Edited by Margaret S. Archer, Unn-Doris K. Bæck, and Tone Skinningsrud

Explaining Morality
Critical Realism and Moral Questions
Steve Ash

For more information about this series, please visit: www.routledge.com/Routledge-Studies-in-Critical-Realism-Routledge-Critical-Realism/book-series/SE0518

BIG PICTURE PERSPECTIVES ON PLANETARY FLOURISHING

Metatheory for the Anthropocene

Volume 1

Edited by Nicholas Hedlund and Sean Esbjörn-Hargens

LONDON AND NEW YORK

Cover image: © Getty Images

First published 2023
by Routledge
4 Park Square, Milton Park, Abingdon, Oxon OX14 4RN

and by Routledge
605 Third Avenue, New York, NY 10158

Routledge is an imprint of the Taylor & Francis Group, an informa business

© 2023 selection and editorial matter, Nicholas Hedlund and Sean Esbjörn-Hargens; individual chapters, the contributors

The right of Nicholas Hedlund and Sean Esbjörn-Hargens to be identified as the authors of the editorial material, and of the authors for their individual chapters, has been asserted in accordance with sections 77 and 78 of the Copyright, Designs and Patents Act 1988.

All rights reserved. No part of this book may be reprinted or reproduced or utilised in any form or by any electronic, mechanical, or other means, now known or hereafter invented, including photocopying and recording, or in any information storage or retrieval system, without permission in writing from the publishers.

Trademark notice: Product or corporate names may be trademarks or registered trademarks, and are used only for identification and explanation without intent to infringe.

British Library Cataloguing-in-Publication Data
A catalogue record for this book is available from the British Library

Library of Congress Cataloging-in-Publication Data
A catalog record for this book has been requested

ISBN: 978-1-138-85624-0 (hbk)
ISBN: 978-1-138-85625-7 (pbk)
ISBN: 978-1-003-14031-3 (ebk)

DOI: 10.4324/9781003140313

Typeset in Bembo
by Apex CoVantage, LLC

This volume is dedicated to Roy Bhaskar (1944–2014). Roy's unique combination of a beaming joyful heart with a fierce philosophical mind touched and inspired all of us. We are deeply grateful for the unwavering support and vision he brought to the CR-IT symposiums and their resulting volumes. May these volumes help carry the bright light of his life into the world serving to inspire the next generation of visionary scholar-practitioners.

CONTENTS

List of Figures and Tables ... ix
List of Contributors ... xi
Acknowledgements ... xv
Preface ... xvii
David Graeber and Steph Grohmann
Foreword ... xxiii
Michael E. Zimmerman

    Introduction: From Metatheory to Metapraxis for
    Planetary Flourishing ... 1
    Nicholas Hedlund and Sean Esbjörn-Hargens

PART 1
Society and Economics ... 27

1   The Quintuple Crisis: How Metatheory Contributes to
    Social Theory ... 29
    Hans Despain

2   Healthy versus Pathological Political–Economic Discourse
    and Policy: An Integral Political–Economic Treatment ... 48
    Kevin Bowman

3   Sustaining Spirit across Complexities of International
    Development in Relation to Indigenous Peoples ... 71
    Neil Hockey

PART 2
Social Psychology — 95

4 Applying Bhaskar's 'Four Moments of Dialectic' to Reshaping Cognitive Development as a Social Practice Using Laske's Dialectical Thought Form Framework — 97
   Otto Laske

5 On Realizing the Possibilities of Emancipatory Metatheory: Beyond the Cognitive Maturity Fallacy, Toward an Education Revolution — 122
   Zachary Stein

PART 3
Education — 149

6 Metatheory: The Ontological Turn in Mathematics Education Research — 151
   Iskra Nunez

7 Coalescing and Potentializing Integrative Higher Education: Complex Thought, Critical Realism, Integral Theory, and a Meta-Matrix — 169
   Gary Hampson and Matthew Rich-Tolsma

8 Getting Theory into Public Culture: Collaborations and Interventions Where Metatheorists Meet — 209
   Zachary Stein and Hans Despain

After Words: The Spirit of Evolution and Envelopment — 231
Frédéric Vandenberghe

Index — 260

FIGURES AND TABLES

Figures

1.1	Wilber's four quadrants	31
1.2	Bhaskar's four-planar social being	32
1.3	Wilber's inward and outward arcs	42
2.1	The portion of economic reality recognized or emphasized by political–economic type	52
2.2	Game 1: Two egoists and their short-term payoffs	58
2.3	Game 2: Two cooperators and their short-term payoffs	59
2.4	Game 3: A liberal cooperator and a conservative egoist and their short-term payoffs	60
4.1	Bhaskar's four eras of adult cognitive development	98
4.2	DTF as bridge between DCR and the language-suffused social world	100
4.3	The four phases of dialectical-thinking development in adults according to Basseches/Laske	101
4.4	The four transforms of dialectical thinking according to Bhaskar (1993)	102
4.5	The four classes of thought forms associated with MELD in DTF (P = 2E; C = 1M; R = 3L; T = 4D)	103
4.6	Cognitive behaviour graph of a manager	106
4.7	Social–emotional stage progression according to Kegan	108
4.8	Nexus between social–emotional meaning making and cognitive sensemaking in CDF	109
4.9	Social–emotional differences between cohorts	110
4.10	Epistemic limits (F) of six developmentally differing cohorts	110
4.11	CDF cohort typology	111

4.12 Cohort differences in the ability of handling complexity 112
4.13 The three DTF dialogue modes as used in teaching, coaching, and consulting 116
A.1 Wilber's four quadrants 246

Tables

2.1 The value and the failures associated with the private and public sectors 51
2.2 Less developed versus more developed agents by political–economic type 53
2.3 Two versions of the immature/mature type fallacy: reductionism and elevationism 54
2.4 Examples of stakeholder deflection of blame by stakeholder group 55
3.1 W(h)ither development post-Rio+20 and post-2015? 73
3.2 Australian Aboriginal and Biblical teachings about spirits and their activities 79
3.3 Community focus, identifying and defining needs 84
4.1 Compact table of DTF thought forms 104
4.2 IDM case study, thought form scoring sheet 114

CONTRIBUTORS

Kevin Bowman, PhD (12 February 1970–4 February 2016) was an Integral Economist and Professor who taught economics at Bloomsburg University, Augsburg College, Loyola University Chicago and at DeVry Chicago. He was the co-author of an economics textbook and published many articles in professional journals. He received his doctorate and master of arts in economics from University of Illinois Chicago and his bachelor of arts in economics from Indiana University. One of his lasting contributions to integrative thought is the work he did around developing an integral field theory.

Hans Despain, PhD, is Professor of Political Economy at Nichols College, where he also teaches courses on Great Ideas in the Western canon. He is a Visiting Professor of Economics and Finance at Saint Joseph University, Macao, China. He has taught at the University of Massachusetts, Amherst, Wesleyan University, and the University of Utah. He has published hundreds of articles in economics, education and pedagogy, and philosophy.

Sean Esbjörn-Hargens, PhD, is Dean of Integral Education at the California Institute of Human Science (CIHS). At CIHS his is also chair of the MA/PhD program in Integral Noetic Sciences. In 2011 he founded the MetaIntegral Foundation, a social impact network that supports change leaders around the world in applying integrative principles to projects and organizations. In 2018 he founded the Exo Studies Institute through which he is pioneering an integral approach to anomalous phenomena including UFOs/ETs. Sean combines a strong academic background in the philosophy of science and integrative metatheories with an open-hearted exploration of the mystery and multi-layered nature of reality. He has published and edited numerous articles, chapters, and books. His most recent books are *Metatheory for the Twenty-First Century* (Routledge, 2016) and *Dancing with Sophia: Integral Philosophy on the Verge* (2019).

David Graeber, PhD (12 February 1961–2 September 2020) was an American anthropologist, anarchist activist, and author known for his books *Debt: The First 5000 Years* (2011), *The Utopia of Rules* (2015), *Bullshit Jobs: A Theory* (2018), and *The Dawn of Everything: A New History of Humanity* (2021) with David Wengrow. He was a Professor of Anthropology at the London School of Economics. Graeber was a leading figure in the Occupy Wall Street movement, and is sometimes credited with having coined the slogan, 'We are the 99 percent'.

Steph Grohmann, PhD, is a Leverhulme Early Career Fellow at the Centre for Homelessness and Inclusion Health, University of Edinburgh. She received her doctorate in anthropology from Goldsmiths, University of London, and is the author of *The Ethics of Space*, an ethnographic monograph on the criminalization of squatting in the UK, and the edited volume *Critical Realism, Feminism and Gender* with Michiel van Ingen, PhD.

Gary Hampson, PhD (aka Neo Elder) was nominated for the Australian national award for his doctoral thesis on a postconventional approach to integral theory and education. As Senior Research Fellow at the Philosophy Department, Palacky University, Czech Republic, he lectured on such topics as the philosophy of quantum mechanics, education of the heart, and transformative higher education. He is currently writing a book of spiritual poetry inspired by Hafiz, developing a post-Jungian archetypal approach to queer theory and praxis, exploring integral exo studies and near-death experience research, and co-designing a strategy board game about dolphin communication. A member of the Ridhwan spiritual community, his creative engagement with life sits in service to deep ecological adaptation, postformal social justice, and human being and becoming. He currently resides in southwest England and London.

Nicholas Hedlund, PhD, is a visionary philosopher working at the nexus of philosophy of science, worldviews, and socioecological transformation. He obtained his PhD in philosophy and social sciences from University College London, studying under the philosopher Roy Bhaskar. Nicholas also holds a master's degree in philosophy and religion, as well as one in psychology. He is director of the Eudaimonia Institute, an emerging social innovations lab for planetary flourishing. Nicholas was an exchange scholar at Yale University, executive director of the Integral Research Center, and organizer of the CR-IT symposia series. His work has appeared in numerous anthologies and peer-reviewed journals. He is co-editor of *Metatheory for the Twenty-First Century: Critical Realism and Integral Theory in Dialogue*. Nicholas has received several academic honors including the Jacob Van Ek Scholar Award, the Honors Graduating Senior Scholarship Award, Best Paper Award at the Integral Theory Conference, and the Yale–UCL Bursary Award. He currently teaches at the California Institute of Human Science.

Neil Hockey, PhD, has over 40 years' community development experience in India, Malaysia, and Australia. With degrees in science, arts, and education, his PhD focused on frameworks for decolonizing research methodologies. His passion is helping transform social institutions, primarily from within marginalized and exploited communities, so as to benefit both Indigenous peoples and the modern societies in which they are now embedded. He remains committed to participatory action research projects strengthening Australasian Indigenous contributions to economies, building on existing links within and between marginalized or remote communities both locally and internationally.

Otto Laske, PhD, is founder and director of IDM, the Interdevelopmental Institute. Since its inception, he has been its Director of Education. In this capacity, he has developed and taught the methodology constructive developmental framework (CDF), a synthesis of adult-developmental research that includes a social–emotional component (ED), a cognitive component (CD), and a psychological component (NP). He has written numerous articles and three books. In his artistic work as a composer, poet, and visual artist, he has demonstrated dialectical thinking in its many forms outside of using verbal language.

Iskra Nunez, PhD, completed her doctoral dissertation at the Institute of Education, University of London under the supervision of Roy Bhaskar and Candia Morgan. Her research interests include philosophy, learning sciences, and mathematics. She has taught mathematics and education at a variety of institutions in the United States.

Matthew Rich-Tolsma, MPhil, FRSA, is an educator, organisational consultant, and independent scholar based in South Africa and The Netherlands. He is a sought after coach, mediator, and thinking-partner and has worked with a wide range of organisations and communities from rural school leaders in India to the board rooms of leading global companies. He has published both books and articles on a wide range of topics concerning transformative learning, leadership, and complex social challenges. Most recently he has critically evaluated the use of adaptive leadership frameworks in central Europe, and explored the use of empathic dialogue as a tool for engaging racism in South Africa. He previously served as a Fellow at the Philosophy Faculty at Palacky University, Czech Republic, and was a Carnegie Visiting Scholar at the Global Change Institute at Wits University, South Africa.

Zachary Stein, EdD, is philosopher of education working at the interface of psychology, metaphysics, and politics. He has published two books, including *Education in Time between Worlds*, along with dozens of articles. Co-founder of a non-profit and think tank; teacher of graduate students at Harvard, JFK University, and Meridian University; sought after lecturer and consultant, currently working on projects intending to roll back pollution and enclosure of the informational commons.

Frédéric Vandenberghe, PhD, is Professor of Sociology at the Institute of Philosophy and Social Sciences of the Federal University of Rio de Janeiro in

Brazil. He has published widely in the field of social theory. His most recent books are *What's Critical about Critical Realism? Essays in Reconstructive Social Theory* (Routledge, 2014); with Margaret Archer *Le réalisme critique: Une nouvelle ontologie pour la sociologie* (2019); and with Alain Caillé *For a New Classical Sociology: A Proposition, Followed By a Debate* (Routledge, 2020).

Michael E. Zimmerman, PhD, is Professor Emeritus at Tulane University and at the University of Colorado Boulder. He is the author of four books, more than 100 book chapters and peer-reviewed articles, and a leading anthology of environmental philosophy. An award-winning teacher, he co-directed Tulane's Environmental Studies Program for a decade, and spent four years as Director of the Center for Humanities and the Arts at the University of Colorado. His research interests include environmental philosophy, integral theory, Buddhism, Heidegger, Nietzsche, and anomalous phenomena.

ACKNOWLEDGEMENTS

This book, like its companion volume, *Metatheory for the Twenty-First Century: Critical Realism and Integral Theory in Dialogue* (Routledge, 2016), is the outcome of multiple years of dialogical engagement between critical realism and integral theory in which many people and a number of organizations and institutions played an invaluable role. First and foremost, we would like to thank our dear friend and comrade Roy Bhaskar—from the bottom of our hearts—for his visionary leadership, contributions to, and support of this project and beyond. Roy played a central role in the inception of this project, helping to shape it on all levels until his untimely death in November 2014. While he did not live to see this project to fruition, he made invaluable contributions to it, for which we are forever grateful. As such, we hereby dedicate this volume to Roy Bhaskar, his elevated and generous spirit in support of the deep dialogue these two volumes represent, and his ever-inspiring vision for a eudaimonistic society.

We would also like to thank Mervyn Hartwig, who played an essential role in the first half of this project, co-editing the previous companion volume with us, before deciding to step down in the wake of Roy's passing. Mervyn made important editorial contributions to the present volume as well, for which we are indebted.

Moreover, these two volumes (and the third forthcoming volume *Integrative Responses to the Global Metacrisis*) likely never would have happened had Mark Edwards not encouraged Sean Esbjörn-Hargens to check out critical realism at the 2008 Integral Theory Conference and had Markus Molz and the Institute for Integral Studies (Germany) not organized an international symposium in Luxembourg that brought together Roy Bhaskar and Mervyn Hartwig, and Sean Esbjörn-Hargens and Nicholas Hedlund. We are thankful to Mark and Markus for this.

In organizing all of the symposia, the lead role was taken by the Integral Research Center, and for this we are most grateful. Special thanks go to Ken Wilber and the

Integral Institute for largely funding the first symposium that got the engagement seriously under way, and to John F. Kennedy University for hosting it. For hosting the second, third, and fourth symposium we must thank the MetaIntegral Foundation, UCL Institute of Education, University College London, and Sonoma State University, respectively.

Other important roles were played by the International Centre for Critical Realism and the International Association for Critical Realism (London) and by the organizers of the 2013 and 2015 Integral Theory Conference, especially Mark Forman and Jordan Luftig (San Francisco Bay Area). Special thanks must go to Roy's partner, Rebecca Long, for her care and support of Roy at the San Francisco and London symposia, and for helping to organize the latter; and to Gary Hampson (AKA Neo Elder) for recording the proceedings in London. Thanks also to the *Journal of Integral Theory and Practice* and the *Journal of Critical Realism* for publishing important exchanges and articles arising from the dialogue.

We are thankful to David Graeber, Michael E. Zimmerman, and Frédéric Vandenberghe for their support of this project and their exceptional contributions in the preface, foreword, and afterword, respectively. We were very sad to have lost David whose passing at the end of this project left a big hole in our hearts. His contributions towards making the world a better place are without parallel. He is missed by many. We also want to acknowledge our friend and colleague Kevin Bowman, who sadly also passed on during this project. We are proud to include Kevin's contribution to this volume and thank him deeply for his life's work and contributions to the political and economic aspects of integral studies. He also left a generous donation to the MetaIntegral Foundation, which was used in part to help with costs associated with this volume.

We are deeply indebted to Alan Jarvis of Routledge (the publisher of a range of book series on critical realism, including the present series) for his warm encouragement and support for our project and his ready willingness to go to a second volume when the first one burgeoned beyond its bounds. Many thanks also to Alice Salt (and her team) at Routledge for her excellent editorial assistance. Finally, we want to thank the many participants in the symposia for their creative input and our co-authors for their lively and brilliant input and patience with the long trajectory of this project.

PREFACE

David Graeber† and Steph Grohmann

This book (both Volumes 1 and 2) is based on a multi-year symposium (2010–2015) that Roy Bhaskar was working on and helping to lead at the time of his passing. This symposium was an ongoing mutually transforming dialogue between two groups of scholar-practitioners: critical realists and integral theorists. Roy was very passionate about this academic encounter as it represented for him the kind of applied philosophical discourse that is needed to transform ourselves and the world around us. In many ways this symposium and its resulting volumes embody and express the core essence of Roy's life and vision of a better world. Thus, it seemed best to preface this volume with a comment on the overall significance of his work.

When Roy Bhaskar passed away on 19 November 2014, after a long period of ill health, the world—certainly the world of philosophy, but also of all disciplines engaged in thinking about their own theoretical foundations—lost one of the most original and prolific contributors to our thinking about the nature of reality and scientific inquiry.[1] It is still somewhat amusing to note that this most philosophical of minds did not actually start out as a philosopher—Roy Bhaskar started his career as a lecturer in economics at Oxford University in the late 1960s, and only later turned his attention to questions of metatheory underlying that field, as well as many others. Despite the highly abstract nature of his resulting work, Roy was driven to it not primarily by theoretical concerns, but rather by a practical problem: his discomfort with the fact that economic science had virtually nothing useful to say about the real-world issues of global inequality and poverty that had inspired him to turn to the study of economics to begin with. That never ceased to be true. Roy always saw his philosophical work as a form of political action. It was meant to change the world. For him this in no way undermined its rigorous nature. In fact, he would argue it meant the work had to be more rigorous, since so much more rested on getting things right.

A word in way of background: born in Teddington, west London, to an Indian father, Raju Nath Bhaskar, a GP, and an English mother, Kumla (nee Marjorie Skill), an industrial administrator, Roy was educated at St Paul's school, London, and gained a PPE degree at Balliol College, Oxford (1966). The Oxford curriculum for PPE—philosophy, politics, and economics—provided, then as now, a training for would-be politicians and civil servants who, he soon concluded, were more likely to contain or even reinforce society's problems than resolve them. It was designed to train the entitled and complacent, and, perhaps, a few lucky souls who, having risen through the ranks, overcome disadvantaged class, race, or gendered origins, and who were supposed to feel grateful effectively, being allowed to join the ruling class, if in a duly subordinate position. Needless to say this did not sit well with him. Roy quickly came to decide he wanted to provide the tools for understanding society's problems in a deeper, structural sense that might allow ways to put them right. Economics seemed more practical, but he soon discovered it to be more complacent yet. Searching, in vain, for a philosophical system that could instead serve as an ethical basis for this kind of work, it became apparent to him that such a philosophy had yet to be written. He thus duly embarked on a programme of research that eventually culminated in the foundation of the philosophical school known as critical realism.

The program, he later remarked, ended up taking him much further than he had originally anticipated. Before long, Roy began to understand that the problem ran deeper than merely a lack of commitment to what today we call 'impact' in the social sciences and humanities—his studies led him to conclude that Western science and social theory itself were based on a series of intellectual mistakes, which created false dichotomies such as those between individualism and collectivism, and scientific analysis and moral criticism. The most glaring of these mistakes he called 'the epistemic fallacy', an error arising from the conventional study of how we can know things, or epistemology. The problem consisted in the fact that almost invariably, philosophers have treated the questions 'does the world exist?' and 'can we prove the world exists?' as the same. As a result, the philosophy of science had ended up essentially divided into two camps: one, commonly called 'positivists', which assumes that since the world does exist, we must, someday, be able to have exact and predictive knowledge of it; and another, referred to as poststructuralist or constructivist (and sometimes, somewhat too generally, as 'postmodernist') which argued that since we cannot have such knowledge, we cannot speak of 'reality' at all. What would appear at first glance as a fairly academic debate had important political implications—especially in the social sciences (but not only there): the positivism/constructivism divide also characterized embittered political controversies around colonialism, Western hegemony and the scientific validity of non-Western views of the world.

Into these debates, Roy interjected with an idea that promised to bridge the gap between reality and human perceptions of it: it is perfectly possible, he argued, that the world might exist and we could not prove it, let alone be able to obtain absolute knowledge of everything in it. Both 'camps', in his view, therefore are just rehearsing different versions of the same fundamental error: in fact, real things are precisely those whose properties will never be exhausted by any description we can make of them. We can have comprehensive knowledge only of things that we have made up. Our very lack of a full appreciation of reality, grounded in our situatedness and necessary perspective, therefore supports, rather than negates, the existence of what Roy came to call 'the Real'.

Roy substantiated this view by adopting a version of Kant's transcendental method of argument, which asks 'what would have to be the case in order for what we know to be true?' For science, he argued that two key questions must be asked simultaneously: first, why are scientific experiments *possible*, and second, why are scientific experiments *necessary*, in order to obtain verifiable knowledge of what scientists call natural laws. How is it possible to contrive a situation where you can predict exactly what will happen, when, say, water is heated to a certain temperature in a controlled environment, but also, why is it that one can never make similar predictions in natural settings—no matter how much scientific knowledge we acquire, we still cannot dependably predict natural disasters. Why, in other words, does it take so much work to create a situation where one does know precisely what will happen?

His conclusion was that the world must consist of independently existing structures and mechanisms, which are perfectly real, but they must also be, as he put it, 'stratified'. His model of 'reality' therefore consists of a number of 'levels of emergence', grouping phenomena according to their respective level of complexity. Each emergent level is ontologically grounded in the previous one, but at the same time, cannot be ontologically reduced to it. Complex phenomena thus emerge from less complex ones, but that does not mean that the more complex level merely 'is' the previous one. As an example, the phenomenon we call the human mind is emergent from the biological entity we call the human brain. Without a brain, there can therefore not be a mind, but that does not mean that therefore, the mind is reducible to the biological brain and can be understood exhaustively by referring to biology—rather, it is a more complex emergent phenomenon that due to its higher complexity exists as a phenomenon in its own right.

This view of emergence came to characterize Roy's entire view of science, as he argued that the disciplinary compartmentalizations we make are actually grounded in real differences between emergent levels of reality. Thus chemistry emerges from physics, in that chemical laws include physical ones, but cannot be reduced to them; biology emerges from chemistry, and so forth. At each level, there is something more, a kind of leap to a new level of complexity, even, as Roy put it, of freedom. A tree, he argued, is more free than a rock, just as a human is freer than a tree. What a scientific experiment does, then, is strip away everything but one mechanism at one emergent level of reality, in order to make this one mechanism observable. To do so takes considerable work, and is the basis of what is commonly referred to as 'The Scientific Method' (capitals), however, experimental settings are actually special cases in that they are what Roy referred to as 'closed systems'—systems set up in such a way that it actually becomes possible to eliminate all but the one mechanism one wants to study. In real-world situations, in contrast, like in the case of natural disasters, there is normally a multitude of different mechanisms from different emergent levels operating at the same time, and thus the way they interact will always be inherently unpredictable. Most real-world settings, including the social world, are therefore 'open systems' and require a different analytical approach than experimental settings—which, however, does not make them inherently less scientific.

The books first outlining these thoughts, *A Realist Theory of Science* (1975) and *The Possibility of Naturalism* (1979), almost instantly made Roy one of the most influential voices in the philosophy of science. But even beyond the ivory tower, Roy's new approach made waves. In the 1990s, he sparked intense debate when he publicly applied his philosophy to a critique of the 'new realism' of Tony Blair. Perhaps Blair's choice of the word 'realism' for what was basically a project of total political surrender to the interests of capital made such an intervention inevitable. Vaunted as a belated adjustment to the facts of political life, Roy said that it fails to recognize the underlying structures and generative mechanisms, such as property ownership and the exploitation of labour, that produce observable phenomena and events such as low pay and intolerable working conditions. In other words, New Labour was based on realism of the most superficial sort, and by virtue of this fact, was unable to solve any of the problems it purportedly set out to solve. Roy presented these and other political implications of his work at the Philosophy Working Group of the Chesterfield Socialist conferences, associated with Tony Benn and Ralph Miliband, in the late 80s, and eventually published it under the title *Reclaiming Reality* (2011).

Roy's interventions in the daily politics of Britain illustrate a facet of his thought that not only made him friends (far from): he was a committed political revolutionary. The unifying purpose of his work, as he never tired of pointing out, was to establish that the pursuit of philosophical knowledge necessarily implied social transformation; the struggle for freedom and the quest for knowledge were ultimately the same. This view certainly made him somewhat unpopular with those parts of the philosophical discipline (and other disciplines) who would rather engage in 'pure'—that is to say, disinterested and detached—thinking, and it made him an outright pain in the side of politically conservative colleagues. Perhaps the most exasperating aspect of Roy's work, from the perspective of these conservative forces, was that unlike a merely ideologically driven approach, it was firmly grounded in a sustained and detailed appreciation of the nature of reality and human sociality. This made dismissing him a challenge, since anyone who wished to do so had to mount a critique of at least the same level of intellectual rigour. Perhaps for this reason, throughout his life and career Roy was less than popular in certain quarters, although he remained refreshingly unperturbed by this fact.

Unlike some of his more cynical compatriots, Roy's way of engaging with the world—of philosophy as much as the world at large—was wide-eyed, playful, often impractical, always evolving and learning. There was always a kind of wide-eyed innocence about him, and irrepressible enthusiasm. He continually announced new breakthroughs, sometimes at a rate that flummoxed his own followers. In the 90s, he announced that the Hegelian dialectic—an assertion, its contradiction, and the resolution of the two—was but an odd and idiosyncratic version of a universal principle that formed the basis of all human thought and learning. This launched the second phase of his philosophy, producing in short order the volumes *Dialectic: The Pulse of Freedom* (1993) and the ambitiously titled *Plato Etc: The Problems of Philosophy and Their Resolution* (1994). Both books marked a watershed not only in Roy's thinking, but also in his appeal to scholars outside of philosophy: while many, especially in the natural sciences, had welcomed his work on naturalism and scientific realism, many found dialectic, that slippery processual engine of German philosophy, decidedly too esoteric. But whoever thought that Roy would take this lack of appreciation as a sign to backtrack was sorely mistaken. On the contrary, Roy kept pushing the envelope—literally in his case, as the metaphor of the 'cosmic envelope' would become one of his central concepts.

Plato Etc. had been inspired by Alfred North Whitehead's famous claim that 'all of philosophy is but a footnote to Plato'. Roy subsequently realized that Whitehead was speaking of only Western philosophy; respect for the full range of human thought, however, required engagement with Eastern philosophy too. This had to mean taking spiritual ideas seriously—a domain of human experience that the left had abandoned to the fundamentalist right. In a number of books, notably *The Philosophy of MetaReality: Creativity, Love and Freedom* (2012), he argued that 'spiritual' experiences should be considered a constant feature of everyday life; that every successful act of communication is, in effect, an example of the spiritual principle of non-duality, where both parties become, momentarily, the same person.

Where *Dialectic* had merely raised hackles among Roy's more scientifically minded readers, the development of the theory of metaReality created heated contention among the core of critical realists, some of whom maintained that Roy had left the path of serious philosophical inquiry. Other embraced the new turn with enthusiasm. Splits occurred. At the point of his untimely passing, these debates were still raging, sometimes in embittered ways—Roy, however, maintained his cheerful generosity of spirit, playing an active role in the Centre for Critical Realism and the International Centre for Critical Realism, always brimming with projects, visions, and ideas. Not least, he remained until the end a helpful, generous, and thoroughly approachable mentor to junior colleagues and students, many of whom made their first forays into philosophy inspired by the promise of critical realism to combine technical analysis with effective social change.

Roy fought against the grain of conventional academic philosophy throughout his career, and it should therefore perhaps not come as a surprise that official academia did not always reward his efforts. Following his time as an economics lecturer at Pembroke College, Oxford, he held philosophy posts at Linacre College, Oxford; Edinburgh University; the Swedish Collegium for Advanced Study in the Social Sciences, Uppsala; and the University of Tromsø, Norway. Despite this illustrious career, towards the end of his life ill health and increasingly idiosyncratic work made Roy an outsider in what is now an increasingly commercialized and stratified academic employment market. After losing a foot in 2008 to Charcot's disease, he made use of a wheelchair, and survived on only a partial and woefully inadequate salary as a world scholar at the Institute of Education in London. He was forced to abandon London. He was often in physical pain. Nonetheless, he remained a figure of unparalleled energy and invention, and of almost preternatural kindness and good humour.

What happened to Roy Bhaskar should be an eternal shame for the current British academic system. Roy Bhaskar grew up in one of those brief moments of human civilization during which it could be assumed that if someone displayed an unmistakeable ability to make important contributions to human knowledge, then, no matter how much they might be lacking in skills of careerism and self-professionalization, even, indeed, if they were obvious eccentrics, they would at least be assured the minimum required to keep them working: a desk, a stipend, and a place to live in the city where they taught. This changed dramatically over the course of Roy's life. A tacit promise that was made to him, and to thinkers like him, was ultimately betrayed. Yet one never saw the slightest trace of bitterness in him. Indeed, the authors of this preface well remember, on meeting Roy, being struck by his remarkable ability to transcend adversity. 'If you think about all his endless troubles', one of us asked, 'you really have to wonder, how can he remain so philosophical about things?' And then we looked at one another, and, realizing we'd just answered our own question, laughed. Just as he would have done.

These last posthumous works now emerging are testimony to Roy Bhaskar's tireless optimism and creativity; constantly finding new fields, movements, and philosophies to engage with, and always, in doing so, coming up with something interesting and unexpected to say. We hope the reader enjoys them as much as we have. May others carry on in his spirit.

London, 2020

Note

1 Parts of this preface were published in *The Guardian*, 4 December 2014. See: www.theguardian.com/world/2014/dec/04/roy-bhaskar

FOREWORD

Michael E. Zimmerman

The tangled and uncertain times in which we live are characterized by palpable urgency, as media bring instantly to our attention far off events that contribute to global instability. Knowledge has become highly specialized, the scope of problems has become vast, and contemporary political discourse and mechanisms are increasingly seen as incapable of finding a way forward. In this anthology, *Big Picture Perspectives on Planetary Flourishing: Metatheory for the Anthropocene* (Vol. 1), contributors maintain that an *integrative metatheory* such as Ken Wilber's integral theory (IT) or Roy Bhaskar's critical realism (CR) or Edgar Morin's complex thought (CT) is required to reveal complex relationships within multi-layered and historically interdependent natural and social realities.[1] A major contention of IT, for example, is that an environmental or social problem must be examined from several different perspectives in order to define the problem and to suggest ways of resolving it. However well supported a theory about transmission of environmental toxins may be, that theory alone is not sufficient to determine how to deal with pollution coming from an aging industrial plant that employs hundreds of people. Scientific and technical knowledge alone cannot determine *praxis*; those who think otherwise are committed to technocracy. Metatheoretical approaches are crucial for addressing 'wicked' problems such as anthropogenic climate change. A problem is wicked when it contains contradictory, changing, and unknown factors that make problem resolution exceptionally difficult. Indeed, efforts to solve such problems often generate new, unanticipated problems. A sound metatheory provides the multiple, overlapping perspectives needed to characterize wicked problems adequately, even while recognizing that some miscues and mistakes are inevitable in the process of wrangling with wicked problems.[2]

I

Integrative metatheory—or just metatheory for short—can be conceived as a sophisticated multi-disciplinary understanding needed to cope with today's problems. A useful metatheory provides the inclusive, integrative, and high-altitude vision needed to discern trends and opportunities that would otherwise remain hidden. Such vision could then, suitably staged-down, allow us to show the limits of given social arrangements and practices, and also give us the opportunity to generate alternatives.

In speaking of the possibility of 'planetary flourishing', the editors of this volume ally themselves with those who call for a 'good' Anthropocene. To achieve such an end, a currently predominant human species would need to re-envision its aims and re-structure its technology, economy, socio-political structures, and cultural values in ways that allow for human well-being as well as for the well-being of non-human life.[3] If we continue business as usual, however, that is, heedlessly mobilizing Earth's resources for economic expansion, while adding two or three billion additional people who want a piece of the action, a good Anthropocene seems unlikely.

For metatheoretical analysis conceived in this way to make effective contributions, its proposals must mesh with what takes place on the ground, as it were. But what's there is often enormously complex, ranging from the molecular structure of a one-celled organism to the human economic relationships that both oppress and allow people to earn a living. One reason that research and practical specialization has spread so widely is that, in many cases at least, the more we learn about something, the more we realize how much more there is to learn about it. Traditionally, research involves analysis, that is, dividing up a given phenomenon into its constituent elements, examination of which is then undertaken by people in various sub-specialties. To understand how a specific mechanism works, for example some complex intra-cellular process, researchers isolate the mechanism from environmental influences ruled as not affecting the mechanism. At some point, additional research may be met with diminishing returns, in part because the excluded influences are in fact not tangential and thus safely ignored but instead play some as yet not understood role in the process under investigation. Recommending action, for example, on a new drug to be used for medical intervention can go astray when based upon incomplete knowledge of how a given mechanism actually works. With hyper-specialization, however, the more encompassing perspective needed to grasp subtle interconnections is missing.[4] Integrative metatheories provide some of the most robust frameworks for understanding these subtle and global interconnections necessary for the kind of actionable analysis needed.

If we take action without understanding how things are interconnected, unintended consequences often occur. Often, however, the only way that we discover that such interconnections even exist is by making some intervention that goes awry. Environmentalists often cite the chain of events triggered when DDT was used to control malaria in Borneo. At one point, cats had to be parachuted into the area. Here is one account of what happened:

> As part of anti-malarial campaign in the northern states of the island of Borneo in the late 1950s, the World Health Organization sprayed DDT and other insecticides to kill the mosquito vector for malaria. During this

campaign, DDT was sprayed in large amounts on the inside walls and ceilings of the large 'long houses' that housed an entire village in these areas. As a consequence of this effort, the incidence of malaria in the region fell dramatically. However, there were two unintended consequences of this action. There was an increase in the rate of decay of the thatched roofs covering the long houses because a moth caterpillar that ingests the thatch avoided the DDT but their parasite, the larvae of a small wasp, did not. Also, the domestic cats roaming through the houses were poisoned by the DDT as a consequence of rubbing against the walls and then licking the insecticide off their fur. In some villages, the loss of cats allowed rats to enter, which raised concerns of rodent-related diseases such as typhus and the plague. To rectify this problem in one remote village, several dozen cats were collected in coastal towns and parachuted by the Royal Air Force in a special container to replace those killed by the insecticides.[5]

The story is instructive for two reasons. First, it demonstrates how well-intended action can result in an unanticipated cascade of events that requires more and more interventions. One way of putting the moral of the story is that today's solution is tomorrow's problem. Horseless carriages, aka automobiles, were once celebrated because they would eliminate the environmental problem caused by piles of horse manure on city streets. Automobiles not only dramatically altered social practices and vastly expanded the land-grabbing reach of suburbs, however, but also generate air pollution and vast amounts of CO2, which contributes to climate change. Electric cars are put forward as a solution, but that electricity must still be generated by power plants, most of which are still dependent on fossil fuels. Some have proposed geo-engineering the atmosphere as a solution to current climate problems, but long experience indicates that such a 'solution' would give rise to serious unanticipated consequences.

Here, one need only contemplate the 'efficiency' dilemma, as explained by David Owens in his insightful book, *The Conundrum: How Scientific Innovation, Increased Efficiency, and Good Intentions Can Make Our Energy and Climate Problems Worse*.[6] As pointed out by nineteenth-century economist William Stanley Jevons, the dilemma is that more efficient use of a resource (for example, more efficient steam locomotives) often lowers the cost for using it. The way to 'sustainability', then, is not necessarily through technological gains in efficiency. A metatheoretical approach would be required in order to suggest some ways around such conundrums, which cannot be understood solely in terms of one or two perspectives, such as economics.

The parachuting cats story is also important because it took decades to get the story right. In some versions 14,000 cats (not a few dozen) were dropped by parachute, and other versions reported (falsely) that plague and typhus carried by rat vectors really did break out. Moreover, although cats did die, it was not because they consumed insects containing concentrated amounts of DDT. The person who interpolated this idea into the story had recently read Rachel Carson's 1962 book

Silent Spring, which attributed decline in bird populations to the mechanism of bio-concentration of DDT and other pesticides. In fact, however, the Borneo cats died because the DDT sprayed on indoor walls of houses left a powdery residue, which got onto the cats' fur when they rubbed against the walls. In cleaning their fur by licking it, they ingested fatal doses of DDT. Even after a series of unintended consequences takes place, then, an accurate reconstruction of events takes time, money, effort, and competence in various domains.

Growing awareness of the unintended consequences—social and environmental—of otherwise well-intended interventions and technologies led to the creation of the Precautionary Principle, an approach to risk management which states that if an action or policy has a suspected risk of causing harm to the public or to the environment, in the absence of scientific consensus that the action or policy is not harmful, the burden of proof that it is *not* harmful falls on those taking an action.[7]

For instance, even though for a time questions remained about how smoking caused cancer, enough was already known about smoking's ill effects that steps should have been taken much earlier to discourage smoking. Critics maintain, however, that the Precautionary (or foresight) Principle could be and has been applied in ways that discourage important new developments that could prevent great human suffering.

The Precautionary Principle has also been called on to justify calls for drastic cuts in fossil fuel use, in order to forestall anthropogenic climate change, a wicked problem that calls out for metatheoretical, integrative approaches. Not long after Sean Esbjörn-Hargens and I published our book, *Integral Ecology: Uniting Multiple Perspectives on the Natural World*, Sean alerted me to the work of climate scientist Mike Hulme, who has developed a multi-perspectival, inclusionary approach to making sense of the climate change debate. That he developed this approach without being acquainted with the work of Wilber, Bhaskar, and other metatheoretical thinkers is a sure indication that metatheoretical thinking is on the rise.

Hulme, Founding Director of the Tyndall Centre for Climate Change Research at East Anglia University (UK) and professor at King's College London, is author of *Why We Disagree about Climate Change*, one of the most important interventions in this hot-button issue.[8] Hulme invites readers to acknowledge and to integrate into their thinking the factors that give rise to disagreements about causes and consequences of climate change; to cease demonizing opposing views; and to respect alternative perspectives that are espoused in good faith. Although himself a scientist, Hulme recognizes that science alone cannot provide the insight needed for people either to understand or to cope with/plan for climate change. Indeed, many perspectives need to be brought into play in order to make sense of the 'mutating idea of climate change' (2009, p. xxxvi). Hulme writes that we must call upon

> the concepts, tools and languages of the sciences, social sciences and humanities, and the discourses and practices of economics, politics and religion. As we examine climate change from these different vantage points, we begin to see that—depending on who one is and where one stands—the idea of

climate change carries quite different meanings and seems to imply quite different courses of action.

(p. xxxvi)

Hulme rightly maintains that climate change disputes often 'end up being used as a proxy for much deeper conflicts between alternative visions of the future and competing centres of authority in society' (p. xxxvii). He is 'uncomfortable' with the fact that, as a result of this super-charged political 'climate', climate change is typically described in terms of 'the language of catastrophe and imminent peril, as "the greatest problem facing humanity", which seeks to trump all others' (p. xxxiii). Many other present environmental and social problems, however, are also already causing widespread death, disease, destruction, and suffering.

Hulme's book clarifies the climate debate by using seven different lenses (or perspectives) to make sense of climate change: science, economics, religion, psychology, media, development, and governance. His goal in each case is to reveal why scientists or economists or theologians *disagree* about climate change. Hulme takes pains to demonstrate that opposing ways of 'framing' issues pertaining to climate change all contain at least a grain of truth. He writes: 'None of these ways of framing climate change can be claimed to be wrong in any absolute sense. Equally, none of them offers a 360-degree view of climate change' (p. 227).

In addition to his productive discussion of alternative ways of making sense of climate change, however, Hulme articulates an important and possibly game-changing stance *vis-à-vis* climate change. Instead of regarding it merely as a threat or as a problem to be solved, he urges his readers to see

> the creative psychological, *spiritual and ethical work that climate change can do and is doing for us*. By understanding the ways in which climate change connects with these foundational human attributes we open up a way of re-situating culture and the human spirit at the heart of our understanding of climate.
>
> (p. xxxvii; my emphasis)

Climate has cultural and emotional meanings from which natural science only recently divorced itself. Our tendency to view climate almost exclusively as a physical system that must be understood on a planetary scale 'simultaneously explains and justifies—in this case—the hegemony of the Earth (or climate) system scientist' (p. 18). Moreover, 'metereological fundamentalism' is at work in the rhetoric of claims that wars, conflicts, and refugees are induced by climate change (p. 20; see also pp. 68–69).

Although not discounting the importance of the scientific study of climate, Hulme calls on readers to include neglected but equally important points of view in order to understand climate and how it changes. He notes that climate has long been the carrier of ideology, including racism (people from the tropics are dullards because of the heat), human mastery of nature (at work in current geo-engineering proposals to control climate), and the idea that 'wild' nature has the most inherent value. If pure or virgin climate is most valued, then maintaining climate stability becomes 'of prime, even sacrosanct importance. Climate thus becomes freighted with the ideology of stability and order in Nature, as opposed to ideas of change and chaos' (p. 26). If we disturb the supposedly stable climate, according to many people, we will end up with 'climate chaos', although in fact ecologists have long since concluded that 'change, dynamism, and instability' characterize not only ecosystems, but also climate itself. The ideology that pristine nature must be protected, however, leads to warnings about climate tipping points, and claims that '(re-)stabilizing global climate following the reckless interference of humans is what must be achieved at all costs' (p. 27).

Hulme acknowledges that thresholds, abrupt and non-linear changes and tipping points are part of the new Earth sciences paradigm. He writes:

> These ideas do not, however, present themselves to us, unambiguously, through observed evidence. As with the Greek idea of *klimata*, the metaphor of Gaia for the Earth system and the idea of 'tipping points' in the climate system *are ways of seeing the world; ways of believing.*
>
> (p. 60; my emphasis)

Scientific perspectives can reveal important aspects of the world, but so can the perspectives offered by social science, cultural anthropology, history, philosophy, and so on. Including insights drawn from these additional perspectives may justify very different courses of action than those dependent solely on the findings of climate science. Hulme notes that many nineteenth- and twentieth-century climatologists underscored the potentially beneficial consequences of global warming, but also discounted the possibility that human activity can alter the global climate. He then explores how the idea of anthropogenic climate change came to prominence so rapidly, and why such change has become depicted so negatively. According to Andrew Ross, 'apocalyptic fears about widespread droughts and melting ice caps have displaced the nuclear threat as the dominant feared meteorological disaster' (cited in Hulme, 2009, p. 63). Additionally, rhetoric originally pertaining to the 'war on terror' became projected onto climate change, thereby generating discourses of fear, calamity, and apocalyptic changes. People are typically unaware that such discourses, long associated with climate change, 'are not imposed by Nature; they are created through Culture' (p. 68).

Hulme denies that natural science has the 'authority to make definitive and universal statements about what is and is not dangerous for people and societies and, ultimately, for the world' (p. 74). The credibility of science is put in jeopardy when people use scientific findings to justify claims not merely about how the world is, but how it *ought* to be. Science thrives on dispute, questioning, and scepticism, but supposed scientific disputes may often 'be rooted in more fundamental differences between the protagonists' (p. 75). Contemporary science takes place in a cultural context, such that climate change is now framed as an environmental risk of global proportions. Climate science, then, is an instance of 'post-normal science' (p. 78).

In today's contentious political context, scientists must more than ever 'recognize and reflect upon their own values and upon the collective values of their colleagues. These values and world views continually seep into their activities as scientists and inflect the knowledge that is formed' (p. 79). Post-normal science also challenges how expertise is understood. People with varying backgrounds want and need to weigh in on important issues of the day, including climate change. Hence, natural science must cede some governance to wider society and some ground to 'other ways of knowing' (p. 81). In post-normal science, moreover, people acknowledge that there is much that we cannot predict; uncertainty is *intrinsic* to climate change issues. The public and their political representatives may want certainty, but it is not available in regard to the behaviour of a chaotic system such as climate (pp. 83–84).

Hulme reviews the debates carried on by people with very different evaluations of what ought to be done about climate change. 'We disagree about climate change because we view our responsibilities to future generations differently, because we value humans and Nature in different ways, and because we have different attitudes to climate risks' (p. 139). Later, he maintains that: 'One of the reasons we disagree about climate change is because we believe different things about our duty to others, to Nature and to our deities' (p. 144). Hulme takes up a host of competing but important views about such duties, including monotheistic stewardship of Creation, the responsibility to care for life, environmentalism as a religious discourse, the moral imperative to care for Gaia, romantic views of nature, and so on. Theologies of blame arise, one of which accuses individuals of responsibility for climate change, another of which accuses socio-economic systems.

> Those in the West hear of 'penances' being paid for 'carbon sins' through the purchase of emissions offsets, read of the personal 'guilt' associated with flying, and are challenged to 'repent' of their profligate consumption. And to 'convert' to low-carbon lifestyles. There is even a new missionary movement of communicators and advocates commissioned on the back of Al Gore's evangelical movie *An Inconvenient Truth*.
>
> *(pp. 173–174)*

Hulme does an excellent job of examining why discourses about climate change tend to emphasize the risk of 'doom and disaster', and how such risk is socially 'amplified' in various ways. Why do people have such different assessments of the risks posed by climate change? Many experts assume that objective, quantified information provided by scientists and economists allows the public to arrive at a generally shared view of such risks. Clearly, however, this assumption is false. To help understand why, Hulme calls on Mary Douglas and Aaron Wildavsky's *cultural risk assessment* model, according to which psychological, cultural, and political factors play crucial roles in how people assess risk. This model, which can be applied to individuals or cultures, is represented as a quadrant diagram that schematizes four preferred ways of life.

The quadrants are classified according to two major categories: 'the extent to which people are group-oriented or individual-oriented, and the extent to which people believe that many rules are needed to control behavior or that only a few rules are necessary' (p. 186). This category scheme yields four ideal types of people or cultures, each with a different way of assessing risk. *Hierarchalists* and *egalitarians* share a strong sense of social solidarity with larger social units, but whereas the former emphasize 'a strong social structure of rank, role, and place, with social interaction governed by multiple sets of rules', egalitarians emphasize the fundamental equality of persons who are 'joined together through purely voluntary associations with few governing risks' (p. 187). Both *fatalists* and *individualists* view society as constituted by relatively few social bonds. Fatalists, however, are hierarchical insofar as they accept that individuals need to be governed by rules and stratified social structures, whereas individualists believe that people can manage their affairs with relatively few such rules.

Three of these four categories correspond to the three ideal types posited in integral theory's developmental model of cultural waves or stages: hierarchalists correspond to *traditional conservatives*, individualists correspond to *rational modernists*, and egalitarians correspond to *postmodern greens*.[9] According to one survey of Americans, egalitarians/greens have the highest perception of climate change risks, while hierarchalists/conservatives and individualists/moderns have a lower perception (pp. 197–198). Given that egalitarians/greens constitute only about a quarter of the adult American population (depending on what survey data you are looking at), it should come as no surprise that most Americans rank climate change low on their list of concerns. Why, however, should egalitarians/greens rank climate change as so much more important than do hierarchalists/conservatives and individualists/moderns? People from all three groups tend to agree that climate change will affect poor people in faraway lands more so than relatively wealthy people close to home. Egalitarian/greens, however, tend to have a greater sense of emotional identification with and concern about those faraway people (and other life forms).

Hulme concludes:

> Rather than passively being told by experts what the risks of climate change 'really are', and then believing them, many people project their world-views outwards, thereby shaping the sorts of risks associated with climate change in which they are prepared to believe. Someone who views the world's climate as fragile and easily destabilized is more likely to believe intimations that we are approaching a 'tipping point' in relation to ice sheets or ocean currents than is someone who views Nature as benign or tolerant. When scientific assessments clash with deeply held values or outlooks, it may not always be science that triumphs.
>
> (p. 208)

In his concluding chapter, Hulme returns to the idea broached in his preface, namely, that we should regard climate change as an opportunity for reconfiguring our identities and projects, rather than as a technical problem to be defined by science and solved by engineering. According to Hulme, human influences on climate are now and probably forever inextricably entangled with natural forces (p. 330). He is not a sceptic about the human contribution to climate change, however. He believes in the 'reality' of IPCC's consensus on this matter (p. 325). Nevertheless, he writes: 'Science may be solving the mysteries of climate, but it is not helping us discover *the meaning of climate change*' (p. 326, emphasis in original). Shifting the debate's emphasis from IT's lower right issues (Earth systems science, climate science) to lower left issues (values, culture, worldview), Hulme maintains that 'the ultimate significance of climate change is ideological and symbolic rather than physical and substantive' (p. 329). That is, climate can 'matter' for human beings—whether as a source of fear or of inspiration—only insofar as it shows up within a particular, historically conditioned cultural framework. Having moved this far from the standpoint of those who emphasize the need for either treaties or markets or engineering to control Earth's climate, Hulme rephrases a famous line from John F. Kennedy: 'We need to ask not what we can do for climate change, but to ask what climate change can do for us' (p. 326).

After entertaining the possibility of viewing climate change as either a 'clumsy' problem or even as a 'wicked' problem (one so complex that some proposed solutions end up undermining other solutions), Hulme concludes that climate is not a 'problem' to be solved at all. Instead, it is an *opportunity* to transform how we understand ourselves and relate to one another. The opportunity favoured by Hulme becomes clear in his discussion of what he calls the four leading 'myths' of climate change: Lamenting Eden, Presaging Apocalypse, Constructing Babel, and Celebrating Jubilee. It is no accident that all four myths are taken from the Judeo-Christian tradition. Hulme is well aware that such myths retain some of their original animating force, even though they have become marginalized in secular Euro-American cultures. Moreover, in his preface Hulme acknowledges his own Christian faith (p. xxx).

Lamenting Eden is the myth adhered to by postmodern greens who bemoan the loss of pristine nature and simpler ways of life. Presaging Apocalypse is the myth adhered to by traditional conservatives who depict climate change in terms of calamities that exact cosmic retribution for human depravity, notions with a long and often critically unscrutinized lineage. Constructing Babel is the myth adhered to by rational moderns who, as in the Genesis myth of Babel, seek to become like God by developing technological power. Whereas the peoples at Babylon sought to build a tower reaching to heaven, contemporary geo-engineers propose technical means to gain control over climate. These myths resemble key aspects of what integral ecology regards as the three most important developmental waves in Euro-American cultures: traditional (Presaging Apocalypse), modern (Constructing Babel), and green/postmodern (Lamenting Eden).

The fourth and final myth, Celebrating Jubilee, is consistent with Hulme's vision of what climate change can do for us. Jubilee takes its name from the Jewish Torah, according to which every 50 years 'soil, slaves and debtors should be liberated from their oppression'. Metaphorically, then, Celebrating Jubilee encourages us think about climate change in terms of morals and ethics, and 'offers hope as an antidote to the presaging of the Apocalypse' (pp. 353, 354).

> For those in social and/or environmental justice movements, climate change is not primarily a substantive, material problem, nor simply—as in the lament for Eden—a symbolic one. Climate change is an idea around which their concerns for social and environmental justice can be mobilized. Indeed, a new category of justice—climate justice—is demanded, and one that attaches itself easily to other long-standing global justice concerns.
>
> (p. 353)

The 'inadvertent and unwanted' climate changes that humans have brought about indicate 'the limits of our science saturated and spiritually impoverished wisdom. Humility thus becomes a virtue' (p. 361). Such humility might steer us away from 'ever more reactionary and dangerous interventions' in the search to solve our wicked problem, interventions ranging from colonizing space with mirrors to colonizing 'the human spirit with authoritarian government' (p. 359). Climate change, Hulme concludes, can serve to harness scientific, artistic, and spiritual capacities in the service of civic and political pursuits that allow us to 'reconcile climate change with our human and social evolution, with our instinct for justice and with our endurance on the planet' (p. 362).

Hulme shows that even to characterize, much less to 'solve', a wicked problem like climate change requires taking into account interpersonal relations and social organization. Doing so, however, leads to exponential growth in complexity of what was already a very complex phenomenon. Given this fact, we may be tempted to withdraw from practical action altogether, thereby joining Voltaire's Candide, who chose to tend his garden rather than to take further part in worldly affairs. Daunting complexity alone, however, is not the only factor that may weaken resolve to stay engaged in the *praxis* needed to improve life for humankind and the biosphere. As Hulme suggests toward the end of his book, perhaps even more pressing is the modern disenchantment of the world, which leads to the challenging problem of *nihilism*.[10]

II

When Nietzsche spoke of 'the death of God', he meant the advent of nihilism. Nihilism comes about when the Platonic-Christian table of values that had long organized Western civilization has been eroded by the acid bath of modern science. Although appreciating science's sober rationality, Nietzsche recognized that the triumph of its mechanistic worldview would be a calamity. As he wrote in *The Gay Science*:

> A 'scientific' interpretation of the world, as you understand it, might therefore still be one of the *most stupid* of all possible interpretations of the world,

meaning that it would be one of the poorest in meaning: ... an essentially mechanistic world would be an essentially *meaningless* world![11]

(Section 373)

A meaningless world amounts to nihilism. Nietzsche writes: 'Nihilism: The goal is lacking: the answer to the "Why?" is lacking'.[12] Metatheories address the problem posed by nihilism. Honouring but moving beyond the mythic gods, and having explored the cold outposts of modernity, each offers its own version of a post-secular spirituality. Such spirituality is consistent with the best aims of modernity, with natural science, and with the deepest insights of major religious traditions. Based on experience and reasoning, IT and CR insist that what we do—and what we fail to do—matters. There is a deep, long-term meaning to human striving for the good insofar as we are capable of understanding it.

Relatively late in his career, Bhaskar began exploring the non-duality associated with various spiritual traditions. This move provoked, as might be expected, considerable criticism and questioning on the part of his leftist colleagues. A leading CR theorist, Mervyn Hartwig, embraced important aspects of Bhaskar's new view. According to Hartwig,

> Evil is unilaterally dependent for its existence (parasitical) on the more fundamental human capacities for freedom, creativity, love, spontaneous right-action, self-realization, enchantment, and awakening to non-duality—an 'unnecessary necessity'. Resolution of the 'problem' of evil is thus identical to the resolution of the antinomy of freedom and slavery, wholeness and alienation. Evil is not a cognitive problem but real emergent levels of being of our own making that have to be got rid of.
>
> *(2015, p. 339)*

To be sure, the world will not be perfected overnight; the scale of suffering, alienation, oppression, and exploitation of human life, not to mention other life forms, shows how far there is to go. For many moderns, however, results must count for everything, since there is nothing beyond the natural circumstances in which we find ourselves. The vertical plane of reality taken for granted by religious narratives was eclipsed by the ideal of progress, which will take place on the horizontal plane of human history. While acknowledging modernity's important achievements, both IT and at least some associated with CR are disinclined to dwell within its wholly disenchanted precincts. Instead, some metatheorists affirm that all phenomena arise within a non-dual, all-encompassing matrix of love, affirmation, and creativity. The interrelated whole of the cosmos, with all its suffering and creative strife, possesses *intrinsic* meaning at the outset and gains further such meaning through evolutionary processes and struggles, at many different levels and time scales. Creative, affirmative, non-dual freedom is both cosmic ground and consequence, the always-already clearing within which entities arise and contribute to the endless process of self-overcoming.

Perhaps a *proviso* for both IT and CR could be taken from the *Bhagavad Gita*: do not be attached to the *fruits* of your efforts, since much lies beyond your control. What you *intend* matters most. Let your intention be inspired by the indescribable taste of divine creativity, within and without.

Whereas IT emphasizes interiority and its development, CR emphasizes social structure and how to change it. Both IT and CR are concerned about human well-being, but they have taken different routes to arriving at such well-being. Both Bhaskar and Wilber are influenced in certain respects by classical philosophy, especially Plato and Aristotle. Wilber's pan-experientialism owes much to Whitehead's neo-Platonic process philosophy, as well as to Aurobindo's evolutionary thought. Whitehead and Wilber ascribe to versions of panpsychism or pan-experientialism, according to which the capacity for experience—no matter how vanishingly meagre—goes 'all the way down'.

Wilber's deep interest in human psychological development attracted him to Whitehead's metaphysics. Like Whitehead, Wilber also emphasizes the cosmological dimension of Platonic *eros*, a kind of 'strange attractor' drawing order (truth, beauty, goodness) out of relative chaos. Perhaps this process has dialectical elements. Because Plato did not ascribe to evolutionary theory, however, one must be cautious in ascribing 'dialectical development' to the cosmos as he understood it.

Plato did not subscribe to a version of the 'new universe story' that figures prominently in Wilber's work, especially *Sex, Ecology, Spirituality*. The title evokes the metaphysical centrality of *eros*, both as the cosmic lure to creativity and concreteness, and insofar as *eros* is not an accidental manifestation of non-dual Omega. The future is open; many unknowable, unimaginable pathways have yet to be opened up throughout the cosmos. Drawing on Buddhist non-dualism, Wilber asserts that Form, the world of configured matter/energy, arises within Emptiness. Form is not other than Emptiness; Emptiness is not other than Form. Within the non-dual matrix arises the erotic urge to move forward, to give oneself over into forms into existence, to surrender to the creative process.

Wilber acknowledges the inherent worth of phenomena, all the way down. As a non-dualist he must also acknowledge that the *Ur-grund* can be conceptually differentiated from the *open-ended* future. Wilber's emphasis is on cosmic development, which he understands to be the unfolding *not* of prefigured possibilities, but rather of how the given world (constituted by actual occasions) is changed by the advent of novelty—what has never been and which could not have been anticipated. In the human world, the emergence of new ideas, new modes of consciousness, and corresponding/enabling new institutions means that the future is radically open ended. We don't know what will be next, even though the enormous inertia imposed by cosmic evolution may limit just how radical cosmic innovation can be.

Wilber is in some respects a nominalist and non-dualist along the lines of Buddhist philosopher Nagarjuna, according to whom there is no fixed substance; instead, everything arises and falls according to ever changing conditions. Value names not something fixed and frozen, but rather qualities that *emerge* as the cosmos evolves in its material and corresponding conscious modes. The non-dual cosmic origin, Alpha, encompasses and grants initial value to all phenomena, but the depth and intensity of value grows throughout cosmic history. What matters to an antelope exhibits greater value-intensity and depth than what matters to a sapling. Both lives matter, but the *worth* of life is intensified by *awareness* of such worth. Value is not merely in the eye of the beholder. Even rocks, or perhaps the molecules constituting them, have *at least* the basic ground value of being, one of the transcendental categories explored in medieval philosophy. Human *apprehension* of the inherent value of cosmos and life includes respect for the often-violent power of negation required to provide a clearing for what comes next in the creative process. In addition to discerning the goodness of the world, humans also recognize instantiations of two other transcendental categories, beauty and truth. Such recognition involves generative *judgments* that the non-human natural world typically cannot make about itself. Creative discernment of beauty and truth belongs to humans, and perhaps to some other beings. In my view, shared by Wilber and others involved in IT, insight into the Good, the True, and the Beautiful are needed in order to allow for the best possible Anthropocene.

I beg the reader's indulgence in the following comments about Bhaskar's admirable work, which I know less well than Wilber's. Bhaskar draws on both Plato and Aristotle, although of course in ways that are mediated by 2500 years of history and his metacritique of the Western philosophical tradition. Aristotle looms large in any thinker with debts to Hegel and Marx. In their understanding of Plato's dialectic, Hegel and Marx emphasize the importance of *negation* of the given. The resolution of conflict and contradiction—interpersonal and social—is inevitably required to actualize our full human potential. Human self-actualization is not inevitable, however. Circumstances can readily be imagined that would extinguish humankind. Nevertheless, humankind is endowed with something like a *telos*, a possible trajectory or rational directionality. Social critique says in effect: 'This is not it. We are not there yet. Let's keep moving'.

According to Bhaskar, the noble ideals and aspirations of socialism and its allies are real possibilities that *can be realized* by human beings acting in concert in accordance with a deep understanding of how things really are. For one thing, there is an, in principle, knowable, human-independent natural reality that allows for animals and human beings to evolve in the first place. Such a highly complex, hierarchically arranged natural order is also necessary for humankind to generate the tools and practices to help generate novel emergent levels. Greater technical competence generates more wealth, but in a social context dominated by power-over relations it also generates social conflict. Humans can change the way in which they organize the social world. Late capitalism is not the end of history.

In rejecting positivism, Bhaskar insists that scientific analysis of empirical events can do more than merely offer a description of phenomenal sequences. Rejecting postmodern constructivism, Bhaskar maintains that science can discover the myriad mechanisms that must work 'just so' if my own body is to live for another minute. In some respects the enduring mechanisms of nature are akin to Platonic universals, but unlike the Platonic forms they are immanent to the cosmos. These mechanisms are the causal powers and tendencies that manifest and sustain the dual world that humans inhabit. In the end there *is* much that humans can know.

When it comes to knowledge of society and its individuals, there is the old problem that trying to understand oneself or one's society can change that which is under investigation. Critical realism claims to resolve this problem with its thesis of *existential intransitivity*. Whether in the natural or social world, once something has come to be it is determined and determinate: nothing can now alter that and why it has occurred; there is thus always an ontological distinction between beliefs and concepts and what they are about, even where this is itself a belief or concept. Humans can of course change their beliefs, concepts and social relations etc., and recommendations for change necessarily arise from critical assessment of how things are currently done, but such change occurs in what is indeterminately taking shape in the present-in-the-future, not in what is determined and determinate. What needs above all to change for humanity is our ignorance that led Rousseau to conclude 'Man is born free, but everywhere he is in chains. One man thinks himself the master of others, but remains more of a slave than they are' (1998, p. 5). We are born free because human intentionality presupposes freedom to carry out projects and because we come from the free, open, creative, non-dual *ground*, Alpha, but we have forgotten our origin. Instead of being radiant, loving, and godlike beings, we let ourselves be deceived by the demi-real and the world's empty promises. Blind to our origin in the infinite ground, we sell others and ourselves short, and we end up enslaving one another and ourselves. If we could but act consistently in and from our ground-states we could build a truly remarkable planetary civilization of universal free flourishing.

According to Plato, knowing is the process of recollecting what we already knew when our souls dwelt among the eternal forms in the ultimate ground. Upon being born into a body, however, our souls forgot everything. Recovering this forgotten knowledge is called *anamnesis*. If we could but restore our relationship to Alpha, much of life's misery could be ended, and authentic human life could begin. Bhaskar immanentizes this transcendent account of the eternal forms. Contra Plato, we do not forget everything when we are born, which we may later recollect. Rather, we are born with the potential to know enfolded within us, a potential that is unfolded or awakened when we learn.

In 'Intimation of Immortality from Recollections of Childhood', William Wordsworth (2018) shares his famous poetic recollection of our origin:

> Our birth is but a sleep and a forgetting:
> The Soul that rises with us, our life's Star,
> Hath had elsewhere its setting,
> And cometh from afar:
> Not in entire forgetfulness,
> And not in utter nakedness,
> But trailing clouds of glory do we come
> From God, who is our home:

Heaven lies about us in our infancy!
Shades of the prison-house begin to close
Upon the growing Boy,
But He beholds the light, and whence it flows,
He sees it in his joy;
The Youth, who daily farther from the east
Must travel, still is Nature's Priest,
And by the vision splendid
Is on his way attended;
At length the Man perceives it die away,
And fade into the light of common day.

III

As Bhaskar is well aware, being in touch with the primal ground and source does not mean reverting to some earlier stage of existence; instead, proximity to the ground makes possible ever more constructive, generous, inclusive, and more compassionate modes of social organization and personhood. Those who confuse the innocence of infancy with higher consciousness commit what Wilber calls the pre/trans fallacy, that is, confusing pre-personal modes of existence with trans-personal modes. Wilber himself committed this fallacy, so he reports, in *No Boundary*.[13]

In *Up From Eden: A Transpersonal View of Evolution* (1982), however, Wilber makes clear that the evolutionary trajectory of humankind, personal and interpersonal, makes possible access to domains of reality that are completely unavailable in our early years.[14] When Jesus said, 'Truly I tell you, unless you turn around and become like little children, you will never enter the kingdom of heaven' (Matthew 18:3), he was not calling for regression to infantile status, but instead to allow ourselves to be touched once again by the creative freedom and spontaneous love from which and as which we arose.

Here, I think of the famous Zen *koan*, 'Show me your original face before you were born'. For a long time, I thought the answer had something to do with getting in touch with myself in a previous lifetime, while waiting in the *bardo* to be reborn. Recently, I have come to see this *koan* very differently. It should be read with this stress: 'Show me your original face before *you* were born'. The 'you' at issue is my fearful, arrogant, power-hungry, manipulative, and confused 'personality'. The joyful, affirmative, creative openness with which we are born all too often allows itself to become shrivelled, self-protective, negative, and grasping. East Asian Buddhism, including Zen, emphasizes that every sentient being is always already endowed with eternal Buddha-nature.

According to the teaching of Buddha-nature, each of us already shares in the creative matrix or womb within which all phenomena arise. Awakening means recollecting our original identity, whereupon our entire mode of being-in-the-world is transformed. Awakening is said to be possible either suddenly or gradually, as the result of extensive practice. Wilber emphasizes the latter path, which speaks of various evolutionary levels attained by one seeking to become a *Bodhisattva*. So far as I can tell, Bhaskar recommends the path of awakening to enlightenment. There is no place to 'go', because Buddha-nature is already always present in every human (creature and thing), merely concealed by the defilements that led to the rise of the atomistic ego.

That Bhaskar started out in philosophy of science and social critique but ended up with non-dual metaReality was a source of consternation for many people influenced by his work. This move did not negate the importance of social critique and action based on it, but it grounded critique in the metaRealist or spiritual conditions necessary for a society of universal free flourishing, and in particular in transformation of the self. This move to non-duality is in part responsible for the interest in his work on the part of integral theorists. In addition, however, a number of integral theorists have come to recognize the limits of too much focus on interior development to the neglect of critique of social institutions that lead to estrangement even as they at times produce wealth for some. Even if IT and CR can never be 'merged', each can learn from the other in ways that make them more effective integrative metatheories. Having these metatheories engage each other as they do in this volume (and its companion volume) is a promising development and one that can serve to help ensure a flourishing planet. The Anthropocene will likely be characterized by a level of psychological, economic, cultural, environmental, and social complexity that far exceeds previous ages. As a result, integrative metatheories can play a clear and important role in weaving together these threads of complexity into a more coherent vision of humanity and its relationship to this planet.

How fortunate we are to have IT, CR, and CT in their various modalities available to us. Exceptional intelligence, combined with wide-ranging interests and a thirst for the ultimate, allowed Wilber and Bhaskar to bring forth inspiring, inclusive visions that provide orientation in a time of confusion, anxiety, and despair. Both thinkers acknowledge modernity for differentiating among domains that had once been conflated (religion, economics, art, and politics, for example), and both see the unfortunate consequences of failure to achieve a higher re-integration of such domains in ways that restore intelligibility to life. Such re-integration is one of the key promises of IT and CR. Both also recognize the importance of postmodern critiques of modernity's failures, including its exclusion of some people and virtually all non-human beings from the domain of those entities possessing moral and legal standing. In rejecting all hierarchy as nothing but an excuse for domination, however, postmodernism fails to make crucial distinctions both between humankind and other life forms, and among various instances of human organization. The universe exhibits a developmental hierarchy, without which it could not be organized as it is. Moreover, some societies are healthier than others, although such an assessment should not be an excuse for invasion or colonization! Each in its own way, IT and CR explore how to allow for the possibility of a post-postmodern world in which all beings can flourish.

The essays in this fine anthology provide excellent examples of how IT and CR can guide the *praxis* needed to free us from ignorance and oppression, on the one hand, and to allow us to bring forth a future commensurate with what we can *imagine*, rather than being forced to settle for the *given*. These thinkers offer us many things, then, but above all they offer us reasoned hope for realizing what *could* be. The chapters in both volumes cover a lot of ground—as one would expect from any collection of essays that takes on such a metaview as this volume does. Topics explored include: climate change, education, economics, politics, dialectical thinking, human development, international development, religious studies, and transdisciplinary research. Individually and together these chapters demonstrate the ways integrative metatheories have a unique and even important role in contributing to a good Anthropocene. They do this by using metatheory to make more visible important interconnections across divergent domains and in the process they shine a light on pragmatic interventions that can lead to more integrative outcomes.[15]

Notes

1. In what follows, IT and CR are both used as umbrella terms that include the conceptual phases undergone by the work of Wilber and Bhaskar respectively. I am intentionally not including or emphasizing Morin's complex thought (CT) as much since it is a minor focus of this volume. However, it is an important third integrative metatheory along with IT and CR and interested readers can find a fuller discussion of CTs relationship with both IT and CR in *Metatheory for the Twenty-First Century* (see especially Chapters 3 and 4, and Chapter 7 in this volume).

    What constitutes an integrative metatheory is discussed extensively in these two volumes and the companion volume, *Metatheory for the Twenty-First Century*. Let me add only this: if someone were to assess competing metatheories, from which vantage point would one undertake such an assessment? Would not someone primarily informed by Ken Wilber's IT interpret Roy Bhaskar's CR in ways that don't really do it justice? Would it not be likewise for someone trained in CR who attempts a critical appraisal of IT? Do we need, then, something like a META-metatheoretical perspective in order to provide a satisfactory comparison and appraisal of IT and CR? If so, we will be disappointed. No such perspective currently exists, although a fruitful dialogue between IT and CR (and CT) could reveal elements of what such a META-metatheoretical platform would require. For an initial exploration and articulation of such a META-metatheoretical view see the work being done on complex integral realism by Esbjörn-Hargens and Marshall in Chapters 3 and 4 respectively in *Metatheory for the Twenty-First Century*. See also Marshall (2016).
2. See Wilber and Watkins (2015).
3. In June 2015 The Breakthrough Institute held a dialogue on 'The Good Anthropocene'. For an account of the event, see http://thebreakthrough.org/index.php/dialogue/agenda
4. Equally important is the extent to which much research, including experiments conducted meeting the methodological 'gold standard', is irreproducible and thus flawed, because scientists have an interest in the outcome of their experiments (see https://en.wikipedia.org/wiki/Reproducibility). As physician and medical researcher John Ioannidis has demonstrated, many drugs continue to be widely prescribed by physicians even though the evidence for their efficacy cannot be replicated. Of course, pharmaceutical companies are happy to earn billions of dollars for medicines that are no more efficacious than sugar pills, and potentially carry deleterious side-effects. See Freedoman (2010).
5. O'Shaughnessy (2009). For more details on the story, see O'Shaughnessy (2008).
6. Owens (2012).

7 For a useful overview of the Precautionary Principle, see https://en.wikipedia.org/wiki/Precautionary_principle
8 Hulme (2009).
9 In our volume *Integral Ecology*, Sean and I briefly discuss these links between cultural theory and integral theory. See endnote 8 in Chapter 11 (p. 662) in Esbjörn-Hargens and Zimmerman (2009).
10 See Zimmerman (2019).
11 Nietzsche (1974, section 373).
12 Nietzsche (1968, p. 2).
13 Wilber (1981a).
14 Wilber (1981b).
15 For the opportunity to write the foreword to this volume, I am grateful to Sean Esbjörn-Hargens and Nick Hedlund. Sean invited me to the original meeting in September 2011 between representatives of the two metatheoretical perspectives, but due to a sudden family emergency I was unable to attend. My thanks to David Storey and Roger Walsh for their very helpful comments on an earlier version of this essay.

References

Bhaskar, R., Esbjörn-Hargens, S., Hedlund, N., & Hartwig, M. (2016). *Metatheory for the Twenty-First Century: Critical Realism and Integral Theory in Dialogue*. Routledge.
Esbjörn-Hargens, S., & Zimmerman, M.E. (2009). *Integral Ecology*. Random House Books.
Freedoman, D.H. (2010). Lies, damned lies, and medical science. *The Atlantic*, November. Available at www.theatlantic.com/magazine/archive/2010/11/lies-damned-lies-and-medical-science/308269/ (Accessed 15 July 2016).
Hartwig, M. (2015). MetaRealism. *Journal of Critical Realism*, 14(4), 339–349.
Hulme, M. (2009). *Why We Disagree about Climate Change: Understanding Controversy, Inaction and Opportunity*. Cambridge University Press.
Marshall, P. (2016). *A Complex Integral Realist Perspective: Towards a New Axial Vision*. Routledge.
Nietzsche, F. (1968). *The Will to Power*, transl. W. Kaufmann. Vintage Books.
Nietzsche, F. (1974). *The Gay Science*, transl. W. Kaufmann. Vintage Books.
O'Shaughnessy, P.T. (2008). Parachuting cats and crushed eggs. *American Journal of Public Health*, 98(11), 1940–1948.
O'Shaughnessy, P.T. (2009). The flying cat story, or 'Operation Cat Drop': A history of this oft-told tale. Available at http://catdrop.com (Accessed 1 September 2015).
Owens, D. (2012). *The Conundrum: How Scientific Innovation, Increased Efficiency, and Good Intentions Can Make Our Energy and Climate Problems Worse*. Riverhead Books.
Rousseau, J-J. (1998). *The Social Contract or Principles of Political Right*. Wordsworth Editions.
Wilber, K. (1981a). *No Boundary: Eastern and Western Approaches to Personal Growth*. Shambhala Publications, Inc.
Wilber, K. (1981b). *Up from Eden: A Transpersonal View of Human Evolution*. Anchor Press/Doubleday.
Wilber, K., & Watkins, A. (2015). *Wicked & Wise: How to Solve the World's Toughest Problems*. Urbane Publications.
Wordsworth, W. (2018). *Intimations of Immortality: An Ode* (T.B. Mosher, ed.). Creative Media Partners.
Zimmerman, M.E. (2019). How does integral theory address nihilism? In M. Schwartz & S. Esbjörn-Hargens (eds), *Dancing with Sophia: Integral Philosophy on the Edge*. SUNY Press.

INTRODUCTION

From Metatheory to Metapraxis for Planetary Flourishing

Nicholas Hedlund and Sean Esbjörn-Hargens

> A crucial function of contemporary metatheories is to address the great social, global, and ecological crises of our time. Our species and our planet are imperiled, and effective metatheories can help us to navigate these perils to avert the very real prospect of ecological and civilizational collapse.
>
> Walsh (2006, p. xvii)

Introduction

This anthology weaves together 11 essays[1] about the future of integrative, big-picture thinking at the dawn of a new era in the evolution of consciousness, culture, and nature. Each of these diverse essays refracts the role of metatheory within the context of the complex global problems of the twenty-first century. It does this by offering a variety of big-picture perspectives on the possibility of planetary flourishing at the beginning of a new geological epoch that many scholars now refer to as the *Anthropocene* (a notion that we will return to below).

This volume, and the essays in Volume 2, are a follow up and companion to *Metatheory for the Twenty-First Century: Critical Realism and Integral Theory in Dialogue* (Bhaskar et al., 2016). All three of these volumes are the dialogical outcomes of a multi-year symposia series wherein critical realists, integral theorists, and other metatheorists deeply engaged each other and their distinct but complementary approaches to integrative metatheory. Through the course of over six years, symposia participants engaged in a process of collaboratively exploring, dialoguing about, constructively critiquing, transforming, and synthesizing aspects of their respective metatheories. Whereas the first book (*Metatheory for the Twenty-First Century*) is more theoretical in its focus, setting indispensable foundations and contexts, *Metatheory for the Anthropocene*, in its two volumes, aims to more concretely and practically address the complex, overlapping, and causally interdependent planetary crises that we call the *metacrisis*[2] (Hedlund, 2021; Hedlund et al., 2016) co-arising with the Anthropocene. It does so by applying the powerful sensemaking and meaning making frameworks of critical realism, integral theory, and their higher-order syntheses[3] to forge integrative responses that might help to shift the trajectory of our imperilled society away from existential catastrophe (Ord, 2020) and towards planetary flourishing or a *eudaimonistic society* (Bhaskar, 2008/1993).[4]

In this first of the two new volumes, participants of the symposia series used an emergent set of principles[5] of what we call *metapraxis* (outlined below) to arrive at and articulate a variety of big-picture visions and transformative interventions in the domains of: *society and economics*; *social psychology*; and *education* (while Volume 2 explores: *climate change*; *integrative research*; and *religion and spirituality*). With one of the defining characteristics of the Anthropocene being the sheer complexity and multi-valent nature of our interconnected global challenges, these volumes crucially present new and potent forms of scholarly sensemaking that can adequately weave together insights from multiple disciplines into new and coherent forms of metapraxis—that is, the integration of metatheory and applied practice—that might be adequate to address these complex demands.[6] Collectively, these chapters form an integrative pluralism that demonstrates how integrative metatheory and its applications offer a sophisticated, 'next-level' approach to sensemaking and meaning making that can make powerful contributions towards the concrete possibilities for planetary flourishing in the face of the metacrisis. Together they can help us to steer the critical global phase shift or bifurcation that the modernist world system is undergoing towards a better, emergent outcome as the intimations of a new, metamodern world begin to take shape. Despite the daunting trends and trajectories of the cascading and compounding crises that we face, integrative metatheory, through its synthesising and realist functions, can offer great clarity and coherence in a time when confusion and even epistemic madness abound in a broken media ecology mired in ubiquitous information warfare. Moreover, through its visionary and concrete utopian capacities, we argue that integrative metatheory can reclaim and ignite a realistic sense of hope in a time of growing despair wherein hope may indeed be an essential resource (and causal force) for the immanent cultural and political transformations needed in the face of the metacrisis. This sense of hope is patently not sanguine or pollyanna; it seems clear to us that at this point we are not going to get out of the metacrisis 'pickle' (Rowson, 2021) we are in unscathed. Life in the Anthropocene will inexorably be challenging and tragic in certain ways as life conditions get substantially worse and increased suffering besets us during this period of great change. But ultimately, through active hope (Macy & Johnstone, 2012)—which is to say a critical mass of *ethical participation* in 'the more beautiful world our hearts know is possible', to borrow Eisenstein's (2013) phraseology—we believe that tragedies can be forged into opportunities for transformation[7] and the maturation of the human soul. Thus, we argue that a sober yet ultimately bright and beautiful '*post-tragic*' Anthropocene, to invoke Zachary Stein's notion, is a concretely actualisable possibility that beckons our higher nature. This volume aims to broadly point us in the direction of a future in which humanity successfully navigates planetary initiation (Kelly, 2021), regardless of our ultimate fate in terms the timeline of our civilizational mortality. Indeed, we believe, following the argument we made in the introduction to *Metatheory for the Twenty-First Century*, that metatheory deployed as applied, collaborative metapraxis carries a cultural key to unlocking the complex dynamics of the metacrisis. Metatheory can potentially play a crucial role in averting near-term civilizational collapse and steering us instead towards a relative utopian trajectory in which a eudaimonistic society—characterized by planetary flourishing—is progressively actualized, even if it is never actually fully realized.

The deepening of the symptom-events of our complex, global crises has also revealed the arguable necessity of the notion of 'metacrisis' for adequately making sense of the world situation. Modern atomistic and mechanistic interventions targeting isolated symptoms of our crises tend to eventually deepen the problem or create new ones through their second- and third-order effects (e.g., superbugs and superpests). The world has now become so tangibly ridden with a barrage of worsening and overlapping problems that it has come to be more and more painfully obvious that the major crises of the twenty-first century cannot be addressed through a late modern gaze, which still deludedly views them as if they were closed-systemic, siloed, disciplinary challenges. However, they are in fact all open-systemic, recursively interdependent, and transdisciplinary fractals of the metacrisis as a whole.[8] Likewise, the experiential intensification of our crises highlights the indispensability of *metatheory* for making sense of our radically entangled and imperilled world. Indeed, 'theory' (from the Greek *theōria*) means 'view, seeing, or looking at'—essentially, a lens or perspective—while the prefix 'meta-' (from the ancient Greek) refers to that which is 'after, behind, between, or beyond' (www.etymonline.com), with 'beyond' arguably standing out as its primary early connotation. Thus, metatheory can be understood in a broad sense as 'a view from beyond' the hyper-specialization and fragmentation of late modernity. Metatheory in its twenty-first-century inflection—what we call 'integrative metatheory 2.0'[9] (Hedlund, 2021; Hedlund et al., 2016)—is a key scholarly channel of an emerging metamodern sensibility (Freinacht, 2017, 2019; Stein, 2018), that seeks a more holistic-systemic view—a 'big-picture perspective' on our complexly interwoven crises and dialectically related possibilities for planetary flourishing.

In short, when we penetrate into the nature of the metacrisis it is—on the deepest and most fundamental level—an epistemic and existential crisis—a *crisis of sensemaking* and a *crisis of meaning making*, respectively. This is not to discount the eco-social or ethical aspects of the metacrisis (we discuss these aspects of the metacrisis in detail in our introduction to Volume 2). Rather, we want to highlight that, epistemically, if our shared capacity to make sense of reality and what is happening in the world is broken—to see and intersubjectively verify it—then there is virtually no chance that we will be able to effectively address our complex global problems at scale. Likewise, without a new vision and ontology of ourselves and the cosmos—a deeper self-understanding of what it means to be human, why we are here, and what our role in the field of nature is—then we are unlikely to muster the ethical and spiritual[10] calling—the sense of ultimate significance—that can give us the deeper motivation and ethos to participate in making sense of our imperilled world and doing all we can to wield our knowledge with the wisdom or *phronesis* needed to enact transformative solutions. In other words, the (epistemic) sensemaking crisis and the (existential) meaning crisis in some ways supervene on the more systemic (eco-social and ethical) aspects of the metacrisis. Put differently, we need to be able to make sense of *what* is happening in the world, *who* we are in the context of the cosmos, and *why* we are here if we are to rise to our planetary initiation and clarify *how* to make the right choices that can actualize the transformative potentials of the metacrisis. The sensemaking crisis is about understanding the following questions of: *What* is going on? What is true? And *how* do we go about developing intersubjective verification procedures and methods that help us develop high-quality knowledge that can provisionally approximate, if not descriptively express, alethic truth?[11] The meaning crisis, in contrast, pertains to existential questions such as: *Who* are we? What is our place in the cosmos? And *why* we are here? What is our *raison d'etre*? Thus, integrative metatheory 2.0 represents humanity's leading-edge cultural technology—our best hope—for understanding the truth of what is going on and why it matters. And the idea of applied metatheorizing, or *metapraxis*, is about how we collectively make the wisest choices in the face of the existential risks and profound spiritual opportunities of the metacrisis. This book therefore aims to develop the field of integrative metatheory as a potent cultural generator function that can help us address the sensemaking crisis and meaning crisis, and therefore the metacrisis at large.

As we touched on in the introduction to the first of the metatheory books (Hedlund et al., 2016), metatheory can help us address the metacrisis by:

1. providing tools and methods for epistemic integration in the face of immense complexity
2. identifying causes of oppression, alienation, and other social pathologies, dialectically implying pathways to emancipation and health
3. providing a critical philosophy of science/depth ontology/metaphysics that establishes a solid foundation for reality and truth, that is also the basis of re-weaving the truth and value (in an ontological-axiological chain), or a rational metaphysics that can correct many of the distortions and follies of modern science while providing the basis for a planetary wisdom culture
4. providing tools for deeper epistemic and axiological reflexivity, thus helping us to correct for our cognitive biases, and make transparent and justify our knowledge-constitutive values and aims
5. enabling new visionary ways of forging plausible concrete and relative utopian futures and pathways of transition
6. helping humanity develop its vocabulary and capacity for self-transformation, particularly the transformation of our self-understanding *vis-à-vis* the field of nature. That is, metatheory can help us to forge a new, re-enchanted, transrational, or post-secular worldview, including a new philosophical anthropol-

ogy that might re-weave the torn fabric of our world, and address the root-level distortions in who we take ourselves to be, why we are here, and what our role is in the unfolding cosmos. In short, metatheory can help us to forge new cultural metanarratives that make comprehensive sense of what is happening in our world and confer a sense of visionary depth of meaning, purpose, and planetcentric solidarity that is so painfully absent in today's world.

What, if not integrative metatheory, holds the promise of helping us to catalyze the cultural transformations that can reinvigorate our atrophying shared sensemaking and fix our broken information ecology? And what, if not integrative metatheory, can help forge new overarching self-understandings or philosophical anthropologies that can help us reconsider our being and place in the cosmic order of things? Metatheory, we argue, is uniquely poised as a force of social innovation and transformation that will play an indispensable role in addressing the sensemaking and meaning crises. Thus, we are making a case that 'big picture perspectives' (i.e., integrative metatheories) will necessarily play a pivotal role in helping us navigate the turbulence of the unfolding metacrisis, steering us toward planetary flourishing.

In the remainder of this introduction, we will discuss the larger geo-historical context of the emergence of a new geological epoch known as the Anthropocene, and the role that metatheory ought to play in terms of meaning making in this perilous and potentiated time. In doing so, we sketch a vision of integrative metatheory with collaborative sensemaking and meaning making at the centre. We then reflect on the multi-year symposium series between critical realists and integral theorists that served as the backdrop to this volume. In the process, we identify key qualities that made this scholarly exchange so generative and highlight how this can go further moving forward so as to serve as a model for other communities of metapraxis to collaborate in emergent collective sensemaking and meaning making that might begin to help bring the dawn of a bright Anthropocene in a metamodern relative utopia or eudaimonistic society. Finally, we introduce each of the chapters of the volume and highlight how each one strikes a resonance in a mosaic vision of big-picture perspectives in the domains of society and economics; social psychology; and education in service of a flourishing planet.

1   Metatheory for the Anthropocene

As the sun rose over the Jornada del Muerto ('Journey of the Dead Man') desert on Monday, 16 July 1945, the world was about to change forever. At exactly 5:30am at the so-called 'Trinity site', the United States military detonated the first ever atomic bomb, releasing 18.6 kilotons of power and instantly turning the surrounding asphalt and sand into green glass.[12] Seconds after the detonation, an enormous shock wave sent a scorching blast of heat across the desert, knocking onlookers to the ground. This detonation released radioactive isotopes into the atmosphere, which eventually spread across the entire planet, impressing themselves into the sedimentary record (Steffen et al., 2015). This crustal deposition of radionuclides left the unique signature of humanity's powers imprinted across the Earth, marking the beginning of 'the Great Acceleration' wherein exponential increases in technology and economic activities have driven key Earth System indicators into a new state—a *phase shift* beyond the relatively stable (and hospitable) regime of the past 10,000 years of the Holocene epoch. As such, many scientists now agree, this very moment, on that early July morning in 1945, marked the dawn of a new geological era known as the Anthropocene.[13]

This new geological era is marked by an emergent and unprecedented level of human impact on the material structure of the Earth system—humanity has inscribed its prowess in its very geological and atmospheric composition. The notion of the Anthropocene, popularized by the Dutch Nobel Prize winning atmospheric chemist Paul Crutzen (see Crutzen & Stoermer, 2000), signifies a new geological epoch, identified by stratigraphic and fossil data, and marked by the profound and far-reaching causal power of human intellectual, cultural, and social life in shaping the evolutionary trajectory of Earth system processes as a whole (see e.g., Merchant, 2020; Steffen et al., 2015). In contrast with previous epochs, the most recent being the generally accommodating and climatically stable Holocene, never before has the trajectory of the Earth system been so radically determined by a single dominant species—a global apex predator *par extraordinaire*. We have reached a critical threshold in the evolution of the physical planet itself (the planetary physiosphere) when the actions of a single species are demarcating a new geological epoch—a time scale that typically describes periods of at least tens of thousands of years or more.[14] We now live in a time when our human powers have become so powerful and ubiquitous that our impact on nature has reached tectonic proportions. Humans can now literally move mountains and cause earthquakes, as research in *Nature* shows that unsustainable human usage of the water table for agriculture in California's central valley is causing changes in elevation in the mountains and valley floor, and thus anthropogenic earthquakes (Amos et al., 2014). When taken as a whole, the Anthropocene itself reveals the human as a literal *geological force*[15] of nature. This is a stunning turn in the evolutionary trajectory of the planet, laden with radical implications for our evolving identity and collective self-understanding.

At the level of the material Earth system, the Anthropocene (or the state of the very geological substrate) is a meta-artefact or embodiment of the deeply sedimented unconsciousness from which we have acted. This unconsciousness has critically destabilized the finely tuned bio-geo-chemical cycles within which we have been graciously granted the hospitable conditions for the possibility of the emergence and perpetuity of human civilization. The profound partiality and *demi-reality* (or falseness which is nonetheless profoundly causally efficacious) of our modern materialistic and atomistic vision of ourselves and the cosmos, expressed through the hubris of our Promethean techno-economic prowess, now returns to feed back to us our own delusions. The Anthropocene is a lucid mirror of the demi-real shadows from which we have acted, revealing the deep ontological contradictions and absences in our dominant worldview and collective self-understanding. It is a clear reflection and detailed historical ledger of our spiritual immaturity—a reckoning and a sobering reminder of the bill that we have racked up on our collective credit card (*capitalism*, to be sure)—which is now essentially maxed out, rapidly compounding, and past due.[16] To redress this, we need to embolden the democratic lifeworld's powers to delimit and bind on the reified systemic logics of capitalism, as Habermas (1987) has argued. We also need, at the very least, a shift from *mono*capitalism to a form of *multi*capitalism that recognizes multiple forms of capital/value (e.g., psychological, social, spiritual, natural, health, financial, manufactured) and multiple bottom lines (e.g., people, planet, profit, purpose) in a dynamic integrative way. Such a shift would do much to help us transition away from the unchecked excesses of contemporary capitalism.[17]

As the myth of Prometheus proclaims, we have been given the stolen fire of the gods—the self-reflexive, radically creative powers of *logos*. But wielding the word—the metacognitive transformative agency to create and forge reality at a level resembling that of the gods (i.e., humanity as a geological force) can only be sustained if we simultaneously develop the wisdom, compassion, care, circumspection, and love of the gods. Otherwise, the asymmetric development of our instrumental intellect (expressed as exponentially more powerful technology) over our moral and spiritual faculties appears to be a self-terminating trajectory for our species, as Daniel Schmachtenberger (2021) and others have argued.

The Anthropocene signals the anointment of humanity to the status of *demigods*. As the prefix 'demi-' denotes, we are 'half' or 'lesser' gods, with the Promethean fire of *knowledge* conferring radical powers to create or destroy worlds;[18] yet we are deeply deficient in terms of our ability to actualize what is of value in life in service of planetary flourishing—that is, we are profoundly deficient in terms of wisdom or *phronesis*. We are also demigods in the sense of Bhaskar's notion of *demi*-reality: that which is false or illusory but nonetheless causally efficacious and therefore real. As stated above, the Anthropocene is, in part, a mirror of humanity's demi-reality: the false or illusory ideas that have nonetheless been so radically causally efficacious as to drive the Great Acceleration and effectively rupture the functioning of the Earth System as a whole. Put differently, humans are also demigods in the sense of being gods (or radically powerful agents) of demi-reality. 'It appears the Earth is being put in our hands and we are not prepared for the responsibility' Stein (2019, p. 67) writes. To further the mythopoetics invoked here, it is as if humanity drank from *Lēthē*, the river of oblivion (unconsciousness or concealment) that flows through the underworld, and that unconsciousness or asleepness is now returning to us through the resurgence of the reality principle, embodied and enmeshed in the Earth system. Taken together in its various inflections of meaning, the notion of the human as demi-god invokes both our deeply unconscious and irresponsible use of our agential powers, as well as our higher collective potentials to awaken to the reality of our integral inter-being[19] with our ecological and cosmological context and evolve into playing a unique role as wise, meta-reflexive participants and stewards of the Earth community. On a deep level, humanity has yet to realize the alethic truth of our self-reflexive, meta-aware nature: we have been given the *logos* of self-reflexive consciousness and the creative and agential powers that it confers. And yet, Stein (2019) goes on,

> [o]ur species is reeling from the shock that comes from realizing that it is up to us to ensure the continuation of the Earth's life support systems. We are existentially intertwined in a common destiny, both as a species and as a biospheric community. A vast web of life now depends on our stewardship.
>
> *(p. 67)*

At another level, the Anthropocene is a *clarion call* and potent opportunity to rapidly transform and evolve our self-understanding and culture towards an *alethic resonance* with the field of nature from which we emerged, are co-constituted, and are ongoingly sustained (Hedlund, 2021). While coming into this resonance is a radical project of holistic-systemic transformation that inexorably envelops all aspects of human society, the core of it, we argue, is a transformation to a new self-understanding that undergirds a new, regenerative cultural and social formation.

'Anthropo' comes from the Greek word *Anthropos* (ἄνθρωπος), meaning 'human', while 'Cene' comes from the Greek word *kainos* (καινός), meaning 'new'. Thus, Anthropocene can be taken to mean the 'new human' or 'the age of the new human', wherein the totality of our life and identity will inevitably undergo a radical transformation. We find ourselves in a dizzying existential confusion about who we are, as our old, siloed identity frays and is revealed to be both an anachronism and a causal force of the great unravelling. At the same time, the first glimpses of a new vision of ourselves and our place in the order of things is beginning to take shape. We lurk, awkwardly and anxiously, in existential liminality. We very well may come to see ourselves as a failed species as we are humiliated by our self-created climate catastrophe, or we may move towards the actualization of our potential as benevolent and wise stewards of our complex socio-ecological systems, tending the conditions for life to flourish. Either way, the Anthropocene ensures that our collective self-understanding will undergo a radical re-appraisal and shift. As Stein (2019) lucidly describes this interrelatedness of the transformation of our shared identity and the planetary crisis:

> Humanity's inability to understand itself is part of a cascading planetary phase shift. Our identity crisis is coinciding with the dawning of the Anthropocene; the educational challenges humanity faces in the coming decades are in large part about reconstructing our self-understanding as a species.
>
> *(p. 73)*

Metatheory, therefore, will play a crucial role in scaffolding our capacity to address the educational challenges of reconstructing our self-understanding in resonance with axiological necessity in the face of the planetary crises of the Anthropocene. We need coherent and compelling big-picture metatheoretical visions in order to give shape to this new identity and understand our new responsibility or ethical imperative to care for all life. Indeed, without our metatheoretically emboldened imagination, we are unlikely to transform from our present default position as a global apex predator species with radically asymmetric powers on a fast track towards self-termination into a new role as a kind of participatory 'capstone' species[20] of wise and benevolent planetary stewards that can reflexively hold a socio-ecological meta-view and take radical responsibility to care for, harmonize, and tend the conditions for the flourishing of each and all through a dialectic of deep 'listening'[21] and attunement.[22]

The Anthropocene is enmeshed in the psychological, cultural, intellectual, spiritual, and social dynamics of the late modern worldview and world system. The Anthropocene signals not only the need for new big-picture visions of ourselves and our relations—new philosophical anthropologies and ecologies that re-situate us in relation to nature and the divine. We need new visions, new maps and mirrors, new frameworks and ways of understanding our purpose and place in the order of things. We are assuming a new mantle of relationship to ourselves and the Earth. Humanity is, as Kelly (2021) states, 'becoming Gaia' and therefore he refers to our present epoch aptly as the *Gaianthropocene*. But from where will such transformative innovations in our self-understanding come? As Stein (2019) notes, 'the resources of the lifeworld for meaning making and identity creation have become almost as depleted as the resources of the natural world' (p. 72). This is where metatheory's power lies: it has *in itself* the power to contribute the crucial intellectual resources that can revivify the lifeworld for sensemaking, deep meaning and ethics, identity creation, and transformation, thereby addressing the complex, twenty-first-century challenges of the metacrisis (Hedlund, 2016). We are in the midst of a collective existential crisis, which is itself a major driver of the global metacrisis. Our identity crisis is concrescing precisely at the dawn of the Anthropocene, a synchronicity imbued with gravitas and numinosity. The Anthropocene also invites a new era of radical self-reflexivity, underscoring our potent transformative agency and responsibility to use it to ethically shape our planetary future. And yet the force of humanity is driven, in large part, by the big-picture perspectives we hold—the worldviews, the metanarratives, meta-memes, and perhaps most aptly, the *metatheories* that constitute the deep 'code' of our cultural and social operating systems (Freinacht, 2017). Because cultural worldviews evolve and cohere through complex collective processes of convergence, iterative reappraisal, and emergence over longer temporal horizons, they are not so much direct functions of transformative agency and therefore cannot be designed. They are, rather, structures that have been shaped by—and are ongoingly reproductively sustained or transformed by—processual flows of collective agency over time. Metatheory, in contrast, functions as the deep code or generator function for the larger streams of cultural negotiation that produce more deeply sedimented worldviews (Hedlund, 2021), as we will revisit in the introduction to Volume 2. It could be said, therefore, that in the context of the Anthropocene, *metatheory itself has become a geological force*.

Similarly, Jason W. Moore (2015) and Christian Parenti (Parenti & Moore, 2016) have argued that the term *Capitalocene* is a more apt name for the new geological epoch we are entering, since it is really, as the argument goes, the effects of capitalism that have primarily driven the changes in the world ecology and geology that constitute the Anthropocene. When you look at the geological substrate, the physical markers in terms of atmospheric chemistry and so forth, what you find there are the externalizations of the capitalist world system. There are stunning changes happening in the relationship between the human being and the Earth. While we would not disagree with Moore and Parenti's argument, by a similar logic, it begs the question as to what has caused capitalism's rise as a nearly ubiquitous force on the planet? While there are many complex contributing factors, capitalism as a reified institutional-systemic logic did not arise out of a vacuum. Rather, as Bhaskar and others have argued, capitalism is a systemic expression, and reification, of positivist metatheory, refracted through the lens of neoclassical economic theory and neoliberalist political economic theory.[23] In this context, humanity's collective self-understanding of human–environment relations and its philosophical response to our global metacrisis rises to the fore. The state of the world is thus deeply instructive with respect to the revelation of the shortcomings of our dominant philosophies and metatheories (e.g., positivism and social constructivism) and the collective self-understanding(s) they have produced. The metacrisis, we argue, can thus be seen largely as reality kicking back at us, showing us what is *absent* or left out in these metatheories: we are witnessing the 'return of the repressed' and the resurgence of the real. Since the dawn of the Anthropocene (and the Great Acceleration in 1945), human beings now constitute a demi-real 'ontological rupture' in the Earth system as a whole (Hamilton, 2017, p. 9). In this way, the inadequacies of our dominant metatheoretical tradition of (post)modern irrealism as a response to the complex global challenges of the twenty-first century are becoming ever more glaring. There is thus an urgent and increasingly recognized need for more sophisticated and efficacious metatheoretical alternatives that can support planetary flourishing in the Anthropocene. The Anthropocene beckons a new kind of responsibility, a new kind of ethical imperative, for our collective sensemaking and meaning making to serve the flourishing of life on Earth. As the French integrative metatheorist Edgar Morin puts it, 'never before in the history of humanity have the responsibilities of thinking weighed so crushingly on us'.[24]

To collectively carry this 'thinking weight' we need metatheorists, in all their guises, coming together to engage in real shared sensemaking and meaning making, while applying their emergent insights and perspectives to address real-world challenges. As such, we now turn to examine the principles of collaborative metapraxis that emerged through the CR-IT symposia series—our six-year experiment in collaborative metatheorizing.

2 The Collaborative Metapraxis of Big-Picture Thinking

Over the course of this multi-year symposia series, a number of overlapping and complementary principles of engagement developed and informally guided the process. We share these here to inspire other collaborative metatheoretical sensemaking initiatives to benefit from and build on these to support their own post-disciplinary aspirations. So, in sharing the results of our experiments of bringing together multiple communities, we hope to inspire progressive communities of practice, dialogue, and inquiry across streams of (meta)integrative thinking to deepen their endeavours and look for natural points of collaboration and synergy with ours. Some of the key principles of our collaborative metapraxis included:

- *Dialogue and dialectical engagement:* Genuine open dialogue is essential, especially the kind where both parties are aiming to create mutual understanding and mutual learning. This takes a certain degree of epistemic humility, or openness to being (at least partly) wrong, and relatively greater alignment with higher, worldcentric principles like learning in service of truth and collective evolution, rather than entrenchment in fixed, egocentric or tribal ideas, identities, and methods. This willingness to dialogue in this open, humble, curious, actively receptive way lays the groundwork for an even more profound possibility—that of dialectical engagement where each party allows themselves and their metatheories to be potentially transfigured on a deep, architectonic level through their engagement with the other party. In other words, dialectical engagement[25] means being so committed to truth, beauty, and goodness in the world that one allows whatever real absences or contradictions that are identified through the dialogue—and the problem fields that they imply—to work their alchemical, transformative magic, leading potentially to deep revisionings and/or emergent, non-preservative syntheses. This requires that we hold our ideas and identities lightly, stay present to the reality of the unknown, and trust in the emergent, hive mind, or collective intelligence at work. It is also worth noting that ontological realism along with epistemic relativity/fallibility and judgmental rationality (i.e., critical realism's so-called 'holy trinity') appear to be necessary presuppositions for such fruitful dialogue and dialectical hermeneutics. Put conversely, if there is not a shared commitment that there is a truth (ontological realism), however much fallibility, (social, historical, or linguistic) mediation, or contingency is involved in trying to know it (epistemic relativity/fallibility), then even trying to adjudicate differences through rational dialogue (judgmental rationality) is an unintelligible fools quest—and engagements typically settle into an implicitly nihilistic 'to each their own' radical relativism.[26] From another angle, a developmental ontology and epistemology is important here for a number of reasons, not the least of which is the fact that such an ideal of dialogue and dialectical engagement across communities certainly presupposes embodied elements of post-formal—namely, metasystematic (Commons et al., 1982, 1984)—levels of cognitive development (Basseches, 1984, 2005). Thus, some individuals and communities may need to undertake long-term integral educational practice as a prerequisite for engaging in an optimally generative process of dialogue and dialectical engagement. However, the dominant discourse of a given conversation can be facilitated in a way that may scaffold individual participants to show up or perform in a more complex way than they would otherwise be capable of, thereby elevating the conversation as a whole. It is important to note that emotional development and psychological healing and integration are probably at least as important as cognitive-developmental complexity when it comes to mature dialectical dialogue and engagement.[27]

- *Learning to speak each other's metatheoretical languages:* It takes time to learn each other's specialized language or lexicon of key terms and concepts. While some notions might be the same on the signifier level (e.g., ontology, liberation, integrate), some have very different referents—distinctions, meanings, and nuances in each metatheoretical system that are referentially divergent. Not to mention the fact that each system has a host of specialized terms and concepts that often elude immediate grasp. Each metatheoretical stream or tradition that has its own emergent or synergistic systemic logic or what A.H. Almaas (2004) calls a 'logos', meaning that it 'possesses a different and unique technical language, logic of experience and understanding, ideals of development or realization, phases of unfoldment of experience and understanding, and kinds of experience, perception, and knowledge' (pp. 568–569). Therefore, he goes on, it is 'not possible to translate the experiences and conceptualization of two teachings in a one-to-one manner' (p. 570). What we can skilfully do is draw general correlative *homologies* between metatheories, while keeping in mind that each tradition possesses a unique *logic field* that cannot be reduced to the terms of the others (in spite of their sometimes similar sounding approaches). This tendency to naively interpret everything through the lens and categories of one's own chosen system (focusing more on the signifier level than on the referent level) is a common mistake when complex metatheoretical systems are wielded without sufficient nuance and epistemic reflexivity.[28] For example, in the CR-IT dialogues, we occasionally saw the tendency to conflate critical realism with a reductionist materialist inflection of 'realism' by virtue of the fact that critical realism refers to real entities as 'objects' and therefore tends to code them as right-hand quadrant exterior-material phenomena (see e.g., Wilber, 2019); in fact, critical realism explicitly defines objects as causally efficacious and therefore real generative mechanisms, tendencies, structures, or forces, whether interior ideas or exterior material things. When we were able to muster the judicious consciousness that it takes to not hastily mistranslate each other's metatheory, really aiming to cultivate overlapping horizons of mutual understanding, the conversation was able to efficiently deepen. However, when coarse translations are hypostatized, the conversation ceases to feel productive, but rather ends up feeling more like 'ships passing in the night'. For an example of the results of inadequately learning to speak each other's metatheoretical language, see the exchange between Wilber and Bhaskar in the *Journal of Integral Theory and Practice* (Bhaskar, 2012; Wilber, 2012a, 2012b).[29] When we take the time and care to really learn the nuances and systemic logics of each other's metatheory, then we can build a genuine epistemic commons and a shared horizon of meaning together.

- *Hermeneutic and ontological generosity:* It is important to lead with a spirit of interpretive generosity and good faith *vis-à-vis* each party's approach. It is hard to get a fruitful conversation off the ground without this kind of 'appreciative inquiry' (Cooperrider et al., 2008) or exchange. There will be plenty of time to go back and further clarify meanings, terms, or examples—as well as for critical examination. But in the initial phase of dialogue, looking for and appreciating common aims or methods, as well as points of contact, resonance, and referential overlap between different systems is important to build a base of positive affect, respect, and connection. This sensibility will provide a foundation of intellectual and emotional good will, mutual support, and solidarity, before broaching the spaces of more cutting or challenging critiques and differentiating contrast between the approaches. Similarly, granting each approach a broad or general sense of ontological purchase on reality is important. In other words, it is very helpful to acknowledge that each approach is built on real distinctions, insight, and understanding and is likely talking about reality in a useful way even if it is not obvious at first. This spirit of generosity does not negate the validity of intense critique or the possibilities for category error, contradictions, absences, aporias, etc.—which is indeed the generative engine of deep transfiguration and metatheoretical evolution (Bhaskar, 2008/1993). To the contrary, as Collins (2000) writes based on a sweeping sociological study of the history of philosophy East and West, '[i]ntellectual life is first of all conflict and disagreement … the forefront where ideas are created has always been a discussion among oppositions' (p. 1). Rather, the idea is that critique—the identification of contradictions, absences, and so on—if it is to deliver on its potential as a primary generative mechanism of metatheoretical development, must be preceded by and complemented with emotional and intellectual rapport-building appreciative inquiries: for example, the places where an approach got it right, and possesses strengths, insights, or methods that are relatively obvious or uncontested. Then and only then can the generative power of ontological negativity (Bhaskar, 2008/1993) and critique 'work its magic'. Conversely, without a phase of engagement in which the emphasis is strongly on hermeneutic and ontological generosity, the subsequent turn to critique is likely to lead to less generative, if not downright distasteful, results. Interestingly, integral theory's approach, based on the principle of non-exclusion and its mantra 'everyone's position is true but partial' (often operationalized as 'everyone is right'), is strong in terms of its hermeneutic generosity, but lacks an underlying depth ontology that includes absence and ontological negativity that would undergird an emphasis on critique.[30] In complementary contrast, critical realism underscores the importance of critique, the generativity of contradiction and absence, etc., but can likewise tend to be somewhat lacking in its hermeneutic and ontological generosity, despite its commitment to 'the critical realist embrace', which is a commitment to ongoingly include and integrate valid findings from various disciplines (Bhaskar, 2016).[31]

- *Working together on real projects in mixed teams:* It is one thing to come together as two or more communities of metatheoretical thought and application to compare approaches, but where things get really exciting and interesting is when one is able to identify practical areas to work in that involve individuals representing different metatheoretical vantage points (e.g., sensemaking on key facets of the metacrisis, innovating new physical or social technologies, strategic interventions in systems, applied socio-political initiatives). This provides a context to 'pressure test' strengths and weaknesses, similarities and differences, between different metatheoretical approaches. And it can be fun and satisfying as you build heartfelt connections with others who are skilled at big-picture thinking. This approach also brings the aims of real-world initiatives to the fore—highlighting what John Heron (1996) calls the 'primacy of the practical' and subjecting each approach to assessment in terms of the Hegelian notion of 'seriousness' (Bhaskar, 2012/2002b), or the coherence of theory and practice. Zachary Stein and Hans Despain's collaborative metapraxis of educational reform, highlighted in this volume, provides an apt example of this kind of working together across metatheoretical streams to address real-world challenges.
- *Epistemic reflexivity at individual and 'team' levels:* Not only is the effort more likely to succeed if individuals have the capacity for epistemic reflexivity (taking their own biases, preferences, and lived experience as an object of reflection), but it is important for this to occur at the level of the team or members of the different approaches.[32] While the members of our symposia had various degrees of alignment or identification with each metatheory, there were new kinds of insight available when we could reflect on the geo-historically situated positionality (e.g., IT emerged out of transpersonal psychology in the US in the 1970s, while CR emerged in philosophy in the UK in the 1970s) and unique strengths and weaknesses of the approaches we were most familiar with or aligned to (e.g., CR's depth ontology and IT's developmental metapsychology and taxonomy of epistemic structures).
- *The cultivation of philia:* We feel that a crucial element of our success with the CR-IT symposia had to do with the cultivation of *philia* or deep friendship. Philia is a Greek word that connotes a sense of brotherly/sisterly love, fondness, mutual support, trust, solidarity, and resonance in a sense of shared values or purpose. In Aristotle's (2014) *Nicomachean Ethics*, philia is often translated simply as 'friendship' or 'affection'. In the curation of the various symposia, we organizers consciously created space for philia to emerge organically by building in ample opportunity to connect as whole people outside of the formal sessions. We broke bread and drank wine together, laughed, exchanged warm-hearted hugs, sipped coffee and tea, and got to know each other beyond our merely professional scholarly personas. As a result, many deep and lasting friendships were forged through the symposia—not strictly professional or collegial affiliations. We feel that intentionally creating these informal spaces for face-to-face, in-person connection did much to help us integrate the personal

and professional in a shared sense of philia or affectionate intellectual and spiritual friendship that bonded us in our shared commitment to the deepening of integrative vision in a fragmented and crisis-ridden world. This backdrop of philia and resonance on the heart and soul level was clearly part of the 'secret sauce' that afforded such intellectual generativity and innovation throughout the process.

In our view, one of the most important aspects of the CR-IT symposia series were our experiments in creating social innovation labs[33] and exploring together the future of metatheorizing across multiple communities of scholar-practitioners. We had 10–15 of the top scholars from each metatheoretical stream involved in multiple ways over many years.

Thus, what in-part makes these three volumes unique is that they are the result of a six-plus year series of experiments in which two communities of practice came together in a collaborative space and fairly successfully advanced each of their approaches, explored similarities and differences, points of resonance and points of dissonance—and also to developed third-way, emergent syntheses of the two (see e.g., Esbjörn-Hargens, 2016; Hedlund, 2016, 2021; Marshall, 2016a, 2016b). In the process, we collaboratively created a variety of new and generative metatheoretical vistas that included both divergence and consilience. In a world full of intellectual fence-building, entrenched career identities, and academic-tribal warfare, something like this seems to have rarely happened.

Through this metatheoretical collaborative inquiry we not only learned a lot about how to engage across the boundaries of our respective intellectual streams, we also learned a lot about how to address the ever-looming metacrisis. Through this collaborative sensemaking process, we went from metatheory to metapraxis—the results of which provide new and important insights into the metacrisis and how to address it. What we did in this context is a collective, co-generated practice of philosophizing. It is our conviction that we are really only going to successfully address the metacrisis in a 'meta' way through exactly this kind of shared metatheorizing. In this regard, we experienced something that was apparently rather unique; as a result, its learnings need to be distilled out so that others can adapt and experiment with them in order to help this kind of process to continue evolving over time and forge new emergent insights and practices that can address the metacrisis. We need a 'meta' playbook—a *social innovation meta-methodology*—for addressing the metacrisis. The planet is on fire—we may be approaching a global cascade of tipping points in the Earth system (see e.g., Lenton et al., 2019)—and we do not have time to lose. It therefore feels important that we have identified some of the key meta-principles that emerged in our experiment which serve as guidelines for how we did what we did so that others can replicate and build on it, in various experimental inflections, at scale. We hope that this can contribute to the growing para-academic community of metamodern[34] intellectuals that are advancing the crucial conversation around how we can reinvigorate and reinvent our shared sensemaking and meaning making, thereby reclaiming and advancing the downtrodden notions of reality and truth in a world gone mad. Needless to say, without a radical revival of our collective intelligence and capacity for high-quality, sophisticated sensemaking, we are, simply put, *f#cked*.

The symposia series gave us an experience of being able to navigate the metacrisis on a microcosmic level. In particular, the series was a fractal of the epistemic crisis, albeit at a high level of academic discourse, in which we had to confront the reality of the multiple sensemaking perspectives on various issues, multiple systems of meaning making, differing metaphysical presuppositions and vantage points, and differing levels of expertise in various domains. In other words, we had to deal with the points of incommensurability in our worldviews, the so-called problem of inter-individual epistemic-hermeneutic variability (Hedlund, 2016). Each approach, CR and IT, brought their chops to the sensemaking table: IT, for example, brought a robust developmental psychology (rich with implications for epistemology that CR could integrate), and CR brought, among other things, a powerful philosophical system of science (a post-post-metaphysical critical ontology *par excellence* that could resolve some of IT's core philosophical contradictions and buttress its realist aspirations in the face of postmodern constructivism and radical epistemic relativism). Each of these, among other complementary elements, contributed to a more robust collaborative sensemaking process. By combining the best of both approaches and exposing the limitations of each, we started to develop a more coherent and powerful mode of meta-level sensemaking—a 'next-level epistemology', if you will—that required we reflect on, and in some cases release, our individual and team identities around our preferred approach. In the face of the terror and opportunity of the metacrisis, that which best does justice to its reality seemed to rise to the fore. These moments of mutual transformation helped us to feel that we were part of an emerging process that was bigger than our particular philosophical commitments and positions.

These kinds of collaborative metatheoretical initiatives are critically important—our hope is that this is only the beginning of a new cultural wave in which we collectively start to experience the effects of such social innovation experiments at scale. Such sophisticated experiments in high-quality, big-picture collaborative sensemaking provide a start to a much-needed road map of how we can collectively begin to address the metacrisis. We hope that this book will set your hair on fire, if you will—igniting and emboldening your soul's blazing passion and purpose to participate in these potent new experiments at the forefront of an emerging culture. The actualization of such a shared dharmic project is among our best hopes for the emergence of a higher-order post-capitalist (or metamodern) sociosphere and a bright Anthropocene, rather than a radical regression to some kind of authoritarian or fascist barbarism and a dark future that could plausibly be nothing short of a civilizational collapse.

In the afterword to *Metatheory for the Twenty First Century*, Markus Molz (2016) emphasizes the critical need for metatheorists to go beyond the hyper-individualistic sensibility of modernist metatheorizing and move rapidly towards collective or shared metatheorizing—particularly in the form of full-on co-creation and group authorship. Similarly, in the afterword to Volume 2 of this anthology, Daniel Görtz[35] (in press) makes a powerful argument for the need to go beyond the archetypal lone wolf metatheorist towards a curation of the generative conditions and processes that allow for effective shared or team metatheoretical sensemaking. We feel that this experiment in metatheoretical collaboration serves as an inspiration and an initial road map for others to take up and carry on—hopefully further potentiating the field of integrative metatheory to be a vector for emancipatory metapraxis and the actualization of our potential and purpose of planetary flourishing in the midst of the Anthropocene.

3 In This Volume: Chapter Summaries

Both volumes are divided into three parts. This volume's chapters are divided into 'Society and Economics', 'Social Psychology', and 'Education', while the chapters in Volume 2 are divided into 'Climate Change', 'Integrative Research', 'Religion and Spirituality', and 'Metaintegrations'. Many of the chapters, due to their integrative approach, could justifiably be placed in more than one of the two volumes' six parts. So, these divisions are fictions as much as they are helpful facts but they do succeed in highlighting a particular emphasis that each chapter holds. As such they are meant to help readers locate specific chapters that they may want to consult given their specific areas of interest.

We begin this volume with the section on 'Society and Economics'. This serves as a way of stepping back and getting a big picture view of the metacrisis. Society is now facing many distinct but overlapping crises, what we call the metacrisis. Multiple systems are at play in this process and the three chapters in this section explore different layers of this. We begin with Hans Despain's 'The Quintuple Crisis: How the Metatheory of Dialectical Critical Realism and Integral Theory Can Contribute to Understanding Our World, Society, and Self' (Chapter 1). In this chapter, Despain develops the concept of the 'quintuple crisis' which involves simultaneously related crises in the socio-economic, political, environmental, and existential/spiritual domains. As a result, this chapter models how to draw on several integrative metatheories to better understand the ways different layers of the metacrisis are recursively related. Despain nicely draws on key concepts from both critical realism and integral theory to develop a more nuanced and sophisticated understanding of the quintuple crisis.

Next, Kevin Bowman presents his Integral Political Economy framework in 'Healthy versus Pathological Political–Economic Discourse and Policy: An Integral Political–Economic Treatment' (Chapter 2). Given the level of polarization present in contemporary politics in the US and beyond this chapter provides some innovative ways to distinguish between healthy and pathological forms of discourse across the political spectrum. This enables us to get out of entrenched stereotypical views of opposing political camps and see how both sides on an issue can engage in either immature or mature forms of discourse. By becoming attentive to this psychological/sociological layer we can begin to move our political processes and their resulting policies in a direction that can benefit from healthier expressions of opposing viewpoints.

The last chapter in this section explores the fascinating domain of taking spirit beings associated with Indigenist worldviews seriously. Neil Hockey's 'Sustaining Spirit across Complexities of International Development in Relation to Indigenous Peoples' (Chapter 3) breaks new ground in exploring the role mythic and mystical elements of Indigenous communities play in individual and collective development. By daring to consider what many secular rational modernists would readily avoid or discount, Hockey models for us a way of honouring and incorporating elements of society that do not always fit in well with a globalist postmodern view of international development.

The next section is on 'Social Psychology' and contains two chapters, both of which explore post-formal developmental stage theories. First, we have Otto Laske's 'Applying Bhaskar's "Four Moments of Dialectic" to Reshaping Cognitive Development as a Social Practice Using Laske's Dialectical Thought Form Framework' (Chapter 4). This chapter illustrates how a Bhaskarian ontology of dialectical thinking can be modelled via a stage theory. Laske's lifelong work, reaching back to his roots in the Frankfurt School, has been to support the development of dialectical thinking in adults and as such provides an important framework for exploring how integral thinking can be cultivated and used in practical settings that serve social transformation. This chapter is situated at the fruitful intersection of Wilber's focus on developmental stage theories and Bhaskar's emphasis on dialectical thinking.

Next, is Zachery Stein's 'On Realizing the Possibilities of Emancipatory Metatheory: Beyond the Cognitive Maturity Fallacy, Toward an Education Revolution' (Chapter 5). This chapter echoes the previous one in that it too is exploring the synergies between Bhaskar's dialectics and Wilber's developmental psychology. Stein explores these themes in the context of education and introduces what he calls the 'cognitive maturity fallacy', which posits that philosophical epistemologies all too often assume a static mature epistemic subject. In contrast, Stein highlights that the epistemic subject evolves over time and the field of education plays a crucial role in the development of said subjects.

Stein's chapter serves as a bridge between the second and final section of the book, which is focused on education. There are three chapters in this section. The first one is Iskra Nunez's 'Metatheory: The Ontological Turn in Mathematics Education Research' (Chapter 6). This chapter draws on elements of integral theory and critical realism to explore the ways integrative metatheory can contribute to mathematics education. In the process Nunez develops a critique of integral theory arguing that it omits dialectical realism.[36] She also examines a number of case studies of integral theory being used in mathematics education.

The next chapter is Gary Hampson and Matthew Rich-Tolsma's 'Coalescing and Potentializing Integrative Higher Education: Complex Thought, Critical Realism, Integral Theory, and a Meta-Matrix' (Chapter 7). Adding French metatheorist Edgar Morin to the conversation, this chapter provides a side-by-side comparison on how all three metatheorists (Bhaskar, Wilber, and Morin) have inspired distinct but complementary approaches to education. With this overview in place, the authors spend the rest of the chapter exploring synergies and potentialities of educational praxis informed by all three.

For our last chapter we have two of the authors of standalone chapters noted above teaming up and co-authoring a chapter. Zachary Stein and Hans Despain's 'Getting Theory into Public Culture: Collaborations and Interventions Where Metatheorists Meet' (Chapter 8) is an appropriate piece to complete this volume as it represents and illustrates the value of metatheorists informed by different metatheoretical traditions working together on behalf of 'real-world' applications. Stein and Despain document their collaboration of 'trans-metatheoretical practice' and present both its successes and challenges. Together they penned a series of published Op-Ed pieces, which aimed to translate and make relevant to the general public metatheoretical insights regarding educational reform.

Conclusion

This book therefore explores the potential of applied metatheory in the age of the Anthropocene, offering a variety of big-picture perspectives in service of the aim of planetary flourishing. The relatively new field of 'Big History' (Christian, 2004) is a scholarly discipline which looks at history from the Big Bang to the present from a big-picture, multi-disciplinary perspective. It resists reductionism, integrating various sciences and fields within the humanities to situate the human project within the larger cosmological context of 'the universe story' (Swimme & Berry, 1992). Such a metanarrative, while formally rooted in scholarly, rational epistemologies, nonetheless offers a kind of creation story (*cosmogeny*) or rational-scientific myth, thereby integrating logos and mythos. In this way, 'Big History and other related conceptual frameworks may themselves provide a foundation for a new more integrated worldview, onto which an almost spiritual dimension could be read'.[37] Integrative metatheory 2.0 is precisely one of these 'related conceptual frameworks'. It is a kind of 'Big Theory' and its associated 'big picture thinking' can deploy potent sensemaking methods to articulate an overarching vision of life and humanity's place and purpose in the order of things. That is, this kind of metatheorizing can catalyze the emergence of a more integrated worldview with a post-rational (Wilber, 1995, 2006) or post-secular (Habermas et al., 2010; Taylor, 2007) spiritual dimension that might function as the deep cultural code for a higher-order, relative utopian or eudaimonistic society, in which the free flourishing of each is the condition for the possibility of the free flourishing of all.

In many ways this volume (and its companion) have emerged out of a similar process as Stein and Despain's collaboration in this volume. All of the authors and their chapters introduced above emerged out of a collaboration across metatheoretical orientations and preferences, searching for both common and novel generative grounds. All the while there has been a shared commitment to translate these big-picture views into practical action that can serve us as global citizens facing the emerging metacrisis of the Anthropocene. Thus, we hope that this volume offers you epistemic resources, perspectives, and practices that can inspire and empower you to seek out and help forge new big-picture vistas from which to make sense of—and wisely respond to—a complex world in great need.

Acknowledgements

We would like to thank Paul Marshall and Olga Sohmer for their keen editorial feedback on this introduction.

Notes

1 Specifically, eight chapters plus a robust preface, and an in-depth foreword and afterword.
2 The notion of metacrisis is addressed in more depth in the introduction to the second, forthcoming volume: *Integrative Responses to the Global Metacrisis: Metatheory for the Anthropocene*.
3 See, for example, the unique inflections of *complex integral realism* pioneered by Paul Marshall (2016a, 2016b) and Sean Esbjörn-Hargens (2016); the *critical realist integral theory*, later dubbed *visionary realism*, of Hedlund (2016, 2021); as well as the *integrative evolutionary realism* of Stein (2018, 2019).
4 A eudaimonistic society is the critical realist notion of a society in which all are free to realize and actualize their unique singularity or purpose—the free flourishing of the deepest purpose or potential, dialectically realized individually and collectively such that 'the free flourishing of each is the condition for the possibility of the free flourishing of all' (Bhaskar, 2008/1993, 2012a/2002; 2012b/2002, inspired by Marx). It is the notion of a society in which heteronomous and false but causally consequential (or demi-real) socio-cultural forms in all four planes of social being (or integral theory's quadrants) are increasingly shed and relations of oppression, alienation, and exploitation ever less prevalent. Put positively, it is a society that is increasingly aligned with alethic truth, and (holistic) health, (non-hedonic/depth) happiness, and (open, evolving) wholeness are evermore actualized. Such a society could be considered a concrete utopia in the sense that it is actualisable within existing constraints—it is not abstract and untethered from the laws of nature and the patterning of social structures. It is also a relative utopia, as Freinacht (2017, 2019) discusses, meaning that it is better than what came before, rather than some kind of ultimate or fixed utopia, since flourishing, in principle, is open-ended. Such a concrete and relative utopia, or eudaimonistic society, will be necessarily in a perpetual state of change or open process and will always be a moving, evolving target—at least until we reach collective self-realization.
5 To be sure, these principles were deployed relatively implicitly during the symposia series, and then later were explicitly coded or identified through reflection and dialogue.
6 We should note that we hold this binary of (meta)theory and practice or application lightly and with a healthy dose of relativity. Of course, metatheorizing is a form of practice that works in the causally efficacious and therefore ontologically real realm of ideas to transform the social world (see e.g., Bhaskar, 1997) of which it is a part. It is only within an irrealist or reductionist-materialist worldview that theory is understood as split off from practice, since theory or ideas are understood to be unreal. The relevant distinction, rather, has to do with a spectrum from abstraction and generality on the one hand to concreteness and substantiveness on the other. All theory *is* practice, and all practice presupposes theory, but some theory operates at high levels of generality and abstraction (e.g., philosophical metaphysics or ontology) and some operates or applies theoretical abstractions at much lower levels (e.g., a critical realist theory of climate science and policy). This understanding of the dialectics of (meta)theory and practice impels us to deploy the notion of 'metapraxis', which implies a more complex interdependent understanding of their relations.

7 See Patten (2018) for an insightful discussion of how tragic events and crises can potentially be opportune moments for decisive and transformative action systems redesign (*kairos,* as the ancient Greeks would have it).
8 This speaks to the holographic quality of the metacrisis: if you penetrate deeply enough into any part of it, following the general method of Goethian science (see e.g., Bortoft, 1996; Steiner, 2005, 2008/1886) the whole is revealed. As such, due to the chains of causal interdependence and recursivity, no part of the metacrisis can be solved in isolation—the deeper holistic-systemic solution pattern must be applied across all its aspects or dimensions, if solutions are to be effective and lasting at scale.
9 The notion of 'integrative metatheory 2.0' is also elaborated in the introduction to Volume 2.
10 Following James Fowler's (1981) work, spirituality has to do with matters of ultimate significance in an existential sense of what matters in the big picture of one's 'ultimate environment' (p. 24).
11 According to critical realism, alethic truth is ontological truth—the truth of things as distinct from epistemic propositions. It is the real reason why something is the way it is, the real ground for something, as encountered by human beings. These real grounds for things can change, especially in the social world, so that alethia is developing and dynamic.
12 See www.energy.gov/lm/doe-history/manhattan-project-background-information-and-preservation-work/manhattan-project-1
13 At the time of writing, in early 2022, the term Anthropocene has yet to be officially approved and ratified as an official Geological Time Scale by the International Commission on Stratigraphy. Its acceptance, however, seems imminent, and the term has gone viral—penetrating the scientific and popular discourse and striking a deep resonance in the zeitgeist. The Anthropocene Working Group (AWG) of the Subcommission on Quaternary Stratigraphy of the International Commission on Stratigraphy (ICS) voted in April 2016 to proceed towards a formal proposal to define the Anthropocene epoch in the official geologic time scale. In May 2019, the AWG voted in favour of submitting a formal proposal to the ICS by 2021. The ratification is still in process, and thus a date remains to be decided definitively, but 'The Great Acceleration'—a massive spike in the data of human impact on Earth systems, including atomic bomb testing in the 1940s and into the 1950s—seems to be highly favoured (see e.g., Steffen et al., 2015), situating the most likely beginning of the Anthropocene at or around the detonation of the first atomic bomb in New Mexico in 1945 (Wikipedia, 2021).
14 The official geological time scale is divided into ages, epochs, periods, eras, and eons, with ages being the shortest of these nested temporalities.
15 Of course, one might object that it was not some homogenous collective called 'humanity' that produced changes in the Earth's geological composition that we call the Anthropocene, but rather was largely due to the wealthy, developed nations (most notably, the USA) and their prodigious consumer economies and bloated militaries that detonated their bombs and burned most of the fossil fuels, and so brought us into the Anthropocene. This is also true, and important to note, but does not preclude making species-level generalizations.
16 As Jason Moore (2015) and others convincingly argue, capitalism has always necessarily depended on the availability of 'cheap nature' to be extracted or exploited. Since 'cheap nature' was either simply taken or acquired at well below its real value, this process can be said to incur compounding 'ecological debt'. Because the capitalist world system creates nominal value from cheap nature without paying the true cost (i.e., internalizing all externalities), it 'kicks the can down the road', continually attempting to avoid paying down the accrued balance, while preferring to pay only the 'minimum due'. But eventually, this endless growth credit card shopping spree must come to an end, since the card itself will get 'maxed out' as we hit the alethic ecological boundaries of our finite Earth system and the balance 'comes due'.
17 See Esbjörn-Hargens' MetaImpact Framework with its ten types of capital, four types of impact, and four types of bottom lines (www.metaintegral.com).

18   Technically, humanity can only create the social world in the sense of transforming, potentially in radical ways, the social structures that we have inherited. But that social world can then supervene on the physical world, and through concept-dependent human activities mediated by exponentially more powerful technologies, can impact—and eventually destroy or catastrophically destabilize—the functioning of the Earth system. Hence, humans can both create and destroy worlds; but, importantly, there is an asymmetric dynamic in which we can only 'create' the social world, but we can impact, destroy, or regenerate the ecological world.

19   The idea of inter-being is increasingly being thematized as a powerful rhetorical frame or narrative that represents a kind of third way between a strictly materialist conception of interconnection via the first-generation sciences of complexity on the one hand, and a strictly transcendent, mystical notion of 'oneness' on the other.

20   This is similar to Tyson Yunkaporta's (2019) discussion of 'Indigenous thinking', which often sees humanity in a unique role as a so-called 'custodial species'—a species that can see and take responsibility for stewarding the many relations that constitute the whole.

21   Listening is understood here in a broad metaphorical sense of epistemic receptivity, rather than a narrow literal sense of auditory perception.

22   In contrast to some traditions of ecological thought, such as deep ecology, this notion of humanity as a capstone species implies a need for humanity to own its unique powers and central role in the stewardship of the planetary ecosystem. In some sense, this implies a kind of transfigured anthropocentrism, wherein humanity understands itself to be burdened and blessed with the heavy responsibility of protecting the health of the whole. Hence, what might be called an 'integral anthropocentrism' is ethically planet-centric, while simultaneously being anthropocentric in the sense of acknowledging our radically asymmetric transformative agency and responsibility *vis-à-vis* the well-being of all other species.

23   These theories are also co-produced by structures of consciousness, specifically Jean Gebser's (1984) deficient mental structure (ratio) and a hemispheric brain imbalance (left-hemispheric dominance; McGilchrist, 2012), among other factors.

24   Quoted in Kelly (2021, p. 75).

25   Dialectical engagement as a second-person, relational mode wherein both parties wield the first-person capacity for dialectical thinking (Basseches, 1984, 2005) stands in contrast to 'being dialectical' in the third-person metatheoretical sense of 'having a dialectical theory'. At the third symposium (at UCL in London), it was quite apparent that these two distinct understandings of 'dialectical' led to a degree of conflict and misunderstanding in various moments, with Otto Laske and other integral theorists emphasizing the importance of (first- and second-person) 'dialectical thinking', while Iskra Nunez, Mervyn Hartwig, and other critical realists emphasized the importance of having a (third-person) dialectical metatheory. Nunez (in this volume) articulates a critique of integral theory that claims that it is non-dialectical according to the terms and criteria of dialectical critical realism. While we would agree with this critique, and feel that it should be taken to heart, we argue that integral theory nonetheless is strong in terms of its emphasis on the epistemic capacity for dialectical thinking, and its highlighting of the educational conditions that support its emergence—realities that critical realism tends to overlook in its explicit ontology and epistemology, yet are clearly presupposed (see, e.g., Stein's critique of what he calls the 'cognitive maturity fallacy' in this volume).

26   The socio-political end game of such radical relativism should be painfully obvious at this point, especially since 6 January 2021, when rioters stormed the US Capitol emboldened by President Trump's misleading rhetoric and post-truth philosophy.

27   Nonviolent Communication (Rosenberg, 2012) and Internal Family Systems (Sweezy & Ziskind, 2013) are notable examples of effective scaffolding processes for emotional and psychological development and integration in service of effective dialogue.

28   Critical realism provides a robust framework of referential detachment between signifier and referent in its semiotic triangle, whereas integral theory, while also offering a

complex theory of semiotics, does not have an explicit philosophy of referential detachment, which can lead in practice to a stronger tendency to focus on the surface signifier level, while potentially overlooking or underemphasizing the referent level.
29 It is worth noting that we tried to facilitate a face-to-face meeting between Bhaskar and Wilber in 2013, but Wilber declined. Their exchange in the JITP seems to reflect the lack of personal connection and rapport, as well a lack of understanding between their respective metatheoretical languages.
30 This also implies, importantly, that 'everyone is wrong'.
31 Curiously, Roy Bhaskar himself never lacked in this generosity, but generalizing from our experience interacting with the critical realism community over many years, such generosity was indeed sometimes lacking. The opposite dynamic was observed too with the integral theory community tending to be generous, while Ken Wilber often was less so.
32 According to Hedlund (2010):

> The following categories could be considered by integral researchers with respect to reflexive epistemological inquiry: axiological (core values and knowledge constitutive interests); emancipatory (normative dispositions, passions for transformational service); soteriological (liberational, spiritual, or religious inspirations and orientations); ontological (theoretical backgrounds and pre-understandings, assumptions about the data, assumptions about how the data is interpreted [e.g., what's meaningful/not meaningful]); cultural (geospatial region [north, south, east, west], national culture, local culture, ethnic background); socio-economic (class, techno-economic milieu); political (partisan orientations/identifications, political milieu); generational (e.g., baby boomer, generation X, generation Y); historical-autobiographical (personal narrative vis-à-vis the research topic); developmental (cognitive, interpersonal, self-identity, values, morals, needs, somatic, emotional, aesthetic, psychosexual); and typological (Enneagram, Myers-Briggs, quadratic orientation).
>
> *(pp. 16–17)*

33 See Tiesinga et al. (2014) for an introduction to social innovation labs.
34 We invoke 'metamodern' as a general, 'catch-all' notion that refers to our current geo-historical epoch, emerging in the wake of modernism and postmodernism. Metamodernism in this sense has numerous inflections in terms of intellectual formations, including both integral theory, critical realism, game b, and the Nordic school of political metamodernism. This meaning stands in contrast to the usage of the term as a particular school or intellectual brand, wherein 'metamodernism' stands in competition to other approaches, such as critical realism or integral theory. Thus, we use 'metamodern' broadly as a rough synonym for post-postmodern, integrative, or integral (in the broad sense).
35 Also known as Hanzi Freinacht: Daniel Görtz and his co-author Emil Friis publish under the pen name Hanzi Freinacht (see e.g., Freinacht, 2017, 2019).
36 See n.26.
37 Voros, J., quoted in (Kelly, 2021, p. 32).

References

Almaas, A.H. (2004). *The Inner Journey Home: Soul's Realization of the Unity of Reality.* Shambhala Publications, Inc.
Amos, C.B., Audet, P., Hammond, W.C., Bürgmann, R., Johanson, I.A., & Blewitt, G. (2014). Uplift and seismicity driven by groundwater depletion in central California. *Nature*, 509(7501), 483–486. doi:10.1038/nature13275
Aristotle. (2014). *Nicomachean Ethics*, ed. R. Crisp (Rev. edn). Cambridge University Press.
Basseches, M. (1984). *Dialectical Thinking and Adult Development*. Ablex.
Basseches, M. (2005). The development of dialectical thinking as an approach to integration. *Integral Review*, 1, 47–63.

Bhaskar, R. (1997). On the ontological status of ideas. *Journal for the Theory of Social Behavior*, 27(2/3), 136–147.

Bhaskar, R. (2008/1993). *Dialectic: The Pulse of Freedom*. Routledge.

Bhaskar, R. (2012). Considerations on 'Ken Wilber on critical realism'. *Journal of Integral Theory and Practice*, 7(4), 39–42.

Bhaskar, R. (2012a/2002). *The Philosophy of MetaReality: Creativity, Love and Freedom*. Routledge.

Bhaskar, R. (2012b/2002). *Reflections on MetaReality: Transcendence, Emancipation and Everyday Life*. Routledge.

Bhaskar, R. (2016). *Enlightened Common Sense: The Philosophy of Critical Realism*. Routledge.

Bhaskar, R., Esbjörn-Hargens, S., Hedlund, N., & Hartwig, M. (eds) (2016). *Metatheory for the Twenty-First Century: Critical Realism and Integral Theory in Dialogue*. Routledge.

Bortoft, H. (1996). *The Wholeness of Nature: Goethe's Way toward a Science of Conscious Participation in Nature*. Lindisfarne Press.

Christian, D. (2004). *Maps of Time: An Introduction to Big History*. University of California Press.

Collins, R. (2000). *The Sociology of Philosophies: A Global Theory of Intellectual Change*. Harvard University Press.

Commons, M.L., Richards, F.A., & Kuhn, D. (1982). Systematic and metasystematic reasoning: A case for levels of reasoning beyond Piaget's stage of formal operations. *Child Development*, 53(4), 1058–1069. doi:10.2307/1129147

Commons, M.L., Richards, F.A., & Armon, C. (eds) (1984). *Beyond Formal Operations: Late Adolescent and Adult Cognitive Development*. Praeger.

Cooperrider, D.L., Stavros, J.M., Whitney, D.K., & ebrary Inc. (2008). *Appreciative Inquiry Handbook for Leaders of Change* (2nd edn). Available at https://yale.idm.oclc.org/login?URL=http://site.ebrary.com/lib/yale/Doc?id=10315423 (Accessed 10 May 2015).

Crutzen, P.J., & Stoermer, E.F. (2000). The 'Anthropocene'. *Global Change Newsletter*, 41, 17–18.

Eisenstein, C. (2013). *The More Beautiful World Our Hearts Know Is Possible*. North Atlantic Books.

Esbjörn-Hargens, S. (2016). Developing a complex integral realism for global response: Three meta-frameworks for knowledge integration and coordinated action. In R. Bhaskar, S. Esbjörn-Hargens, N. Hedlund, & M. Hartwig (eds), *Metatheory for the Twenty-First Century: Critical Realism and Integral Theory in Dialogue*. Routledge.

Fowler, J.W. (1981). *Stages of Faith: The Psychology of Human Development and the Quest for Meaning*. Harper San Francisco.

Freinacht, H. (2017). *The Listening Society: A Metamodern Guide to Politics* (Vol. 1). Metamoderna.

Freinacht, H. (2019). *Nordic Ideology: A Metamodern Guide to Politics* (Vol. 2). Metamoderna.

Gebser, J. (1984). *The Ever-Present Origin*. Ohio University Press.

Görtz, D. (in press). Afterword: Metatheory and those who seek it. In N. Hedlund & S. Esbjörn-Hargens (eds), *Integrative Responses to the Global Metacrisis: Metatheory for the Anthropocene* (Vol. 2). Routledge.

Habermas, J. (1987). *The Theory of Communicative Action: Lifeworld and System*, transl. T. McCarthy (Vol. 2). Beacon Press.

Habermas, J., Reder, M., Schmidt, J., Brieskorn, N., & Ricken, F. (eds) (2010). *An Awareness of What Is Missing: Faith and Reason in a Post-Secular Age*. Polity Press.

Hamilton, C. (2017). *Defiant Earth: The Fate of Humans in the Anthropocene*. Polity Press.

Hedlund, N. (2010). Integrally researching integral research: Enactive perspectives on the future of the field. *Journal of Integral Theory and Practice*, 5(2), 1–30.

Hedlund, N. (2016). Rethinking the intellectual resources for addressing complex twenty-first century challenges: Towards a critical realist integral theory. In R. Bhaskar, S. Esbjörn-Hargens, N. Hedlund, & M. Hartwig (eds), *Metatheory for the Twenty-First Century: Critical Realism and Integral Theory in Dialogue*. Routledge.

Hedlund, N. (2021). *Visionary Realism and the Emergence of a Eudaimonistic Society: Metatheory in a Time of Metacrisis*. PhD Thesis, University College London.

Hedlund, N., Esbjörn-Hargens, S., Hartwig, M., & Bhaskar, R. (2016). On the deep need for integrative metatheory in the twenty-first century. In R. Bhaskar, S. Esbjörn-Hargens, N. Hedlund, & M. Hartwig (eds), *Metatheory for the Twenty-First Century: Critical Realism and Integral Theory in Dialogue*. Routledge.

Heron, J. (1996). *Co-Operative Inquiry: Research into the Human Condition*. SAGE Publications.

Kelly, S.M. (2021). *Becoming Gaia: On the Threshold of Planetary Initiation*. Integral Imprint.

Lenton, T.M., Rockström, J., Gaffney, O., Rahmstorf, S., Richardson, K., Steffen, W., & Schellnhuber, H.J. (2019). Climate tipping points—Too risky to bet against. *Nature Comment*, 575. doi:10.1038/d41586-019-03595-0

Macy, J., & Johnstone, C. (2012). *Active Hope: How to Face the Mess We're in without Going Crazy*. New World Library.

Marshall, P. (2016a). Towards a complex integral realism. In R. Bhaskar, S. Esbjörn-Hargens, N. Hedlund, & M. Hartwig (eds), *Metatheory for the Twenty-First Century: Critical Realism and Integral Theory in Dialogue*. Routledge.

Marshall, P.A. (2016b). *A Complex Integral Realist Perspective: Towards a New Axial Vision*. Routledge.

McGilchrist, I. (2012). *The Master and His Emissary: The Divided Brain and the Making of the Western World*. Yale University Press.

Merchant, C. (2020). *The Anthropocene and the Humanities: From Climate Change to a New Age of Sustainability*. Yale University Press.

Molz, M. (2016). Afterword. In R. Bhaskar, S. Esbjörn-Hargens, N. Hedlund, & M. Hartwig (eds), *Metatheory for the Twenty-First Century: Critical Realism and Integral Theory in Dialogue*. Routledge.

Moore, J.W. (2015). *Capitalism in the Web of Life: Ecology and the Accumulation of Capital*. Verso.

Ord, T. (2020). *The Precipice: Existential Risk and the Future of Humanity*. Hachette Books.

Parenti, C., & Moore, J.W. (2016). *Anthropocene or Capitalocene? Nature, History, and the Crisis of Capitalism*. PM Press.

Patten, T. (2018). *A New Republic of the Heart: An Ethos for Revolutionaries*. North Atlantic Books.

Rosenberg, M.B. (2012). *Living Nonviolent Communication: Practical Tools to Connect and Communicate Skillfully in Every Situation*. Sounds True.

Rowson, J. (2021). Tasting the pickle: Ten flavours of meta-crisis and the appetite for a new civilisation. Available at https://systems-souls-society.com/tasting-the-pickle-ten-flavours-of-meta-crisis-and-the-appetite-for-a-new-civilisation/ (Accessed 28 May 2021).

Schmachtenberger, D. (2021). The power of gods. *Conversations with Coleman*. Available at www.youtube.com/watch?v=XQpoGL0yIFE (Accessed 16 March 2022).

Steffen, W., Broadgate, W., Deutsch, L., Gaffney, O., & Ludwig, C. (2015). The trajectory of the Anthropocene: The great acceleration. *The Anthropocene Review*. doi:10.1177/2053019614564785

Stein, Z. (2018). Love in a time between worlds: On the metamodern 'return' to a metaphysics of Eros. *Integral Review*, 14(1), 186–220.

Stein, Z. (2019). *Education in a Time between Worlds: Essays on the Future of Schools, Technology, and Society*. Bright Alliance.

Steiner, R. (2005). *Goethean Science*, transl. W. Lindeman. Mercury Press.
Steiner, R. (2008/1886). *Goethe's Theory of Knowledge: An Outline of the Epistemology of His Worldview*. SteinerBooks.
Sweezy, M., & Ziskind, E.L. (2013). *Internal Family Systems Therapy: New Dimensions*. Routledge.
Swimme, B., & Berry, T. (1992). *The Universe Story*. Harper San Francisco.
Taylor, C. (2007). *A Secular Age*. Belknap Press of Harvard University Press.
Tiesinga, H., et al. (2014). *Labcraft: How Social Labs Cultivate Change through Innovation and Collaboration*. Labcraft Publishing.
Walsh, R. (2016). Foreword: The potentials of metatheory. In R. Bhaskar, S. Esbjörn-Hargens, N. Hedlund, & M. Hartwig (eds), *Metatheory for the Twenty-First Century: Critical Realism and Integral Theory in Dialogue*. Routledge.
Wikipedia. (2021). Anthropocene. Available at https://en.wikipedia.org/wiki/Anthropocene (Accessed 28 July 2021).
Wilber, K. (1995). *Sex, Ecology, Spirituality: The Spirit of Evolution*. Shambhala Publications, Inc.
Wilber, K. (2006). *Integral Spirituality: A Startling New Role for Religion in the Modern and Postmodern World*. Integral Books.
Wilber, K. (2012a). Critical Realism Revisited. Available at https://vdocuments.mx/download/critical-realismrevisited-1pdf (Accessed on 15 July 2021).
Wilber, K. (2012b). In defense of integral theory: A response to critical realism. *Journal of Integral Theory and Practice*, 7(4), 43–52.
Wilber, K. (2019). Afterword: Realism and idealism in integral theory. In M. Schwartz & S. Esbjörn-Hargens (eds), *Dancing with Sophia: Integral Philosophy on the Verge*. SUNY Press.
Yunkaporta, T. (2019). *Sand Talk: How Indigenous Thinking Can Save the World*. Text Publishing Company.

PART 1
Society and Economics

1
THE QUINTUPLE CRISIS

How Metatheory Contributes to Social Theory

Hans Despain

Introduction

The importance of this volume is the efforts of the contributors to relate the *events* of the early twenty-first century to a larger existential context. Metatheory is to theorize about theories and how theories about reality interconnect. Thus, the contributions are certainly cross-disciplinary; the real contribution, however, is that these contributions are *transdisciplinary*. As individuals we necessarily tend to *partialize*[1] reality in order to grasp and navigate it. The aim of science and academia is to understand reality more objectively, and events and experiences as aspects of a greater *totality*. However, whereas science and academia have succeeded in objectivity, they have been far less successful in totalizing knowledge of reality. Disciplinary fragmentation within the academy too often leads to a lack of connections between events and experiences. Science and academia suffers from over-specialization, an absence of metatheory informing scientific understandings of reality, even dissuasion from approaching inquiry of reality informed by robust and ambitious metatheory to understand social being and natural reality as greater totalities.

The aim of this chapter is to sketch a metatheoretical approach to several urgent dilemmas facing human beings in the twenty-first century. This chapter argues the world is currently facing quintuple crises, socio-economic, political, environmental, personal, and existential/spiritual. Two partly complementary metatheories are employed in order to bring the quintuple crises into conceptual and ontological *totality*. Roy Bhaskar's philosophy of dialectical critical realism is employed to understand the economic *structural* conditions causing most immediately the socio-economic, political, and environmental crises. Ken Wilber's integral theory is employed to grasp most immediately the existential/spiritual, mental health/personal, and environmental crises at the level of agency.

The first task is to briefly explain the urgency of metatheory to practical and personal problems. Next the quintuple crises will each briefly be described. The rest of the chapter argues that the quintuple crises are best understand as a totality, each symbiotically related to the others, and how the work of Bhaskar and Wilber can be synthesized (see Despain, 2013a, 2014) to help us understand this *symbiotic totality* of the crisis-ridden twenty-first century.

1 Metatheory and Existential Crises

The quintuple crises are certainly overdetermined.[2] However, the argument here is that the crises can be best understood as a *totality*. Moreover, the crisis is rooted in the power$_2$[3] relations of corporate capitalism. This is not to suggest that absenting corporate capitalism will automatically solve the dilemmas facing human beings in the twenty-first century. It is to suggest that the political economy of corporate capitalism has explicitly shaped how these problems have manifested. Consequently, any 'solution' to the human problems and *crises* facing humanity *must* understand how the political economy of corporate capitalism shapes, maintains, and produces them.

It is contended here that most natural scientists and social scientists, indeed most human beings, tend to view the rise of terrorism and war separate from political economy (Despain, 2004); that the environmental crisis is not related to the rise in drug use, suicide, and crime. The ubiquitous use of anti-anxiety and anti-depression medication is viewed as a personal 'psychological' problem, rather than a social crisis of social relations and power. There is a general lack of understanding between personal development and social institutions; likewise for the interconnections and inner-connections between the quintuple crises.

This chapter proposes we understand the quintuple *crises* as *a* quintuple *crisis*. The urgency of the metatheory of dialectical critical realism and integral theory is that each underscores the inner- and interconnections between, and within, things and events.

Integral theory is built from the insight that humans are complex beings. Integral theory emphasizes there is complexity and depth to what a (human) being is. Wilber illustrates this complexity and depth of being in his 'all-quadrant, all-level' model, or AQAL (see Figure 1.1). Wilber is underscoring in the AQAL model the value spheres of human beings. Sometimes Wilber speaks of these value spheres as Beauty, Goodness, and Truth; other times as subjective, intersubjective, and objective; and as I, We, and It.

The details, intricacies, and multifariousness that Wilber intends to capture in the AQAL model, and illustrated in Figure 1.1 (as one simple representation of AQAL), need not detain us. What is important for our purposes is that the AQAL model proposes that Being in general, human being in particular, are ontologically constituted by internal aspects (inside) and external aspects (outside), the interrelational dimension (we/culture), and the inner-relational dimension (its/systems).

What then is important for our purposes is that what happens at the environmental, social, cultural, or personal level necessarily affects symbiotically each

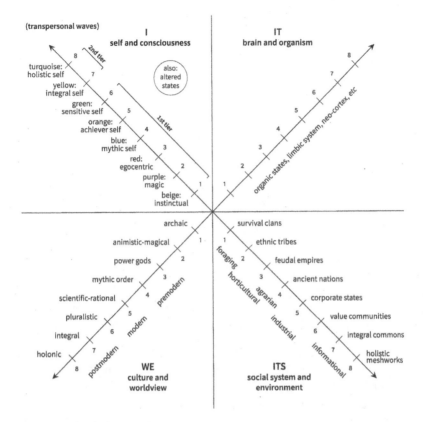

FIGURE 1.1 Wilber's four quadrants

level. In other words, integral theory evokes a perspective that would argue that the manifestation of a crisis at any-level or within any-quadrant, is a crisis for all-quadrants, all-levels.

Critical realism proposes a very similar perspective. Critical realism has promoted two important models that capture the inner- and interconnections of social being. The first model is the transformational model of social activity, or TMSA (Bhaskar, 1986, pp. 122–129) and the second (an elaboration of the first) is the four-planar model of social being (see Figure 1.2). The TMSA features the dualities of structure and praxis,[4] and generates two interconnected social scientific problems: (1) how social practices are to be identified, i.e. as motivated by the cultural and social structural physiology and/or by individual beliefs and action; and (2) how the individuated practices are interlaced and intricated, i.e. what are *tendencies emergent* from exchanges of practices and how do the individuated practices relate and/or *cause* other practices (Bhaskar, 1986, p. 154). Bhaskar extends the TMSA model by developing the four planar model of social being. This extension of and development of TMSA is necessary so as to include and accentuate social relations/culture, and to underscore that human praxis always occurs in time and space, and has effects and

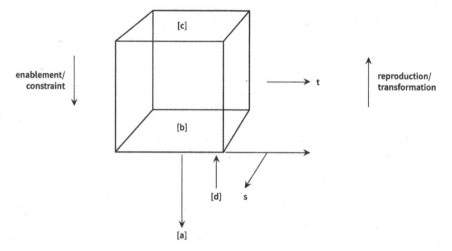

[a] = plane of material transactions with nature
[b] = plane of inter/intra-subjective [personal] relations
[c] = plane of social relations
[d] = plane of subjectivity of the agent

FIGURE 1.2 Bhaskar's four-planar social being

consequences on the individual, between individuals (and groups), on transactions between individuals (and groups), and nature (Bhaskar, 1986, p. 128).[5]

What is important for our purposes, according to both Wilber's AQAL schema and Bhaskar's four-planar model of social being, individual human beings, the Self, is in part constituted by (1) human psychology and natural personal development,[6] (2) cultural and social interactions,[7] (3) institutions, social structure, and other systems,[8] and (4) biology, nature and other material transactions.[9]

The importance of the AQAL model and the model of four-planar social being is that the quintuple crises should be understood as a totality. At the very least each crisis is affecting all dimensions (quadrants and planes) of Being. More strongly, these models suggest that researchers, scientists, policymakers, and *all* citizens should be aware of the possibility of not only inter-inner-related effects, but *also* inter-inner-related causation.[10]

It is within the sights of inter-inner-connectivity that we now turn to, first, the false promises of peace and prosperity and then the brief description of the quintuple crises, before returning to integral theory and dialectical critical realism to better understand it as *a quintuple crisis*.

2 The (False) Promise of a Teleological Manifest Peace and Prosperity

Triumphantly several prominent social theorists have argued that human beings are becoming more peaceful. Steven Pinker has made the argument from a psychological/cognitive perspective, Jared Diamond from an anthropological/cultural perspective, Francis Fukuyama from both a political/institutional *and* philosophical/rationality perspective (this list could be significantly extended, see Wilber, 1995, pp. 311–312). Their arguments are persuasive. Yet there are depressing and blatant *existential contradictions*. Human beings today have the capacity to both annihilate the human race and to destroy the planet. Worse, the *current* destruction of Earth by human beings is as you read these words 'running Genesis backward, decreating' (McKibben, 2010, p. 25).

The blatant existential contradictions and global crises make Fukuyama's thesis of the 'End of History' and the 'Last Man' indefensible. Nonetheless, most people within the developed, US hegemonic world are Fukuyamean. In other words, most people more or less accept that liberal-democratic society settles all of the 'really big questions'; all that remains is to extend Hegelian mutual recognition between nations, between groups, between individuals, etc. and make the social being of liberal-democratic capitalism a little more just, tolerant, patient, aware, accepting, etc. The 'there is no alternative' dictum is softened by Pinker, Diamond, and Fukuyama to 'there is no need for an alternative' because the world is getting better, more peaceful, more just, thanks to the historical development of liberal-democratic capitalism. The premise here is that there are strong reasons to be *both* optimistic and pessimistic about the future of human life and planet Earth.

We can agree with theorists such as (those above, and) Ken Wilber that there is a *telos* to human life and the Kosmos more generally, both a teleological pull, and a teleonomic push (Bhaskar, 1993, p. 22; also see Wilber, 1995, pp. 310–316). However, this *telos* should be understood to offer *only* a '*tendential rational directionality*' to the development of consciousness (Wilber, 2001/1979, italics in original) and to geo-history (Bhaskar, 1993). For both Bhaskar and Wilber the *tendential rational directionality* of geo-history and consciousness finds its origin in Aristotle, Hegel, Marx, Freud, and Piaget. More specifically, the *tendential rational directionality* is a function of Bhaskar's and Wilber's respective conceptions of human agency as involving non-identity with, *and* dialectical dependence between, the self and society, self and nature, and subject and object most generally. Moreover, the principle of Adornoian/Bhaskarian non-identity is the basis for the potential of *alienation* (Despain, 2011), the principle of dialectical dependence is the basis for a fundamental drive or a *telos* to overcome alienation through Aristotelian self-actualization (Wilber, 2001/1979) and Hegelian self-realization (Sayer, 2003).

This optimism is both contingent and 'tendential', *and* hard work, having to overcome master–slave-like power$_2$ relations (Bhaskar, 1993, p. 367 n.). Against Fukuyama's thesis, it is arguable that liberal-democratic capitalism blocks Hegelian mutual recognition rather than manifests it. The master–slave dialectic can result in an acquiescence of reconciliation that is consistent with oppressive power$_2$ relations, rather than a reconciliation that overcomes oppressive power$_2$ relations. Geo-history evolution and the historical development of consciousness is radically incomplete (Wilber, 1995, p. 313; Bhaskar, 1993, p. 367 n.). Power$_2$ relations and oppressive institutional forms can function as a *block* to conscious development of thought and well-being (Bhaskar, 1993, pp. 252–254; Wilber, 1995, p. 313).

The potential for alienation denotes that the relationships between subject/object, self/nature, and self/society can be hellish, terrifying, and enslaving. In *The Atman Project*, Wilber explains the temporal development of human ontogeny as an evolutionary process from an infantile state of an unconscious Hell, to a conscious Hell, to (potentially) a conscious Heaven (Wilber, 1996/1980, p. xii). However, this ontogenic process can be constrained, arrested, and reversed. When the developmental process is constrained, arrested, or a reversal of the developmental process manifests, it can be dubbed involution$_2$. This terminology is usurped from Wilber (Wilber, 1996/1980, pp. 185–203). However, Wilber's use of the term is developmentally progressive. For Wilber when involution is achieved it is necessarily a deeper personal enlightenment, however, usually out of phase with conventional modes of being. It is a deepening and extension of *mind* and personal power$_1$.[11] Wilber's use of the term is here embraced and labelled *involution$_1$*. Involution$_2$ then is the tendency of spiritual development to acquiesce to power$_2$ and coming to believe spiritual development is secondary to cultural modes of being, and must be reconciled with current social practices. For example, the pursuit of money has cultural priority to cosmic or religious awareness. Typically this is more tacit acquiescence, due to the lack of philosophical/spiritual awareness, than it is a conscious choice.

Involution$_2$ is the belief that spiritual enlightenment is exhausted by the practice of commercial relations. It is well captured by what Marcuse called 'one-dimensional man'. Marcuse (1991/1964) maintained that particular dimensions of human existence have disappeared or been eliminated by commercial capitalistic society. Marcuse argued certain spheres of existence, formerly considered as private and emancipatory (e.g., sexuality, artistic creativity, spirituality), are now part of the systemic social oppression and domination. Technological change offers the material bases of human freedom, but has instead been employed to serve the interest of the wealthy and powerful and suppress human freedom. Marcuse's primary warning is that totalitarianism and economic and political domination can now be imposed without outrage and resistance. In other words, *involution$_2$* dominates. Existing social relations and technology are denying the *real* possibilities inherent in them and freedom and ethical life is severely circumvented.

Bhaskar's *Dialectic*, although not employing the terms, is a meditation on socioeconomic involution$_2$ and the process of becoming 'one-dimensional man'. Bhaskar theorizes the ubiquitous historical presence of master–slave-like relations throughout recorded history, the hegemonic-hermeneutical struggles of oppressive modes of praxis as ideologies informing Hegelian unhappy consciousness and the absence of fully critical self-consciousness. Bhaskar very explicitly develops what Marcuse called 'negative' or dialectical thinking, whereby existing things are argued to be other-than-they-appear, tending to serve hidden power$_2$ and interests.[12]

The argument of this chapter is that the current (global) social circumstance is one of Bhaskarian *blockism*, a Wilberian-like involution of social consciousness. Bhaskar employs the term 'blockism' to refer to theories of space, time and space-time that cannot sustain a realist theory of causality, hence universalizability is blocked, or 'block universalism', blockism for short (1993, pp. 252–254). Here I want to extend its use. It is not simply theory that blocks our ability to achieve universalizability, but social structural and cultural forms function as blockism to our personal development. When it is theory that blocks universalizability, it will be labelled *blockism₁*. When it is social relationships, political powers₂, institutions, or social structures that block personal development it will be labelled *blockism₂*.

3 Quintuple Crises: Wilberian Involution₂ and Bhaskarian Blockism₂

The quintuple global crises are a type of Wilberian involution₂ and Bhaskarian blockism₂. The quintuple global crises are manifest as socio-economic, political, environmental, personal, and spiritual calamities.

This quintuple global crisis needs to be understood as a *totality*. Although overdetermined, the quintuple global crisis needs to be understood as symbiotic *causal* relationships between *events* and episodes. In the political realm the globe is plagued by wars, acts of terrorism, political protests, and socio-political uprising. In 2011 alone the world saw the rise of the Arab Spring in the Middle East, and the Occupy Movement in the developed West. From New York to Paris, from Egypt to London, from Libya to San Francisco the world imploded in political protest. Tens of thousands of protests have emerged throughout Asia and within China. South and Central Americans have experienced a resurgence of socialistic politics, all in the wake of the fall of the Soviet Union and socialistic Eastern Europe. Politically the world is in turmoil.

The environmental circumstance, at best, is grim. According to the UN GEO-4 report (UN, 2007), climate change has now become 'urgent' (p. 6), but the report declares 'a remarkable lack of urgency' and a 'woefully inadequate' (p. 66) response, including the refusal of severe-polluting countries to ratify the Kyoto Protocol (p. 72). Several 'industrial sectors that were unfavourable to the Protocol managed successfully to undermine the political will to ratify it' (p. 74). There has been a significant extinction of species (according to the UN report, extinction of species is 100 times faster than the rate shown in the fossil record. Over 30 percent of amphibians, 23 percent of mammals and 12 percent of birds are threatened), decline of fish stocks, loss of fertile land through degradation, overconsumption of many natural resources, declining supplies and increasing demands of fresh water, populated urban air, acute problems of human hunger and severe poverty, and unsustainable patterns of human consumption. The UN report suggests that wealthier populations are living beyond their means. 'Humanity's footprint is 21.9 hectares per person while the Earth's biological capacity is, on average, only 15.7 ha/person' (pp. 163–201). The United Nation's Intergovernmental Panel on Climate Change has confirmed there is a strong correlation between climate change and changes to the global supply (IPCC, 2022, Chapter 5). The report is yet another urgent alarm bell, underscoring the real dangers and current crises in nations across the globe. Climate change is bringing severe consequences from increasing floods and failing dams that endanger entire communities, to droughts and tapped-out water supplies that put people, industries, economies, and ecosystems at high risk.

The crises we have are manifesting all too personally. Recent reports have underscored the rise of suicide in the United States: 28 percent increase in overall suicide rates, 40 percent spike among whites, and 48 percent jump among men in their 50s. There have been similar rises in suicide throughout Europe, South Korea, China, and Japan. There is increasing evidence of a growing mental health crisis in the United States. The lack of labour rights, instable income and employment, long hours of work, unemployment, poverty, and inequality have been strongly linked to substance abuse, gambling, anxiety, depression, anger, and violence. Within capitalist relations, mental health systems are driven by market economics and the profit motive. This means that the quality and quantity of mental health services is dependent on access to money, income, and insurance. Wealthy people have reasonable access to the best mental health services available. However, working class populations, unemployed, and poor have little, if any, access to mental health services. Richard Sennett (2007) has written of the rise of anxiety and the 'spectre of uselessness' now pervasive in the 'new culture' of capitalism. Well before the 'age of anxiety' identified by Sennett, Sigmund Freud contemplated if civilization itself might have 'become neurotic' under the pressure of civilizing trends. Erich Fromm answered 'yes'. Indeed according to Fromm 'The world in the middle of the twentieth century is mentally sicker than it was in the nineteenth century' (Fromm, 1990/1955, p. 102). Robert E. Lane (2000) has demonstrated that in recent years there has indeed been an increase in depression and anxiety, a decline in happiness, marital satisfaction, work satisfaction, and financial satisfaction.

There is a lack of leisure time to pursue relationship needs for many American citizens. The higher needs of worship are often neglected and not pursued, although expressly desired (Taylor, 2005). There seems to be a lack of existential meaningfulness. Capitalistic culture has become radically and dangerously secularized and disenchanted. For far too many Americans, life's meaning has been reduced to going to work, watching TV, and attending sports events. Existential absurdism seems culturally widespread. Fred Hirsch (1976, p. 12) has declared that capitalism 'exhibits a pronounced proclivity toward undermining the moral foundations on which any society, including the capitalist variety, must rest'. Karl Polanyi (2001/1944) saw this pronounced proclivity as a duality. On the one hand capitalism leads to material progress and creates the conditions for material social well-being, but on the other hand market activity undermines the very moral and communal foundations upon which material progress depends. Polanyi called this capitalism's 'double movement'. The double movement is the basis of socio-economic crisis.

4 Political Economy as the Primary Generative Mechanism of Crisis

As stated above, the quintuple crisis is overdetermined. There are mechanisms at work at many levels of social and natural being. However, the contradictory nature of capitalism, its double movement, its proclivity to undermine moral foundations and the conditions for a more spiritual existence can be argued to be a primary cause of the quintuple crises. We here embrace the following:[13] (1) the Keynesian/Minskyian notion that the financial sector is radically unstable; (2) the new Keynesian/Polanyian thesis that price adjustments, for which the system depends, do not equilibrate the system; (3) the institutional/neoclassicist position that the American economic system is dominated by megacorporations; and finally (4) the institutional/Marxian thesis that capitalism is prone to stagnation, not because of its failures, but its successes. If these premises have warrant, then it is quite easy to understand that the contradictions generated will cause socio-economic crisis, political turmoil, tensions, and mistrust, personal overwork, unhappiness, depression, anxiety, existential meaninglessness, and spiritual disenchantment.

American capitalism collapsed into a financial crisis in 2008, well anticipated by post-Keynesian and stagnation economic theorists. Today the economy remains stuck in an 'Endless Crisis'. The little 'recovery' that has occurred has been jobless, unemployment remains at 8 percent, and underemployment at 17 percent. Even mainstream economists have urged that inequality in the United States is at a level that puts in peril our economy, our democracy, and our very system of justice.

American workers are now desperate for a transformation, and democratization, of the workplace and an alternative economic arrangement. Margret Thatcher in the 1980s proclaimed there is no alternative (TINA) to free-market capitalism. But for the majority of Americans, capitalism is itself no alternative (CINA) for making a living or for living a life (Despain, 2013b). American workers need an alternative to low-paying jobs, lack of benefits, and the lack of economic security. The political avenue is blocked. Austerity and fiscal deficits occupy the minds of American politicians.

Ronald Reagan proclaimed that 'Government is not the solution to our problem, government is the problem'. As paradoxical as this statement is, Reagan was 100 percent correct that fiscal policy by the government is not the solution. This is because the problem is economic, structural, and systemic. No employment policy and spending programme is going to fix the problem that is the capitalistic mode of production.

Thus, the political gridlock and obstruction in Washington simply underscores the fact that any solution will at this moment in history necessarily come from outside of Washington. Stagnation is the normal state of monopoly capitalism. Financialization has only further destabilized the economy and augmented the boom and bust cycles. The rise of the neoliberal state and the Washington Consensus has simply exported to the rest of the world the form of monopoly capital, oligopolistic hegemony, finance capital and its boom and bust cycles.

Americans have a very clear conception that something is amiss. They understand there are problems in various industries, especially the financial industry. They also have a clear understanding of the obstruction in Washington. Americans understand that market concentration, predation, and rent-seeking are now an integral part of the American economic system. They also voted Barack Obama into office twice on the conception of 'hope' and the promise of change. Most Americans now interpret Obama's campaign slogans as mere political rhetoric.

There is a remarkable lack of outrage and protest. Initially after the financial collapse and the Herculean bailouts of the financial sector there was both outrage and protest in the form of the Occupy movement across the country. In June 2012 the leftist social theorist and Harvard University Professor Theda Skocpol declared the Occupy 'movement over'. Indeed the outrage and protest has dwindled and appears to continually fade. Many bloggers, columnists, and activists have claimed it is because Americans lack any trust in the ability of the public sector to address our economic problems. Others have embraced a Chomskyesque explanation that mainstream media, right-wing pundits, and Fox News have obscured the real problems and confused the public. Jeff Faux (2012, p. 13) offers a very interesting explanation by pointing out that polls reveal

> a gap between people's perception of the nation's economic fate and their own. The same polls that reported that Americans were pessimistic about the country's future and believed that the next generation would be poorer also showed that they were optimistic about their own prospects.

Faux dubs this the 'Lake Wobegon effect'. It certainly helps to explain why polls time after time report a majority of Americans, typically between 70 and 80 percent, believe themselves to be doing better than average. Distrust in government, Chomskyesque views of the media, and the Lake Wobegon effect have significant merit but do not go anywhere near far enough to explain how we as Americans acquiesce to the perpetuation of joblessness, household debt, government deficits, economic insecurity, and the reproduction of capitalistic social relations and its totalitarian workplace relations.

I believe the primary explanation is fourfold. First, the particular master–slave-like power$_2$ relations, in short big business generally, and big finance in particular, have economic hegemony that has transformed into political hegemony.[14] Second is the lack of economic literacy. Third is the absence of any conception of alternatives to undemocratic workplaces and capitalistic social relations in the minds of the majority of Americans. Fourth is providing the conditions for more Eros, an extension of one's personal and existential Atman Project. In short we need greater cosmic or spiritual awareness. More philosophically, we respectively fail to fully understand: (1) the *structural* and *institutional conditions*; (2) the *hermeneutic hegemonic/counter-hegemonic struggles* of the contemporary situation; (3) *agency* and the *open totality* of social being. All of these need to be fundamentally mended for real change and social transformation to occur.

Theda Skocpol is wrong to declare the Occupy movement 'over'. This is because the nation's socio-economic maladies and hardships facing citizens and workers persist. Given the problems of unemployment, underemployment, poverty, inequality, lack of benefits, lack of security, and countless other injustices generated by the American oligopolistic economy, the Occupy movement is better understood as merely latent! The movement initiated in September 2011 may well be only the beginning of a revolutionary era.

Rick Wolff (2011) reports that the Occupy movement is a good indication that post-crisis-2008 'people are realizing that they have to understand the economics if they want to be part of the debate on how to turn things around' (p. 103).

Economic literacy requires a deep understanding of distributional trends and shifts in labour compensation and job security. For example real wages in the US have been stagnating for 80 percent of American workers for 40 years; 30 percent of Americans (100 million people) either endure poverty or have incomes just above the poverty level (approximately $23,000 annual income for a family of four). Pensions have all but disappeared for American workers, while they also endure cuts in health care insurance and other benefits. Meanwhile worker productivity rises, working hours increase, and leisure and vacation time diminish.

Taxes have been cut for corporations and wealthy Americans in promise for higher growth rates and trickle down effects for workers which have not manifested. Corporate production is highly undemocratic and designed to benefit shareholders and upper management with little or no benefit for American workers and citizens.

The lack of economic literacy does not necessarily mean Americans fail to learn 'economics'. Rather they are learning economics—neoclassical economics. What can be learned from neoclassical economic are the distributional trends and the shifts in labour compensation and job security. This should be encouraged and embraced. However, more economics, and better economic theory, is needed. Specifically what is needed, and not provided in neoclassical economics, is class analysis in a historical context and a Sweezyian political economy and theory of stagnation as a structural explanation of the historical quagmire and the impossibility of capitalist social relations improving the lives of the majority of Americans and the majority of world citizens.

Capitalism should be condemned for its injustices and inequalities on the grounds of morality, ethics, and politics. However, the condemnation of capitalism includes understanding that the injustices and inequalities generated by capitalism are the basis of the financial and economic instability, unemployment, and crises. In other words, the crises of capitalism are absolutely systemic.

Economic literacy requires a fundamental understanding of class formations and historical alliances manifest in the last four decades. The alliance between 'popular classes' and management class following the Great Depression of 1930 was severed following the profitability crisis of 1970. A new alliance emerged wedding the management class with the 'capitalist classes' (i.e. corporate (stock) ownership and financial agents). Financial enticements and financial innovation reconfigured compensation incentives and corporate personnel motivations consummated the marriage between capitalist classes and their corporate management teams. At the same time, according to Duménil and Lévy (2011), this consummation constituted a 'divorce' between ownership/finance and the actual production processes in the domestic economy. This was essentially a delocalizing of financial incentives for corporate management, the sales effort, and financial intermediation.

The political arrangement of 'neoliberalism' and the 'Washington Consensus' expedited the 'divorce' between ownership/finance from the actual production process of domestic economies via deregulation, helping to develop securitization, and other forms of financial innovation. Two of the economists to first realize the importance of the developments of this so-called 'financialization' were Paul Sweezy and Harry Magdoff (1980).

For several decades *Monthly Review* has been interpreting the historical development and crises around the theory of monopoly capital (as developed by Paul Baran, Paul Sweezy, and Harry Magdoff). Contemporary circumstances have proven the effort to be crucially important and historically urgent. Most recently John Bellamy Foster, Fred Magdoff, and Robert W. McChesney have demonstrated that the theory of monopoly capital is powerful for interpreting the triple crisis human beings are confronting, a socio-economic global crisis, world political crises (of war and ineffectual fiscal austerity), and environmental crisis.

One interesting aspect about the work of the *Monthly Review* social thinkers is that their work is an extraordinary and sophisticated synthesis of political economy. The strengths and insights from mainstream, Marxism, institutionalism, post-Keynesianism, feminism, and environmentalism have been incorporated and developed into a powerful and very fruitful explanation of the quintuple crises human beings are facing across the globe. Thus, the really revolutionary achievement of the *Monthly Review* effort is the depth and breadth of understanding contemporary historical political economic circumstances and the global Triple Crises.

In their most recent book *The Endless Crisis: How Monopoly-Finance Capital Produces Stagnation and Upheaval from USA to China*, Foster and McChesney argue the institutional and industrial organization of oligopolistic capitalism or monopoly capital is plagued by severe stagnation as the normal state. Stagnation gives rise to financialization and conglomeration as a means to escape the normal state, generating financial bubble after financial bubble within a financial institutional arrangement which has effectively transformed oligopolistic financial markets into a massive gambling casino. The only viable escape is expansion into foreign markets, but the intense profit motive of oligopolistic capitalism and the Veblenesque predation and 'superexploitation' facilitated by and politically institutionalized as neoliberal policy blocks this avenue and turns foreign investment strategies into systems of debt peonage(-like) circumstances for domestic populations and generates horrific levels of political, economic, and social inequality, both within nations and between nations, generating a new imperialism.

The *Monthly Review* literature is spontaneously a call for action with the potential of transforming the political dysfunction that is American political economy. With monopoly-finance capital theory as the foundation of economic literacy we have (partially) addressed two of the four primary reasons for the remarkable lack of outrage in protest in America today.

Recall the third reason for the remarkable lack of outrage and protest is that most Americans lack any conception of an alternative. This impedes the public will and prohibits (potent) action and political will. It also is the basis for acquiescing to capitalistic social relations.

The most extraordinary aspect concerning the absence of an alternative is that it is fallacious. The fallaciousness of alternative ways of economic organization and social interaction needs mending.

To repeat for emphasis, the financial system has not been restructured, thus another financial collapse is imminent. Moreover, the problems of capitalistic social relations have not been mended, and cannot be within the undemocratic workplace relations and undemocratic/tyrannical capital markets. This means that in addition to an imminent financial crisis, we can expect the continuation of inequality, unemployment, underemployment, overwork, lack of benefits, poverty, undemocratic/tyrannical workplace and capital market decisions, and environmental destruction.

The capitalistic system itself must be transformed. To put it into a slogan: capitalism is no alternative—CINA.

5   From TINA to CINA, to EASE

Recently I have explained how alternatives to capitalism already exist; in other words, real alternatives to, and realistic mechanisms of transformation from, capitalism are now occurring (Despain, 2013b). In recent work including Rick Wolff's *Democracy at Work: A Cure for Capitalism* (2012), David Schweickart's *After Capitalism* (2011), Gar Alperovitz's *America Beyond Capitalism: Reclaiming Our Wealth, Our Liberty and Our Democracy* (2011), and Dada Maheshvarananda's *After Capitalism: Economic Democracy in Action* (2012) an alternative to capitalism is constructed and a political bridge to achieve it developed. Thus, there are alternatives to capitalism. These alternatives are in existence currently. In an acronym, these alternatives can be dubbed 'existing alternatives starting emancipation', or EASE.

I won't here repeat the details of these alternatives, first, because my article can be read in *Monthly Review* (Despain, 2013b), and second, because they are only meant as highly selective examples of practical calls to action capable of transforming the economy and democratizing the workplace. The conclusions are broadly that there is a severe *real contradiction* between democratic politics and highly undemocratic workplaces. The historical manifestation is inequality, insecurity, low pay, lack of benefits, etc. for significant numbers of American workers. Private property, exploitation, labour laws, segmentation of the labour force—the labour/capital nexus—have created a situation whereby personal development has been disrupted and suspended for millions of persons, agency and self-efficacy have been significantly circumvented, and involution$_2$ tendentially triumphs over evolution and involution$_1$ of personal development.

What here is important is that EASE means not only overcoming socioeconomic crisis and an extension of democracy into the workplace, but also, based on AQAL and the four-planar model of social being, a mending of personal crises, a decrease in the current forms and reasons motivating terrorism and war, a transformation in how human beings relate to nature, and new possibilities for finding *meaningfulness* and *purposefulness*, with the possibility of deeper, multiply-dimensional, being.

6 Personal Development: From Involution$_2$ to Involution$_1$

When master–slave-like power$_2$ relations predominantly prevail, involution$_2$ is the dominant tendency. Ken Wilber has given the most complete picture of this process of personal development by synthesizing the work of dozens of researchers on the topic. *The Atman Project* is one of Wilber's early developmental syntheses. It is a highly ambitious work that traces human development from (pre-)birth to the 'Formless'. The book describes the path that human development takes as essentially described by psychoanalysts, such as Freud, Erikson, Maslow, and developed by Piaget, Vygotsky, existential philosophers, and others. Wilber calls this process of human development the 'outward arc'. It describes the development of a pre-conscious baby to cultural 'normality'.

For Wilber (1996, p. 5) the outward arc is only the beginning of the story! Human development becomes most interesting when consciousness of the individual strives for the *beyond normal*. Normal today is the tragic 'one dimensional' human being. This 'beyond normal' aspect of human development Wilber calls the 'inward arc' (see Figure 1.3).

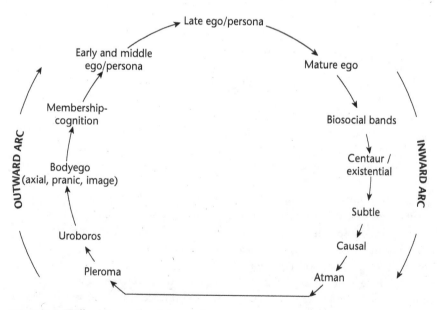

FIGURE 1.3 Wilber's inward and outward arcs

Wilber emphasizes that human development requires both (personal) *growth* and (a type of) *death*. The death of course is our 'one dimensional' self. Emancipation requires the death of the 'one dimensional' self, who unconsciously serves and tacitly reproduces the power$_2$ of big business and big finance.

Personal development proceeds in a progressive evolution, as long as the *self* can 'accept the death of its present structure, disidentify with it, and transcend it to a higher structure, more unified, less substitutive' (Wilber, 1996, p. 194). If the *self* does not accept the death of the present structure of self, personal development is arrested, can even regress, or suffer psychotic breakdown (Wilber, 1996, p. 184). The late ego/persona is to achieve socio-cultural 'normality'.

Once the self reaches socio-cultural 'normality' she begins to develop a 'mature ego' that is able to critically apprehend socio-cultural normality and reach beyond normality, toward a higher self(-awareness), unfettered by socio-cultural normality and historical cultural relativity. What the self is striving for is a less cultural relative meaning to life. The self strives for what Kohlberg called universalism, or a more universal meaningfulness to life. Bhaskar argues the same thing. Human beings desire a universal existence, but the current master–slave-like power$_2$ relations 'block universalism', or *blockism$_2$* for short.

Wilber maintains that twentieth-century developmental psychology and nineteenth- and twentieth-century philosophy (especially the existential tradition) have fully grasped the striving for *beyond normality* and meaningfulness to life that is more universal, i.e. a striving for universalism. In Figure 1.3, the pleroma, uroboros, bodyego, membership-cognition, and early and middle ego/persona stages roughly map onto the five Freudian stages. Wilber has changed both the Freudian names and developmental descriptions to free these development stages from biological reductionism and from being overly driven by libido as in Freudianism. Instead of the biological and libido being the primary drive, Wilber underscores the ever-presence of existential concerns and the necessary relationship between subject and object or human being and nature/cosmos.

The basic structure of development, (personal) evolution, and transcendence is remarkably similar.

> As evolution proceeds, however, each level in turn is differentiated *from* the self, or 'peeled-off' so to speak. That self, that is, eventually *disindentifies* with its present structure so as to *identify* with the next higher-order emergent structure. More precisely (and this is a very important technical point), we say that the self detaches itself from its *exclusive* identification with that lower structure. It doesn't throw that structure away, it simply no longer exclusively identifies with it.
>
> (Wilber, 1996, p. 94, italics in original)

To reach the existentialist level of consciousness is a remarkable achievement, both individually and culturally. It is to endeavour for *universalism* concerning morality and the meaning of life. It is what Maslow, Rogers and Perls, following Aristotle, called 'self-actualization' (Wilber, 1996, pp. 169, 55) and what Fromm and

Riesman called 'autonomous' individuals (Wilber, 1996, pp. 210, 53). For Wilber this is only half of the story of the inward arc. The other half of the inward arc is the Atman Project proper which is grossly underdeveloped in Western science and philosophy. Thus, for the Atman Project proper Wilber develops his insights from the mystic and religious traditions from the West and East.

As interesting as the entirety of the Atman Project on both the outward arc and inward arc is, it need not detain us here. Our purpose is to introduce and begin developing language, concepts and theories for understanding the *block universalism*, i.e. *blockism$_2$*, beguiling human beings.

Blockism$_2$ is another expression for the current existential/spiritual crisis. Recall above, we suggested that capitalistic social relations generally fail to provide the social environment for personal and mental health development. This is because capitalism is based on exploitation, profit maximization, and cost minimization. Market interaction and pecuniary motive generates a particular type of mistrust between individuals. Moreover, the inequity, poverty, and low incomes mean that individuals remain stuck in the lower levels of Maslow's hierarchy of needs, that involution$_1$ is arrested and involution$_2$ prevails. One-dimensional human beings proliferate and tacitly replicate.

Conclusion

What then we have initiated in our sketch above is what Bhaskar calls metacritique. First, we have made a contribution to the development of metacritique$_1$ by developing new concepts and theories for understanding the quintuple crises confronting human life. We began with the insight, based on Wilber's AQAL and Bhaskar's four-planar model of social being, that the quintuple crises are symbiotically related and better understood as *a* quintuple *crisis*. In short, it is a shift toward a more *totalizing* conception of the twenty-first-century dilemma. Secondly, it was argued that there currently exists well-developed political economy theory very capable of providing a partial explanatory critique. In a desperate effort for brevity it was claimed that *Monthly Review* monopoly capital theory provides a *depth* analysis to conventional economic theorizing. More ambitiously and more realistically, it will require a further synthesis of several currents within political economy theorizing.[15] Third, it was asserted that TINA is false, CINA is more accurate, and EASE is real concrete possibility.[16] Finally we extended the meaning of Wilber's notion and process of involution and Bhaskar's notion of blockism, respectively to involution$_2$ and blockism$_2$, to explain how currently existing power$_2$ relations reinforce 'one-dimensional' existence and the reproduction of power$_2$ relations at the expense of deeper personal development, self-awareness, and cosmic enlightenment.

Notes

1 This term is borrowed from Otto Rank (1989/1932). It implies that human beings can only take in part of reality at any one time. For Rank 'partialization' was primarily a psychological process of repression. However, the critical realist ontological position of 'stratification' suggests that partialization is at least partly ontological. In other words, it

is not that reality is necessarily repressed, but human access to reality is circumvented, necessitating the activity of science as an intervention to understand reality.
2. This fragmentation of academic disciplines is not simply a metaphysical mistake. Rather it is function of human knowledge and causality within reality. Multiple-causation is characteristic of events and experiences. Reality is overdetermined. Human beings all too often cannot determine the correlation and causes, hence the need for specialization and reductionism to identify a real cause. In a sense, it is fair and accurate to say all science must be necessarily reductionist (non-identity). Metatheory is to first remind us of this necessity, second to pull science upwards towards construction of greater totalities. Metatheorists maintain that this effort not only provides greater scientific understanding, but also better informed policy.
3. The subscript is in reference to Bhaskar's (1993) distinction between two different notions of power. Power$_1$, or the abilities of human agents to think, communicate, feel, act, care, etc., and power$_2$, characteristic of societies to both (1) enable and enhance individual agents and (2) to coerce and constrain individual agents.
4. Duality of structure maintains that society is both the ever-present condition (material cause) and the continually reproduced outcome of human actions. Duality of praxis maintains human action is work, or conscious production, and (normally unconscious) *reproduction* of the conditions of production and society (Bhaskar, 1998, pp. 34–35).
5. Dialectical critical realism further extends the insights of the TMSA and the four-planar model to include new ontological and epistemological insights. Bhaskar (1993, Chapter 2) emphasizes three primary philosophical insights of *absence*, *contradictions*, and *non-identity*. These insights have important implications at the level of praxis and ethical living. Otherwise, the basic insights of TMSA and four-planar model, underscored above, are maintained. The primary implications for praxis concern 'what is to be done' and who's responsibility is it to do it (see Bhaskar, 1994, Chapter 5) and how to live well and practice real morality and ethics (see Bhaskar, 1994, Chapter 7).
6. Wilber's upper-left quadrant and Bhaskar's plane [d].
7. Wilber's lower-left quadrant and Bhaskar's plane [b].
8. Wilber's lower-right quadrant and Bhaskar's plane [c].
9. Wilber's upper-right quadrant and Bhaskar's plane [a].
10. The *really revolutionary* moment in transcendental realism concerns Bhaskar's (1997) new conception of causation, based on powers, tendencies, and emergence. Bhaskar strongly and brilliantly develops and defends a multiple causation model (Bhaskar, 1997, p. 72) based upon causal power tendencies of real 'things' and effects generated by the interaction between real 'things' (Bhaskar, 1997, pp. 96–102).
11. The subscripts are in reference to and correspond respectively to Bhaskar's distinction between power$_1$ or abilities of human agents to think, communicate, feel, act, care, etc., and power$_2$, characteristic of societies to *both* (1) enable and enhance individual agents and (2) to coerce and constrain individual agents.
12. The hidden aspects of reality are the very essence of ontological stratification (i.e. the realms of the empirical, actual, and real). The development of dialectical critical realism is necessarily an extension and amplification of the realm of the real, and the implications this has for better understanding the realms of the actual and empirical, or its hidden causes. It is a perceptional shift, with the normative aim of changing everyday one-dimensional action toward greater emancipation from power$_2$ relations and self-awareness and self-enlightenment. In Bhaskar's terms this is elaboration and strengthening of power$_1$. In Wilber's terms it is involution$_1$ and expansion and progression of Eros.
13. The intended audience is the non-expert in economic theory. However, it is important to understand that there exists well-grounded economic theory to support respectively: (1) economic instability; (2) mechanisms generating market disequilibrium; (3) power$_2$ relations in the economic sphere in the form of the oligopolistic firm; and (4) as the system generates economic growth, more and more people are left out from participating in the benefits, effectively leading to 'stagnation' for millions of households.

14 Moreover there is not currently a comprehensive explanatory critique, or what Bhaskar calls metacritique$_2$, that offers alternative conceptions and theories that are capable of explaining the generative mechanisms and modes of behaviour reproducing the power$_2$ relations causing the crises, blockism$_2$, and involution$_2$. The very purpose of metatheory is to enable, underlabour on behalf of, and be a midwife for metacritique$_2$.

15 The stagnation theory in particular, but a synthesis of political economy literature more generally, is both an initiation and a development of *metacritique$_2$*, or the ability to provide a more comprehensive theory to some aspect of being, in this case political economy, and explain the conditions giving rise to the misunderstanding of reality.

16 EASE is also in part a contribution to metacritique$_2$.

References

Alperovitz, G. (2011). *America Beyond Capitalism: Reclaiming Our Wealth, Our Liberty, and Our Democracy*. Democracy Collaborative Press.

Baran, P., & Sweezy, P. (1966). *Monopoly Capital: An Essay on the American Economic and Social Order*. Monthly Review Press.

Bhaskar, R. (1986). *Scientific Realism and Human Emancipation*. Verso.

Bhaskar, R. (1993). *Dialectic: The Pulse of Freedom*. Verso.

Bhaskar, R. (1994). *Plato Etc.: The Problems of Philosophy and Their Resolution*. Verso.

Bhaskar, R. (1997). *A Realist Theory of Science*. Verso.

Bhaskar, R. (1998). *The Possibility of Naturalism: A Philosophical Critique of the Contemporary Human Sciences*. Routledge.

Despain, H. (2004). Economic policy and the rise of global violence and terrorism. *The Humanist: A Magazine for Critical Inquiry and Social Concern*, July, 26–30.

Despain, H. (2011). The pulse of freedom and the existential dilemma of alienation. In M. Hartwig & J. Morgan (eds), *Critical Realism and Spirituality*. Routledge.

Despain, H. (2013a). Integral theory: The sublabrious chalice? *Journal of Critical Realism*, 125(4), 507–517.

Despain, H. (2013b). It's the system, stupid: Structural crises and the need for alternatives to capitalism. *Monthly Review*, 65(6), 39–44.

Despain, H. (2014). Integral theory and the search for earthly emancipation: On the possibility of emancipatory and ethical personal development. *Journal of Critical Realism* 13(2), 183–188.

Diamond, J. (2013). *The World Until Yesterday: What Can We Learn from Traditional Societies?* Penguin Books.

Duménil, G., & Lévy, D. (2011). *The Crisis of Neoliberalism*. Harvard University Press.

Foster J.B., & McChesney, R. (2012). *The Endless Crisis: How Monopoly-Finance Capital Produces Stagnation and Upheaval from USA to China*. Monthly Review Press.

Fromm, E. (1990/1955). *The Sane Society*. Henry Holt and Company.

Fukuyama, F. (1992). *The End of History and the Last Man*. Avon Books, Inc.

Hirsch, F. (1976). *Social Limits of Growth*. Routledge.

Intergovernmental Panel on Climate Change (IPCC) (2022) *Sixth Assessment Report: Impacts, Adaptation and Vulnerability*. Available at www.ipcc.ch/report/ar6/wg2/ (Accessed 16 March 2022).

Lane, R. (2000). *The Loss of Happiness in Market Democracies*. Yale University Press.

Maheshvarananda, D. (2012). *After Capitalism: Economic Democracy in Action*. InnerWorld Publications.

Marcuse, H. (1991/1964). *One-Dimensional Man: Studies in the Ideology of Advanced Industrial Society*. Beacon Press.

McKibben, B. (2010). *Eaarth: Making a Life on a Tough New Planet*. Henry Holt and Company.

Pinker, S. (2011). *The Better Angels of Our Nature: Why Violence Has Declined*. Viking.
Polanyi, K. (2001/1944). *The Great Transformation: The Political and Economic Origins of Our Time*. Beacon Press.
Rank, O. (1989/1932). *Art and Artist: Creative Urge and Personality Development*. W.W. Norton and Company.
Sayers, S. (2003). Creative activity and alienation in Hegel and Marx. *Historical Materialism*, 11(1), 107–128.
Schweickart, D. (2011). *After Capitalism*. Rowman & Littlefield Publishers, Inc.
Sennett, R. (2007). *The Culture of the New Capitalism*. Yale University Press.
Sweezy, P., & Magdoff, H. (1980). *The Deepening Crisis of US Capitalism*. Monthly Review Press.
Taylor, C. (2007). *The Secular Age*. Harvard University Press.
United Nations (UN) (2007). Global Environment Outlook: Environment for Development 4. Available at www.unep.org/resources/global-environment-outlook-4 (Accessed 28 May 2021).
Wilber, K. (1977). *The Spectrum of Consciousness*. Quest Books.
Wilber, K. (1995). *Sex, Ecology, Spirituality*. Shambhala Publications, Inc.
Wilber, K. (1996/1980). *The Atman Project: A Transpersonal View of Human Development*. Quest Books.
Wilber, K. (2001/1979). *No Boundary: Eastern and Western Approaches to Personal Growth*. Shambhala Publications, Inc.
Wolff, R.D. (2012). *Democracy at Work: A Cure for Capitalism*. Haymarket Books.
Wolff, R.D., & Barsamian, D. (2011). *Occupy the Economy: Challenging Capitalism*. City Lights Publishers.

2
HEALTHY VERSUS PATHOLOGICAL POLITICAL–ECONOMIC DISCOURSE AND POLICY

An Integral Political–Economic Treatment

Kevin Bowman[†]

Introduction

This chapter argues that an integral (metatheoretical, transdisciplinary, and developmental) approach to the analysis of economic decision-making aids in the recognition of how conflicting special-interests across the major stakeholders in American society act and defend their actions via a highly distorted and unjustified use of economic theory. A large disjuncture exists between sound policy and policies that have created, worsened, or prevented adequate responses to the Triple Crises in the US (the global financial crisis that originated in the US and peaked in 2008–2009; the ongoing global environmental crisis, a crisis that American has done little to address; and an inequality crisis in the US that contributes to stakeholder antagonism).

This chapter further argues that unhealthy political–economic discourse helps explain the choice of suboptimal policies over relatively sound ones that are readily available. This reflects a condition in which collective development in the political–economic learning line lags relative to what is capable given general development in other lines that theoretically feed into the political–economic line (especially cognition, morals, and values). Therefore, there exists a high, unexploited return to healing and developing the political–economic line.

The approach here is offered as a way to work for healthier interaction within the present system with insights from integral theory and, to a lesser extent, critical realism as to what an integral-stage economy may look like. The recent, healthier discourse and relations between stakeholder groups in Denmark, which allowed for its economic transformation, is contrasted with the Triple Crises in the US case.

I will use some key portions of the Integral Political Economy (IPE) framework (Bowman, 2008, 2010a, 2010b, 2010c, 2011), which is grounded in the integral philosophy of Ken Wilber (1995, 2000a, 2000b, 2000c, 2002, 2006). IPE has been

DOI: 10.4324/9781003140313-4

used to examine the partial ways in which economic theory has been created and used. This chapter sharpens and deepens the focus on relatively healthy versus unhealthy stakeholder interaction by level and type of development and how the Triple Crises (financial, environmental, and distributional) interact to discourage development in the political–economic learning line despite advances in other lines.

According to Habermas,

> social pathologies occur when one of [his specified] rationalization complexes [similar to Wilber's lines of development] are not cultivated to the same degree as the other rationalization complexes or when learning in one rationalization complex is not allowed to interact with learning in another complex.
>
> *(as cited in Ingram, 2010, p. 319)*

The cognitive line of development is a necessary, but insufficient ingredient to development in many other lines of development. Success in economics should be highly dependent on cognitive maturity as the economy is a highly abstract and complex object. Given the nature of the subject of economics in which distribution and social welfare (though underplayed by the mainstream teaching of the subject) are central issues, values and moral development should also be important inputs into economic understanding (normative economics).

In cognitive terms, Americans have developed remarkably over the last century gaining three intelligence quotient (IQ) points per decade on both the Stanford-Binet and Weschler Intelligence Scales (Flynn, 1984). This has been both the response to, and input into, the rising complexity of everyday social life. The rise (the 'Flynn Effect') has been broadly felt throughout American society as the success has occurred at the higher and lower ends of the IQ distribution.

Despite these advances, Gorton and Diels (2011) find, counter to their expectations, that presidential debates have not become more scientific since 1960. Topics analyzed were economics, foreign policy, and health care/education. They conclude that the use of abstract scientific terms and employing them in logical and causal analysis (formal/orange or post-formal/post-orange rather than concrete/amber or pre-concrete/pre-amber cognition) has decreased significantly over time in the economics realm, but not in matters of foreign policy and health care/education, which remained statistically stable. They found no difference overall between Democrats and Republicans. The authors were surprised and puzzled by their findings. Economics discourse, the authors hypothesized, was particularly well suited to increase in complexity given the abstract requirements to conceptualize the economy and economics being a long-established field within social science. It has developed rich, abstract terminology and logical, causal mechanisms.[1]

Although this is just one narrow measure of economic policy discourse in the US, in my IPE analyses, I have provided many observations consistent with the view that political–economic discourse in the US is showing resistance to the learning opportunities afforded by the Triple Crises—enough evidence to warrant serious study of the political–economic learning line and its general health. Although there are sure to be healthy and unhealthy influences in all countries, this chapter argues that the collective, American political–economic learning line (which helps examine the subject disclosing the economy) and the American political–economic system (object of enactment) are mutually influencing one another (dynamically interacting) in unhealthy ways to a degree that is causally efficacious and economically significant. To make the argument, it is useful to contrast the difficulties the US has had (financially, environmentally, and distributionally) with the achievements made in Denmark. While the financial imbalances were growing, with little or no progress environmentally, and as inequality continued to expand in the US, Denmark, on the other hand, was the only developed economy to have reduced its greenhouse gas emissions. And this was a time that Denmark experienced a successful, broad economic transformation, fairly resilient to the global financial crisis and benefitting a broad swath of the citizenry.

I argue that increasingly antagonistic and polarized policy pressures from various interest groups at different levels and types of development in the US represent resistance to the needed cultural transformation in important segments of the population. Informational-stage technological change and globalization pressures in the social domain require a cultural shift that can contribute to institutional political–economic upgrades. The relatively unhealthy interactions resist learning opportunities through the reinforcing influence of their short-term, narrow interests and their preferred modes of consciousness. The clearer it has become scientifically to reasonable observers that significant change was needed financially and environmentally for a more just and sustainable distribution of investment and consumption, the more dogmatic the discourse has become. This represents a psychological denial of the underlying behaviours across groups that have caused the imbalances and that require change.

1   Key Components of Integral Political Economy

In my IPE framework, I have developed several metatheoretical categorizations of economics. For the objective of this chapter, I will focus on just a few of them. Table 2.1 provides a simple metatheoretical categorization of many of the mainstream economic principles. They are organized by the strengths and weaknesses of the public and private sectors.

See Bowman (2010a, 2010b) for a categorization of the microeconomic and macroeconomic principles of economics, respectively, by eight zones. Bowman (2008) presents a four-quadrant approach to capital and a Wilberian-augmented, marginal theory of value. See Bowman (2011) for a grouping of the mainstream and heterodox schools of economics by quadrant and political–economic type. There you will also find aspects of the economy by level of development. The critical realist economist Tony Lawson (1997) argues that economies are open systems, agents have choice, and thus economists will not find any significant causal regularities. The closed modelling of mainstream economics, however, does transparently

TABLE 2.1 The value and the failures associated with the private and public sectors

Sector	Value (Positive)	Failures (Negative)
Private	Invisible hand	Externalities
	Competitive allocation of scarce resources	Financial contamination
		Short-term incentives and inattention to aggregate risk
	Hard budget constraint	
	Cost reduction in firms	Borrowing constraints for education
	New product development including financial innovation	Anti-competitive consolidation
		Rent seeking
		Sticky prices
Public	Taxing negative externalities and natural resources	Special interest persuasion
		Logrolling
	Anti-trust regulation	Moral hazard
	Financial education. Public goods provision	Pandering populism
		Imperfect modelling of the economy
	Inflation-output monitoring	
	Regulation of excessive risk	Soft budget constraint
	Deposit insurance	
	Short-run stabilization of aggregate demand	

reveal results based on simplistic assumptions. They teach us sufficient conditions needed to reach what are often testable, practical conclusions, but not the existence of universal laws. The metatheoretical approach is a way to contextualize isolated, closed models such that their assumptions can be more appropriately applied. A metatheoretical framework that ties together a series of closed models is arguably more powerful than an open approach with extreme uncertainty about the relationships between all the variables. As Brown et al. (2002) state, 'It is one thing to say that the social world should be understood as a unified whole. It is quite another to show how this can be achieved in practice' (p. 777).

These tools can be used as an integral methodological input to help the subject scientist or economic participant avoid reductionist and elevationist views of the object economy. Although it is important to synthesize mainstream and heterodox schools (a project partially taken up in IPE elsewhere), primarily, I will be making use of only mainstream principles in this chapter. This will demonstrate that a balanced view of mainstream economic theory does not support the policies that have led to or exacerbated the Triple Crises. I'll also show that combining mainstream principles aids in the formation of sophisticated radical arguments.

A critical feature of IPE needed to examine the relative health of political-economic discourse is the notion of the learning line of political-economic understanding and its three political-economic types of conservative, liberal, and

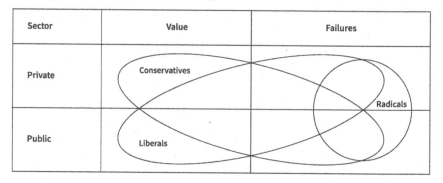

FIGURE 2.1 The portion of economic reality recognized or emphasized by political–economic type

radical. Political–economic conservatives tend to favour the market mechanism in allocating scarce resources. This view is associated with recognition or emphasis on the beneficial aspects of the private sector and the adverse aspects of government involvement in economic affairs. Alternatively, liberals tend to prefer a larger role for government involvement in redirecting resources. This view recognizes or emphasizes the positive aspects of government and the limitations of markets. Radicals recognize or place greater emphasis on the negative aspects of the capitalist system. These types are shown in Figure 2.1.

IPE claims that the individual typologies of conservative, liberal, and radical can each be expressed as relatively less or more developed (Bowman, 2010a). I theorized that less developed agents *tend* to acknowledge or recognize only their two preferred areas of Table 2.1. For example, less developed conservatives only acknowledge the value of private markets and the failures of government. Therefore, they will not make the fine differentiations of Table 2.1. Unlike less developed agents, more developed agents do not suffer from sector absolutism (in the case of liberals or conservatives) or shadow absolutism (in the case of less developed radicals). More developed types recognize aspects of all four spaces in Table 2.1, but they do tend to emphasize the two areas they prefer. The overwhelming consensus in the fields of economics and political economy is that there is value to both sectors in directing the economy, but that each sector has its particular strengths while also being prone to failure in specific ways. Table 2.2 provides common examples of less and more developed versions across the three types.

I will define healthy discourse or policy as discourse or policy that tends to promote meaningful and sustainable development. Unhealthy discourse or policy constrains this sort of development. The more developed versions may be associated with higher or healthier development. In theory, I do not a priori associate them with absolute levels of development or Wilberian fulcrums.

Table 2.3 describes the immature/mature type fallacy in which more developed types are erroneously reduced by less developed agents of another type. Less

TABLE 2.2 Less developed versus more developed agents by political–economic type

	Conservative	Liberal	Radical
More Development	Markets are often efficient. Some market failures exist. Government policies often make matters worse. Open to less distorting, public corrective measures.	Emphasizes market failures. Acknowledges failed liberal policies of the past. Sees development as not occurring without sound public corrective measures and investment.	Market and government failures are interrelated (such as the goal of oligopoly power may interact with special interest persuasion to allow over consolidation). Need evolution in both sectors for a new stage of economic development with better stakeholder balance.
Less Development	Deregulate always. Always cut taxes. Typically sees no role for government.	Fix prices to help us (or poor) now with no regard to unintended consequences. Profit incentive is the problem. No acknowledgment of government failures.	May advocate revolution, not reform. Favours one change as a panacea such as state ownership of capital and land (communism), no hierarchies (anarchy), or abolition of the fractional reserve system.

developed types can simultaneously and irrationally elevate their own views by pointing only to the limitations of other types.

This epistemological aspect of IPE is sorely lacking in economics. How agents disclose necessarily partial aspects of the economy is a strength of an enactive approach where interior methodologies are employed. For example, less developed agents more often see reality in absolutist ways. Holarchical embeddedness or Kosmic address helps determine the expression of various agents. See Bowman (2011) for further elaboration. Consistent with a critical realist qualification, the common expressions shown here are not presented as ahistorical and universal. The expressions are seen as important surface tendencies influenced by the interaction of relatively antagonistic first-tier, deep structures as they tend to interpenetrate these days. These specified tendencies paint useful corners between which other tendencies fall. Furthermore, the analysis of this chapter does not prioritize, on one hand, economic reality as determined exclusively by our subjective experience and enactment of it (idealist), or on the other hand, holarchical, economic potentiality independent of our perceptions and choices (realist).

Table 2.4 focuses on the unhealthy nature of stakeholder interaction. Although there are also relatively healthy stakeholder tendencies as well, a culture of deflection of blame by the important stakeholder groups in the economy emerges as an important force.

TABLE 2.3 Two versions of the immature/mature type fallacy: reductionism and elevationism

Reductionism	More Developed Conservative	More Developed Liberal	More Developed Radical
(Examples of more developed agents reduced to less developed)	Concern of unintended consequences of improper liberal reform seen by *less developed liberal* as selfish defence of the privileged business class.	Desire to regulate a market failure seen by *less developed conservative* as ignorant encroachment of freedom and the right to pursue prosperity.	Critique of policy formed by mutually reinforcing self-interests of Political and business leaders assumed to be motivated to implement state communism or to throw off any benefits of the present system (seen as a 'commie' or 'crazy conspiracy theorist'). The reduction can be by a *less developed conservative or less developed liberal*.
	Either a **more developed conservative or liberal** approach may be met by a *less developed radical* as unwitting support of corrupt elites preventing the overthrow of the status quo.		

Elevationism	Less Developed Conservative	Less Developed Liberal	Less Developed Radical
(Examples of less developed agents elevated to more developed)	Use unsound liberal regulations to elevate their position for no regulation as if there is no theory and evidence for sound regulation.	Refer to the conservative lobbying for deregulation to elevate the liberal position that the crisis was all due to corporate greed without acknowledging government failures or specifying specific, sound regulations.	Use the systemic collapse to elevate their position that the fractional reserve system itself (what they call the debt-based money system) causes unsustainable and speculative lending ignoring the scholarly literature that sustainable borrowing can coexist with sound government policies such as adequate reserve requirements, loan-to-value ratios, debt-payment-to-income ratios, and environmental regulations, taxes, and subsidies.

Critical realism broadens the targeted scope of economic science as it points to, among other things, the unnamed underlying causal mechanisms and stratified structures that are overlooked by methodologies employed in economics. This major critique has been relatively more deconstructive than reconstructive. Integral theory provides some reconstructive access to uncovering some of these important causal mechanisms and stratified structures. In his effort to describe a methodology for economics informed by critical realism, post-Keynesianism, and grounded

TABLE 2.4 Examples of stakeholder deflection of blame by stakeholder group

Stakeholder Group	Example of Deflection of Blame
Republican Leadership	McConnell stating that he 'will oppose any climate program' implying that any government effort to combat climate change is an unneeded, inefficient largesse to the green lobby group (Strassel, 2008).
Democratic Leadership	Pelosi arguing that 'Health care companies are immoral' rather than discussing specific market failures, how government intervention may be needed, and how government failures must be overcome for sound policy (Hamburger & Geiger, 2009).
Average Voter	A survey showed that the majority of Americans support a treaty to reduce carbon emission, but not if it results in higher energy bills (Slate, 2009). This view is despite economic theory, which suggests energy prices should internalize the currently external pollution costs.
	Also, Fed Chairman Paul 'Volcker was everyone's favorite scapegoat' in 1982 (Ullmann, 1983). This is despite the conventional wisdom in economics today that high inflation required Paul Volcker to raise interest rates in the early 1980s. The cost was a severe recession, but the long-term benefit was the defeat of high overall inflation.
Media	Spin is often used in the media to appease extremes rather than informing readers (Mullainathan & Shleifer, 2005). For example, the inheritance tax is referred to as an 'estate tax' in liberal news (as it sounds like it will affect only the rich) or a 'death tax' in conservative news (because it sounds unfair or that it will affect everyone) (The Economist, 2008).
Business Leaders	Business lobbying against any regulation rather than supporting sound regulation arguing that the government cannot know better than the market what are sound practices. Even after the financial crisis, the banking industry lobbied aggressively to prevent even modest reform proposals with these sorts of arguments (Immergluck 2009; Cohen, 2009).

theory, Lee (2002) describes the need to expand methodologies for economics. His uncategorized list touches on the main components of the synthetically explicit integral methodological pluralism.

This section provided the essential aspects of the IPE framework needed to more closely compare healthy versus pathological political–economic discourse and policymaking in the next section.

2 Introducing Game Theory within IPE

Long-Run versus Short-Run Outcomes

This section makes distinctions between long-run and short-run outcomes from relatively less mature versus more mature economic policies. These distinctions are needed in order to justify the game theory setup of the next section. IPE characterizes government-imposed price and wage supports, tariff protection of industries, and subsidies for production (without significant positive externalities) as relatively less mature liberal policies. These policies have greater distortionary effects in the long run. They discourage competitiveness. As the markets change, prices do not signal needed change. Unions that support wage distortions have become less popular among US workers during the era of intensified globalization because firms will more likely outsource or invest in labour-saving mechanization (The Economist, 2009). Alternatively, retraining will increase productivity and wages of workers, but again, disproportionately in the long run. Unlike protectionism, a consensus exists in economics that governmental assistance for education and retraining is justified based on market imperfections to human capital formation (such as credit market constraints and positive externalities). Retraining is especially important today. Increased inequality, in significant part, reflects skill-biased technological change that has outpaced the increase in the supply of skilled workers (Autor et al., 2008; Aghion et al., 1999). Unions that provide better services such as lobbying for retraining assistance for displaced workers allow for skills to complement modern physical capital investments.

Indiscriminate deregulation (from less mature conservatism), lack of public investments, and lack of taxes on carbon and natural resources also have great long-run costs. The surest defence against over-regulation, nationalization, less mature liberal policies, etc., is sound regulation and sound public investments. Sound policies prevent the perceived need for radical overreactions or populist responses to the long-run outcomes of inadequate regulations and public investments. But in the short run, total deregulation can be profitable for certain interests. The financial sector, for example, was very profitable in the short run as it overleveraged homeowners and helped create longer-term systemic collapse. The share of corporate profits going to financial firms increased dramatically during the bubble years. The share rose from 21.1 percent in 1979 to 41.2 percent in 2002 and 37.2 percent in 2006 (Kotz, 2009). Yet without government bailouts much of the financial sector would have gone bankrupt during the Financial Crisis of 2008–2009. Mature policies and investments are also consistent with the cognitive, moral, and needs development of humans. This sort of personal development has long-run benefits but can require difficult life changes and educational work in the short run.

Carbon taxes decrease carbon emissions (a negative externality) to help deal with future costs of global warming. Taxes on natural resources help us incorporate the future value of natural-resource depletion to better incentivize renewable resources. Although economists generally argue marginal tax rates should not be too high, many support progressive taxes because of the diminishing marginal utility of income and to help fund worthy public expenditures. Inadequate taxes and excessive pork spending can result in unsustainable debt levels with longer-term costs.

In conclusion, less mature policies will look relatively more attractive when agents are focused on the short run. Unfortunately, behavioural economists have shown that a majority of agents heavily and irrationally discount the long run (Davis, 2008). Since economic theory does not support policies that overly discount the long run in the ways described in this section, then the immature/mature type fallacies are used as an attempt for economic agents across major stakeholder group to justify their continued, long-run irrational behaviour.

The immature/mature type fallacy is a specific manifestation of the more general critical realist account of ideology or false consciousness, which is influenced by the Marxist tradition. What is unique to IPE is the demonstration that all major stakeholder groups in a mass-consumption, postmodern economy, when weighed down by the immature centre of gravity, can interact from ideological positions that are not necessarily or not fully driven by elite manipulation and exploitation of the common people. Rather, it is the flourishing of the depth-realist, higher-order, longer-term interests of all major groups that can be oppressed by the opposing, widespread ideological positions that shelter the short-term, unjustified interests from the deeper truth. This argument is flushed out further below.

Demonstrating the Need For, and Difficulty in Achieving, Coordination

Here I will use game theory to demonstrate the suboptimal outcomes associated with less mature political–economic culture relative to the benefits of maturity. In Game 1 (a version of the prisoner's dilemma game), let us assume that there is one liberal group (L) and one conservative group (C). Radicals are not a socially acceptable typology in US culture and are not well represented by our two-party system and mainstream media. Thus we can focus on liberal and conservative influences. First I'll assume that both L and C are at a relatively less mature level in the political–economic line. They behave in a manner that deflects blame while avoiding mature compromise. The liberal group could include amber-stage, low-skilled workers that benefit from protectionism. Also in the liberal camp are some green-stage liberals who sympathize with the marginalized workers in the US economic system and who prefer high corporate taxes to carbon taxes and other regulations that raise the cost of living of the average consumer in the short run. The conservative group could include orange-stage, relatively skilled workers that benefit from a laissez-faire economy in the short run. The conservatives may also have support from some amber-stage workers whose short-term benefits are allied with, not necessarily laissez-faire, but with the bundle of policies that tend to be grouped together. Small government conservatism tends to be allied with broader social policies that preserve traditional ways of life. Figure 2.2 presents the short-term payoffs of these two groups.

C has two choices. Strategy 1 (S1) is to support sensible regulation, progressive taxes, carbon and natural resource taxes, and sound public goods like needed infrastructure spending and grants for basic research. Strategy 2 (S2) is to lobby for no significant regulation, less progressive taxes, and no carbon or natural resource taxes. L also has two strategies. Strategy 1 is to support flexible wages based on productivity, generous retraining assistance, carbon and natural resource taxes, and sound public goods. Strategy 2 is to support tariff protection, and price and wage

FIGURE 2.2 Game 1: Two egoists and their short-term payoffs

		Liberal Group (L)	
		S1. Retraining, flexible wages/prices, carbon and natural resource taxes, sound public goods.	S2. Tariffs protection, fixed wages/prices, no carbon or natural resource taxes, high taxes on corporate profits.
Conservative Group (C)	S1. Proper regulation, progressive taxes, carbon and natural resource taxes, sound public goods.	3 / 3	1 / 4
	S2. No regulation, less progressive taxes, no carbon or natural resource taxes.	4 / 1	2 / 2

supports. In IPE, S1 for each agent is a mature preference (mature conservative for H and mature liberal for L). S2 are less mature policy preferences (less mature conservative for H and less mature liberal for L).

C finds that S2 is preferred no matter what L chooses (4 > 3 if L chooses S1, and 2 > 1 if L chooses S2). L also finds S2 to be their dominant strategy (4 > 3 if H chooses S1, and 2 > 1 if the H chooses S2). Therefore the Nash equilibrium (an outcome in which neither of the groups can improve their situation by changing their individual strategy given the choice of the other agent) is for each group to choose its S2.

The less mature, beggar-thy-neighbour policies (S2 for each) can be the dominant strategy for each particular group because costs from these policies are greater in the long run and these agents are assumed to be short-term oriented. L is best off in the short run, in this example, with protection and price supports (L chooses S2), and with progressive taxes (C chooses S1). Since they disagree on carbon and natural resource taxes, in this scenario, they may or may not be implemented. Therefore, let us assume that these taxes would not be very high if implemented, so this reduces the short-term cost for L to choose S2. L still prefers protection and price and wage supports even with less progressive taxes. H is best off with just the opposite; with less progressive taxes, no regulation, flexible wages and prices, and so on. Even with tariffs and prices supports, H still prefers less progressive taxes and no other regulation besides the tariffs and price supports. Less mature conservative arguments can be used to defend C's decision while L may use less mature liberal arguments. Exogenous to this game is the relative political strength of these two groups. These payoffs are consistent with a high-skilled worker who needs no protection. Support from some amber-stage conservative agents may support the conservative position of S2 for ideological reasons, not necessarily for economic reasons if they could also benefit from protection and wage supports.

In Game 1, the Nash equilibrium is suboptimal. Despite the greater costs of less mature policies in the long run, even in the short-run game above, a Pareto improvement can be made if they cooperate and each choose S1 (3 > 2). Firms can be competitive and C can be more willing to support progressive tax levels if workers' wages reflect their productivity. C can receive a greater share of firm revenue when low-skilled wages do not exceed their productivity. Workers can support flexible wages if progressive tax levels are used for retraining. The progressive taxes benefit L in the short term. Here, coordination of multiple sound policies can increase the likelihood that they are short-run beneficial for both stakeholder groups. Political clustering and extremism where agents are not encouraged to engage in cooperative behaviour with other types and stakeholder groups can theoretically reinforce the suboptimal state represented by the Nash equilibrium of Game 1.

Alternatively, even if the long run was still ignored, high-level cultural capital, which includes an expectation that groups in our society will cooperate for the greater good, would allow for the socially optimal outcome as described by IPE (S1 for each). This is demonstrated in Game 2 presented in Figure 2.3. Here two groups that are more morally mature interact. They each personally value following a constructive norm (as is done in Ostrom, 2005). Call them cooperators rather than egoists. If the intrinsic value of cooperating was equal to two units, then that would increase the value of S1 by two units whether or not the other agent cooperated. This would be enough for S1 to be the dominant strategy for each, thus the new Nash equilibrium.

In laboratory experimental games, some agents behave like calculating, materialistic egoists. But many act as if they are conditional cooperators (Ostrom, 2005, pp. 127–131). They get satisfaction from the attempt to cooperate. Yet, if faced

FIGURE 2.3 Game 2: Two cooperators and their short-term payoffs

		Liberal Group (L)	
		S1. Retraining, flexible wages/prices, carbon and natural resource taxes, sound public goods.	S2. Tariffs protection, fixed wages/prices, no carbon or natural resource taxes, high taxes on corporate profits.
Conservative Group (C)	S1. Proper regulation, progressive taxes, carbon and natural resource taxes, sound public goods.	5 5	4 3
	S2. No regulation, less progressive taxes, no carbon or natural resource taxes.	3 4	2 2

with egoists who repeatedly take advantage of the conditional cooperator's good will, the conditional cooperator will undergo costly effort to punish egoists so that in the future they are more likely to cooperate. If outcomes continue to be bad for cooperators, their behaviour will then change to mimic egoists. If only one group was a conditional cooperator, let us say L, then the game can be represented as Game 3 in Figure 2.4.

In Lawson's critical realist economic science, an important dimension of abstraction in economic theorizing is the vantage point of the theorist. This will 'depend on the knowledge, understandings, values, and interests of the individual scientist or research group involved' (Lawson, 1997, p. 229). One can add that the vantage point is also important for understanding economic agents' behaviour as is demonstrated in the game theory of this section. An integral epistemological pluralism can aid in further understanding cognitive, moral, and values development plus socio-cultural incentives and other influences involved (Esbjörn-Hargens, 2010; Bowman, 2012).

In Game 3, L chooses S1 and C chooses S2. In a repeated game scenario, eventually the cooperator group, if they are conditional cooperators, would lose the value they attach to cooperating. Then the game would move to the original short-run, suboptimal Nash equilibrium of Game 1 (where both groups choose their S2). This is essentially how I will describe the dominant US political–economic culture of the last decade in the next section. Conditional cooperators have not had much reason to cooperate and policies are enacted from less mature tendencies across both types. These games illustrate a critical importance of cultural capital, which includes in IPE the value of healthy public political–economic discourse. A subset of cultural capital is civic capital, which was recently defined by Guiso et al.

FIGURE 2.4 Game 3: A liberal cooperator and a conservative egoist and their short-term payoffs

		Liberal Group (L)	
		S1. Retraining, flexible wages/prices, carbon and natural resource taxes, sound public goods.	S2. Tariffs protection, fixed wages/prices, no carbon or natural resource taxes, high taxes on corporate taxes.
Conservative Group (C)	S1. Proper regulation, progressive taxes, carbon and natural resource taxes, sound public goods.	5 3	4 1
	S2. No regulation, less progressive taxes, no carbon or natural resource taxes.	3 4	2 2

(2010) as the set of values and beliefs that help cooperation. Collective development in the political–economic line theoretically, therefore, helps develop civic and cultural capital and vice versa. Denmark's transforming reforms beginning in the mid-1990s will be discussed below as an outgrowth of relatively healthy discourse and substantial civic and cultural capital compared to that of the US.

This analysis shows how the functioning of the economy can diverge from its more justified management as judged by a sober reading of sound theory and evidence. What is sound is judged in the sense of Wilberian partial truths that are dependent on our current state of understanding and ability to apply them justly. IPE's particular stab at this is engaging with mainstream economic principles in a way that critical realist political economists typically have not. Nielsen (2002) argues that 'critical realists to a large extent misrepresent the great political economists by separating philosophy and science (or levels of abstraction) and by focusing almost exclusively on the philosophy of political economy' (p. 732). This relates to why critical realist critiques tend to be deficient in concrete real-world economic analyses. An exception of this is from, interestingly enough, the integrally informed, critical realist economist and contributor to this volume, Hans Despain, who does engage multiple and specific proposals of reforming the capitalistic system (Despain, 2013).

3 Recent Historical Cases: Relative Pathology versus Health

More on a US Collective Pathology

Given the importance of the political–economic dynamics between less mature individuals across stakeholder groups in US culture that has led to suboptimal policies, I argue that to a significant degree, US culture has a collective pathology around economic policymaking. Various stakeholder groups often use less mature political–economic arguments to support policies that look out for their own short-term interests and to deflect their partial blame for bad economic outcomes that were co-created by political pressures coming from all major stakeholder groups, although usually in varying degrees.

We saw the less mature blame game in strong force during the Financial Crisis of 2008–2009. I argued (in Bowman, 2010b) that the crisis was caused by policies that least offended both less mature conservatives and less mature liberals. For example, (conservative) lax regulation played a very significant role and was, in large part, the result of aggressive lobbying from financial firms (Lewis, 2005). This contributed to short-term speculation, overleveraging of banks and households, and over-consolidation of banks, while also facilitating fraud (Stiglitz, 2010; Immergluck, 2009; Kotz, 2009; Lewis, 2005). Fighting against regulation efforts, less mature conservatives made arguments such as 'the government cannot know better than the private sector what lending instruments are wise or not' (Immergluck, 2009). These arguments were made despite the evidence of unsustainable bubbles in asset markets (Shiller, 2010) using measures of sustainability (e.g., price-to-earnings ratios and ratios of average wages to housing valuations). Liberal political leaders, however, did not provide a coherent alternative to the conservative (neoliberal) trend. Instead, cheap credit from loose lending standards, excessively loose monetary policy, and government loan guarantees on worsening underwriting standards contributed to the severity of the crisis (Thompson, 2009; O'Driscoll, 2009) and found support among liberals.

Globalization has weakened the political strength of relatively low-skilled workers given that it is easier to outsource their work while physical capital complementary to low-skilled labour has diffused to lower wage countries. In the games of the previous section, this would help explain an S2 outcome for C without having to provide as many S2 benefits for low-skilled workers during the period from 1980–2008. This is consistent with the rising income and wealth inequality during this time. This trend, however, placed pressure on the economic system to make consumption activities for the liberal camp palatable. This helped fuel the consumption-driven economy while providing political support for the relatively neoliberal (conservative) economic system.

In my view, analyses by pundits and politicians have failed to foster maturity in US culture despite the potential of the sobering crisis to do so. The conservatives tend to fault the government entirely without acknowledging the role of government-bashing that contributed to lax regulation; liberals tend to blame free market ideology or the greed of business without proposing specific, theoretically and empirically supported regulations, and without acknowledging the need to overcome government failures in implementing proper regulations; and radicals tend to blame the internal contradictions of the system so that the bubbles and busts are inevitable without providing theoretically and empirically supported guidance for reform as opposed to their resignation or their offers of simple panaceas for systemic overhaul (such as communism, anarchy, or abolition of the fractional reserve system). The economics discipline should better communicate that there are more mature arguments coming from each of these various political–economic types to encourage sound theory and evidence, rather than oppositional rhetoric, to guide economic policymaking.

This unhealthy rhetoric contributes to the suboptimal outcomes demonstrated in the (prisoner's dilemma) games of the previous section. Civic and cultural capital, on the other hand, can help overcome these problems. In the American democracy, when politicians speak to the public or when political action committees advertise on behalf of issues or candidates, it is not socially acceptable to admit certain individuals or groups are only looking out for their own self-interest at the expense of the collective good (Scharpf, 1997, p. 163), even though many less mature policies can be characterized this way. And given that there is academic consensus on many issues that are highly controversial politically, then this places pressure on partisan actors to develop or deepen their pathology. As the evidence mounts of the environmental, inequality, and financial imbalances, more pressure is exerted on the ego to change. If the ego refuses to make behavioural changes and sacrifice in the short term for the long-term greater good, then the ego may avoid or repress the evidence that the ego is acting selfishly, hence the growing social pathology.

Habermas's definition of social pathologies, from above, matches my description of the US political–economic learning line since learning in the political–economic line in culture at large is not benefiting from advances in other lines. In a pathological social realm, for Habermas, claims are not made subject to adequate validation. This problem is better understood with IPE. Immaturity in the political–economic line becomes expressed through the immature/mature type fallacy in stakeholder deflection of validating claims in discussions of, and actions associated with the enactment of, economic policies.

Future studies can employ integral methodological pluralism (IMP) to further study ways in which agents in various positions within the economy tend to view their actions and the economic theory that justifies it. Thus IMP can serve to respond to critical realism's rightful concern for mainstream economics' difficulty in uncovering generative mechanisms that may require a wider focus than that usually related to observables detected by mainstream methods in economics (Lawson, 1998; Boylan & O'Gorman, 2005). IMP can expand the scope of observables and provide added theory to point to important unobservables that may lead to fruitful investigations to better account for them.

At the individual level, a strongly averted or overly critical response to more mature or opposing views may be indicative of shadow projections. An upbringing in an oppressive or dogmatic setting where absolutist thinking around economic policy prevailed may repress intellectual questioning in this area. This may induce projection of one's own inability to be open to the exploration of more mature views onto others. One views an opposing type only in its less mature version because less mature types cannot differentiate less from more developed versions of each type. More mature views by others are emotionally (often angrily) reduced to the less mature version of that type by the projector. This allows one's own less mature views to be elevated by leveraging immaturity in another type (using black versus white, good versus bad, conservative versus liberal dualism characteristic of this type of thought). This relatively unhealthy, first-tier consciousness defends against all opposing views while keeping aspects within the projector repressed and disowned.

Unfortunately, less mature political–economic agents do not have to work hard to feel fully validated at the collective level. There is considerable evidence of clustering of politically like-minded people in social networks, the media, and the internet (Sunstein, 2008; Gentzkow & Shapiro cited in The Economist, 2008; McPherson et al., 2001). This can contribute to political–economic extremism or what IPE would describe as immaturity across political–economic types. We are even taught that discussing politics is not wise when in a new social setting, showing that we have difficulty in having respectful political disagreements. Agents who are relatively highly developed in other lines may be stunted in the political–economic line by individual and collective pathology. I wrote of our unhealthy collective responses to the Financial Crisis at its peak in the fall of 2008 for *Integral Life* where major stakeholder reactions were even more ideological and extreme. Looking back, this seems prescient. Notice that in response to status-quo gridlock and polarization in our political institutions, since 2008, popular movements stretched the nation further to the less developed extremes with the Tea Party movement on the right and Occupy Wall Street on the left. We need collective healing.

This does not mean that pathology is equally distributed among individuals in the US culture. Helpful here is the discussion of holarchical embeddedness in Bowman (2011). Those organizations that have the most to lose in the short run draw in ideological types and encourage those types as part of their group cultures. The political system also reproduces the pathology to the extent financial and electoral support depends on short-term, obstructionist interests.

Cooperation and the Case of Denmark

When participants can communicate, it can help them overcome commons dilemmas (Ostrom, 2005, p. 113). In the games of the previous section, communication might help agents develop trust that each would be willing to act as a conditional cooperator. Yet if the less mature level of debate in culture makes oppositional less mature conservatism and less mature liberalism appear as the only alternatives, then it is important to work for the maturation of the level of public discourse around policymaking. This can theoretically foster improved communication among stakeholders and help build constructive norms around stakeholder contributions to public economic policy.

Here I will use the recent case of Denmark as an example of relatively healthy political–economic discourse fostered by stakeholder balance. Campbell and Pedersen (2010) have described Denmark's economic transformation. Denmark experienced lackluster economic performance during the late 1980s and early 1990s by measures of GDP and productivity growth, unemployment, inflation, budget deficits, and national debt. Since then, there has been considerable improvement in all of these indicators along with low inequality.

Campbell and Pedersen (2010) largely credit Denmark's economic turnaround to its labour market reforms dubbed 'flexicurity' (flexible but secure). Firms were given more freedom to hire and fire (unlike in Germany or France, but like the US). This increased worker mobility and firms were not afraid to invest in physical capital that complemented new workers. Before its reforms, Denmark had generous health insurance and welfare benefits. In the 1990s the country continued with these universal benefits, but they tied them to job seeking and the benefit levels were reduced to encourage finding new jobs. New and generous retraining benefits (more than in any other country besides Sweden) were implemented during the early 1990s. These benefits were empowered by institutional decentralization. For example, legislation in 1993 allowed retraining programmes to be tailored at the local level to fit the needs of local employers.

These reforms are supported by sound economic theory and evidence. Stakeholder interaction, however, is not typically analyzed by mainstream economists. The reforms were accomplished through decentralized negotiations among unions, employer groups, municipal authorities, academics, and other relevant actors at the regional and local level. This therefore reflects relatively healthy stakeholder representation and policy discussion working for the validation of claims. The reforms helped upgrade worker skills needed for the information age with increased flexibility of the economy and economic confidence of workers rather than specific job security. Flextime was an added outcome making it easier for individuals to manage their work, family, and educational and retraining needs. Even though unionization was among the highest in the world, decentralization of bargaining contributed to unions supporting sound policies. Increased training during economic downturns is particularly wise because it allows for needed labour churn while also decreasing labour supply during a time of diminished labour demand in certain sectors. The retraining allows growth in competitive areas of the economy aided by structural adjustment. Denmark's willingness to train the unemployed is in contrast, during this time, with Germany, who retrained only those already working, and with the US, who disqualified the unemployed for unemployment benefits if they enrolled in education.

Retrained workers gave Danish firms an incentive to invest in complementary machinery and technologies. They did not want their workers to leave for more interesting, better paying jobs. Denmark already had vocational schools in place, but the reforms increased demand for them. The negotiating process chose and expanded programmes that met the needs of employers. Prior to the 1990s, Denmark engaged in more state policy to direct the economy. In the 1990s, they deregulated and decreased state subsidies. So the reforms were neither completely laissez-faire, nor were they a case of the government picking winners with subsidies which can lead to crony capitalism. Rather they were 'a discovery process where firms, unions, other interest groups, experts, and the state learn about costs and opportunities and then engage in strategic coordination' (Campbell & Pedersen, 2010, p. 323). This process contributed to upward mobility for Danes. Economist Markus Jantti found that 42 percent of American men raised in the bottom fifth of incomes stay there as adults compared to 25 percent of Danes (DeParle, 2012).

Denmark is also the only country to achieve a 15 percent reduction of carbon emissions from 1990 to 2005 without relying on nuclear energy. According to Northwestern University sociologist Monica Prasad (2008), they did so by taxing carbon and subsidizing clean alternatives during a period of strong economic growth as their companies were not put at a competitive disadvantage because those carbon tax revenues were given back to firms that were environmentally innovative. A 2009 briefing by the Environmental and Energy Institute (ESSI, 2009) and the Embassy of Denmark credited Denmark's success to

> carbon pricing (through energy taxes, carbon taxes, and the 'cap and trade' EU Emissions Trading Scheme), strict building codes, energy labeling programs, and other policy measures. Denmark has spurred renewable energy development by establishing feed-in tariffs and modernizing the electric grid.
> *(ESSI, 2009)*

The Danish case contrasts sharply with the US in this area as well. The US has made no significant progress in dealing with climate change since backing out of the Kyoto Protocol.

Even with regards to the global financial crisis, Dougherty (2008) reported that Denmark's sound underwriting standards have prevented the level of losses there relative to those related to subprime lending in the US. The stress on the financial system in Denmark was blamed more on international financial contamination than on any policies originating within the country.

The healthy stakeholder balance and more mature economic policies in Denmark shared similarities with the reforms contributing to the high growth era of the High-Performance Asian Economies described by Campos and Root (1996). Autocratic leaders chose shared growth strategies, in part to avoid communist uprisings. Institutions such as economic councils were developed to bring together representative stakeholder groups. This helped communication for needed public policies to contribute to the shared growth strategy. Broad investments in health, education, and infrastructure contributed to shared growth and prevented unproductive beggar-thy-neighbour policies. With Bhaskar's (1998) transformational model of social activity in mind, this IPE analysis hopes to shed some light on the unhealthy actions that can reproduce suboptimal economic outcomes and social arrangements.

4 Critical Realism's Eudaimonia and Recent Discourses of Modernity Related to IPE

Elsewhere I have written of the cognition, values, and guiding strategies of economic agents by major level of development represented in US culture (Bowman, 2010a, 2010b). Distinctions were made between their influences in our relatively unhealthy culture wars versus their potential when healthily and deeply included in a second-tier socio-culture. This follows Wilber's (2000b, p. 169) prime directive to 'facilitate the health of the entire spiral of development without unduly privileging any particular wave'. Here, I will briefly describe how IPE adds to the insights of critical realism on the subject of heteronomy, dialectics, and eudaimonia. Following the prime directive is consistent with working towards what Bhaskar calls a eudaimonistic (good, human) society. This is where the 'free development of each [is] a condition of the free development of all' (Hartwig, 2007, p. 213). A dialectic of self- and mutual-esteem leads to existential security to ergonic efficiency to empowerment to universal emancipation and then to eudaimonia (Bhaskar, 2008, pp. 120–121).

In IPE, the political–economic collective pathology affects the centre of gravity of all major stakeholder groups and thus it is our healthier and higher selves that are being marginalized by the pathology. IPE seeks to decrease heteronomy by shedding light on the pathology. The continual evoking of the immature/mature type fallacy shows that most of us are not free from our unconscious resistance (implanted in us by socio-cultural influences) to a more just, sincere, and true exchange of economic ideas and their consequences. Healthier stakeholder interaction and discourse can contribute to holarchical investments that improve ergonic efficiencies, improve sustainability, and improve workers' and consumers' capabilities of engaging and enacting a better economy thereby improving their self-esteem and self-actualization. Since multiple stakeholder groups would be in healthier interaction and would mutually benefit, mutual self-esteem and self-actualization would be improved. More sincere, just, and true discourse and policy should lead to greater existential freedom due to the exposure of shadow elements and their healing. Integral change agents, highly productive and transparent as they are known to be, will do well to work for leadership positions in major stakeholder groups. Their willingness to dialogue and their ability to reconcile polarities position them to improve efficiency and competitiveness of their stakeholder group while aligning stakeholder actions to serve the greater good. This will provide the role models for mature green agents to improve their relations with other first-tier groups as they transition from opposition to incumbent with the new centre of gravity currently transforming from orange to green.

IPE also adds some insight into Bhaskar's critique of the discourses of modernity. The regressive bourgeois triumphalism (Harwig, 2007, pp. 349–352) corresponds to the pathological regression in the political–economic line and the dominance of the immature conservative view during the neoliberal period (and the neoliberal capitalistic social structures of accumulation) that held the most sway as the Washington Consensus was implemented. IPE shows, however, that this period required a new allegiance with liberal tendencies to supplant the postmodern discourse of modernity and its correlated post World War II social structures of accumulation (see Bowman, 2010b, for more on social structures of accumulation theory as included within IPE). Although blue-collar production workers, a portion of which is an important segment of the liberal voting bloc in the US, have lost negotiating strength with the rise of the newly industrialized countries and globalized technologies and organizational structures, liberal tendencies (including many sympathetic green agents) had to be assuaged with the rising inequality that benefited conservative interests. As described above, the bubble economy was the result of a new, mostly unconscious alliance between the less developed conservative and less developed liberal blocs that dominated American political–economic culture.

Conclusion

This chapter contrasted the relatively unhealthy or pathological US political–economic discourse and policy with the relatively healthy discourse and policy of Denmark over the recent time period. Game theory was used to show the suboptimal policies that can result in less mature, strategic, short-term-focused behaviour of agents from two broad stakeholder groups. The game theory, motivated and contextualized by the integral political economy approach, also showed how constructive norms can foster political–economic maturity and help overcome suboptimal policy. IPE can therefore be used as a tool to shed light on collective dynamics and encourage more mature political–economic dialogue and policy. This helps demonstrate that applied integral metatheories can be of aid in serving and strengthening national and international commons to address the global issues of this century.

Note

1 Abstract economic terms that may be used as markers of scientific thinking do not guarantee sound thinking. Examples of abstract terms include inflation, recession, market, and the business cycle. Examples of causal relationship could include an increase in the money supply increases inflation or a fall in investment spending may induce a recession.

References

Aghion, P., Caroli, E., & Garcia-Penalosa, C. (1999). Inequality and economic growth: The perspective of the new growth theories. *Journal of Economic Literature*, 37(4), 1615–1660.

Autor, D., Katz, L., & Kearney, M. (2008). Trends in US wage inequality: Revising the revisionists. *The Review of Economics and Statistics*, 90(2), 300–323.

Bhaskar, R. (1998). *The Possibility of Naturalism*. Routledge.

Bhaskar, R. (2008). *Dialectic: The Pulse of Freedom*. Routledge.

Bowman, K. (2008). Integral neoclassical economic growth. *Journal of Integral Theory and Practice*, 3(4), 17–38.

Bowman, K. (2010a). Integral Political Economy. *The Journal of Integral Theory and Practice*, 5(3), 1–27.

Bowman, K. (2010b). The Financial Crisis of 2008–09: An integral political–economic analysis. *The Journal of Integral Theory and Practice*, 5(3), 39–67.

Bowman, K. (2010c). Integral Political Economy, rejoinder: A response to Scott. *The Journal of Integral Theory and Practice*, 5(3), 33–38.

Bowman, K. (2011). Holarchically embedding Integral Political Economy: Helping to synthesize major schools of economics. *The Journal of Integral Theory and Practice*, 6(2), 1–29.

Bowman, K. (2012). Integral scientific pluralism. *Journal of Integral Theory and Practice*, 7(1), 54–66.

Boylan, T., & O'Gorman, P.F. (2005). Fleetwood on causal holism: Clarification and critique. *Cambridge Journal of Economics*, 30(1), 123–135.

Brown, A., Slater, G., & Spencer, D.A. (2002). Driven to abstraction? Critical realism and the search for the 'inner connection' of social phenomena. *Cambridge Journal of Economics*, 26(1), 773–788.

Campbell, J., & Pedersen, O. (2010). The varieties of capitalism and hybrid success: Denmark in the global economy. *Comparative Political Studies*, 40(3), 307–332.

Campos, J., & Root, H. (1996). *The Key to the Asian Miracle: Making Shared Growth Credible*. The Brooking Institution.

Cohen, N. (2009). Regulation: Doubts over political resolve for reform. *The Financial Times*, 5 October. Available at www.ft.com/content/5cf43a1a-b14b-11de-b06b-00144feabdc0 (Accessed 6 May 2016).

Davis, J. (2008). The conception of the socially embedded individual. In J. Davis & W. Dolfsma (eds), *The Elgar Companion to Social Economics*. Edward Elgar.

DeParle, J. (2012). Harder for Americans to rise from lower rungs. *The New York Times*, 5 January. Available at www.nytimes.com/2012/01/05/us/harder-for-americans-to-rise-from-lower-rungs.html (Accessed 6 May 2016).
Despain, H. (2013). It's the system stupid: Structural crises and the need for alternatives to capitalism. *Monthly Review*, 65(6). Available at https://monthlyreview.org/2013/11/01/its-the-system-stupid/ (Accessed 6 May 2016).
Dougherty, C. (2008). No quick solution to financial crisis, Denmark shows. *The New York Times*, 27 October. Available at www.nytimes.com/2008/10/27/business/worldbusiness/27iht-denmark.4.17287933.html (Accessed 6 May 2016).
The Economist (2008). A biased market. *The Economist Magazine*, 30 October. Available at www.economist.com/finance-and-economics/2008/10/30/a-biased-market (Accessed 6 May 2016).
The Economist (2009). In from the cold. *The Economist Magazine*, 12 March. Available at www.economist.com/business/2009/03/12/in-from-the-cold (Accessed 6 May 2016).
Environmental and Energy Study Institute (ESSI) (2009). On the road to Copenhagen: Telling Denmark's story. Available at www.eesi.org/road-copenhagen-telling-denmark%E2%80%99s-story-24-nov-2009 (Accessed 6 April 2011).
Esbjörn-Hargens, S. (2010). An ontology of climate change: Integral pluralism and the enactment of multiple objects. *Journal of Integral Theory and Practice*, 5(1), 143–174.
Flynn, J.R. (1984). The mean IQ of Americans: Massive gains 1932 to 1978. *Psychological Bulletin*, 95(1), 29–51.
Gordon, W., & Diels, J. (2011). Is political talk getting smarter? An analysis of presidential debates and the Flynn effect. *Public Understanding of Science*, 20(5), 578–594.
Guiso L., Sapienza, P., & Zingales, L. (2010). Civic capital as the missing link. European University Institute Working Paper ECO 2010/08. Available at http://cadmus.eui.eu/bitstream/handle/1814/13659/ECO_2010_08.pdf?sequence=1 (Accessed 24 February 2012).
Hamburger, T., & Geiger, K. (2009). Health insurers set to benefit from overhaul. *Los Angeles Times*, 24 August. Available at www.latimes.com/archives/la-xpm-2009-aug-24-na-healthcare-insurers24-story.html (Accessed 28 May 2016).
Hartwig, M. (ed.) (2007). *Dictionary of Critical Realism*. Routledge.
Immergluck, D. (2009). Core of the crisis: Deregulation, the global savings glut, and financial innovation in the subprime debacle. *City & Community*, 8(3), 341–345.
Ingram, D. (2010). *Habermas: Introduction and Analysis*. Cornell University Press.
Kotz, D.M. (2009). The financial and economic crisis of 2008: A systemic crisis of neoliberal capitalism. *Review of Radical Political Economics*, Summer. doi: 10.1177/0486613409335093
Lawson, T. (1997). *Economics and Reality*. Routledge.
Lawson, T. (1998). Economic science without experimentation. In M. Archer, R. Bhaskar, A. Collier, T. Lawson, & A. Norrie (eds), *Critical Realism: Essential Readings*. Routledge.
Lee, F.S. (2002). Theory creation and the methodological foundation of Post Keynesian economics. *Cambridge Journal of Economics*, 26(6), 789–804.
Lewis, J. (2005). Monster banks: The political and economic costs of banking and financial consolidation. *Multinational Monitor*, January/February. Available at https://tinyurl.com/yhmhyzwt (Accessed 28 May 2016).
McPherson, M., Smith-Lovin, L., & Cook, J.M. (2001). Birds of a feather: Homophily in social networks. *Annual Review of Sociology*, 27, 415–444.
Mullainathan, S., & Shleifer, A. (2005). The market for news. *The American Economic Review*, 95(4), 1031–1053.
Nielsen, P. (2002). Reflections on critical realism in political economy. *Cambridge Journal of Economics*, 26(6), 727–738.

O'Driscoll, G.P. (2009). The Financial Crisis: Origins and consequences. *The Intercollegiate Review*, 44(2), 4–12.

Ostrom, E. (2005). *Understanding Institutional Diversity*. Princeton University Press.

Prasad, M. (2008). On carbon, tax and don't spend. *The New York Times*, 25 March. www.nytimes.com/2008/03/25/opinion/25prasad.html (Accessed 28 May 2016).

Scharpf, F. (1997). *Games Real Actors Play: Actor-Centered Institutionalism in Policy Research*. Westview Press.

Shiller, R. (2010). *Irrational Exuberance* (2nd edn). Princeton University Press.

Slate (2009). Majority back climate treaty. *Slate Magazine*, 15 December. Available at http://sslaest.slate.com/id/2238656/?wpisrc+newsletter (Accessed 28 May 2016).

Stiglitz, J. (2010). *Freefall*. W.W. Norton & Company.

Strassel, K. (2008). How to block the liberal agenda. *The Wall Street Journal*, 7 November. www.wsj.com/articles/SB122603073121807985 (Accessed 28 May 2016).

Sunstein, C. (2008). The law of group polarization. In J.S. Fishkin & P. Laslett (eds), *Debating Deliberative Democracy*. Blackwell Publishing.

Thompson, H. (2009). The political origins of the financial crisis: The domestic and international politics of Fannie Mae and Freddie Mac. *The Political Quarterly*, 80(1), 17–24.

Ullmann, O. (1983). Will Paul Volcker seek another 4-year term? *Ludington Daily News*, 19 March. Available at https://news.google.com/newspapers?nid=b0M2c_1WBrUC&dat=19830319&printsec=frontpage&hl=en (Accessed 28 May 2016).

Wilber, K. (1995). *Sex, Ecology, Spirituality: The Spirit of Evolution*. Shambhala Publications, Inc.

Wilber, K. (2000a). *Integral Psychology*. Shambhala Publications, Inc.

Wilber, K. (2000b). *The Theory of Everything: An Integral Vision for Business, Politics, Science, and Spirituality*. Shambhala Publications, Inc.

Wilber, K. (2000c). *Sex, Ecology, Spirituality* (Rev. edn). Shambhala Publications, Inc.

Wilber, K. (2002). *Kosmic Karma and Creativity*. Available at http://wilber.shambhala.com (Accessed 10 July 2004).

Wilber, K. (2006). *Integral Spirituality: A Startling New Role for Religion in the Modern and Postmodern World*. Integral Books.

3
SUSTAINING SPIRIT ACROSS COMPLEXITIES OF INTERNATIONAL DEVELOPMENT IN RELATION TO INDIGENOUS PEOPLES

Neil Hockey

Introduction

Grounded in commitments to social justice, I have engaged in local and international community development throughout more than four decades of adult working life. I have often reflected on the generative mechanisms of social being. Such mechanisms operating in both natural and social sciences exemplify the notion of natural necessity, central to critical realist arguments on causality. Alan Norrie's (2010) work on dialectical critical realism and the grounds of justice rearticulated Roy Bhaskar's dialectical account of natural necessity. First, it gives rise to the 'material meshwork' of social process and social product or structured being and becoming. Second, natural necessity as moral reality works itself out through fluctuations within constellational relations between the ethical and the historical. Third, to affirm rather than deny natural necessity represents a way between the two poles of Habermasian structural abstract universalization and Derridean post-structural radical particularization.

In a previous paper[1] I translated and further articulated Norrie's argument with both regional and local expressions of Indigenous principles, philosophies, and spiritualities. My purpose there was to strengthen my own life and work context, a specific geo-historical struggle for decolonization as self-determined development with culture and identity, a depth-struggle oriented to reclaiming Indigenous contributions to economies. The urgency of that task seems to grow by the day, with governments and religious leaders questioning how to limit *self-radicalization* in specific contexts. In contrast, our work focuses on *radical self-emancipation* as necessarily grounded in a culture of mutual listening and solidarity rather than opposition and conflict.

This current chapter, then, draws on critical/metaRealist praxis from my own context,[2] with a focus on Spirit prompted by Gail Hochachka's accounts of her

DOI: 10.4324/9781003140313-5

integralist work.[3] Ken Wilber's integralist analysis of the emergence of 'flatland'[4] might well resonate with many community workers lamenting the loss of soul, of connections or spirit-in-community work.[5] Others point the way toward revitalizing such spirit, a journey with undeniable roots in earlier streams of spirituality, belief, and political engagement.[6] However, both the ambiguous Western resurgence of religion and spirituality amidst a necessarily ongoing resistance to theism in general[7] and the tremendous resilience of Indigenous political philosophies[8] raise further questions for me.

My purpose here is to utilize the notion of Spirit or spirit(s) as generative mechanisms in extending the dialogue regarding neo-integrative worldviews[9] beyond issues of God, Spirit, the Divine, or consciousness and spirituality, even of community soul or spirit. Our dialogue must embrace Indigenist and related traditions of discerning the spirits and gods[10] as entities operative at the nexus between politics, culture, religion, and spirituality. I argue that if we fail to so discern, we not only miss a core problematic within local and international development, but also risk both losing key resources and becoming victims of further spiritual oppressions.

One well-known proponent of the strength of Indigenist stances and resources is Ward Churchill.[11] Others have written regarding Indigenous research paradigms or methodologies,[12] radical Indigenist scholars,[13] and an Indigenist critique of Marxism.[14] Central to all of these is the utmost importance of relationality, of connectivity, mediated at their core by spirit beings, guardians, powers, or animals. Hence in what follows I outline several key Indigenist implications for ongoing transformative dialogue between those applying critical realist and integralist metatheoretical approaches to international development.

The chapter is arranged in four parts as follows. Section 1 presents an Indigenist standpoint that articulates questions around discerning spirit(s) within the international development field confronted by complex and urgent challenges. From tentative answers to these questions, Indigenist bases for participation in mutually transformative dialogue give rise to implications for the contemporary CR-IT dialogue. These implications are developed in three steps. Section 2 first portrays, from within my own depth-investigative participatory research, the necessity for discerning Spirit in struggles over land and resources. Section 3 then engages with integralist questions raised by Gail Hochachka on issues of an 'ultimate concern' in a dialectic of faith in animism, in a theistic God and in postmodern secularism. In light of the preceding, I review in section 4 specific points raised in the ongoing CR-IT dialogue. The conclusion revisits the methodological nature of my argument.

1 An Indigenist Standpoint: Discerning Spirit(s)

By portraying contemporary development scenarios in the light of challenges and problems besetting us locally and globally, I begin in this section to draw implications for twenty-first-century international development. An assessment of hope for greater engagement with Indigenist concerns within development circles is undertaken by means of Indigenous responses to local development globally. The spiritual heart of their political philosophy thus articulated presents challenges to our dialogue.

Urgency and Complexity in Contemporary Development Scenarios

Whether we utilize critical realist dialectical explanatory argument[15] or an integralist holarchical[16] approach in prioritizing responses to future possibilities, Wladawsky-Berger's identified needs[17] in the face of unpredictable, complex and chaotic futures appear mild compared to the problems in Table 3.1. However, both of these metatheoretical approaches would draw us back, I argue, to the urgency of solutions to such basic but complex problems of lifelong learning and reasonable standards of living for all, especially in relation to health care needs and the aged.

TABLE 3.1 W(h)ither development post-Rio+20 and post-2015? Some most urgent and complex emerging issues as factors calling for integrating approaches to development[18]

Before It's News[19]	Martin[20]	UNEP[21]
Global economic collapse	Excessive population growth	Six cross-cutting issues[22]
Overpopulation	Extreme poverty	Four food, biodiversity, and land issues
Poverty	Growth of shanty cities	
Oil and gas resource crises	Unstoppable global migrations	
Terrorism	Non-state actor with extreme weapons	
Proliferation of WMDs	Violent religious extremism	
	New dark age, a global cocktail including pandemics (deliberate or not)	
Climate change	Global warming	Three climate change issues
Water scarcity	Water shortages, famine, and wars	Four energy, technology, and waste issues
	The spread of deserts	
	Mass famine in ill-organized countries	
Specific species extinction	Destruction of life in the oceans	Four freshwaters and marine issues

Furthermore, following the thrust of Radha D'Souza's 'Justice and governance in dystopia',[23] if this chapter is to fulfil its purpose (to utilize the notion of Spirit/spirit(s) as generative mechanisms) it must not only ground any philosophical dialogue in everyday experiences, but also sustain a unity of perspectives on cultures, structures, and being, so as to strengthen psychological and cultural predispositions to challenge power and knowledge.[24] To do so certainly requires global restoration of a sense and practice of community.[25] Yet there are inbuilt problems when governments attempt to promote what they see as the *techniques* of community development, since such efforts frequently destroy a community's sense of responsibility.[26] Is it possible that at heart, the real problems of sustainability in community development (and therefore in international development as in Table 3.1), arise from a lack of soul or spirit?[27] Peter Westoby is not alone in calling for 'depth participation'[28] in development, a perspective resonating with Indigenous communities.[29] For the most marginalized, it's a question of discerning hope for the future despite their everyday experiences.

Discerning Hope for Indigenous Concerns

Set against future scenarios could be international analyses such as those from recent years of the journal *Development and Change*. These provide plenty of stories with which to engage the challenge of development alternatives.[30] Here though, 'it may be useful to recall that the engagement of stakeholders ... in international policymaking has broadly been along four different but complementary sets of actions'. The first two are rare, being overtly political: *pushing against* the agenda or *pulling* the agenda in strategic directions. More prosaic forms of engagement are to *help* the agenda by accepting and supporting inter-governmental work, or to *rally* stakeholders through alliances and movements. Yet whether you are a member of civil society, government, or a global citizen's movement, the problem today is that '*Push is incoherent, Pull is blind, Help is paralyzed, and Rally is overstretched*' (italics in original).[31] This resonates with my own experience of working alongside Indigenous communities at local levels across many sites.

However, shifts toward a greater embracing of spirituality in development circles[32] seem to provide hope that Indigenist concerns might increasingly be taken up. To express Indigenous hopes from a comparative account across three countries (Australia, New Zealand, and North America), in an earlier work I drew upon five selected Indigenous authors' concepts of purpose and scope in writing[33] and suggested two options for engaging with those purposes.

First, it is possible to use the parameters of emergent properties of culture, agency, and structure[34] in order to grasp the collective impact of the selected documents. Thus the authors' transformative intentions could be viewed collectively as a set of processes (in brackets following) whereby:

- *Socio-cultural transformation* (countering the politics of racial abuse; minimizing confusion; identifying research as a significant site of struggle; restoring

balance to the relationship between language and thinking; grasping the deep meaning of the traditional teachings)
- *in ways that include material conditions and concerns* (the quality of daily life; interests, and ways of knowing and of resisting; marginalizing authority; crippling welfare; trauma; culture/future shock)
- *can be brought about by taking action as agents* (establishing an Aboriginal research paradigm; supporting better understanding of cultural differences; balancing form and meaning in languaging; giving an account of how, and why, Indigenous perspectives on research have developed)
- *within and between structural groups* (reclaiming cultural values; renegotiation with education power bases; persuading people to consider drawing on traditional teachings to create an appropriate framework for governance).

Second, there is the possibility of using the authors' own elaboration of the concepts put forward as a means of developing categories that appear to be more basic. Which concepts appear to represent 'building blocks' or underlying structures? Which represent the properties or powers of those underlying structures? Which concepts represent mechanisms likely to trigger the powers to produce outcomes? Which appear to be effects or outcomes in themselves?

This second, retroductive approach produced a way of assessing hope through Indigenous responses.

Assessing Hope through Indigenous Responses

A number of Indigenous studies courses highlight five core components of spirituality pervading Indigenous political philosophy. These are Land, Language, Law, Kinship, and Ceremony. My own initial assessment of Indigenous hopes for sociocultural transformation as decolonization was undertaken by means of Indigenous responses to local development globally. That assessment is portrayed in *Learning for Liberation*.[35] I adapt its retroductive procedure here, emphasizing (in italics) the five core components as they appear in one form or another. Every phrase in the entire text that follows is as presented by one or more of the Indigenous writers.

> *Deep Indigenous kinship* as manifesting through *continually developing songlines* is accessible, including via the lived experience of a non-dual element of solidarity within family activities and interventions of everyday life. Strengthening participation in this kinship involves becoming more at one with a *complete, complex system of holistic law* through languaging[36] gifts of the Creator in all of life. Prerequisites of effective access to and sustainable participation in kinship are the impartation of *a set of culturally premised constitutional procedures* of oral history (linguistic, spiritual, and social) and the *continual, contiguous (collective) physical and spiritual application of a matrix* of all (eight) dimensions.[37]
>
> Becoming more at one with a complex system of holistic law is a process of daily responding to situations and circumstances (to holistic reception of

sensory confrontations) through instantly positioning oneself in the manifested and manifesting. It is to become committed to government for and by the people through *practice of the principle of unity of mind, body and spirit amongst family and clan leaders*, being aware of the *oneness of the Law* throughout generations, entailing a social conscience logistic.

Social conscience logistics are given operative meaning by the inference that a basic characteristic of deep Indigenous kinship is a *balance between love, spirituality, authority, and compliance*. Thus, oneness of the Law accesses the intrinsic value of being as political, family-based, and interwoven through and beyond a tapestry or field of *country and thought* through spirit. Social conscience logistics have three dynamics:

1   A re-orientation of *one's attitude towards one's cultural personality*, one's inner self (manifesting responses toward the totality of the Law as accessed).
2   A re-orientation of *one's everyday activity*, drawing on public-domain and ontological/theocratic, confidential cultural principles, with implications for the *transformation of academic, anthropological, archaeological and other structures* based in devaluation, neutralization and exploitation of cultural constructs, in conflict, aggression, etc.
3   A momentum toward *expanding activity toward the self-rejuvenation of others* (since their trauma and abuse means that your own social fabric is also torn).

    Articulating better understandings and explanations of barriers to realizing potential, along with breaking cycles of colonization policy, therefore requires a non-duality of solidarity within and between cultural groups, emergent from *discipline of individual and collective being* in entirety and from respect for life, community, and cosmos in entirety.

This analysis emerged from my participation across Indigenous communities in Australia, drawing from global Indigenous writings used extensively in our region. Over the years since, I have reflected deeply on its relevance through participation amongst communities and writings associated with agencies such as the Centre for Orang Asli Concerns (COAC)[38] in Malaysia, the regional Asia Indigenous Peoples' Pact (AIPP),[39] based in Thailand, and the global Tebtebba,[40] based in Baguio, the Philippines, all of whom I liaised with while working in Malaysia from 2009–2011. I will return to the five core components in section 4.

Articulating Questions toward Dynamic Dialectical Dialogue

The above set of complex and urgent challenges, contemporary development scenarios, and Indigenous responses to these are now the stage for further dynamic and dialectical interplay with ongoing critical realist and integral theorist dialogues, and with each of our explanatory and interpretive horizons as readers. The challenge and encouragement to engage Spirit[41] as ground-state[42] or Emptiness[43] pervades both parties to the dialogue.

A primary question that emerges is how to go about the dialectical process of locating commonalities and particularities across Indigenist spiritual beliefs. I portrayed in 'Assessing Hope through Indigenous Responses' above to some degree my own outcome from such a process, with a focus on deep Indigenous kinship, a universal holistic law, social conscience logistics, and non-duality.[44] Indigenous communities remind us that the realm of Spirit, indeed our world experienced as pervaded by spirit beings, is on the one hand inescapable and conducive to human (even cosmic) well-being, while on the other hand, it is a realm demanding healthy respect and capable of enacting dire consequences for those acting contrary to its law. In terms of international development, this first point articulates further questions to the ongoing dialogue, questions that arise from an Indigenist standpoint on the all-encompassing reality, powers, and potentials of Spirit and spirits interpenetrating our world.

Second, then, taking the Indigenist given of spirit beings, what might be their roles and functions in sustaining well-being or flourishing, in pursuing or resisting truth, oppression, condolence, emancipation and revitalization across all spheres of personal and social life?[45] As a means of engaging this broad question, the work of Yong (2003) on discerning spirits[46] is pertinent, raising a third key question that asks how best to explore the 'processive, ambiguous, and dialectical nature'[47] of discerning 'the diversity of human, social and even "demonic" spirits'?[48]

I turn now to applying the work of discernment to my own context of depth-investigative[49] participatory action research and evaluation (PARE) tending toward (in critical realist terms) emancipatory axiology.[50]

2 Discerning Spirit (the Divine at Work) within Depth-Investigative PARE

Discerning spirits can be messy, confronting and is hard work, for the spirits we encounter are not always good, true, or beautiful. But then neither are they always harmful, destructive, false, evil, or ugly. Neither divine presence nor absence is a simple category with clear lines between them. Our responsibility includes working out the 'dynamic and mediational' divine activity as 'things move continuously either to or away from their divinely instituted reason for being' at various levels in space and time. Just as important however, is 'the capacity to follow the trajectory of that phenomenon's movement and historical evolution—whether that be identified in moral, religious, spiritual or theological terms—precisely what the category of divine activity points to'.[51] Discerning Spirit in my own life-work draws from animistic-Biblical analogies as I reflect in solidarity. A key focus of my reflections is our strategic questioning vision for protecting children, in both State and global political contexts.

Some Animistic-Biblical Analogies

A central dialectic in the past 500 years of Western colonization's global trajectory has been the nexus between politics, culture, spirituality, and religion within frequently violent struggles over land and resources. The clashes with Indigenous peoples continue through globalization by corporations,[52] often aided and abetted by internal colonization, whether through various forms and combinations of Christian, Hindu, Islamic, Buddhist, Marxist, Atheistic, New Age, and other movements including Indigenous. However, apparent bastions of oppression can also contain within them sources of resilience and resistance to the brutalities of colonization.[53] Consequently criteria, norms, and means for discernment of spiritual states or of the work of spirits vary tremendously. In the West until relatively recently, a primary basis for discriminating between truth and error, good and evil has been the Bible.[54] Graham Paulson's *Towards an Aboriginal Theology*[55] is a recent example of advocating the use of Indigenous animistic spiritual traditions in holding together with integrity Indigenous and Christian identities.

A Banjalung man with historical connections to the various Indigenous people where I live in southeast Queensland, Paulson also draws from his years of living with the Warlpiri people in Central Australia. In his own words, he offered a series of comments on the pervasiveness and strength of his spiritual roots, 'in the hope that some collaboration might be fostered among all the animistic Indigenous populations of the Pacific'. I show in Table 3.2 his initial tentative comparison between some Biblical and animistic teachings on spirits and their activities.

In our own work contexts, nearly all conversations around the activity of spirits occur informally and, depending on the range of people in the conversation, it is with regard to one or more aspects of our family and community practices as strategic critical enquiry.

Solidarity in Transforming through Strategic Critical Enquiry

Our specific project is an Aboriginal community-based response to the over-representation of local Indigenous people in statutory systems such as child protection and the juvenile and criminal justice systems.[56] Our Jymbi (family or relations) Centre Vision Statement commits us to living out vital and inclusive community development. Our focus is on engaging and addressing the causes and consequences of (ongoing) colonization and invasion. The challenge is to contribute to building on individual and collective strengths, establishing sustainable self-determining systems, family and cultural structures, and reducing over-representation.

We know some of our real problems are our shattered links with country, family, Aboriginal lore and ways of learning. We know the heavy impacts on our personal and cultural identities and on our ability to control our own lives. We know some violent histories of our community and Australian society, physical and sexual abuse of all kinds.

Knowing all this, what do we do as a team, with our children, parents, families and communities experiencing chronic stress and conflict, in order to see further growth in our knowledge and ability to understand and to cope, our strength of personal and cultural identity, our self-esteem, confidence and belief in our ability to contribute to change at all levels? What must we do to help everyone involved

TABLE 3.2 Australian Aboriginal and Biblical teachings about spirits and their activities

Spirit Beings in Aboriginal Spirituality	Spirit Beings in Biblical Spirituality
Populate our world pervasively and include ancestral and totemic spirits.	God's *ruach* or Spirit in Gen 1:2 'hovered' (like an eagle) over the unshaped earth and waters (cf. Exod 19:4 and Deut 32:11). Is God like a totemic eagle in this case? All creation shares both the frustration and the liberation of the 'children of God' (Rom 8:20–25).
Specific 'hero' beings are human in emotions and intellect; animal, bird, or reptile in shape; super-human in power and creative ability; and were interactively responsible for the shaping of creation and animating of all life. Specific physical sites are sacred for local groups, but every part of living creation is animated by a spirit being.	God's Spirit exists within a plurality 'Let us make humankind in our image' (Gen 1:26, cf. 3:22, 11:7). All living things have a spirit given by God (e.g., Gen 1:30; Ps 104), but the 'holy ones of the earth' (Ps 16:3; 1 Sam 28:13) could be ancestral spirits associated with specific sites.
Are linked to space and place in their emergence from hidden worlds, their traveling and interacting with other spirits beings.	As the Spirit brought life, the earth was called upon to produce vegetation and to bring forth living creatures (Gen 1:11,24).
Are linked to human identity and experience through totems allocated in relation to conception, birth, skin, clan, and moiety, etc. Spiritual and physical responsibilities through songs, dances, and management practices are linked to totems.	Angels are spirits sent to serve those to be delivered by God (Heb 1:14), whether in human or animal appearance (1 Kings 19:5–8; 17:4–6). With Yahowah are 'holy ones' in a heavenly council, with different nations each having a representative spirit being (2 Kings 3:27; Mic 4:5; Deut 32:8).
Are arranged hierarchically, reflected in human society in an oligarchy where higher knowledge, responsibilities and participation rights are reserved for those with appropriate maturity of personality and character.	Are arranged in a hierarchical order (Eph 1:21; Col 1:16), with the power to help or hinder human interests as granted (Job 1:6–12).
Have the power to help or hinder human interests in relation to weather, hunting and gathering, choosing partners, etc. Supernatural powers and abilities may be granted to older people who habitually observe spiritual law, for the purpose of sustaining or enforcing spiritual and/or social law in their community, through ceremony.	The world is populated by other spirit beings, whose activities have significant impact on human societies, which in turn have responsibilities through ceremonial praying to influence those activities appropriately (Daniel 10:13,21; 12:1; Eph 6:12). The foundation and pinnacle of ceremonial praying is living in the Spirit (Rom 8, esp. 26–39).

by strengthening our sense of safety, of being more connected, our experience of mutual respect and of being more in control of our own futures?

A broad answer is—we must demonstrate the developmental core of our transformational work through holistic emphasis on three intertwining processes: enabling individuals and families to access service systems and structures; alleviating stress and illness by enabling healing from multi-generational legacies of trauma and thus supporting a restoration of effective agency; and engaging culture through key leaders or representatives from within each extended family group.

Consequently, as well as engaging with local community people, other key partners in collaborative activities necessarily include agents of local, state, or federal government systems and structures. Queensland State government departments with whom we regularly engage include: child safety; communities; community corrections; legal services; education; emergency services; employment and training; health; housing; natural resources and mines; main roads; police. Australian federal departments include: family and community services; attorney generals; education, science, and training. In all, we find that any one individual might be engaging over 35 different agencies. Forging solidarity with whichever workers are empathetic is key to moving forward. This necessity that we face every day is reinforced by the June 2013 report on the Commission of Inquiry into Child Protection in Queensland.

Queensland Child Protection Commission of Inquiry

An estimated 50 percent of Indigenous children in Queensland are known to the Department of Child Safety while almost 40 percent of children in out-of-home care are Indigenous. The Commission recognizes the need to address broader historical and systemic factors through governments and local communities integrating strategies in health, housing, education, and skilling for work.[57] It also notes, in particular, the strong evidence for community development approaches that unite all stakeholders at regional levels, directly contributing to improvements in life outcomes at the local level.

The Commission's Recommendation 11.7 (pp. 375–376) addresses the need for a ten-year 'capacity development plan' so as to promote partnerships, mentoring and secondments with the department and other agencies. This plan should include: developing skills and expertise within communities; developing a sustainable funding model to support establishing an alternative pathway for children in out-of-home care; establishing sustainable, accountable, and effective governance and business arrangements; and developing innovative partnership arrangements with mainstream service providers delivering out-of-home care services.

Our agency is well placed in relation to each point here. We initiated such a partnership ourselves in 2012, are working on alternative pathways, and the Mununjali Housing and Development Company was declared runner-up from amongst Indigenous regional finalists in a national mainstream process to evaluate the best employer of 2013. Of most significance we feel is the recommendation that Aboriginal controlled agencies such as ours 'have the option of coordinating family group meetings and working more closely with the department officers to develop cultural, case and transitions plans' (p. 387).

The effective development of cultural plans for children or young people in out-of-home care is an issue our staff members have long identified as a gap in the services meant to be provided by statutory bodies with whom we work. In regard to this point, much can be learnt from the experience and models being developed by Indigenous agencies throughout Australia and globally. Space does not allow here, but reference must be made for example to many of the papers in *Towards an Alternative Development Paradigm*, which relate the core role of spiritual practices in the development models described.[58] For all such communities, these are indeed questions of ultimate concern.

3 Questioning an 'Ultimate Concern'

My focus on Spirit in this chapter on sustainable international development was influenced since its inception by Hochachka's integralist questions about issues of ultimate concern. Reasonably familiar with the entire spread of critical realism, I initially had only a surface familiarity with integral theory. Since this book's context is a metatheoretical dialogue considering the most urgent and complex global problems, and since localities are global microcosms, my central focus is on localizing Wilber's theme of Spirit-in-action. Furthermore, against all criteria Indigenous contexts and struggles are urgent and complex, hence my inclusion of Indigenist worldviews and stances as political, rational, material, and above all spiritual.[59] I then framed my own context of participatory action research around discerning the presence, absence, and activities of the Great Creator Spirit[60] and of the lesser spirits.

I now engage briefly with integralist questions raised by Hochachka (2011b) in relation to an evolving 'ultimate concern' via simultaneously present and at times messily intersecting faith in animism, in a theistic God and in postmodern secularism. She first asks, 'How can our understanding of faith and spirituality be more skillfully included in international development?' Then, 'What might be a postsecular approach to development practice that includes both secular and spiritual truths in development work?'

Personally it's a matter of relentlessly going deeper into the Spirit so as to be restored in my own spirit while engaging stress and tension in my/our world, no matter where I am at the time. Stress can lead to restfulness as I meditate on Truth at all levels and from all perspectives. Only in doing so am I sustained to continuously challenge friends and colleagues to likewise contemplate their own historical trajectories and socio-cultural realities.

From this perspective, I suggest that Hochachka's noted points of relevance to international development appear to resonate with many Indigenous communities globally. First, exploring the relationship between seemingly Western faith and faith-inspired development work could move forward in a number of directions by considering histories of development work over two millennia. Don Richardson's *Eternity in Their Hearts* (1981) comes to mind in relation to its focus on Indigenous groups. There are other rarely acknowledged non-Western sources of history and cultural roots. For example Philip Jenkins' *The Lost History of Christianity* (2008) concludes that the largest and most influential churches of Christianity's youth were Eastern, covering the world from China to North Africa, ruled over the Middle East for centuries, and produced chief administrators and academics within the Muslim empire. Not only did those people of faith encounter a full spectrum of responses ranging from acceptance to persecution under Islamic rule, but their 'reign' lasted until a thousand years after Constantine.

Second, the extent to which Indigenous beliefs and practices have been transcended or included by, or have themselves transcended or included Christian faith in practice, is a topic for ongoing reflection and dialogue. It is certainly a point of conversation amongst a great number of communities across Australasia, as exemplified in Table 3.2 of this chapter. Third, there are indeed potential risks that atheistic assumptions/biases might overlook important components of faith- or Spirit-powered resilience and recovery from trauma and oppression. Yet there is also the risk that unless people of faith engage authentically with those claiming no faith, important perspectives could be overlooked by both parties as well.

Fourth, there is a reality that Indigenous peoples are very much aware of: while institutional faith appears to be declining rapidly in the Global North (the West), faith-centred movements and development are expanding even more rapidly amongst people in the Global South. Yet such movements too often struggle with making that faith relevant to the whole breadth of their concerns around land security, language reclamation, upholding their customary law, and maintaining their kinship systems and ceremonial practices to the extent they see as consistent with such faith. Hochachka's fifth point of relevance to international development relates to possible links between the practice of deeper states of consciousness and peoples' capacity for resilience through practicing faith and hope. My comments on this are presented as questions raised by the current dialogue, giving rise to implications, as in the next section.

4 Indigenist Implications for Dialectical CR-IT Dialogue

One broad motivation for this book arises from connections, divergences, incommensurabilities, difficulties, drawbacks, and potential for mutual enhancement in the emerging CR-IT dialogue. I select now some dialogue of relevance to the nature and focus of my dialectical explanatory argument and draw out some implications for that dialogue.

Outlining Some Dialogue to Date

First, Hedlund's 'Situating the mapmaker', Paul Marshall's 'The meeting of two integrative metatheories' and Timothy Rutzou's 'Integral theory: A poisoned chalice?' agree regarding IT's need to explicitly thematize a realist ontology and weaken its social constructivist position. Second, directionality is a pivotal issue, since for CR, it is geo-historical and tendentially rational (powered by the dialectic of freedom and issuing in emancipatory axiology) while in IT directionality is characterized by Spirit 'involving' itself in the material world of evolution on the basis of both involutionary and evolutionary givens.[61]

Third, for an ongoing dialogue around both ontology and directionality, my view is that Hedlund's paper has much to contribute, with its clarifying some personal-historical and strategic-intentional factors that have likely affected Wilber's map-making in such a way as to explicitly devalue subtle forms of development and restrict a truly cross-cultural, deep structural, integral synthesis. His paper expresses the hope that more integralists will engage in a deeper critical-sympathetic discourse in relation to Wilber's metatheoretical enactment. He also hopes that more perspectives on subtle practice will be incorporated by what some see as a 'frankly somewhat elite integral community', so enabling more effectiveness 'in serving humanity and the planet and actualizing the broader Integral vision in the world'.[62]

My fourth point relates to Hedlund highlighting the 'highly controversial status of the subtle' and of what is perceived as a pre-rational, mythic worldview, in the eyes of the academic mainstream.[63] But is Wilber's recommendation to discard 'pre-rational' 'unnecessary metaphysical dogmatisms' really consistent with his Integral Post-Metaphysics and Integral Methodological Pluralism which advocate the use of eight basic methodological families, the three (or four) strands of valid knowledge, within developmental levels or structures in broad or deep empiricism?[64] I see definite value in the detail of such mapping, but urge great caution and sensitivity in its application to divine activities in the real world of oppressed and exploited communities, especially Indigenous, as I now elaborate.

Practicing Dialectical Explanatory Argument

Some 13 years of further community work after writing *Learning for Liberation*, I am stronger than ever in my convictions on a number of points. My earlier *transcendental* argument for developing an ontological schema, the conditions of possibility of decolonization,[65] I now see as more of a *dialectical explanatory* argument.[66] First, I had explained contradictory forces in terms of both, some errors associated with the role of families in protective intervention and the causes of those errors. I then expanded the conceptual field by engaging a meta-reflexively totalizing (self-)situation,[67] nurturing reflexivity about our reflexivity so as to strengthen totalizing depth-praxis. I am also more convinced of the urgency for correctly discerning spirits.[68] Our challenge and responsibility involves striving to discern beyond the exteriors of concrete particularities to dynamic and relational vectors, to the inner habits, dispositions, tendencies, and powers[69] of structures associated with notions, concepts, or models of freedom, power, agency, solidarity, oppression, and emancipation.[70] It is further to not only discern the presence and nature of spirit entities or beings in this complex dynamic, but also to know how to respond so as to nurture personal and community well-being.

Some Implications for the Dialogue

One key theme in this chapter—that of going deeper, further, and higher, through in-depth community work, deep Indigenous kinship, depth-investigative PARE, and strategic critical enquiry—illustrates the hard work of discerning spirits. The following short extract (Table 3.3) from my retroductive analysis is a tiny indication of the breadth of totalizing depth-praxis by Indigenous communities,[71] who across the globe generally encounter entrenched resistance from and exploitation by the academy and its research programmes. That, in fact, was the motivating force behind the request nearly 20 years ago from local Indigenous community leaders for me to contribute to their pursuit of justice through community learning, by doing further studies under their guidance. The table also indicates something of the enlightening benefits of suffering, and the necessity for connections with land or country.

Overall, this chapter no doubt has many implications for the dialogue. My purpose has been to further expand the spaces for Indigenous participation in it. Major implications I feel have to do with the nature of our depth-praxis with Indigenist leaders and communities, specifically in terms of the three dynamics of social conscience logistics identified (in 'Assessing Hope through Indigenous Responses' in section 1) in relation to reorienting one's attitude to one's inner self and everyday activity with a view to expanding activity directed at the self-rejuvenation of others. There is considerable resonance here with the current CR-IT dialogue. In particular, the dynamic of the five core components of Indigenous political philosophy discussed in 'Assessing Hope through Indigenous Responses' in section 1 opens up dialogue around my four points in 'Outlining Some Dialogue to Date' in section 4.

TABLE 3.3 Community focus, identifying and defining needs

Author	Range or Focus Community	Needed Sources of Determination and/or Means of Defining and Identifying Objective Needs
West	Aboriginal 'members of the world community', writing as one for whom English is his 'unfortunate first language'.	'Cultural currency and humanity' are both denied to the owners of first knowledge, by 'the guardians of the dominant paradigm: the Academy', to communities needing connections with 'traditional lands, seas and the ether'.
Trudgen	East Arnhem Land Yolnu, for whom English is often a fourth or fifth language.	'Trust and insight' come from the 'pain of living with suffering' within everyday life. Primary need is to regain control over life.
Alford	Native American communities in general, although with a focus on an emerging network of representatives of Native American peoples, quantum physicists, linguists and others.	A 'complete cognitive circle', where the 'most current thought' is joined with 'archaic thought, finding a balance which honours both in respect, lifting us to a higher level of complementary thinking, which dismisses neither'.

How do Indigenous dynamics and trajectories of Spirit and spirits as beings, guardians, powers, and animals intersect with realist ontology, with the personal extensions and intentions of our social constructions, with our stances on geo-historical directionality and our immersions in mythic and mystic environments? What some could consider 'pre-rational' 'unnecessary metaphysical dogmatisms' of Spirit-in-action for example might fall within the realm of the functioning of ceremony, of kinship patterns and connections with land, of languaging and of a complete, complex system of holistic law. This in turn raises questions of the possibility of universal paradigms of rationality and spirituality. Such paradigms operate through and beyond a tapestry or field of country and thought, uniting law, land, and leaders through spirit.

Conclusion

The project of spelling out specific Indigenist implications relevant to some of the most complex and urgent challenges of international development can, I suggest, serve three main purposes. First, it has the potential to help sharpen the focus of contemporary international development.[72] Second, it has the practical benefit of contributing to the strengthening of both CR and IT as metatheories. Finally, it could help enable a more genuine and effective engagement with movements built on solidarity throughout the twenty-first century.

At heart, my claim is a methodological one: that the Indigenist implications raised both confront us with the necessity for engaging the contested realm of Spirit and further enable us to do so with growing levels of confidence. The dynamism of Spirit is a liberating influence for deepening dialogical praxis around dialectical questions and concerns. Extending such dialogues within emancipatory axiology will involve at the very least a deepening engagement with Wilber's four faces of truth as Spirit-in-action[73] and with the diversity of dialogue and debate around critical realism, integral theory, and sustainable international development.

My purpose in this chapter has been to extend specific dialogue regarding neo-integrative worldviews, expanding spaces for Indigenist participation in it, by utilizing the notion of Spirit or spirit(s) as generative mechanisms operating at the nexus between politics, culture, religion, and spirituality. We urgently need to learn further from Indigenist and related traditions how to discern and engage the operations of these entities. Ultimately this requires immersion in solidarity with decolonizing ways of life, wherever we can, however we must, whatever the cost.

I presented in section 1 an Indigenist standpoint on the urgency and complexity in contemporary development scenarios, beginning with not only Indigenous willingness to question whether development even has a future, but also a resolute commitment to hold fast to their spiritual heart of self-determined development. This core focus on spirit pervades Indigenous political philosophies of land, languaging, law, kinship, and ceremony. Reflecting deeply on this hope led me to articulate and direct questions to the dialogue between critical realists and integral theorists. First, how do we as dialogue participants dialectically locate commonalities and particularities of belief and practice across the diversity we encounter, including our own? Second, what might be the roles and functions of spirit entities in pursuing or resisting well-being, truth, and flourishing across all spheres of personal and social life? We need to explore here experiential accounts of impersonal ethereal essences, as well as of personal beings, whether in the global West or East, the North or South. This question must also cover both any universal Spirit (whether as Person, abstract Essence, or Emptiness) and particular localized spirit beings. Third, how might we best explore together the processive, ambiguous, and dialectical nature of discerning the diversity of personal, social, and even 'demonic' (absenting the divine) spirits?

In section 2, I applied the work of discernment to my own context of depth-investigative participatory action research and evaluation. Both divine and demonic activity is dynamic and mediational. We need to trace the trajectory of any phenomenon's movement and historical evolution, whether in moral, religious, spiritual, or theological terms. If each phenomenon is comprised of a tapestry of human, social, divine, and demonic powers, then effective discernment will always tend to be messy and confronting. It involves struggle in solidarity and, for us, frequently drawing from animistic-Biblical analogies in our strategic questioning vision for protecting children and nurturing flourishing. The struggle is, essentially, to become more at one with a complex system of holistic law, to practice more consistently the principle of unity of mind, body and spirit amongst family leaders. Awareness of the oneness of the Law throughout generations is tempered by the harshness of its contemporary fracturing. Hence the challenge of strengthening social conscience logistics: re-orientating our attitudes toward our cultural personalities; re-orientating our everyday activities, with implications for the transformation of diverse structures based in devaluation, neutralization, and exploitation of cultural constructs; and thus expanding activity toward the self-rejuvenation of each other and all others. I noted that for vulnerable children and young people, there is a massive gap in services meant to be provided by statutory bodies and other agencies with whom we work. Policymakers, heeding calls from Indigenous community agencies such as ours, now highlight the necessity for effective development of cultural plans for those in out-of-home care. In developing and implementing such plans, spiritual concepts, principles, and practices must remain at the core of development with culture and identity.

My third step in developing Indigenist implications for the contemporary CR-IT dialogue was to engage with integralist questions raised by Gail Hochachka. These are issues of an 'ultimate concern' in a dialectic of faith in animism, in a theistic God and in postmodern secularism. Hochachka noted five points of relevance to international development. I outlined how the resonance of these points with many Indigenous communities globally could be nurtured (1) by considering the history of development work over recent centuries; (2) through dialogue between Indigenous people and those of diverse faiths regarding dialectics linking their respective beliefs and practices; (3) through insistence on surfacing and challenging various assumptions or biases by all people whether of faith or no faith, so as to engage with care every factor contributing to resilience and recovery from trauma and oppression; (4) by strengthening struggles in both the faith-weak Global North and the faith-expanding Global South to make faith relevant to the whole breadth of concerns around land security, language reclamation, upholding customary law, maintaining kinship systems, and ceremonial practices; and (5) specifically exploring the dynamic of deepening consciousness practices, resilience, faith, and hope.

Finally I briefly reviewed in section 4 specific points raised by Hedlund, Paul Marshall, and Timothy Rutzou in the ongoing CR-IT dialogue: realist ontology versus social constructivism; our stances on geo-historical rational directionality, toward a truly cross-cultural, deep structural, integral synthesis; our immersions in mythic and mystic environments via authentic valuing of subtle forms of development. I then called for radical commitment to appropriately discerning and responding to spirit entities or beings through dialectical explanatory argument. There are profound implications for each of us in attending to the dynamics of social conscience logistics in our structured being and becoming, our immersion in constellational relations between the ethical and the historical, and our holding fast to a third way between the two poles of structural abstract universalization and poststructural radical particularization. We cannot afford either to further neglect key resources or to become victims of further spiritual oppressions.

Notes

1 Hockey (2013).
2 See Hockey (2007, pp. 2–10, 19–40).
3 See Hochachka (2005, 2011a, 2011b).
4 See Wilber (1996, pp. 123–130, 151–154, 243–339; 2001, pp. 41, 86, 160 n.1). Flatland denotes scientific materialism, a world of quantity devoid of quality, with mere peeks at peak experiences rather than relentless commitment to sustainable transformation in everyday life.
5 See Andrews (2012a, pp. 1–37).
6 Andrews (2012a, 2012b).
7 Hartwig and Morgan (2012); Wright (2013).
8 See Hockey (2007) and Tebtebba Foundation (2010), for example.
9 Benedikter and Molz (2012).
10 Wink (1992); Yong (2003); McDermott (2007). Besides responses to or applications of Bhaskar's or Wilber's emphases to be referenced in this chapter, see also a diverse range in Archer et al. (2004), Pinchbeck (2009), Creaven (2010), Hampson (2010), Visser (2010), and Smith (2012).
11 Churchill (2008/2000) states that by 'Indigenist' he means

> that I am one who not only takes the rights of indigenous peoples as the highest priority of my political life, but who draws upon the traditions—the bodies of knowledge and corresponding codes of value—evolved over many thousands of years by native peoples the world over. This is the basis upon which I not only advance critiques of, but conceptualize alternatives to the present social, political, economic, and philosophical status quo. In turn, this gives shape not only to the sorts of goals and objectives I pursue, but the kinds of strategy and tactics I advocate, the variety of struggles I tend to support, the nature of the alliances I am inclined to enter into, and so on.

12 See West (2000) and Phillips (2011).
13 Hart (2010, pp. 6–12).
14 See Contreras (n.d.).
15 See 'Practicing Dialectical Explanatory Argument' in section 4.
16 Where sets of holons (wholes/parts), each with its own capacity for agency, communion, self-transcendence and self-dissolution, necessarily form hierarchies in which each holon emerges from the one on which it then depends.
17 Drawn from observations, news and resources on the changing nature of innovation, technology, leadership, and other subjects, three trends are highlighted: the need for life-long education; the impact of globalization in raising the standards of living in emerging and developing economies; and the challenges to health care and social benefit programmes posed by aging populations around the world.
18 SID's *Development* journal (SID, 2013) on the one hand identifies the policy world as actively engaged in redefining the shape of the contemporary development agenda, while on the other hand, interrogating whether—given the overall context of insecurity, the combination of environmental limits, flawed institutions, and fraying solidarity—development does even have a future, especially for the poor.
19 Before It's News' (2013) portrayal of ten most urgent, pressing, global issues, with the least likely (not shown in Table 3.1) being potential meteorite impact.
20 Martin (2013): Interconnected twenty-first century mega-problems resulting from bad management and absence of foresight, including pandemics such as AIDS, runaway computer intelligence, risks to human existence through scientific experiments, and a new dark age of unending hatred and violence through a combination of all the other mega-problems.
21 United Nations' Environment Program's (UNEP, 2012) vivid picture of 21 issues for the twenty-first century, drawn from their Biennial Foresight Process, informs the UN and the wider international community about the most important emerging global environmental issues for action. These are grouped under five themes, as shown in Table 3.1.
22 Identified as: Aligning governance to the challenges of global sustainability; Transforming human capabilities for the twenty-first century – meeting global environmental challenges and moving towards a green economy; Broken bridges – reconnecting science and policy; Social tipping points? Catalysing rapid and transformative changes in human behaviour towards the environment; New concepts for coping with creeping changes and imminent thresholds; Coping with migration caused by new aspects of environmental change.
23 D'Souza's (2013) review essay focuses on three books' methodological approaches to contemporary socio-cultural and political economy problems.
24 D'Souza (2013, pp. 534–536).
25 Andrews' thesis (2012a, p. 13) is that '(o)ne of the biggest problems we face in the twenty-first century is to reweave the broken threads of the fabric of our communities' and notes the many already encouraging signs of renewed interest in community across the fields of physics, biology, philosophy, psychology, sociology, and politics (pp. 13–34).
26 Andrews (2012a, pp. 32–35); cf. Banuri (2013), highlighting the need to move from a technocratic approach to a more political conceptualization of development where policy discussions prevail over the mere use of quantitative targets and technicalities. But is this, I ask, sufficient?
27 Peter Westoby, in Andrews (2012a, pp. 35–36).
28 As in CR regarding depth-investigation and totalizing depth-praxis, and in IT where holarchy is the basic principle of holism. See Bhaskar (2008, pp. 261–270) for an extended discussion of totalizing depth-praxis, especially his elaboration of a typical dialectic of morality on pp. 265–266. See also my own analysis in Hockey (2007, pp. 203–240) of earlier debates and critiques within critical realism itself regarding the theorizing of spirituality and metaReality in the context of Western bourgeois triumphalism.
29 As in concepts of 'dadirri' or deep listening—see Judy Atkinson's *Trauma Trails* (2002).

30 Bebbington et al. (2008).
31 See Banuri (2013, pp. 7–8), especially endnotes 1–3. For more specifically Indigenous perspectives along these lines see initially UN (2009), Tebtebba (2010), and consider further links from those sites in the light of the 1992 Rio Earth Summit with its introduction of Agenda 21, the Rio+20 Summit and the post-2015 agenda.
32 See Hochachka (2005, p. 9).
33 See Hockey (2007, p. 72).
34 As in Archer (2000).
35 Hockey (2007, pp. 159–160).
36 See Hockey (2007, pp. 127–129), in support of a realist, dialectical linguistics (Sapir and Whorf) against Chomsky's idealist, reductionist research programme that consistently committed the epistemic fallacy.
37 West (2000, p. 106). The eight dimensions are cultural, spiritual, secular, intellectual, political, practical, personal, and public.
38 See www.coac.org.my
39 See www.aippnet.org
40 See www.tebtebba.org. and especially Tebtebba Foundation (2010).
41 I use the capitalized form here, because (1) many Indigenous communities globally refer to the universal Great Creator Spirit, as well as particular spirits connected to specific places or regions (whether involved in creation stories or otherwise), besides each person being also a spirit and possessing a spirit from their place of conception; (2) my own belief in and commitment to *Ruach HaKodesh*, the universal clean and pure Spirit of *Yahowah* and of *Yeshua HaMashiach*, and my understanding of particular spirits whose intended function is to serve the well-being of the cosmos; and (3) my belief in common with many Indigenous peoples that the universal Spirit is to be both distinguished from (as transcendent) and yet is (immanent as) 'the life breath of all human interpersonal and communitarian activity' (Yong, 2003, p. 184). Overall, this latter point undergirds my retroductive analysis of selected Indigenous writings that, given the 'all-encompassing reality, powers and potentials of the spiritual world interpenetrating ... the material (including human) world', emancipatory activities must 'fully engage material realities of oppression within and through their spiritual world context' (Hockey 2007, pp. 204, 238). I also note that Wilber (1996) uses 'Spirit' throughout.
42 Bhaskar's metaRealist term.
43 A key Buddhist term used by Wilber, interchangeable not only with 'Spirit' (as in Wilber 2013) but with 'consciousness', 'depth' etc. (as in Wilber, 1996, p. 41).
44 For further elaboration, see such Indigenous publications as UN (2009) and Tebtebba (2010), and other Indigenous texts covered in my own work, along with Hochachka's descriptions.
45 I note reference to a number of Indigenous communities with whom I have had direct or indirect involvement. These have to do with overwhelming terror amongst the Semai of West Malaysia (Dentan, 2009), rapid cultural, social, and political transformation amongst the Kelabit of Sarawak (Bulan & Bulan-Dorai, 2004), widespread inversion of the devic versus asuric dialectic amongst a range of tribals and so-called 'backwards' across India (Khyati, 2013), and holistic transformation and growth amongst diverse groups throughout Mozambique and elsewhere in powerful demonstrations of Spirit-in-action (www.irisglobal.org/about/history).
46 Yong (2003, pp. 132–137) takes up the Peircean triadic metaphysics of: 'firstness—(a thing's) simple, felt qualities of suchness, function and appearance; secondness—its concrete (form or) particularities and actualities; and thirdness—its spiritual vectors or fields of force' (p. 136), or 'inner spirit ... the laws, habits, tendencies, and energetic force that shape its processive actuality and direct its temporal trajectory' (p. 134). Hence with regard to oppression, exploitation, etc. (see Hockey, 2007, pp. 102–104, 108, 113–114, 136–137, 143–144, 150), Yong (2003, pp. 138–139) asks 'what distinguishes demonic spirits from non-demonic—human, institutional—spirits?' He delineates three

characteristic features: a destructive field of force attempting to 'influence the course of things and events'; a destructive means or dynamic, 'developing inauthentic relationships between things', subverting 'the divinely constituted relationality' of harmony between things so as to produce 'strife, violence, isolation and desolation'; and a destructive effect of perverting 'the divine intentions for things' so that they claim more for themselves than their 'reason for being'.

47 Yong (2003, p. 169).
48 Yong (2003, p. 164).
49 See Hockey (2007, pp. 199–200) for my summary of Bhaskar's delineation of depth inquiry as a co-operative inquiry involving an external agent.
50 See Hartwig (2007b), Hockey (2007, pp. 224–240).
51 Yong (2003, pp. 165–166). There are clear parallels here with the Indigenous description of decolonizing processes in the section 'Assessing Hope through Indigenous Responses' above.
52 As an ongoing, dynamic, historical process, as in Bello (2013).
53 Harris (1990) concludes for example that, overall, 200 years of Aboriginal encounter with Christianity in Australia has been a story of hope.
54 Mangalwadi (2009, 2011) concludes that the Bible not only 'created the soul of western civilization' and hence of many of their colonies, but also contains 'a manifesto for ailing nations'. (cf. Hartwig & Morgan, 2012; Wright, 2013).
55 Paulson (2006).
56 See in particular Hockey (2007, pp. 2–10, 31–40). In 2018 I ceased full-time employment with that project, after 15 years.
57 This section is summarized from Chapter 11 of the Commission's report (pp. 349–394). I focus on elements of most direct relevance to our workplace.
58 Tebtebba Foundation (2010), see in particular Chapters 5–7, 10–11, and 14–16. Pages 603–605 present a brief summary of spiritual concepts, principles, and practices, along with challenges in maintaining Indigenous spirituality toward development with culture and identity.
59 See the discussion in Benedikter and Molz (2012).
60 See Hockey (2007, p. 152, Table 4.2), where some Native American terms are quoted as 'Dwells Above', 'Thinks Breath Creates', 'Great sacred mystery of life', or signing such as 'big, large, great' + 'medicine' + 'pointing up', and these are understood to have underlying common meanings of 'Great(ly) Mysterious(ing)' (cf. also Tables 3.1, 3.2, 4.1, and 4.3 in the same thesis). See also Tebtebba Foundation (2010, pp. 603–604), for example, on the roles and functions of the Creator as supreme being and of lesser spirits.
61 Marshall (2012, pp. 205–206).
62 Hedlund (2011, p. 16).
63 Hedlund (2011, p. 11).
64 Hedlund (2011, pp. 16–18; cf. Wilber, 2001, pp. 3–5, 17–28).
65 Hockey (2007, pp. 158–161), and the thesis as a whole.
66 See Hartwig (2007a).
67 See Hartwig (2007c). The concept of a meta-reflexively totalizing (self-)situation provides a rational resolution to the problem of subjectivity and objectivity without conflating the two dimensions, as in the work of Wilber.
68 A good range of examples of discerning of spirit(s) in community work is to be found in Andrews' *Down Under* (2012a), where he explores the significant in-depth difference to be made by amateur, radical, and revolutionary activists along with persistent and resilient rebel practitioners, as well as in his *Out and Out* (2012b), where he explores the dynamics of Christian mystic community work and its heritage in 'Initiatives of Change' and 'The Twelve Step Movement'. However in Andrews' work there is no discussion of relationships between the spirit of community work and spirits as entities, powers, or beings.
69 Yong (2003, p. 151).
70 Hockey (2007, pp. 92–98).

71 Adapted from Hockey (2007, pp. 74–78). The entire thesis gives a more comprehensive view.
72 In terms of strategic features or goals of a post-2015 development perspective, Walden Bello (2013, pp. 98–101) outlines four international- and 14 national-level features, from which he identifies seven that could serve as realistic goals. He calls for indicators to be developed for each goal, in order to assess any advance in reversing corporate-driven globalization as well as in *managing and superseding global capitalism*. His proposed concrete goals are: (1) stabilize the climate; (2) re-regulate finance and cancel development country debt; (3) reduce inequality; (4) ensure food security; (5) de-commodify the commons; (6) provide comprehensive social protection; and (7) promote industrialization. At our local level we are working at articulating some of these goals, with Japanangka West's five core components of spirituality.
73 Wilber (1996, pp. 105–119).

References

Andrews, D. (2012a). *Down Under: In-Depth Community Work*. Mosaic Press.
Andrews, D. (2012b). *Out and Out: Way-Out Community Work*. Challenge Books.
Archer, M. (2000). *Being Human: The Problem of Agency*. Cambridge University Press.
Archer, M.S., Collier, A.C., & Porpora, D.V. (2004a). *Transcendence: Critical Realism and God*. Routledge.
Atkinson, J. (2002). *Trauma Trails, Recreating Songlines: The Transgenerational Effects of Trauma in Indigenous Australia*. Spinifex Press.
Banuri, T. (2013). The future of development. *Development*, 56(1), 1–9.
Bebbington, A.J., Hickey, S., & Mitlin, D.C. (eds) (2008). *Can NGOs Make a Difference? The Challenge of Development Alternatives*. Zed Books.
Before It's News (2013). *Top 10 Most Urgent Problems in the World*. Available at http://beforeitsnews.com/alternative/2013/03/top-10-most-urgent-problems-in-the-world-2603780.html (Accessed 1 June 2013).
Bello, W. (2013). Post-2015 development assessment: Proposed goals and indicators. *Development*, 56(1), 93–102.
Benedikter, R., & Molz, M. (2012). The rise of neo-integrative worldviews: Towards a rational spirituality for the coming planetary civilization? In M. Hartwig & J. Morgan (eds), *Critical Realism and Spirituality* (pp. 29–74). Routledge.
Bhaskar, R. (2008). *Dialectic: The Pulse of Freedom*. Routledge.
Bulan, S., & Bulan-Dorai, L. (2004). *The Bario Revival*. Home Matters Network.
Churchill, W. (2008/2000). *'I Am Indigenist': Notes on the Ideology of the Fourth World*. Available at www.zcommunications.org/i-am-indigenist-by-ward-churchill (Accessed 4 July 2013).
Contreras, F. (n.d.). *Marxist Probematics from an Indigenist Perspective: The Case of the h'Mong*. Available at www.globalsouth12.wordpress.com/an-indigenist-critique-of-marxism/ (Accessed 1 July 2013).
Creaven, S. (2010). *Against the Spiritual Turn: Marxism, Realism and Critical Theory*. Routledge.
Dentan, R.K. (2009). *Overwhelming Terror: Love, Fear, Peace, and Violence among Semai of Malaysia*. Strategic Information and Research Development Centre (SIRD).
D'Souza, R. (2013). Justice and governance in dystopia. *Journal of Critical Realism*, 12(4), 518–537.
Edwards, M. (2004). Good for business: An integral theory perspective on spirituality in organisations. *Journal of Spirituality, Leadership and Management*, 3. Available at www.slam.org.au/wp-content/uploads/2013/06/JSLaMvol3_2004_edwards.pdf (Accessed 30 June 2020).

Hampson, G.P. (2010). Western-Islamic and Native American genealogies of Integral Education. In S. Esbjorn-Hargens, J. Reams, & O. Gunnlaugson (eds), *Integral Education: New Directions for Higher Learning* (pp. 17–33). SUNY Series in Integral Theory. SUNY Press.

Hart, M.A. (2010). Indigenous worldviews, knowledge, and research: The development of an Indigenous research paradigm. *Journal of Indigenous Voices in Social Work*, 1(1), 1–16.

Hartwig, M. (2007a). Dialectical argument. In M. Hartwig (ed.), *Dictionary of Critical Realism*. Routledge.

Hartwig, M. (2007b). Emancipatory axiology. In M. Hartwig (ed.), *Dictionary of Critical Realism*. Routledge.

Hartwig, M. (2007c). Reflection. In M. Hartwig (ed.), *Dictionary of Critical Realism*. Routledge.

Hartwig, M., with Morgan, J. (eds) (2012). *Critical Realism and Spirituality*. Routledge.

Hedlund, N. (2011). Situating the Mapmaker: An Imminent Critique of Wilber's Cartography of the Transphysical Worlds. Philosophy, Cosmology, and Consciousness Program, School of Consciousness and Transformation, California Institute of Integral Studies.

Hedlund, N. (2012). Critical realism. A synoptic overview and resource guide for integral scholars. Resource Paper, MetaIntegral Foundation.

Hochachka, G. (2005). *Developing Sustainability, Developing the Self: An Integral Approach to International and Community Development*. Drishti-Centre for Integral Action with Funding from IDRC.

Hochachka, G. (2011a). Enacting a Post-Secular Spirituality: Or, Why Yoga Is So Cool. Available at http://beamsandstruts.com/articles/item/249-enacting-a-post-secular-spirituality-or-why-yoga-is-so-cool (Accessed 1 June 2013).

Hochachka, G. (2011b). Post-Secularity, Climate Change, and Spirit. Available at http://beamsandstruts.com/essays/item/572-post-secularity-climate-change-and-spirit (Accessed 1 June 2013).

Hockey, N. (2007). *Learning for Liberation: Values, Actions and Structures for Social Transformation through Aboriginal Communities*. PhD Dissertation, Queensland University of Technology. Available at www.eprints.qut.edu.au/16520/ (Accessed 23 February 2022).

Hockey, N. (2013). Dialectic, decolonising and the spiritual heart of Indigenous self-determined development. Paper presented at the IACR Conference, Nottingham, 29–31 July.

Jenkins, P. (2008). *The Lost History of Christianity: The Thousand-Year Golden Age of the Church in the Middle East, Africa and Asia—and How it Died*. Lion.

Khyati, S. (2013). Tribals, backwards seek own voices in Durga Puja this year. *The Indian Express*, 14 October. Available at www.indianexpress.com/news/tribals-backwards-seek-own-voices-in-durga-puja-this-year/1182314/ (Accessed 20 October 2013).

Mangalwadi, V. (2009). *Truth and Transformation: A Manifesto for Ailing Nations*. YWAM Publishing.

Mangalwadi, V. (2011). *The Book that Made Your World: How the Bible Created the Soul of Western Civilization*. Thomas Nelson.

Marshall, P. (2012). The meeting of two integrative metatheories. *Journal of Critical Realism*, 11(2), 188–214.

Martin, J. (n.d.). *The Megaproblems of the 21st Century*. Available at www.jamesmartin.com/book/megaproblems.cfm (Accessed 1 June 2013).

McDermott, G.R. (2007). *Why Has God Allowed Different Religions? Insights from the Bible and the Early Church*. InterVarsity Press.

Norrie, A. (2010). *Dialectic and Difference: Dialectical Critical Realism and the Grounds of Justice*. Routledge.

Paulson, G. (2006). Towards an Aboriginal theology. *Pacifica*, 19(October), 310–320. Available at www.pacifica.org.au/old/files/vol19no3article7.pdf. (Accessed 4 March 2013).

Phillips, D.J.M. (2011). *Resisting Contradictions: Non-Indigenous Pre-Service Teacher Responses to Critical Indigenous Studies*. Available at eprints.qut.edu.au/46071/1/Donna_Phillips_Thesis.pdf (Accessed 30 June 2020).

Pinchbeck, D. (2008). Meeting the Spirits. In D. Pinchbeck & K. Jordan (eds), *Toward 2012: Perspectives on the New Age*. Jeremy P. Tarcher/Penguin. Available at www.nytimes.com/2009/02/06/books/chapters/chapter-toward-2012.html (Accessed 30 June 2020).

Queensland Child Protection Commission of Inquiry (2013). *Taking Responsibility: A Roadmap for Queensland Child Protection*. Available at www.childprotectioninquiry.qld.gov.au/__data/assets/pdf_file/0017/202625/QCPCI-FINAL-REPORT-web-version.pdf (Accessed 14 August 2013).

Richardson, D. (1981). *Eternity in Their Hearts: The Untold Story among Folk Religions of Ancient People*. Regal Books.

Rutzou, T. (2012). Integral theory: A poisoned chalice? *Journal of Critical Realism*, 11(2), 215–224.

Smith, P. (2012). *Integral Christianity: The Spirit's Call to Evolve*. Paragon House.

Society for International Development (SID) (2013). The future of development. *Development*, 56, 1.

Tebtebba Foundation (2010). *Towards an Alternative Development Paradigm: Indigenous People's Self-Determined Development*. Tebtebba Foundation.

Trudgen, R.I. (2000). *Why Warriors Lie Down and Die: Towards an Understanding of Why the Aboriginal People of Arnhem Land Face the Greatest Crisis in Health and Education since European Contact*. Aboriginal Resource and Development Services Inc.

United Nations (UN) (2009). *State of the World's Indigenous Peoples*. United Nations, Department of Economic and Social Affairs, Division for Social Policy and Development, Secretariat of the Permanent Forum on Indigenous Issues. Available at www.un.org/development/desa/indigenouspeoples/publications/2009/09/state-of-the-worlds-indigenous-peoples-first-volume/ (Accessed 1 June 2013).

United Nations Environment Program (UNEP) (2012). *21 Issues for the 21st Century: Results of the UNEP Foresight Process on Emerging Environmental Issues*. Available at www.unep.org/publications/ebooks/foresightreport/Portals/24175/pdfs/Foresight_Report-21_Issues_for_the_21st_Century.pdf (Accessed 1 June 2013).

Visser, F. (2010). The 'Spirit of Evolution' reconsidered: Relating Ken Wilber's view of spiritual evolution to the current evolution debates. Paper presented at the Integral Theory Conference, John F. Kennedy University, San Francisco, 31 July. Available at www.integralworld.net/visser33.html (Accessed 30 June 2020).

West, J.E. (1998a). *Speaking Towards an Aboriginal Philosophy*. Unpublished Thesis, Southern Cross University, extract, 11 pp.

West, J.E. (1998b). *Views on the Place and Import of Indigenous Knowledge*. Unpublished Thesis, Southern Cross University, extract, 40 pp.

West, J.E. (2000). *An Alternative to Existing Australian Research and Teaching Models—The Japanangka Teaching and Research Paradigm—An Australian Aboriginal Model*. PhD Dissertation, Southern Cross University. Available at http://epubs.scu.edu.au/cgi/viewcontent.cgi?article=1015&context=theses (Accessed 1 June 2013).

Wilber, K. (1996). *A Brief History of Everything*. Hill of Content.

Wilber, K. (2001). *A Theory of Everything: An Integral Vision for Business, Politics, Science and Spirituality*. Gateway.

Wilber, K. (2012). In defense of integral theory: A response to critical realism. *Journal of Integral Theory and Practice*, 7(4), 43–52.

Wink, W. (1992). *Engaging the Powers: Discernment and Resistance in a World of Domination*. Fortress Press.

Wladawsky-Berger, I. (2013). *A Few Really Tough 21st Century Challenges: A Collection of Observations, News and Resources on the Changing Nature of Innovation, Technology, Leadership, and other Subjects*. Available at http://blog.irvingwb.com/blog/2013/02/a-few-really-tough-21st-century-challenges.html (Accessed 1 June 2013).

Wright, A.W. (2013). *Christianity and Critical Realism: Ambiguity, Truth and Theological Literacy*. Routledge.

Yong, A. (2003). *Beyond the Impasse: Toward a Pneumatological Theology of Religions*. Baker Academic.

PART 2
Social Psychology

4
APPLYING BHASKAR'S 'FOUR MOMENTS OF DIALECTIC' TO RESHAPING COGNITIVE DEVELOPMENT AS A SOCIAL PRACTICE USING LASKE'S DIALECTICAL THOUGHT FORM FRAMEWORK

Otto Laske

1 Short Definition of the Dialectical Thought Form Framework

The dialectical thought form framework (DTF) provides the structure for practicing a dialogical epistemology, both for establishing metatheories and for solving practical problems. It provides links between dialectical critical realism (DCR) and the language-suffused social world by way of conjointly supporting developmental and dialectical thinking. As a research instrument, DTF helps witness and discern how, and to what extent, the world's ontological structure (seen as grounded in Bhaskar's MELD) unfolds in an individual's mind and speech during a one-hour semi-structured *cognitive* interview. The epistemology is based on the developmental assumption that human consciousness progresses toward dialectical thinking through four eras of cognitive development Bhaskar calls *Common Sense*, *Understanding*, *Reason*, and *Practical Wisdom*. In Figure 4.1, I show in detail how during the transition from Understanding to Reason consciousness encounters its own dialectic.

In terms of present scientific knowledge, the capability of entering into dialectic is rooted in the mind's bi-hemispheric constitution that delivers two very different, if not opposed, 'takes' on what for humans is 'real' in the world, an *experiential* and *representational* one. The second mimics the first in categorical, abstract ways at the constant risk of getting stuck in a hall of mirrors we in our app-centred world are well acquainted with. Crossing over from Understanding to Reason poses the challenge not to mistake what is essentially an abstraction for the experience of the real world itself that the abstraction tries to replicate. Historically, this crossing—which occurs naturally, without warning—was first documented in the transition from

DOI: 10.4324/9781003140313-7

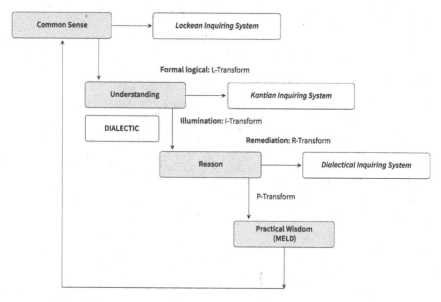

FIGURE 4.1 Bhaskar's four eras of adult cognitive development (Bhaskar, 1993)

Kant to Hegel in the quarter-century between 1781 to 1807, first in Kant's *Critique of Pure Reason*. According to developmental research done at the Harvard Kohlberg School from 1975 to 1995, the unfolding of the mind into dialectic begins ontogenetically in late adolescence and ends only with the end of individual life.

As an instrument of complex thought, DTF is a tool made for DCR to flourish. Pragmatically, it provides a bridge for human agency making an impact on the language-suffused social world through expert user's deep listening practice.

Pedagogically, DTF is employed by the instructor of study cohorts whose members interview others (clients) for the sake of scrutinizing the logical and dialectical thought-form structure of recorded dialogue. The interview is geared towards focusing on clients' real-time thinking about organizational functions, professional agendas, role assignments, and team membership but could be focused on any topic whatsoever, including metatheory. Administering and recording a semi-structured cognitive interview makes it possible to lay bare the dialectical structure of an interviewee's real-time utterances in interchange with a DTF-schooled interviewer.

DTF cognitive interviews are dialogues, not assessments. They follow the assumption that speech flow does not simply issue in describing but *creating* individuals' 'reality', and that it is straightforward to determine empirically differing degrees of clarity in which MELD manifests epistemologically in an individual mind's utterances. Although such an interview is co-created by both interviewer and interviewee (e.g., an executive), the resulting *cognitive profile* is considered as being that of the latter, something made possible by case study cohort interview evaluation.

In order to determine the degree of clarity of dialectical thinking in a client's speech empirically, a DTF expert collaborates with members of a study cohort whose task it is to scrutinize traces of MELD in spoken language based on text selections from recorded interviews. The entire cohort (including the instructor) evaluates ('scores') interview transcripts, aware of the transposition of a real-time into an ideal-time domain. Collaboration assures inter-rater reliability based on the fact one can give valid feedback to clients over and above the purposes of cognitive developmental research itself, either for the purposes of psychotherapy, coaching, or consulting.

Specifically, in the DTF framework, evaluating cognitive interviews happens in terms of *four classes of thought forms*, referred to as CPRT (C=context; P=process; R=relationship; T=transformation). As shown below in greater detail, these classes instantiate and unfold Bhaskar's MELD (Laske, 2008). The evaluation yields empirical data useful in scaffolding the dialectic-thinking capabilities of an individual or team.

The above outline of DTF positions epistemology within ontology. It sees the thinker as part of the real world, not as a purveyor of it as in integral thinking. As shown below, dialectical thought forms as tools of epistemology are therefore not simply perspectives in the sense of logical thinking. Rather, they are *mind openers* that open gates to right-hemisphere vigilance surpassing left-hemisphere focused attention and stare (McGilchrist, 2009). Use of DTF is cogent only when referencing a real world 'pervaded by absences', that is, as being in constant transformation, as intimated by Bhaskar's UDR movement and Hegel's *Aufhebung*.

Following Piaget, in designing DTF I made the assumption that in speaking, humans reveal not only the *contents*, but the (dialectical) *structure* of their movements-in-thought, in a way that refers to the MELD-structure of the real world. In this chapter, I detail how specifically ontological MELD-structures show up in DTF-schooled listening to human speech. As shown in Figure 4.2, a DTF listener-thinker builds rainbow bridges between complex thinking and the actual world to arrive at what is *real* in the sense of Bhaskar's design of dialectical critical realism. Below, I detail in what way M. Basseches' work, published in *Dialectical Thinking and Adult Development* 35 years ago, permitted me to build a bridge between Bhaskar's ontology and dialectical epistemology in the sense of Hegel and Bhaskar himself.

In so doing, my emphasis will fall on my teaching practice with cohorts whose members, by scrutinizing a specific client's speech, 'wake themselves up' to their own mind's dialectic (that heretofore they were unable to grasp). I will reflect on how and why such a cohort functions as a pedagogical context for developing within DCR a dialectical social practice of real-world interventions that are open to truth claims, not just problem solutions. I view a DTF case study as a template for in-depth work in the social sciences, practically as the beginning of integral collaborations poised to solve real-world problems.

In this way, I am linking what Cook-Greuter has called *construct awareness* to collaborative action, but will use this term in a more strongly cognitive, rather

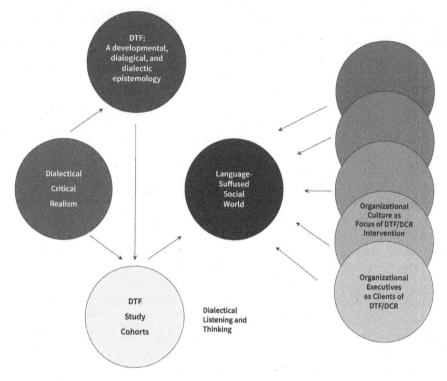

FIGURE 4.2 DTF as bridge between DCR and the language-suffused social world

than exclusively social–emotional way, as she does. I envision dialectical thinking as becoming the central practice of the integral community, to the extent that this community can actually shift from reductive logical thinking to the recognition of the mind as an integral component of the real world rather than as its quadrant- and lines-empowered surveyor.

2 Operationalizing Bhaskar's MELD Based on Basseches' Dialectical Schema Framework

As suggested by Figure 4.2, the DTF builds bridges between DCR and the language-suffused world of society's organizations and their constitutive cohorts (teams). For this purpose, it comprises a social–emotional component following Kegan, a cognitive component following Basseches and Bhaskar, and a psychological component following Henry Murray. Its methodology is part of an inter-participatory framework by which to further adult mental growth at work and in life through dialogue-based scaffolding rather than armchair philosophy.

Although the systemic connectedness of CDF's three components is the focus of IDM teaching and consulting, here I will restrict myself to the cognitive component of CDF, namely DTF. DTF was developed in 1999 in a thesis on developmental coaching that for the first time linked Bhaskar's MELD to Basseches' dialectical schemata framework.

Using DTF professionally requires mature dialectical thinking and the interview-schooled ability of developmental listening in real time. Its dialogue-propelled functioning derives from Basseches' work that focuses on interview dialogue. Basseches presents his findings in a way summarized in Figure 4.3.

For the purposes of his qualitative research, Basseches created a semi-structured interview as a protocol for dialoguing with staff and students of a US college about issues of education. His purpose was to answer the genuinely pioneering question 'how does dialectical thinking develop over an individual's life span?' Basseches asked this question based on the hypothesis that cognitively more highly developed individuals, represented by teaching staff, would show higher levels of dialectical thinking than students. He measured the developmental difference between faculty and students by way of a *fluidity index* indicating fluidity in the use of four classes of thought forms. He did not realize that Bhaskar would conceptualize these classes as building blocks of DCR in 1993, thus that they constitute the epistemological shadow of Bhaskar's 'four moments of dialectic' as I showed in Laske (2008).

By evaluating recorded interviews Basseches found that one can speak of four *phases* (rather than stages) of dialectical-thinking development, where each phase is defined by a maximal fluidity index (phase 1 = < 10, phase 2 = >10 < 30, phase 3 = > 30 < 50, phase 4 = > 50). Simplifying Basseches' findings considerably, one can say that each phase of thinking-development toward dialectic is characterized

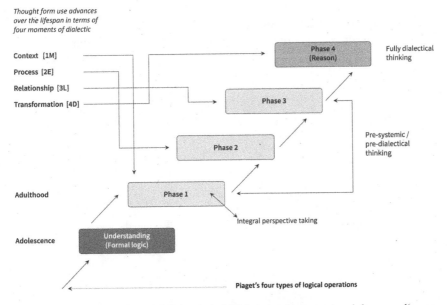

FIGURE 4.3 The four phases of dialectical-thinking development in adults according to Basseches/Laske

by the emergence of one of Bhaskar's four moments of dialectic, in the order of 1M, 2E, 3L, and 4D. The multitude of possible paths toward dialectic has never been ascertained empirically, but see first steps made toward that research goal in De Visch and Laske (2020, Section 7).

In DTF, MELD is epistemologically represented by four classes of dialectical thought forms called *schemata* by Basseches. The most advanced dialectical thought forms, called *transformational*, entail an understanding of negativity (Bhaskar's 'absence') that fully emerges only in phase 4 of cognitive development. *Negativity* has to do with Bhaskar's UDR movement and Hegel's *Aufhebung* (lifting-up) both of which far transcend Wilber's logicized 'transcend and include' metaphor.

When viewing epistemology as embedded in ontology as done in DTF, one is set free to explore how MELD maps into spoken thought via concepts in real time in social dialogue but also written text. In actual usage, each MELD component, represented by a thought form class, serves as a tool to lay bare a speaker's or writer's category errors (such as, e.g., de-stratification when elaborating contexts or embeddedness when exploring processes). The assumption is that by highlighting and giving feedback on such errors to a client or team, s(he) can be helped to move from Bhaskar's *actual* to the *real* world by strengthening internal dialogue with self.

When we put Basseches' findings in a context familiar to readers of Bhaskar, we see that the four phases of dialectical-thinking development referred to in Figure 4.3 differentiate the transition from Understanding to Reason. Pragmatically, they give rise to different forms of illuminative and remediatory commentary, whether exercised during real-time dialogue (interviews) or in hermeneutic text analysis (see Figure 4.4).

Both the I- and R-transform utilize Basseches' four classes of dialectical thought forms, referred to in DTF as C, P, R, and T—a representation of Bhaskar's MELD geared towards exploring the dialectical structure of real-time dialogue or written text (Context = M1; Process = 2E; Relationship = 3L; and Transformation = 4D).

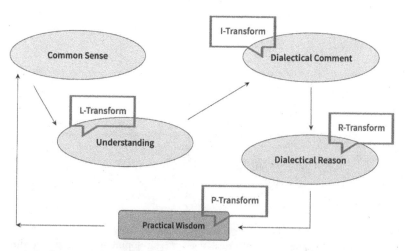

FIGURE 4.4 The four transforms of dialectical thinking according to Bhaskar (1993)

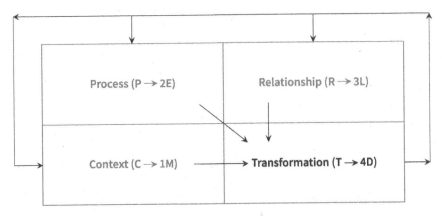

FIGURE 4.5 The four classes of thought forms associated with MELD in DTF (P = 2E; C = 1M; R = 3L; T = 4D)

As Figure 4.5 indicates, *transformational* thought forms (class T) reside on a meta-level relative to CPR thought forms. They are tools for remediation, not illumination, and thus complete the UDR movement by making the loop back from left- to right-hemisphere thinking (Rh→Lh→Rh). Their relationship to CPR thought forms is intrinsically dialectical in that transformational thought forms not only ground CPR but are also enabled by them. This is indicated in Figure 4.5. In this figure, two sets of arrows are used to indicate the intrinsically dialectical relationship between CPR and T thought forms as far as is possible in two dimensions.

While the external arrows indicate the grounding of CPR thought forms in transformational thought forms (T>CPR), the internal arrows indicate that transformational thought forms depend for their full realization on the coordination of CPR thought forms (T<CPR). We can speak of a snake biting its own tail. Transformational thought forms that are not strongly rooted in the coordination of CPR thought forms are considered as *hollow*, i.e., only *espoused*, as for instance when lip-serviced by purely logical thinking that tries to mimic Bhaskar's UDR movement without making Hegel's effort of the concept.

It is the task of DTF experts to discern, and then showcase, what thought forms are used by an interviewee (or speaker generally) in real time, or in the text of a writer. DTF experts do so by pointing to specific category errors, retroducing them where they occur. In each of the four classes of thought forms, a *specific* category error is paramount: de-stratification in C (1M), denial of negativity in P (2E), de-totalization in R (3L), and de-agentification in T (4D).

The Dialectical Thought Form Framework

Table 4.1 shows a two-dimensional table of 28 DTF thought forms. Following Basseches' (1984) precedent, the number of thought forms in DTF is limited to a manageable size. Each of Bhaskar's moments of dialectic is associated with exactly

TABLE 4.1 Compact table of DTF thought forms (adapted from Basseches & Bopp, 1981)

1. **Unceasing** motion, negativity	8. **Contextualization** of part(s) within a whole; emphasis on part	15. **Limits** of separation. Focus on existence and value of relationship	22. **Limits** of stability, harmony, durability (incl. quantitative into qualitative changes)
Contrast: 22	*Contrast: 10–13*	*Contrast: 10–13*	*Contrast: 10–13*
2. **Preservative** negation, inclusion of antithesis (non-A)	9. **Equilibrium** of a whole; emphasis on whole	16. **Value** of bringing into relationship	23. **Value** of conflict leading in a developmental direction
Contrast: 27	*Contrast: 10–13*	*Contrast: 15–17*	*Contrast: 2, 22, 24*
3. **Composition** by interpenetrating opposites, correlativity	10. {**Description of**} structures, functions, layers, strata of a system	17. **Critique** of reductionism and 'de-totalized', thus isolated, entities separated from their shared common ground	24. **Value** of developmental potential leading to higher levels of individual and social functioning
Contrast: 19–22	*Contrast: 8–9, 11–13*	*Contrast: 18–21*	*Contrast: 1, 23*
4. **Patterns of Interaction**	11. {**Emphasis on the**} hierarchical nature of layers systems comprise	18. **Relatedness** of different value and judgment systems	25. **Evaluative** comparison of systems in transformation
Contrast: 2, 19–20	*Contrast: 9*	*Contrast: 20*	*Contrast: 10, 14, 26, 28*
5. **Practical,** active character of knowledge	12. **Stability** of system functioning	19. **Structural** aspects of relationship	26. **Process** coordinating systems
Contrast: 23	*Contrast: 9, 22*	*Contrast: 4, 15–17, 20–21*	*Contrast: 15–16, 25*

6. Critique of arresting motion (reification)	13. Intellectual systems: frames of reference, traditions, ideologies	20. Patterns of interaction in relationships	27. Open self-transforming systems
Contrast: 7, 28	*Contrast: 9, 28*	*Contrast: 4, 21*	*Contrast: 2, 22–24*
7. Embedding in process, movement	14. Multiplicity of contexts (non-transformational)	21. Constitutive, intrinsic relationships (logically prior to what they relate)	28. Integration of multiple perspectives in order to define complex realities; critique of formalistic thinking
Contrast: 3–4, 6	*Contrast: 25, 28*	*Contrast: 2–3, 15–20*	*Contrast: 2, 6, 16*

seven thought forms. All thought forms have integer names that signal the class of thought forms with which they are associated (P = #1–7; C = #8–14; R = #15–21; T = #22–28). DTF thought forms differ from Basseches' *schemata* only in appearance, not essence. In the listing shown, each thought form is accompanied by *contrasts*. Contrasts are alternative thought forms one needs to consider before assigning to an utterance or text a definitive score and weight. They thus point to alternative interpretations of a speaker's speech flow or written expression.

The underlying idea in DTF is that MELD components are expressed in speech or text in various forms and to different degrees of clarity of articulation. For this reason, their use is *weighted* from weak (1) to strong (3). Thought form weightings are summed over an *entire* interview (not locally), 3.0 being the maximal weight any of the DTF thought forms can assume across an interview. The weighting of individuals' thought form use in interviews is both an art and a science.

When we move from an argument- to a dialogue-based epistemology as in DTF, the uses thought forms can be put to multiply. The five most important uses of DTF thought forms are the following:

1. Dialectical listening tools
2. Dialectical text analysis tools
3. Cognitive (interview) prompting tools
4. Mind opening (retroduction) tools
5. Mind-Truth expanding tools.

By using DTF thought forms as listening and assessment tools, an adult's *movements-in-thought*, articulated in an interview or written text, can be empirically assessed, both in terms of the DTF fluidity index and other cognitive indexes deriving from it (Frischherz, 2014a), as illustrated in Figure 4.6. This shows the movement in thought of a manager's interview, associated with DTF cognitive scores (Frischherz, 2014a).

Sentence No.	Process	Context	Relationship	System
1	6			
2				→ 22
3	(5) ←	(9) 14 ←	→ 15	
4			20	→ 22 (24)
5				27, 28
6			19 ←	→ 25
7				22
8		14 ←		
9		8	→ 19, 20	
10	5 ←			→ 26, 27
11				28

FIGURE 4.6 Cognitive behaviour graph of a manager

In the cognitive behaviour graph, the flow of movements-in-thought is indicated by the transitions from one thought form to another in real time, while the result of text analysis of an interview is indicated underneath the graph in terms of four different cognitive scores on which feedback is given.

The most general finding regarding the phase of dialectical thinking an interviewee or author is presently in is the *fluidity index*. This index expresses the total weighting of thought forms used by an interviewee during a one-hour semi-structured conversation (about any topic whatsoever). By contrast, the *cognitive score* expresses this finding in terms of the proportional weight of each thought form class used (i.e., moment of dialectic referred to). This score's fourth part (T), the *systems thinking index*, indicates the client's *potential* for future growth into dialectical thinking. Finally, the *discrepancy index*, which distinguishes between *P/R-* and *C/T-related* thought forms, expresses the strength of an individual's *critical* (left-hemisphere) versus *constructive* (right-hemisphere) thinking.

For further details on DTF see Laske (2008), including the extensive *Manual of Dialectical Thought Forms* included therein. For organizational applications of DTF see Laske (2015).

3 Finding Salient Epistemic Structures in Wilber's Work: Epistemic Limits of Integral Cohorts

From a DTF perspective, it is a fair assumption to make that both individuals and teams, depending on their social–emotional level of meaning making, are limited in their dialectical thinking capability. This has special relevance for present attempts to import integral themes and ideas into DCR in the absence of a focus on dialectical thinking—a self-contradictory proposal.

Asking the question of which epistemic structures 'found' in Wilber's (or anybody else's) work might have salience for DCR sounds like an administrative or archival, rather than a metatheoretical, one which one could equally ask of the Bible. The crucial question that arises is rather how far any such artifacts surpass purely analytical reasoning, thereby strengthening the path towards dialectic. To qualify epistemic structures simply as *integral* would amount to a *quid pro quo*. What is required is to review their potential for dialectical thinking in real time. Salience is not a quality of single concepts (that in isolation have no meaning by themselves), except in purely logic-definitional thinking. Rather, their salience depends on how they are used in real-time dialogue, and what, consequently, is their function in constellations of movements-in-thought, spoken or written.

The pervasiveness of thought forms in spoken language is not in doubt. When filtered through the lens of CDF (i.e., analyzed both social–emotionally and cognitively), natural language expressions used in interviews show clear and measurable structural differences in thought complexity, both between individuals and within the same individual longitudinally. When evaluating CDF case studies, one finds that specific Kegan-stages have been reached by specific dialectical thinking paths and are associated with specific limits of dialectical thinking (see Figure 4.7). Such

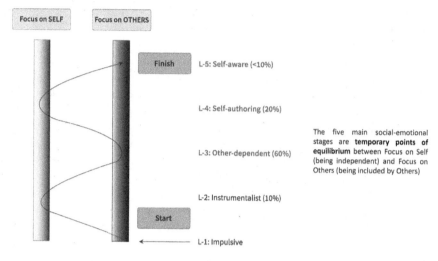

FIGURE 4.7 Social–emotional stage progression according to Kegan

epistemic limits, both of individuals and teams, can be precisely assessed through DTF. In what follows, I will focus on the epistemic limits of cohorts the integral movement can be thought to be composed of and view them as candidates applying for entering DCR from where they are developmentally.

Given that members of any cohort make meaning along Kegan's trajectory of social–emotional stages while simultaneously residing in a specific phase of dialectical-thinking development, we can speak of cohort-specific *epistemic limits*. In DTF, these limits show up in the form of low fluidity indices as well as imbalances in the proportional use of thought form classes (moments of dialectic). To what extent these limits are purely cognitive or are equally rooted in social–emotional maturity levels is presently empirically unknown, due to a lack of research on the intrinsic linkage between the two strands of adult development. However, in teaching and carrying out organizational interventions, the intrinsic nexus between a social–emotional stage of *meaning making* and a particular phase of *making sense* of the world through dialectical thinking clearly comes into view, as intimated in Figure 4.8 (see Laske, 2009, p. 253; for more details, see Laske, 2008, Chapter 8).

Now that members of the integral movement (and of CR) are beginning to absorb dialectical ontology, substantive questions regarding a 'synthesis' of Bhaskarian and integral thinking arise. One such question is: what kinds of teaching programme are required to broaden integral toward dialectical thinking? And furthermore, how can integral thinkers be supported by scaffolding that facilitates a

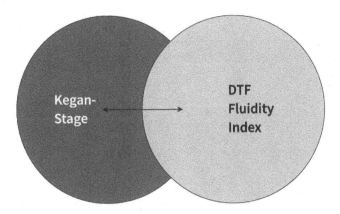

FIGURE 4.8 Nexus between social–emotional meaning making and cognitive sensemaking in CDF

shift from an argument-based (monological) to a dialogue-based epistemology? The first transition is a precondition of the second one. In both cases, empirical proofs would be of great value pedagogically. DTF delivers a straightforward metric for scrutinizing empirically to what extent an integral (or CR) cohort succeeds or fails in making either of these transitions, no different as can be ascertained in organizational teams.

Given that developmentally unified teams—whose members operate from the same developmental level—belong in phantasy land, we can begin to understand the *cognitive profile of integral cohorts* by investigating how they are composed in terms of minority and majority within specific social–emotional ranges (2–3, 3–4, 4–5). This makes it possible to distinguish cohorts whose majority is either more, or less, developed than the minority. We can call the first type *upwardly*, and the second one *downwardly*, divided, to indicate that in cohorts lacking a highly developed majority, less developed members are likely to sabotage the cohort's agenda by reducing it to the lowest possible denominator (their own), to the effect that the cohort enters into a downward dynamic due to insufficient self-organization and thus collaboration.

Applying these team-typological criteria to integral cohorts, we can distinguish the following six types of cohort shown in Figure 4.9, further detailed in Figures 4.10 and 4.11:

1 *Upwardly divided level-2 cohorts (UD2);* majority at level 2, minority at level 3
2 *Downwardly divided level-3 cohorts (DD3);* majority at level 3, minority at level 2
3 *Upwardly divided level-3 cohorts (UD3);* majority at level 3; minority at level 4
4 *Downwardly divided level-4 cohorts (DD4);* majority at level 4, minority at level 3
5 *Upwardly divided level 4 cohorts (UD4);* majority at level 4, minority at level 5
6 *Downwardly divided level 5 cohorts (DD5);* majority at level 5; minority at level 4.

110 Laske

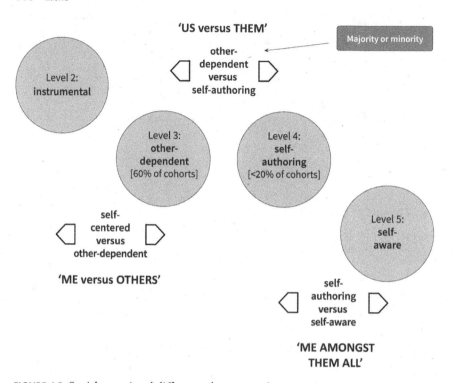

FIGURE 4.9 Social–emotional differences between cohorts

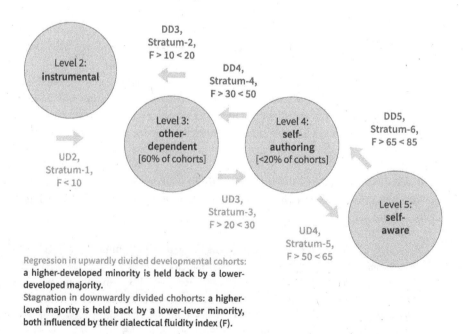

Regression in upwardly divided developmental cohorts: a higher-developed minority is held back by a lower-developed majority.
Stagnation in downwardly divided chohorts: a higher-level majority is held back by a lower-lever minority, both influenced by their dialectical fluidity index (F).

FIGURE 4.10 Epistemic limits (F) of six developmentally differing cohorts

Type of team	Focus of universe of discourse	Predominant moment of dialectic	Need for thinking dialectically
Stratum-1, UD2	Service and execution excellence	Context thinking; focus on present	Present
Stratum-2, DD3	Service differentiation and optimization of practices	Start of process thinking working with difference (negativity)	
Stratum-3, UD3	Rethinking operational processes: new value streams, change management	Advance process thinking; beginnings of relationship thinking	
Stratum-4, DD4	Creating breakthrough by developing and testing alternative strategies	Strengthening of relationship thinking; beginning coordination of C,P,R thought forms	
Stratum-5, UD4	New business models, reshaping of competitive position	Increased coordination of C, P, R thought forms, leading to transformational thinking	
Stratum-6, DD5	Repurposing industry by provoking unconventional uses of services and tools offered	Equilibrated thinking in terms of all four moments of dialectic	Future

FIGURE 4.11 CDF cohort typology

In each cohort, the developmental tension between majority and minority results in idiosyncratic social–emotional cultures characterized by specific *epistemic limits* that stem from the different levels of *cognitive development toward dialectic* of cohort members. In Figure 4.10, I consider these thinking limits as establishing different *strata*, thereby differentiating the level of complexity management that members of a particular cohort are capable of, as well as the specific thematic focus of their universe of discourse. The epistemic limits (F) of these six developmentally differing cohorts are calibrated in terms of the DTF fluidity index.

As we move from UD2-Stratum-1 cohorts (in which the cohort majority resides on Kegan-level 2) to DD5-Stratum-6 cohorts (in which the cohort majority resides on Kegan-level 5), lack of dialectical thinking capability is dramatically lessened.

For example, a *downwardly* divided level-4 cohort (DD4; in which most members reside at Kegan-stage 4 while a minority remains at level 3) has a surer grasp of absence and negativity than an *upwardly* divided level-3 cohort (UD3). Importantly, this differential is likely to determine the relationship of a cohort's *interpersonal* process to its *task* process, whether in academic or organizational work. The task process ('how to get the job done') is determined by cohort members' phase of dialectical thinking, and in more immature cohorts tends to become overwhelmed by their members' interpersonal process.

We can say, then, that each of the six cohort types distinguished in Figure 4.11 is characterized by a peculiar *quality of discourse* expressive of its epistemic limits. For instance, according to Figure 4.10, even logical debate is unlikely in a UD2-Stratum-1 cohort, while a UD3-Stratum-3 cohort can be expected to have a beginning grasp of absence (Bhaskar 2E; DTF process thought forms), having begun to acquire thought forms articulating negativity that are missing from a more immature consciousness. Each of these subgroups has its own epistemological ecology which, in turn, demands a specific pedagogical approach to strengthening cohort members' dialectical thinking.

As shown in Figure 4.12, the higher the cognitive stratum of a cohort, the more cohort members are capable of handling complexity in terms of MELD and its DTF thought-form equivalents. As Figure 4.12 illustrates there are cohort differences in the ability to handle complexity as a function of social–emotional cohort structure and phase of dialectical thinking measured through DTF. Consequently, they will be increasingly open to conceptualizing issues referring to future potential and the creative potential of conflict, rather than being wedded to the status quo, thus differing in terms of transformational thinking capability. Simultaneously, true dialogue will increasingly become possible and so will an autonomous *task* process that is not derailed by a cohort's *interpersonal* process, based on their cognitive-developmental level alone.

These assessment-based considerations of developmentally different cohorts lead to the question of how to guide integral and CR cohorts on a developmental journey toward DCR that amounts to a mental growth assignment. Put differently,

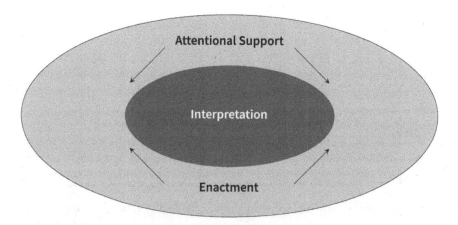

FIGURE 4.12 Cohort differences in the ability of handling complexity

transition to DCR is not an ideological or political issue but one of developmental assessment giving rise to a specific pedagogical, initially experimental, strategy for helping cohorts mentally grow toward DCR.

4 Two Training Programmes for Scaffolding Dialectical Thinking: IDM's Case Study Cohort Method

What is presently lacking both in schools and universities are strategic mental growth assignments that permit individuals to transcend purely analytical reasoning beginning in late adolescence. This lack reflects a one-sided, overly left-hemisphere oriented culture (McGilchrist, 2009) that is unable to make Bhaskar's UDR movement based on MELD. As a result, most individuals' *real world* is a woefully, merely representational, replica of real-world experience that is increasingly lost in a hall of mirrors. The same can be said of most so-called *metatheories* that only pay lip service to dialectic—a tradition in the integral movement it is time to overcome.

The need to break away from left-hemisphere monotony and stare is addressed by IDM's *case study cohort method* of teaching dialectical thinking (see www.interdevelopmentals.org). The name of the method derives from the fact that IDM study cohorts are organized around the pedagogical goal of writing a developmental case study on a single organizational client of the student's choice whose outcome the entire cohort including the instructor is taking responsibility for.

Case studies involve a broad range of mind-opening activities, from semi-structured interviewing to evaluating and scoring interviews and—based on evaluation outcomes—giving feedback to interviewees with the option of further coaching, mentoring, or consultation. The studies are carried out under the supervision of the Director of Education. The latter functions as a cohort leader and guarantor of assessment inter-rater reliability. Along the IDM certification track, writing such a case study requires nine to ten months of study of both dialectical and social–emotional thinking and listening exercised in work with interviewees coming from both for-profit and non-profit organizations. Organizational clients' pragmatic concerns provide the real-world environment for students' mental growth assignments comprising both meaning making and sensemaking. Students' development is supported by clients in positions of high organizational responsibility who, by participating in case studies, function as midwives of students' adult development as well as their own.

At IDM, we use this method of teaching in two forms:

1 An artisan (esoteric) form for educating CDF/DTF trainers.
2 An applied (exoteric) form for those not intending to become CDF or DTF experts, but rather want to use these orienting frameworks in immediately rewarding applications, including that of starting a new business.

In full recognition of the pragmatic demands of students' organizational clients, a case study is about people-in-context, especially executives and team leaders. This mandate is reflected in the structure of the cognitive interview that explores executives' *internal workplace*, i.e., the way in which they conceptually represent their role identity, tasks, work environment, and professional agenda (Laske, 2008; Jaques, 1998). These clients form the *invisible cohort* associated with IDM study cohorts. Metatheoretically, each case study takes on clients' epistemic fallacies and category errors which condemn clients to positivistic thinking and downloading, rather than allowing for deep, dialectical thinking. (This orientation is equally helpful to members of the integral community. Evidently, by using DTF for assessing their own movements-in-thought and receiving feedback, they could move closer to acting as an *educational* force within society as they profess to want to do.)

As my colleague J. De Visch has shown in two recent books (2010, 2013), absence of dialectical thinking in executive (or other) teams not only obstructs social change, but eventually leads to companies' sub-performance or even demise. Executives' epistemic fallacies, which ultimately sabotage emancipatory change in and outside of companies, clearly come to light in one-hour recorded and transcribed cognitive interviews scrutinized by IDM cohorts. Structurally relevant interview fragments are weighted in terms of the clarity of thought forms articulated therein, a method of qualitative research that when applied to written texts such as annual reports is referred to as *dialectical text analysis* (Frischherz, 2013, 2014a). It is a hallmark of dialectically complex texts that they invite to be scored not only in terms of single thought forms, but constellations of thought forms linking different classes (Adorno, 1999, 134 f.), as shown by the example in Table 4.2. This table shows a fragment of a transcribed cognitive interview, cohort-evaluated for the purpose of establishing the interviewee's (executive's) cognitive profile as a basis of feedback to her about the structure of her present thinking, taken from a 2009 IDM case study.[1]

In a society caught and confined in culturally approved and thus thoughtless analytical reasoning, retroductive scaffolding of clients' cognitive development is difficult since it encounters many psychological and institutional obstacles including counterarguments. In my experience, learning cognitive (DTF) interviewing is the royal road for mastering these difficulties. Acquiring the ability for such

TABLE 4.2 IDM case study, thought form scoring sheet

Bit Number and Thought Form	*Questions to Ask Yourself*
(weighted from 0 to 3)	1. What structural evidence leads you to selecting this thought form?
	2. If several thought forms are applicable, explain your choice.

Note: *Weights are assigned to thought forms only across the entire interview, not individually.*

Cognitive Interview, Task House

(Base Concept #1 = 'forcefield'; #2 = 'stability')

Reshaping Cognitive Development as a Social Practice 115

Bit #3,

TF 21 [weight = 1] (Constitutive, intrinsic relationship)

TF 22 [weight = 1] (Limits of stability, harmony, and durability)

TF 17 [weight = 0.5] (Critique of reductionism)

Interviewer: You seem to be taking into account force fields that play a role in this company, and the circumstances under which this project has started ...

Interviewee (Consultant): Well yes, I was referring to certain forces, some tearing things apart, others holding things together, and the conflict energy needed to transform the status quo.

Interviewer: If you look at those force fields more closely, what do you see?

Interviewee: Well, the dilemma lies in that efficiency should be increased while no one would lose their job. This is a human resource problem since probably some people do not have the competences needed to be peak performers. So, management wants to lift up the organization towards a more service-oriented organization. One issue is the accountability level on which people should perform in their new roles. Another issue is to prepare these people to take a quantum leap. However, they will probably not be able to make this leap under the present reward system or given what their competences are. So, there are many conflicting forces I am seeing, but I doubt that my clients are seeing them. I see a gap between reality and how it is viewed by my clients. But I cannot close this gap for them; I need to educate them so they can see it.

Interviewer: What does that say, you think, about the system's stability?

Interviewee: We will have to consider that there is an external force field as well, and together with the internal one, it may rip the company apart. We are now in a financial crisis, and we haven't seen the deepest point yet. So, people are looking at the efficiency and they have never, never been confronted with the fact that they will have to lay-off people. They won't be able to do it before the end of 2009 because they signed an agreement with the union. So, they won't risk that. Except if they would be confronted with extreme situations. Until now they have government support. But I expect they will be asked to take hard measures by the first half of 2010. And they are not at all preparing for that.

Justification of the Scoring

In constructing his internal workplace, the speaker sees individuals determined by the constitutive relationships they are in that have defining quality (relationship TF 21); he also points to the overall systemic context as a factor determining the issues that will need to be considered by clients (transformational TF 22). Finally, he articulates a weak critique of reductionism (TF 17), highlighting that his clients are not looking at the outside world.

interviewing amounts to a revolution of one's way of conceptualizing what Bhaskar would call the 'real', rather than merely the 'actual', world.

Cognitive interviews centre on laying bare clients' category errors and epistemic fallacies that hinder the speaker's world from showing up in its full, right-hemisphere, complexity. Category errors come to light in the process of differentiating the base concept that a specific thought configuration is structured around (e.g., 'role identity' in an organizational, 'quadrant' in an integral, context). In the interview fragment quoted in Table 4.2, the *base concepts* of *force field* and *system stability* are explored by the interviewer. By way of a cognitive behaviour graph such as Figure 4.6, members of a study cohort mentally reconstruct a client's cognitive world construction from a third-person perspective for the purpose of scoring and giving empirically based feedback.

As this demonstrates, work with CDF/DTF is based on dialogue, not argument or debate. There are no winners except the cohort as a collaborating team. Such work is focused on the unpacking of assumptions that lead to category errors in the sense of Bhaskar's retroduction, for the purpose of assisting clients in their work or life in real time.

DTF dialogue is differentiated in favour of one of three dialogue modes shown in Figure 4.13.

In different DTF pursuits, one of these modes—attentional support, interpretation, enactment—is typically the dominant one, the other two functioning as support tools. For instance, attentional support dominates interviewing while interpretation is paramount in interview evaluation, and enactment (modelling of thought form use) is the focus of critical facilitation of cohorts and teams.

All modes require deep listening, but in different ways. In *attentional support*, the focus is on discerning the dialectical thought form structure of a client's speech

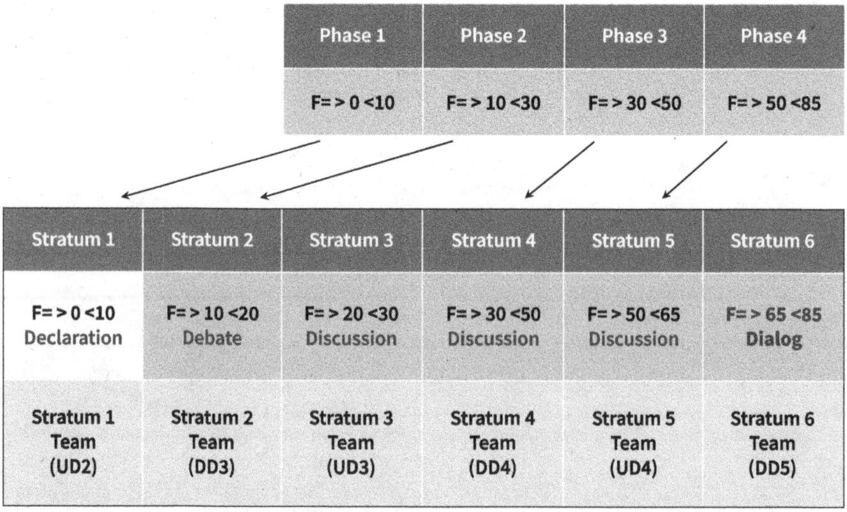

Phase 1	Phase 2	Phase 3	Phase 4
F=> 0 <10	F=> 10 <30	F=> 30 <50	F=> 50 <85

Stratum 1	Stratum 2	Stratum 3	Stratum 4	Stratum 5	Stratum 6
F=> 0 <10 Declaration	F=> 10 <20 Debate	F=> 20 <30 Discussion	F=> 30 <50 Discussion	F=> 50 <65 Discussion	F=> 65 <85 Dialog
Stratum 1 Team (UD2)	Stratum 2 Team (DD3)	Stratum 3 Team (UD3)	Stratum 4 Team (DD4)	Stratum 5 Team (UD4)	Stratum 6 Team (DD5)

FIGURE 4.13 The three DTF dialogue modes as used in teaching, coaching, and consulting

flow, while *interpretation* seizes upon the client's category errors. Once these have been revealed to the client through commentary or questions, the DTF interviewer proceeds to remediate them, enabling the client to proceed to UDR movements (*enactment*). In this way, not only is analytical reasoning critiqued, but *novel experiences* leading to cognitive development are created in and for clients.

Case study cohorts differ in developmental composition and structure as do teams. Their success is not guaranteed. The success of a case study cohort hinges on whether cohort members form a downwardly or upwardly divided team, and thus on the extent that they make effective use of the instructor's developmental modelling. The quality of such modelling determines the degree of cohort members' ability to balance the three dialogue modes they are taught in carrying out a case study. Each of the three dialogue modes is rehearsed separately, before linking it to others. This stepwise learning in case study work is structured as follows:

1. In the first step, **interviewing**, emphasis lies on *attentional support* for the purpose of discovering the thought form structure of a client's utterances. Interpretation and enactment function as support tools.
2. In the second step, **interview text analysis**, the cohort dialogue focuses on the *interpretation* of structurally relevant interview fragments in terms of DTF thought forms. Enactment in the narrow sense happens in each member's internal workplace where developmental thinking is brought to bear on text fragments.
3. In the third step, **writing the case study itself**, *enactment* (in the broad sense) is accomplished. Each cohort member's task is to pull together in a coherent synthesis all empirical evidence gathered about a client's cognitive and social–emotional profile including the linking of the two profiles from a metaperspective.

The case study culminates in a written feedback report supervised by the IDM Director of Education and formulated on a level the client can readily understand. Through this report, the client herself is given the opportunity for enactment in subsequent (team) coaching or mentoring sessions. Those who have made one or more case studies are able to as *critical facilitators* modelling the use of DTF for others.

More generally, IDM case studies school adults at various stages of social–emotional and cognitive development as *critical facilitators* of themselves (initially) and others (eventually). How far this purpose is realized by a specific study cohort or organizational team depends on the cohort's developmental profile, thus on whether it is upwardly or downwardly divided and in what way. Cohort members can opt for learning about their own present developmental profile. If they do, a longitudinal study can be requested two to three years later (Frischherz, 2014a) which also holds for clients. In my year-long experience, clients informed of their developmental profile by IDM cohort members often became promoters of high-quality dialogue in organizational teams, thereby contributing to the effective collaboration of team members (De Visch & Laske, 2020).

5 Dialectical Thinking as the Integral Movement's Central Social Practice: Esoteric and Exoteric Programmes for Teaching Dialectical Thinking

It seems bizarre that a philosophical movement like the integral one, as it is trying to embrace DCR, has not yet embraced the very tools that make dialectic possible, usually referred to as dialectical thinking. Dialectical thinking has a long tradition that has been thoroughly reviewed and superbly worked through by Bhaskar. Evidently, I see dialectical thinking as the essential tool for developing DCR, as well as the principal tool for integrating epistemic structures deriving from integral and/or CR into DCR. For the integral community, which is more accomplished at concocting 'models' than investigating the structure of its own thinking, the need for developing a practice of dialectical thinking seems to be a novel issue. This chapter is meant to move working on that issue along. DTF dialectic is no ideology, but is pragmatic, hands-on, learned by doing: what is a dialectical ontology or epistemology without a pervasive practice of dialectic?

I have shared some details of the DTF *Train the Trainer* certification programme in dialectical thinking in the larger environment of CDF. In doing so, I largely dwelt on the 'artisan' form of teaching dialectical thinking, to make clear how the manifestation of MELD in human speech is assessed by using four classes of dialectical thought forms. I have not found a more effective method of sponsoring mental (including social–emotional) growth than to teach study cohorts dialogical dialectic, at least in an academic environment. In my experience, this approach is the royal road to learning dialectical thinking, superior to using meditation, discussion, hosting, holacracy, or something even more fashionable. This is the case because in such teaching, students' subjective experience of DTF is balanced against the pragmatic goal of understanding a specific interview text by making use of the three DTF dialogue modes. Learning to consciously separate and combine these modes amounts to raising the level of adult awareness as no other method does.

There exists a second, 'exoteric' or peer form of teaching dialectical thinking through DTF whose adepts are managers and executives, rather than DTF trainers. This second form of teaching is already being carried out by those IDM students who work in organizations as consultants, coaches, mentors, and managers (De Visch & Laske, 2020). In my view, DCR could begin to show its educational relevance for the organizational world once it takes up DTF tools in both forms of teaching here distinguished, something I have not seen even a beginning of.

Conclusions and Outlook

Work with CDF/DTF has amply demonstrated that severing developmental from dialectical thinking—characteristic of the integral community's present work—makes as little sense as separating social–emotional meaning making from cognitive sensemaking (Laske, Forthcoming). In each case, intrinsically related dimensions are ripped apart. In addition, the epistemic structures accumulated by neo-Piagetians since the 1970s to a large extent manifest purely analytical reasoning and thus only reinforce the present predicament the integral community as a whole is in.

My counterproposal, therefore, would be to use DTF thought forms (Table 4.1) as seeds for developing new, DCR-instantiating, epistemic structures now found lacking, instead of borrowing from the neo-Piagetian storehouse. Whether such new structures are argument- or dialogue-based, we can develop and teach them while honouring the four phases of dialectical-thinking development integral cohorts will need to pass through to mature in their ability to handle metatheoretical complexity.

As we know empirically, there exist four different human *Inquiring Systems* that gradually emerge and merge over the human lifespan (Figure 4.1; for details see Laske, 2008). While the Lockean (empirical) Inquiring System helps individuals transcend Common Sense, Hegel showed 200 years ago that this transcendence remains epistemologically weak. Even when we move to a Kantian Inquiring System, as the sciences do, we fail, as Bhaskar's work has shown, to move closer to the real world because of falling prey to epistemic fallacies. It is thus imperative that we take advantage of the early stirrings of dialectic in the adolescent mind that Basseches' research revealed and build on its momentum, to secure a broader constituency of dialectical thinkers, both in academia and the world of organizations and politics. What is foremost needed, therefore, is a group of DTF trainers stemming from the integral community who have been thoroughly educated in developmental as well as dialectical thinking. Such an education would help them appreciate the present limits of integral thinking and make them venture out into dialectical territory beyond merely paying lip service to dialectic as Wilber has done.

In my 20-year teaching experience at IDM, a student who has submitted two CDF case studies based on the 'artisan' (rather than the 'peer') schooling path described above is ready to enter a programme for becoming a DTF trainer. Such a person has internalized the dialogue s(he) partook in during the case study learning process, and has, in addition, committed to spelling out her understanding of transcribed interviews in deep dialogue with herself, thereby nurturing the *internal dialogue* on which dialectical listening is based. Not only such a person's way of thinking, but her way of listening to others and communicating with them, has been substantially transformed: she can now see the real world as being in unceasing transformation, with herself as embedded in it. She cannot easily be convinced that 'integral thinking' without dialectic is even a possibility. Once she is so aware, she has become a *transformational thinker* who is motivated to become an agent working on behalf of the global issues that beset humanity at this point in history.

I would see DTF trainers certified by IDM as ambassadors of dialectical thinking as much as of DCR. Dialectical epistemology and ontology make a good marriage. DTF practice having become part of students' professional life, such students can help not only individual clients, but commercial organizations and political factions *get real* about the real world. In addition, DTF-trained individuals can begin to influence the social, not only the developmental, sciences, and promote a dialogue between sciences based on dialectical thinking, something presently lacking. Metatheory by itself will not do it.

DTF training is also of relevance longitudinally. If, after individuals' mid-20s, analytical reasoning is not given a chance to move on to dialectic, developmental arrest sets in even in the social–emotional domain of meaning making (as my own studies bear out). The ensuing stasis only deepens individuals' helplessness on account of feeling trapped in the administered world that Adorno predicted 75 years ago, which now takes the algorithmic form of pervasive control. The cause of this helplessness, easily covered up by dazzling 'integral' contents, is the structure of adults' thinking that is presently not on a par with what the contemporary world cognitively requires of citizens. The blueprint of pedagogical action I have shared in this chapter can certainly be refined and adapted to changing circumstances.

Executive Summary

My ultimate concern in this chapter has been that of extending DCR into social practice through adoption of DTF as a vehicle for fully embracing Bhaskar's legacy within the integral movement. I do not know a better way to honour Bhaskar's legacy. *E-ducere* means *to lead out of*, and if there is one thing to lead out of, it is the absence of dialectical thinking in Western culture, already diagnosed by H. Marcuse in the early 1960s (Feenberg & Leiss, 2007). Since, due to Bhaskar's work, dialectical thinking is no longer viewed as a form of 'salon communism', there is perhaps a chance for establishing institutes of dialectical thinking as think tanks of the twenty-first century, threatened as our century now is by global crises encountering mainly feeble analytical minds.

If developed as part of the Institute of Education at the University of London, a *Center of Dialectical Epistemology* could establish a pioneering agenda: to teach dialectical thinking in an administered world shaped nearly entirely by analytical reasoning acting as the thought master, rather than the emissary of the right hemisphere's holistic thinking. Before addressing the thinking limits of contemporary organizations and institutions with integral thinking in the conventional, non-dialectical, sense, however, such an institute would first have to address the thought limits of present-day integral cohorts whose grappling with Bhaskar's legacy has only just begun.

Acknowledgements

I want to thank Brendan Cartmel for his metacritique of this chapter and his moral support in writing it.

Note

1 The 2009 IDM case study was documented in IDM Working Paper No. 102, written in 2013. This paper contains confidential data and is therefore unpublished.

References

Adorno, T.W. (1999). *Negative Dialectics*. Fischer.
Basseches, M. (1984). *Dialectical Thinking and Adult Development*. Ablex.
Bhaskar, R. (1993). *Dialectic: The Pulse of Freedom*. Verso.
Bhaskar, R. (2006). *Reflections on MetaReality*. Routledge.
Bopp, M., & Basseches, M. (1981). *Manual of the Dialectical Schemata Framework*. PhD Dissertation, Suffolk University.
De Visch, J. (2010). *The Vertical Dimension: Blueprint to Align Business and Talent Development*. Connect & Transform.
De Visch, J. (2013). *Leadership: Mind(s) Creating Value(s): Developing Deep Thinking to Better Manage Complexity and to Create Possibilities*. Connect & Transform.
De Visch, J., & Laske, O. (2020). *Practices of Dynamic Collaboration: A Dialogical Approach to Strengthening Collaborative Intelligence in Teams*. Springer Link.
Feenberg, A., & Leiss, W. (2007). *The Essential Marcuse: Selected Writings of Philosopher and Social Critic Herbert Marcuse*. Beacon Press.
Frischherz, B. (2013). *Dialektische Textanalyse und Textentwicklung—Teil II*. Available at www.zeitschrift-schreiben.eu/cgi-bin/joolma/index.php?option=com_content&task=view&id=95&Itemid=32 (Accessed 28 April 2014).
Frischherz, B. (2014a). From AQAL to AQAT: Dialogue in an integral perspective. Integral European Conference, Budapest, 10 May. Available at www.didanet.ch/wp/wp-content/uploads/2011/07/dialog_in_an_integral_perspective.pdf (Accessed 10 September 2014).
Frischherz, B. (2014b). *Constructive Developmental Framework*. Available at http://en.wikipedia.org/wiki/Constructive_Developmental_Framework (Accessed 28 April 2014).
Jacques, E. (1998). *Requisite Organization*. Cason Hall & Co.
Laske, O. (1966). *Über die Dialektik Platos und des frühen Hegel*. DPhil Dissertation, Mikrokopie.
Laske, O. (1999). *Transformative Effects of Coaching on Executives' Professional Agenda*. PsyD Dissertation, Massachusetts School of Prof. Psychology. Available at http://il.proquest.com/brand/umi.shtml (Accessed 28 April 2014).
Laske, O. (2005). *Measuring Hidden Dimensions* (Vol. 1), Sections B1 and C. IDM Press. Available at https://interdevelopmentals.org/?page_id=1974 (Accessed 28 April 2014).
Laske, O. (2008). *Measuring Hidden Dimensions* (Vol. 2), Sections B1 and C. IDM Press. Available at https://interdevelopmentals.org/?page_id=1974 (Accessed 28 April 2014).
Laske, O. (2015). *Dialectical Thinking for Integral Leaders: A Primer*. Integral Publishers.
Laske, O. (Forthcoming). On some crucial issues of adult-developmental theory. *International Leadership Review*.
McGilchrist, I. (2009). *The Master and His Emissary*. Yale University Press.
Murray, H. (1938). *Explorations in Personality*. Oxford University Press.

5
ON REALIZING THE POSSIBILITIES OF EMANCIPATORY METATHEORY

Beyond the Cognitive Maturity Fallacy, Toward an Education Revolution

Zachary Stein

Introduction: Education in the Anthropocene[1]

> After the bifurcation, after say 2050 or 2075, we can thus be sure of only a few things. We shall no longer be living in a capitalist world economy. We shall be living instead in some new order or orders, some new historical system or systems. And therefore we shall probably know once again relative peace, stability, and legitimacy. But will it be a better peace, stability, and legitimacy, or a worse one? That is both unknown and up to us.
>
> *Immanuel Wallerstein (2000, p. 45)*

Bhaskar's (1993) *Dialectic* is at its core a political book. Building out from basic issues in ontology toward characterizations of the emancipatory possibilities implicit in current geo-historical dynamics, *freedom* stands as the concept that unites humanity with the directionality of an evolving universe propelled forward by dialectical tension and contradiction. The arguments in *Dialectic* provide essential underlabouring for a fundamentally *revolutionary politics*. The possibility of universal human emancipation is revealed as presupposed in every human action. The pulse of freedom, as it were, is shown to be irrepressible, ubiquitous, and indefatigable. These ideas suggest a view of social justice in which a dialectic of human liberation catalyzes *the rational directionality of geo-history* toward universal human flourishing, or a eudaimonistic society in which the free development of each concrete singular individual is the condition for the free development of all. A new form of agency—totalizing depth praxis—is shown to possible now, in the *hiatus* or *pause* between social structure and individual action. *Dialectic* provides a new and profound vision of the human capacity for initiating radical transformations of self and society.[2]

This kind of politically emancipatory metatheory has an essential role to play as our species careens toward planetization. Humanity is confronting the absolute limits of capitalism's domination of nature, both human nature and the biosphere.

In the midst of this crisis, the culture of late-capitalism continues to churn out irrealist and irrational philosophies that

> reify and naturalize knowledge, chiming with the logic of commodification, and cutting the ground from under critique [by] normalizing past and local changes, ideologies and freedoms [and] denying change ... They detotalize, divide, and rule ... [These philosophies are] made for empire-builders, manipulators, and the masters of subjects$_2$ who want to distract their eyes from the top of the power$_2$ relations on which they sit ... As they permeate down from the rarefied stratosphere of philosophy, irrealist ideologies act to disempower and fragment the agent.
>
> (Bhaskar, 1993, pp. 305–306)

We desperately need new metatheories because the lack of a coherent worldview has become a source of repression and a cause of alienation.

This 'recalls Adorno's famous adage that not just theory, but the *absence* of theory, becomes a material force "when it seizes the masses"' (Bhaskar, 1993, p. 159). The *lack* of metatheory can become a force that distorts and undermines our abilities to understand our true needs and the realities of the natural and social worlds. In the past, forms of false consciousness were generated by totalizing worldviews that imposed on us the meaning of everything; today false consciousness results from fragmented and de-totalized worldviews that impede us in making meaningful sense of anything. This idea has echoed on the fringes of the academy and in a few leading minds since the great sociologist Daniel Bell (1960) first declared 'the end of ideology'. Many were not fooled by the eventual decline of the hegemonic Cold War rhetoric that followed the end of actually exiting socialism. On the edges and in the wings were theorists who saw what was emerging, and what has since come to pass: a 'new normal' characterized not by repressive world order, but by de-repressive world disorder, not by the spectre of total submission through integration, but of radical dissolution through fragmentation.

The future depends on the articulation of a new vision of humanity and a new sense of what is possible for the planet and everyone on it. The encounter between Bhaskar and Wilber taking place in these volumes represents one of the most sophisticated attempts to forge just such an emergent metatheory. The metatheory aspired to in these volumes is one suitable for framing a planetary meta-ethics that could justify and motivate the truly revolutionary changes that are necessary if generations to come are to have anything like a life worth living. I take as a given that the years between 2000 and 2050 represent a critical turning point in the history of humanity and the planet. Fundamental transformations of our social structures (economies and institutions), ecosystems (biosphere and agriculture), and consciousness (culture and identity) are upon us.

As this book makes clear, a growing body of scientific research suggest that we have entered a new geological epoch known as the *Anthropocene*. This term was brought to prominence by Paul Crutzen, a Nobel Prize winning atmospheric chemist, and has been reverberating through scientific, cultural, and political discourses ever since.[3] From the Greek roots *anthropo* meaning 'human' and *-cene* meaning 'new', this term is now being used to mark a formal unit of geologic epoch division, suggesting that humanity has so impacted the Earth's basic physical constituents (especially its atmospheric and chemical composition) that our age constitutes a new geological phase of planetary development.

This is only one of the latest scientific concepts to show the extent to which humanity's fate is now intertwined with the fate of the planet itself. Our decisions in the next decades will determine the future of the biosphere, the Earth's geological trajectory, and, of course, our survival as a species. This is not some controversial science. Even climate change sceptics have to recognize the power of nuclear weapons to wipe the biosphere from the face of the planet's hard rock mantel. It is also impossible to overlook the sheer scope and impact of massive human infrastructures, such as cities, dams, canals, and highway systems, which impact whole landscapes and ecosystems. An important fact here, just to get a sense of scale: between 2011 and 2013 the Chinese poured 50 percent more concrete than was poured in the United States during the whole of the twentieth century. Imagine all the vast urban expanses of the US, and now expand them by half—and build it all in three years. The Chinese also have plans to dig another Panama Canal and to link the Southern and Northern tips of South America and Africa with a transcontinental rail line. The Earth is being impacted on a scale today that is almost impossible to comprehend.[4]

It appears the Earth is being put in our hands and we are not prepared for the responsibility. Our species is reeling from the shock that comes from realizing it is up to us to assure the continuation of the Earth's life support systems. We are existentially intertwined in a common destiny, both as a species and as a biospheric community. A vast web of life now depends on our stewardship. This is a profound educational challenge and a historical opportunity.

It is important to understand that the recent genesis of the Anthropocene is a direct result of the modern capitalist world system, which began to emerge during the sixteenth century, and which today represents the largest functionally integrated social unit the human species has ever created.[5] Human societies have always organized the use of nature. Nature has always then worked back upon society. Capitalism has unfolded *within* and as a part of the web of life, not outside it or somehow set apart.[6] Humanity is nature. Even as we somehow manage to 'destroy nature'. How is that even possible? It is possible because humanity has already destroyed many *historical natures*. The capitalist world system in particular has run through multiple distinct world ecologies, each with its own science, technics, and culture. The idea is in some ways simple: every historical era of the capitalist world system has also involved a related *historical nature*—a way of mapping the biological world, including plants, animals, weather, oceans, continents, and even 'human nature'. There have been many world systems during the course of human history, and thus there have been many visions and versions of nature.

While I leverage the language of crisis here and suggest that we have reached the ecological and geographical limits of capitalism,[7] I mean only to point to the limits of the nature we know now, the limits of our current historical nature, in which nature is understood as providing energy that is scarce and food that is produced for profit. Nature, including human nature, is more than is dreamt of by human capital theory and neoclassical economics. Educational futures will take us into institutional forms beyond schooling and curricula content and learning praxis that reveals a new Nature (Stein, 2016).

Today, we are witnessing simultaneous and interactive crises playing out amongst our broadest social structures and their biospheric corollaries. The human-biosphere relationship is being fundamentally renegotiated. In the midst of all this *external* transformation there are, of course, related changes in human consciousness, culture, personality, and capability. Our global crises have an *interior* dimension as well. Social media and popular culture suggest that we live in a time of *identity crises*, a time in which *the self-understanding of humanity is changing*. Throughout the world, basic institutions of government, finance, and education are suffering a crisis of legitimacy as the basic principles upon which public culture is founded deteriorate. In many places there is no shared sense of purpose or common ethical worldview upon which to base constitutional governance. The resources of the lifeworld for meaning making and identity creation have become almost as depleted as the resources of the natural world. Humanity's inability to understand itself is part of a cascading planetary phase shift. Our identity crisis is coinciding with the dawning of the Anthropocene. The educational challenges humanity faces in the coming decades are in large part about reconstructing our self-understanding as a species. Future educational configurations will require a response not only to the current global environmental and economic crises, but also to the current global identity crises. This is another educational challenge and opportunity unique to our time, and the reason we need metatheories to make good on their promises for educational emancipation.

1 Two Meta-Theories; One World in Crisis

In the context of the metatheoretical encounters collected in these volumes, many questions have been raised about how to best interanimate these two philosophical systems. This chapter offers one approach to *constellating* several essential facets of dialectical critical realism (DCR) and integral theory (IT).[8] I argue that the two systems actually need each other, but focus most of my attention on the *lacks* in DCR than can (and ought to) be filled by IT. The guiding theme of this chapter is the primacy of educational activism as a political instantiation of emancipatory metatheory, and the essential unanimity of these two theories on this point. While Bhaskar provides a dialectical social ontology that locates decentralized (non-national/non-corporate) educational initiatives at the epicentre of contemporary revolutionary possibilities, Wilber provides a theoretical developmental psychology that reveals the profound impact of education on human capacities. Both theories highlight the role of education as a revolutionary catalyst as well as the injustices of contemporary educational systems (which reflect the broader social and economic systems in which they reside) that radically truncate our humanity, sometimes to the point of undermining the very possibility of totalizing depth praxis. This term is used in DCR to refer to a merger of theory and practice that reflexively changes and negates the given conditions of personal and social life. This form of praxis stands opposed to or beyond praxis that reproduces given personality structures and social forms, as most conventional human praxis does (Bhaskar, 1993, pp. 157–158).

The idea that oppressive and unjust educational systems can undermine the very possibility of totalizing depth praxis points directly at the lacks in DCR that must be filled by IT. Make no mistake: DCR has a lot to say about human development,[9] and in places provides essential philosophical underlabouring for the field of developmental psychology. This thoroughgoing developmentalism will be discussed below. I show that whole sections of *Dialectic* are ostensibly about the dynamics of psychological growth, as exemplified by the concept of primary polyadization, which brings us from the primal scream of the infant first separated from the (m)other through a dialectic of universalization that leads to the emancipation of all concrete singular individuals from alienation. Yet in DCR the development of human capacities is taken as unproblematically leading to a certain basic form of maturity. De-agentification, distortions of personality, and the forfeiture of self-actualization are all explicitly mentioned and lamented as possibilities. Nevertheless, the basic models of the person and their capacities for reasoning and reflection in DCR assume as given what are actually hard-won developmental achievements contingent upon the availability and utilization of educational resources. This, unfortunately, puts DCR in league with most of the philosophical tradition it seeks to overcome. As Piaget (1932, 1965) first pointed out well over half a century ago, the majority of philosophy is based on assumptions about the basic cognitive endowments of average individuals that totally disregard what is known about human development. This is discussed below in terms of the *cognitive maturity fallacy*: assuming as given capacities for thought and action that are in fact hard-won developmental accomplishments that require the availability and utilization of specific educational resources (education being defined here very broadly, and in no way limited to what takes place in schools). This is a ubiquitous problem in philosophy generally and contributes to the ineffectual, parochial, and elitist position of the discipline, its irrelevance to the concerns of ordinary people, and its frequent retreats into merely academic exercises.

Thankfully, a solution is readily available for DCR, which entails the adoption of a *diachronic emergent capacities developmentalism* (DECD), to be fit inside and expand upon the *synchronic emergent powers materialism* that already serves as the linchpin of a still-nascent DCR philosophical psychology. Wilber's (1980, 1999) work is by far the best place to look for the essential components of this DECD, given that it is a metatheoretical summation of nearly a century of research into the development of human capacities. This tradition of research refashions the models of human personality and reason in DCR, revealing these models to be contingent universal *possibilities* for individuals, as opposed to always already present actualities. It also suggests ways of expanding these models to include an accurate sense of the major qualitative reorganizations of thought and action that have been shown to characterize the development of human beings, from birth to maturity and beyond (i.e. into trans-normal capacities, which also stand as a universal, if rare, possibility for all individuals). Wilber's developmental metatheory provides insights into the ways by which capacities emerge in individuals, stressing the bio-psycho-social dynamics of cognitive growth, and thus the socio-political prerequisites necessary for the *accomplishment* of human maturity. These additions to the DCR model further clarify the primacy of education in the project of human emancipation, while also clarifying some of the impediments to revolutionary political movements in contemporary society, where the educational resources needed to enable maturity and autonomy are becoming increasingly scarce due to the continued push of neoliberal and neoconservative political agendas (Apple, 2013). The *contradictory* nature of education as a social practice becomes apparent in light of the dynamics of this DECD—education can be a source of oppression or a source of liberation; we can be educated towards greater freedoms or away from them. Education, like the term development, is often blindly used as if it only had one side, as if education could only ever be a force of good. Quite the contrary, as I show here, we must take responsibility for the right use of *teacherly authority* and actively promote new forms of education, beyond what schooling would be and has been given by first the church, then the state, and now the market.

2 Human Development and Human Emancipation

> [In] a dialectical kinetic pluriverse *to be* is not only just to be able to do, but *to be able to become* ... *being is becoming* ... A *dialectical life* would be a kind of sequence of immanent critiques, comprising the self-reflective overcoming or non-preservative sublation of a concretely singular self ... dispositionally identical with its changing (developing and waxing and waning) causal powers and tendencies, naturally interconnected with a changing fabric of contingences, accidents, mediation, rhythmics, and contradictions.
>
> Bhaskar (1993, pp. 77, 105; italics in the original)

To accuse DCR of committing the *cognitive maturity fallacy* and to recommend remediation through the adoption of a DECD is to give DCR a taste of its own metacritical medicine. According to its own terms, DCR should already be out to explicitly avoid the cognitive maturity fallacy and should already involve some kind of DECD. DCR is a philosophy that emphasizes process, evolution, generative contradictions, emergence, radical negation, and other development motifs; making DCR the developmental philosophy *par excellence* (although see Whitehead, 1929; Wilber, 1995). There are, in fact, many arguments in *Dialectic* that would be invaluable for developmental psychology as a field if it ever intended to get its ontology straight (which is no small task, given that no major developmentalists since Baldwin and Piaget have addressed the ontological issues implicated by the field). In this section I will look at the arguments in *Dialectic* that can be taken as philosophical underlabouring for developmental studies. In part this is a way of clarifying the nature of my questions and expansions of DCR. But it is also a way of clarifying just what kinds of models of human development I intend to bring into the picture. DCR can actually help in weeding out the wrongheaded and simplistic forms of developmental psychology that have given the field a bad reputation and contributed to its dismissal by many philosophers. This sets the stage for seeing the *absence* of developmental considerations in DCR's models of the self, personality, and reasoning capacities of individuals, which are discussed in the next section.

The simplest place to begin is with one of the most basic notions entailed by DCR: 'Dialectic is at the heart of every learning process' (Bhaskar, 1993, p. 43). This way of understanding learning is fundamentally different from behaviouristic ideas of learning as conditioned response and other related reductive models. DCR positions human learning and development in the context of certain universal dynamics of dialectical growth and evolution. This is an essential idea in the development tradition, which runs from Baldwin, through Piaget, to Kohlberg, Fischer, and Wilber: development proceeds through the dialectical growth of psychological structures, propelled forward by contradictions, absences, and self-transformative agency. As implied by the passage that began this section, development is best thought of as a series of immanent critiques, or as the iterative self-reflective overcoming of a concretely singular self, resulting in the repeated and sequential emergence of qualitatively new capacities for thought, action, perception, and emotion. This is the model of development that Wilber builds upon in extending the tradition of development theory, i.e., it is *not* one based on the mere quantitative accumulation of ideas or skills, nor one based on simplistic ideas of maturational inevitabilities. Many contemporary and past developmental researchers could learn from these basic insights into the dialectical nature of learning and development, so clearly shown by Bhaskar to be ubiquitous ontological realties; this would put an end to the methodologically limited and theoretically truncated approaches to development that have come to dominate some regions of the field.

Moreover, the dialectic of psychological development is also dialectical in the sense that it bridges the space between subject and object, proceeding through the actions of individuals on the world. This is one of Piaget's (1932, 1979) primary contributions: that thought and action are inseparable, that 'logic' does not reside merely in the head of the growing child, but in the evolving sets of operations the child carries out on the world. As Bhaskar says (1993, p. 72), in terms that could be Piaget's: '*Logic does not determine the nature of being, but at best establishes what the world must be like if we are to perform certain operations successfully*' (italics in the original). This basic idea is repeated again later where Bhaskar (1993, p. 304) lays out a formula that summarizes one of the basic tenants of the cognitive developmental tradition: 'to reason = to cause = to negate = to absent = to contradict = to (negatively) constrain'. This 'metatheoretical equation' summarizes what Bhaskar previously established as a ubiquitous ontological reality, and points to the autocatalytic nature of reasoning—an idea that Piaget and others would make much of, arguing that reasoning is by its very nature auto-subversive, that learning takes primacy over knowing, that development is the natural state of cognitive operations.[10]

Importantly, the most sophisticated models of emergent capacities that can be found in this tradition (e.g., Piaget, 1976; Fischer, 2006; Wilber 1999) do not hold to 'the tradition of neo-Platonic-eschatological-Hegelian-vulgar Marxist thought' that characterizes emergence and higher-order structuration in terms of 'assumptions of originarity [sic], uni-linear directionality and teleological necessity of an empirically and conceptually untenable kind' (Bhaskar, 1993, p. 51). This is an important point, because many developmental models associated with IT *do* fall prey to simplistic growth-to-goodness assumptions and untenable ideas about unilinearity and cross-domain developmental synchrony (Stein, 2010). And while Wilber is careful to use these models in the context of his broader theory, which does not harbour these liabilities, the models are nevertheless often discussed outside his proposed metatheoretical context. In fact, as Wilber (1999) argues for clearly, development is a radically messy affair, fitting well with Bhaskar's (1993, p. 50) caveats concerning the nature of emergence, which are worth quoting at length:

> Before I praise emergence, I must bury Hegelian versions of it. In the real world, whether we are dealing with conceptual, social ... or entirely natural terrain, ontological dialectical processes are not generally a product of radical negation alone, let alone that of the linear kind to which Hegel leans. For our world is an open-systemic entropic totality, in which results ... are neither autogenetically produced nor even constellationally closed, but the provisional outcome of a heterogeneous multiplicity of changing mechanisms, agencies, and circumstances. Moreover, in real emergence the processes are generally non-teleologically causal ... and have an inverse that does not figure in the entelechy of the Hegelian scheme, *viz.* disemergence, the decay, demise or disjoint detachment of the higher level. Further, emergence may involve a substantial degree of non-preservative, rather than simply additive, superstructuration. And the result may be internally complex and differentiated, consisting in a 'laminated' system, whose internal elements are necessarily 'bonded' in a multiplicity of structures (perhaps composed of their own structured hierarchies and sub-totalities). Such systems may be ... asymmetrically weighted, and contextually variable ... composing an internal pluriverse ... populated by a plurality of narratives, internal discordance and even palpable contradictions.

These ideas about the sheer diversity and complexity of emergent processes are strongly aligned with advances made by the so-called neo-Piagetians, especially their work using dynamic systems modelling techniques as a part of research into individual development (Fischer & Biddle, 2006; Van Geert, 1993). This work characterizes the development of the mind in terms of a 'complex evolving ecosystem of skills and capacities'. According to these models capacities and skills are hierarchically and heterarchically related in competing and complimentary ensembles, with different sets of capacities developing at different rates, some sets growing in synchrony while others asynchronously diverge, as the whole 'cognitive ecosystem' remains continually and inextricably enmeshed within cultural, social-structural, and interpersonal dynamics. These models, on which Wilber draws heavily, provide tools for understanding the life of the mind as an evolving dialectical 'internal pluriverse' (to borrow Bhaskar's redolent phrase, as he borrowed it from Della Vope). This is far from the simplistic linear growth-to-goodness models that are often used to stereotype the field, such as the versions of Piaget's model found in most psychology textbooks, which presents development as an inevitably unfolding staircase of four levels from the crib to pure reason (this is both patently false as a characterization of Piaget's model (Smith, 2001) and is such an obvious oversimplification of development that it can only be taken as a straw man to be burnt in effigy by behaviourists and nativists).

This brings us to the final set of issues that display the profound confluences between the field of development studies and DCR: 'thematizing *the presence of the past [and the future* ... in terms of] process-embodied-in-product' (Bhaskar, 1993, pp. 139–140, italics in original). Human beings are never complete. And what is past is never gone. 'We may be said to contain possible futures within us, and these may be vital to our being' (p. 143). Developmental models offer a thoroughgoing processual view of the individual, which show (often with great diagnostic detail) the continued legacy of prior achievements (and failures) as well as the tangible futurity of present behaviours. This profoundly augments the ways that individuals should be thought about and their lives and actions evaluated. As Baldwin (1906) first put it: we must learn to understand the personality as a *trajectory*, not an entity. With the idea of *developmental consistency*, Bhaskar echoes this notion and offers what is one of the most important lessons from *Dialectic* for developmentists, insofar as the idea integrates the field's ontological-descriptive moments with its normative-evaluative ones.

> To be developmentally consistent is to know when to be inconsistent, when to grow, when to mature, when to apply a dialectical comment on dialectical comments, when to wait until the agents concerned have made up their own minds into what their freedom consists. Dialectical processual consistency recognizes the authenticity of every concretely singular agent's own narrative or story no less that the rights of her being ... The point about [developmental or dialectical] consistency here is that no general formula for it can be given: the criteria are necessarily *intrinsic* to the processes concerned.
>
> (Bhaskar, 1993, pp. 170, 270)

These ideas on the evaluation of developmental trajectories get us directly into the educational implications that would follow from a sustained encounter between DCR and developmental theory as exemplified by IT. Both can be understood as revealing the emancipatory power of catalyzing the development of the concrete singular individual, and thus both can be understood as *philosophies of education and liberation*. But the scope of arguments about the revolutionary implications of this new theoretical constellation must await the concluding section of this chapter. First it is necessary to see that DRC lacks some of what it needs to make good on its commitments to understanding and catalyzing individual development and to sketch the contours of what it would take to 'absent these absences' in DCR—namely, the importation from IT of a *diachronic emergent capacities developmentalism*.

3 The Cognitive Maturity Fallacy: Growing Up Is Hard to Do

> The average-expectable level of psychocultural development in any given society acts as a *pacer of development* up to that level but does not guarantee that development in all individuals will so proceed. Very few people even in 'developed' countries reach a firm base in worldcentric, postconventional awareness (one study found only 4 percent of the American population at the higher postconventional stages ...) ... Even if society collectively evolves to the average-expectable level of [the postconventional], every single person born in that society will nevertheless still *start development at square one*, as a single-celled zygote: and have to begin the arduous developmental climb ... The pace of this climb can be accelerated, but the fundamental stages cannot be bypassed ... And at *every* stage in development, *things can go wrong*. The more stages, the more nightmares of possible developmental miscarriages.
>
> *Wilber (1995, p. 654, italics in original)*

Surrounding the passages about developmental consistency quoted above, Bhaskar offers several very important reflections, which get directly to the heart of the questioning and expansions that will be unfolded in this section. He argues that universalizability is a test for consistency and a criterion for truth, and thus sets the *directionality* for dialectical rationality as it develops (Bhaskar, 1993, pp. 170, 220). This echoes arguments in other places about the dialectic of universalizability and the dialectic of desire to freedom (pp. 279–280). The idea here is that *all* human action and speech contains within it a drive towards both universalizability and universal freedom; that by simply intending to say something true or satisfy my own desires I am initiating an autocatalytic process toward saying things that are universally true and doing things that contribute to universal emancipation. Norrie (2010, pp. 123–124) is correct in interpreting this line of thought as a radicalization and generalization of Habermas's formal pragmatics, which also claims to reveal the universalizing commitments implicit in every speech act that drives humans toward the universalization of their practical and epistemological orientations and eventually to hold explicit (worldcentric) ethical and epistemic views.

Norrie (2010, pp. 232–237) is also correct in linking this up with Bhaskar's (1993, pp. 177, 221) account of the judgment form, which is his account of what takes place when we are asked to make a judgment (e.g., to give advice to someone about a complex state of affairs). Bhaskar argues that there are four core elements that characterize a human judgment: it will be 'expressively veracious', 'imperatival-fiduciary', 'descriptive', and 'evidential'. The first two concern the nature of the *relationship* between addresser and addressee, the second two concern what the judgment is about. All together they entail the establishment of a relationship of trust between two people, based on a shared understanding about the world. They say: 'trust *me*, on the available evidence, this is the best thing for *you* to do' (Norrie, 2010, p. 134).

The point here is that in the very nature of human judgment are universal commitments to both solidarity and truth. The dialectic of universalizability takes off from what is implied every time we give advice or act on it. The very form of our judgments compels us toward ever expanding circles of emancipatory truth stating, solidarity-enhancing praxis. That is, 'we can ... proceed ... directly from the axiological commitment implicit in the expressively veracious judgment ... straight to ... the goal of universal human emancipation ... The eudaimonistic society is implicit in every desire, assertoric remark or successful action' (Bhaskar, 1993, p. 286). This is only one of several places in *Dialectic* where Bhaskar relies upon the ubiquity of the four-part judgment form as the catalytic kick-starter of a dialectical process toward the totalizing depth praxis that is the ultimate demand of DCR as a philosophy of revolutionary political action. This is best summarized by one of the many 'general schema' (p. 179):

> Axiological commitment in expressively veracious moral judgment → fiduciariness → solidarity → totalizing depth praxis (including inquiry) → content given by explanatory critical theory → emancipatory axiology = [transformed transformative (trustworthy) totalizing transformist (transitional) politics/praxis].

But here is the problem (and the opening for an important expansion of DCR): this starting point of the four-part judgment form is actually the outcome of a long developmental process.[11] That is, individuals have a lot of growing up to do *before they can even begin* the reflective dialectic of universalization (and other related dialectical progressions, such as the dialectic of freedom). This is one case of the cognitive maturity fallacy as it plays out in DCR; and there are others as well, as we will see.

Even a cursory familiarity with any number of developmental models clearly shows that this form of judgment is very far along the course of epistemological development, which can itself be thought of as *a developmental progression of judgment forms*. For example, the models of Fischer (2006) and Kitchener and King (1990) confirm what Piaget (1928) first showed nearly a century ago, that human judgment begins as fundamentally egocentric, lacking all four aspects of the judgment form. These early (but often quite persistent) forms of judgment do not function to establish a relation of trust between addresser and addressee relative to a shared understanding of the world. This is not because the individual is unwilling or deceptive, but because of *limits in their capacity for judgment*—they are unable to coordinate the need for evidence and adequate description with the perspective taking necessary to establish an imperatival-fiduciary relation and the self-reflectiveness needed to claim expressive veracity.

In the earliest and most rudimentary forms of judgment, individuals are unable to even understand the need to justify their judgments, in part because, as Piaget (1928, pp. 21–22) showed in a series of breathtakingly simple experiments: 'the child is incapable of differentiating clearly between relations of causality, of sequence, and of justification ... which means that he is incapable of assigning a fixed function in speech to each of these relations'. Moreover, perspective-taking incapacities contribute to this early epistemic solipsism and related forms of incoherent (or simply absent) justifications:

> It is because it is not detached from the ego that this sort of thinking does not know itself ... There is nothing in egocentrism that tends to make thought

conscious of itself ... The successive judgments that constitute the child's talk are not connected by explicit relations but are simply stuck together ... This absence of direction in the successive images and ideas is itself the outcome of that lack of self-consciousness that characterizes all egocentric thought. Only by means of friction with other minds does thought come to be conscious of its own aims and tendencies ... This is why every act of socialized intelligence implies not only consciousness of a definite thought-direction (as, for instance, of a problem) but also consciousness of the successive statements of a narrative (relations of implication) or of those between successive images of the object of thought (causal relations) ... We have on many occasions stressed the point that the need for checking and demonstration is not a spontaneous growth in the life the individual; it is on the contrary a social product. Demonstration [and justification] are the outcome of argument and the desire to convince. Thus the decline of ego-centrism and the growth of logical justification are part of the same process.
(Piaget, 1928, pp. 11–14)

This quote can be taken to stand in for dozens of others that could be taken from Piaget's numerous studies on the development of logic and morality (for an overview see Piaget, 1977). It also stands in for the hundreds of quotes that could be taken from the theorists that followed him and confirmed and expanded on his findings (see e.g., Kohlberg, 1981; Fischer & Biddle, 2006). The implications of these models are that (1) the four-part judgment form cannot be assumed as a given or as an ideal that always already (even if counterfactually) guides practice (even as especially the practices of adults); (2) the emergence of the four-part judgment form in individuals requires a host of educational resources, which cannot be assumed as a given; (3) the four-part judgment form is a historically emergent human capacity, which must re-emerge in the individuals of each new generation (and could, by implication, potentially cease to broadly characterize human judgment if the requisite educational resources are not in place). I will return to this last point in the final section as part of a discussion of the contradictory role of educational systems, which are at the same time our greatest potential source of oppression and our greatest hope for emancipation. It is the first two topics that are the jumping off point for the rest of this section and the next.

Importantly, the points above should be taken as part of a questioning and expansion, because Bhaskar (1993, p. 220) knows this in a way:

> End-states, which should be universalizable, are not always realizable by agents (e.g., one can't get from x to everywhere and one can't go to y from just anywhere). However, in general it is plausible to suppose that one can progress towards them, or mitigate regress away from them.

There are other places in *Dialectic* that echo this sentiment and where can be found arguments about the irreducible uniqueness and positionality of concrete singular individuals (Bhaskar, 1993, pp. 170–171) as well as the contingency and complexity of individual development, which is recognized as being prone to truncation, forfeiture, and regression (p. 285). Yet even with these insights the cognitive maturity fallacy plagues DCR's models of the human individual and personality. Make no mistake: these models are hierarchical, processual, and stratified, which makes them vastly preferable to most accounts of the human individual and personality offered by philosophers. Nevertheless, they are all *synchronic* characterizations of human capacity, and take as a given what are actually hard-won developmental achievements contingent upon educational resources. The same version of the cognitive maturity fallacy committed in the account of the four-part judgment form can be seen to spread throughout the system.

Take for example the 'Stratified Model of the Self' presented in *Dialectic* (Bhaskar, 1993, p. 149, Figure 2.20). It presents a set of hierarchically structured strata that constitute the self, beginning at the bottom with the 'biological substratum/constitution', on top of which is the 'unconscious' then the 'preconscious' and then 'consciousness (self-consciousness = sentient socialized self-awareness)'. On top of this bias are then layered the structures of an 'agent's praxis, set in material, intersubjective and social context', which is presented as another synchronic hierarchy, beginning with 'agency (transformative negation of the given)' on top of which is 'conscious absorption in the task at hand' on which is put 'reflective monitoring of everyday (or exceptional) spatio-temporalized activities', on top of which is 'meta-reflexively totalizing [awareness of] self-situation', and finally 'subjectivity' is perched atop the whole. Crucially, this whole model is presented in the context of a discussion concerning the importance of the capacity for *a meta-reflexively totalizing awareness of the self-situation*, which is suggested as necessary for truth seeking as well as providing the distance necessary from social-structural determinations to enable emancipatory action (i.e., this capacity, like the four-part judgment form, is a condition for the possibility of totalizing depth praxis). It is worth quoting at length to get a sense of what this capacity entails:

> Consider an agent N's participation in, say, an experimental programme. Amidst a multiplicity of practices and spatio-temporal paths she engages in a distanciated and self-reflexively monitoring participation in a particular aspect of it. Suppose she has to test, as a member of a research team, a particle's spin. She is focusing on untying a knot in a cord. She is competently doing so. She is aware of the role of her task in the context of the overall programme and in the context of the hierarchy and plurality of projects with their own rhythmics in her life. She could recall last night's TV, she is aware that she has an unconscious, that the sign has a trace structure, of the metaphoricity of language use, the very language she is using now, that she is subject, in a multiplicity of dimensions, to the internal drag of the past and its delayed casual efficacy. She knows she will die as so much cosmic dust at the same time as she is untying the knot and attending to the matter at hand ... She knows all this in a meta-reflexively totalizing (reflection on her praxis and) situation of her life ... The same concept of a meta-reflexively totalizing situation allows the agent to understand both that her engagement with

reality is inexorably linguistic and that reality must be referentially detached from her language use ... It is also the concept of a meta-reflexively totalizing situation that allows us to appreciate how we can have a future despite the saturation of social (and to an extent natural) life with the past.

(Bhaskar 1993, pp. 148–150)

It should take very little thought to realize that the capacity being described here is developmentally extremely complex and assumes a great deal of education. Put to one side that this agent is testing a particle's spin, a choice of activity that at once reveals the profound distance between this example and the everyday experiences of the vast majority of humanity. The forms of reflexivity, meta-linguistic, meta-autobiographical, and meta-historical awareness described greatly surpass the four-part judgment form in requiring developmental achievements contingent upon the availability and utilization of educational resources (and recall the four-part judgment form was already shown to be placing the bar too high). For example, this type of meta-linguistic awareness—where language itself is taken as an object, understood as giving structure and texture to experience, while also being epistemologically problematic—this has been shown empirically to appear only at the highest levels of epistemological and personality development (see Broughton, 1975; Wilber, 1999). Moreover, this is only one of several equally complex capacities that make up this meta-reflexively totalizing awareness of the self-situation. Yet this form of awareness is built right into the model of the stratified self and discussed in this example *as if it was a common or universal human endowment*—a near-perfect example of the cognitive maturity fallacy.

The very same problem occurs in other places in the text. Take the discussion and figures presenting models of the stratification of agency and action (Bhaskar, 1993, pp. 265–267, Figures 2.28 and 2.29). These present the human as not only fully grown, but as well educated, suggesting that we can take as given capacities for self-reflection, accountability oriented self-monitoring, and expressive veracity. And again, it is the assumed presence of these capacities that lays the groundwork for the arguments that follow concerning the potentials of totalizing depth praxis for human liberation. These capacities are taken as the *starting point* for the unfolding of a dialectical life and as much-needed catalysts for enlivening social transformations. Not to beat a dead horse, but these capacities presented as the starting point are, in fact, the *outcome* of a long developmental and educational trajectory, which is in no way guaranteed to unfold toward such a socially and personally advantageous culmination.

I can almost hear the protests from DCR scholars 'But *of course* these capacities are very sophisticated, require education, and cannot be assumed to be universally available to all; the whole thrust of *Dialectic* makes clear the contingency and messiness of developmental processes, as well as the oppressive power$_2$ relations that can undermine potentials for human flourishing'. To which my response is: *that is exactly my point!* I am simply pointing out that, given the overall arguments in *Dialectic*, it makes no sense to present these kinds of capacities as if they are simply given.[12] More importantly, because of the emancipatory and political thrust of the text, and the essential role these higher-level capacities play in the central arguments, it stands to reason that a great deal more about the development of these capacities needs to be said. If DCR suggests that it is a long and complex road for individuals to get to where they can *exercise* the freedoms that are their birth right, why does it not offer any road maps, or even any suggestions and elaborations concerning the lamentable detours and potential cul-de-sacs? According to its own terms, the DCR project *requires* insights about what can go wrong in individual development (beyond passing mentions concerning the internalization of power$_2$ relations), as well as insights into how to ensure healthy and full development (beyond platitudes about human flourishing and dialectical life projects). Without substantial insights along these lines we are left unequipped to undertake the meta-critical analyses and concrete utopian theorizing necessary to fundamentally alter the existing social realities that radically impact the shape of human development.

4 Diachronic Emergent Capacities Developmentalism: A Gift from IT to DCR

> This emancipatory component of [developmental] structuralism is a fruitful area of inquiry ... If development in general moves from pre-conventional to conventional to post-conventional ... then a profound motivation of doing adequate [developmental] structuralism is to help individuals and cultures move from egocentric and ethnocentric stances toward more worldcentric levels of compassion, care, and consciousness ... On the other hand, simply asserting that we should all learn a worldcentric ecology, or embrace global compassion, is a noble but pragmatically less-than-useful project, because worldcentric levels are the product of development, not exhortation ... The 'new paradigm' approaches exhort a goal without elucidating the path to that goal—they are cheerleaders for a cause that has no means of actualization, which perhaps explains the deep frustrations among new-paradigm advocates who know they have a better ideal but are disappointed at how little the world responds to their calls.
>
> *Wilber (2003, p. 109)*

It is easy to trace the cognitive maturity fallacy found in *Dialectic* back to Bhaskar's (1979) earlier pre-dialectical work *On the Possibility of Naturalism*. This work provides unrivalled philosophical underlabouring for both sociology and psychology, and is similar to Habermas' (1970) *On the Logic of the Social Sciences*, being written around the same time to address the same issues. Both of these books can be read as primarily written to reveal the emancipatory power of the human sciences, which are characterized as intrinsically tied into possibilities for emancipation, liberation, and the subversion of demi-realities. Most important for our purpose here, and being the central move that puts distance between himself and Habermas, are Bhaskar's arguments that psychology as a science must be based on a *synchronic emergent powers materialism* (SEPM). SEPM argues for the real casual efficacy of reason (and thus the ontological irreducibility of human agency and mental life) in the material world as an emergent property of natural systems of sufficient complexity. Whereas Habermas reproduces the neo-Kantian *division* between humanity and nature, leaving unaddressed essential ontological issues concerning the place of mind in the material world, Bhaskar provides transcendental arguments that ontologically position humanity *within* nature and place psychology on a firmly naturalistic basis. However, the point here is that, as important as the SEPM model is, it begins the trend that would be carried forward into DCR of modelling the human individual *synchronically*.

It is illuminating to compare SEPM with the model of the 'compound individual' that Wilber developed, which has played a major role in his theorizing beginning with his first work *Spectrum of Consciousness* (1978) all the way through to the nearly full blown articulations of IT found in *Sex, Ecology, Spirituality* (1995). The model of the compound individual, a phrase taken from Whitehead (1929), is very similar to the SEMP model, insofar as it is an attempt to characterize the human individual as a nested hierarchy, beginning with a naturally determined material substrate, leading up though ever more complex biological organization, resulting eventually in the emergence of the *sapience* characteristic of human psychological qualities and traits. Some of the ontological distinctions between the two models are beside the point here.[13] What is important is that the hierarchical strata of Wilber's compound individual *evolve into place* during the course of the lifespan and, moreover, Wilber identifies the processes by which emergent capacities emerge from previously emergent capacities in an iterative expansion of embodied consciousness, skill, cognition, and emotion.

Recall the quote above where Wilber states, 'every single person ... will *start development at square one*, as a single-celled zygote'. What is implied here is an essential point: *even the biological substrate that supports human consciousness is an outcome of individual development*. We all begin development in utero. And as the tragedies of birth defects and poverty-stricken mothers teach, the normal development of even our most basic biological endowments cannot be taken for granted. This is why many insightful educational reformers argue that educational reform begins with the care of the pregnant future mother (Shonkoff & Phillips, 2010). It can be too late if we wait for the child to reach school age, after years of nutritional deprivation and toxic stress—often starting in the womb—have left their nervous system literally unable to learn.

The point here is that SEPM deals with emergence in a strictly *synchronic* manner (as the name itself implies). It may be a useful way to consider the ontological status of human psychological powers, but it assumes the prior normal development of (at least) the biological substrate of the individual nervous system. More importantly, *new capacities and powers keep emerging throughout an individual's life*, and while each time a new power emerges the SEMP model can put it in its ontological place, the model does not account for the *diachronic* processes that are necessary for any and all psychological powers and capacities to exist. This is why I suggest working toward articulating the constellational unity of SEMP with some form of a DECD.

The shape and details of this DECD should be determined through a concerted effort on the part of those working with DCR to grapple with the developmental tradition, and IT in particular. IT is worthy of specific focus, as opposed to focusing just on Piaget or Kohlberg, or any other individual developmental researcher, because IT provides a set of invaluable metatheoretical distinctions as part of a developmental meta-model, an *Integral Psychology* (Wilber, 1999). IT is also by far the most philosophically sophisticated and wide-ranging expansion and deepening of developmental studies to date. So while there is not one model or even one research programme within the developmental tradition that can satisfy what DCR needs in a DECD, IT can provide an orientation to the field particularly amenable to the task.

For the rest of this chapter I will simply take off from Wilber's DECD and *begin* to explore the patterns that appear when it is brought into the constellational structure of DCR. I am not even going to touch the epistemological and ontological issues raised as a result of interanimating these two metatheories.[14] Instead, my project is political. Namely, to begin to articulate the emancipatory philosophy of education that emerges during the encounter between DCR and IT, specifically that aspect of the encounter that results in DRC's overcoming of the cognitive maturity fallacy through the insertion of Wilber's DECD into Bhaskar's SEMP.

Conclusion: Teacherly Authority in Crisis

> Philosophers in general, although they are themselves usually teachers, have not taken education with sufficient seriousness for it to occur to them ... that philosophizing should focus about education as the supreme human interest in which, moreover, other problems, cosmological, moral, logical come to a head.
>
> *Dewey (1930, p. 156)*

In rejecting the cognitive maturity fallacy and adopting a DECD we immediately face questions surrounding the problem of *teacherly authority*. A philosophy aiming to promote totalizing depth praxis must face the fact that although everyone is potentially able, most are not currently capable of this form of agency. Thus we must argue in favour of actions that will foster the development of this ability. This follows from the broader insight stemming from the adoption of a DECD: *not everyone knows what is good for them* (usually because what is good for them has been occluded absent, or misunderstood). The implication is that we have an educational responsibility to others; those with greater knowledge and capacity *must* act so as to raise others into the fullness of their capacities.[15]

I have already suggested that politically relevant differences in cognitive ability are a taboo subject in Leftist discourse, which has contributed to the perpetuation of the cognitive maturity fallacy. Too often this stems from a sense that teacherly authority (or any authority for that matter) is *always* an unnecessary stance taken up by oppressors in the context of power$_2$ relations, being necessarily tied into the use of force and leaning towards forms of coercive human engineering. And indeed, this has often been the case; as will be discussed below, the Right often embraces just such a form of politics through educational policy and innovation. Nevertheless, the educational implications of a DECD suggest that *constraining freedom is a necessary part of enabling greater future freedom*. If we take as given things like the capacity for a meta-reflexively totalizing awareness of the self-situation (or even the four-part judgment form) we can end up abnegating our educational responsibilities and leaving others to have more freedom than is healthy and appropriate. That freedom is unhealthy and inappropriate, the exercise of which disallows future freedom. Dewey (1916) understood this very clearly and was at pains to make this point to those in the progressive educational movement who took up his name while creating educational environments that were so 'free' they damaged students' future prospects for living a fully autonomous life (e.g., students not 'naturally drawn' to reading and mathematics being allowed to remain illiterate and unable to multiply).

The fact the autonomy of the child is in some way overridden through education is a very important issue (in education at any level and in developmental work in general—it is part of *all* student/teacher dynamics). Indeed, children and many adults don't know what is good for them (or what is good for them is occluded, absent, or misunderstood); people often can't be recruited to their own cause. The point here is that there are more and less acceptable ways to impinge upon anyone's burgeoning autonomy. This difference between negative and positive forms of teacherly authority becomes extremely important when we introduce a DECD into DCR, because now we must deal with the fact that individuals need to be educated *into* freedom in the context of complex power$_2$ relations. Lack of education or exposure to the wrong kinds can imprison the mind, while access to the right kinds of education can liberate the mind. The question here is how to characterize the difference between educational relationships and processes that are oppressive and those that are emancipatory. I argue that this difference can be directly intuited in the form of the educational relationships established between concrete singular individuals (Stein, 2010, 2013).

There is a difference between doing something *to* someone, doing something *for* someone, and doing something *with* someone. Ideally, education is undertaken *with* someone. Beyond a certain level of maturity, individuals can often be reasoned with about what is in their own interest, in which case teacher and student collaborate in a mutually educative undertaking (all good teaching requires that the teacher learn from their student, even if only to understand where they are coming from). Of course, this cannot always be the case. When it is clear an individual is not willing or able to take responsibility for his or her own development then we are obligated to override this individual's autonomy to some degree. This is done unjustly when they are treated in ways they would not consent to under the condition of full knowledge—it's unjust when something is done *to* them, not *for* them. However, it is possible *to act in ways we believe they could not reasonably object to* (if they knew enough to make a decision that would be in their own interest). That is, it is possible to limit the autonomy of another without it being merely a result of coercive power$_2$ relations (although, in most cases power$_2$ relations are in play, e.g., laws that require school attendance). The difference between coercive education and emancipatory education is the difference between doing something *to* someone and doing something *for* someone. This is close to the classic parental 'You'll thank me some day'—it is a kind of thought experiment in which considerations concerning the probability of future consent are informed by a recognition of the concrete singular individual before you, the validation of whose unique life trajectory requires the use of broad standards of reasonableness, as well as an abiding and explicit desire to establish a cooperative relation with them *as soon as possible* (Habermas, 2003). Importantly, this is also a way of considering the ethical issues involved in educational power$_2$ dynamics that transcends but includes questions about *justice between generations*, as often this form of educational activity must be done between members of the same generation.

Make no mistake: in today's educational institutions the problem is usually *not* an excess of freedom resulting from an abnegation of educational authority, but rather a profound lack of freedom resulting from the infantilizing and oppressive exercise of educational authority. The point here is that the inability of the Left to understand and embrace educational power$_2$ dynamics has resulted in a failure of nerve and a strategically significant inarticulacy and ineffectiveness in the field of education. This inability to clarify the differences between liberating and oppressive forms of teacherly authority has led to a certain postmodern squeamishness concerning the educative use of power$_2$ relations and thus opened the door for the authoritarian modernization of schooling by the Right, who understand the political significance of teacherly authority, and thus have mounted a concerted multi-decade effort to use education to their own ends (Apple, 2013).

There was a time when public school systems raised the cultural centre of gravity, and in some places they still do, but on the whole this time has passed. At this point schools (from kindergarten through university) are literally being designed so that students end up less developed than they would be if they spent the equivalent amount of time doing something else; education is done *to* them, not *for* them—there is no reason to believe they would ever consent to the way they are treated if they had full knowledge of their situation and the full potential of their latent human capacities. Elsewhere I have discussed the dominance of *reductive human capital theory* (RHCT) as an orienting metatheory of education in late-capitalist societies (Stein, 2013, 2016). We are also witnessing the simultaneous widespread hijacking of education by forms of fundamentalism, extremism, and nationalism, which are designed to perpetuate violence and terror, and which create humans with grotesque personalities who are bound and imprisoned in ideology—bringing to mind the theological notion that the opposite of the human is not the animal; the opposite of the human is the demonic (Blumenthal, 1993). It is important to understand that these educational configurations (that go way beyond mere schooling) have arisen as a result of complex and well-coordinated forms of educational activism, usually justified by DECD-like insights into the profound malleability of the most essential human dispositions and capacities. These forms of activism have stepped into the void created by the aforementioned failure of nerve on the part of the Left, who now protest all forms power$_2$ and authority, instead of embracing their appropriate and necessary uses as part of the process of human emancipation.

Beginning in the 1980s and leading up through the first decades of the twenty-first century, educational systems around the world became subject to a form of authoritarian modernization, wherein neoliberal RHCT aligned with conservative (and in the US) religious fundamentalist political actors to create a hegemonic block (Apple, 2001, 2013). During these decades educational systems became increasing characterized by career-oriented technical knowledge, conservative social values, standardized forms of curriculum and testing, authoritarian social relations, privatization, and marketization. One of the essential pillars of this *global education reform movement* (aka GERM; see Sahlberg, 2012) has been sophisticated and self-conscious political organization and activism on the Right, which reflects their implicit rejection of the cognitive maturity fallacy and related recognition of the realities of a DECD. That is, they understand the formative impact of education on essential capacities, claim to know what is good for others and the world, and are willing to use coercive and strategic means to exert as wide an educative influence as possible. These trends are compounded by the efforts of the so-called 'billionaire boys club' (Racvitch, 2013) who have leveraged their positions as captains of industry to wield unrivalled influence over the shape of educational reform, so drastically shaping the funding landscape that many self-ascribed liberals have embraced policies that would previously have only appealed to conservatives (e.g., charter schools, school choice, marketization, accountability-oriented testing). A few wealthy individuals are drastically and unilaterally impacting the shape of schooling, displaying undisguised the interests and power of capital in shaping human development; all this supports the ideas of those who fear a return to the patterns of the Gilded Age (Piketty, 2014), which was the only other time in history that the power of capital to shape education was so extreme.

All this also makes clear the essentially *contradictory* role of education, which can be either a liberating force or a force of oppression. While the drive to freedom cannot be totally vanquished, and remains always latent even in the most oppressed and 'wretched of the earth' (Fanon, 1961), it is also true that oppressive forms of education can radically *disable* individuals, undercutting the development of capacities that are a precondition for the exercise of totalizing depth praxis. Because of the ineliminable innate freedom of all humans, some will develop these capacities *despite* the system; counter hegemonic practices are always present, even in the most repressive educational regimes (Apple, 2013). Nevertheless, any true DECD should convey a sense of *urgency* concerning the cultural transmission of certain essential capacities—which are not guaranteed to re-emerge with each new generation—as well as providing insights into the necessary future emergence of unprecedented capacities, as humanity continues to grow up and into the full stature of its freedom. As discussed above, many of the capacities that we take for granted (even ones as fundamental as the four-part judgment form) are, in fact, historically emergent, were at one time unprecedented, and remain reliant upon the continuation of complex processes of cultural transmission and education. And just because these capacities have emerged to become taken-for-granted aspects of social life does not rule out their widespread disappearance due to socio-cultural regression or organized repression through oppressive education.

However, what we have seen in the recent political events of 2016–2017 is not organized repression through mass education but the hijacking of teacherly authority in the public sphere by small groups interested in large-scale cultural and political disruption. In the case of 'the Trump Insurgency',[16] this was accomplished through a combination of innovations in the use of social media, the intentional adoption of a simple and divisive political strategy, and the shameless use of the rhetorical power of media spectacle and scandal, which regress whole discourses below the four-fold judgment form. Facts and truths, let alone deeper structures, patterns, and realities, have no impact in the maelstrom of a 24-hour news cycle dominated by contrived scandal and crisis. Repeated cycles like this lead to a decline in trust and coherence between spectacle and spectator, and thus to a diffusion and undermining of teacherly authority ('Who knows what/who to believe anymore?'). This was possible in part because the postmodern Left cannot locate or justify its own teacherly authority, especially in the context of social media and the new decentralized news and content production platforms. These forms of communication technology are importantly different from those historically used in the interest of modern and postmodern teacherly authority. They have unique educational affordances that make obsolete many conventional ways of thinking about teacherly authority and it appropriate use.

Take for example the internet communications and political strategy company Cambridge Analytica, which had a hand in both the election of Trump and the Brexit campaign. Founded by an expert in psychometrics, this company leverages Big Data from social media to facilitate customized ad and content delivery, targeted to an individual's psychological dispositions and vulnerabilities, as mined from their personal data.[17] Into the postmodern vacuum of teacherly authority—the space of 'who knows what/who to believe anymore?'—can be inserted any number of beliefs, and the longer the state of unknowing lasts, the greater is the emotional desire to get clear answers. The techniques of Cambridge Analytica and those like them are to put into this space not reasons and resources, but politically charged advertisements and ideological 'edu-tainment' videos, with an emotional and cognitive combination that has been customized to known aspects of an individual's psychological makeup.[18] The result is that many individuals resolve the crisis of teacherly authority by relinquishing the demands of the four-fold judgment form and accepting the so-called 'alternative facts'. The recent eclipse of reason in the public sphere has sprung from the misuse of new and powerful educational technologies.

The implications could not be more serious given all that has been said here about the development of human capacity and the centrality of education in the project of emancipation. This way of understanding the function of education in social reproduction and individual development, which is foregrounded in the interanimation of IT and DCR, leads me to echo Dewey and argue for *the primacy of education as a philosophical concern*. Whereas Aristotle argued that metaphysics was to be taken as *first philosophy*—the most important branch, the one from which all else follows—Kant argued it was epistemology. More recently following the linguistic turn, it was semiotics and philosophy of language that were given philosophical primacy. However, as suggested by Dewey in the quote that began this section, all aspects of philosophy come to a head in the problem of education; it may be that the philosophy of education should be taken as first philosophy, as synthesizing all other branches and dealing with the most essential tasks of philosophy in its service to humanity.

It is interesting to note in this light that the word 'education' does not appear in the index of *Dialectic*. Yet there are places in the text where Bhaskar (1993, pp. 158, 262) is fully aware of the unique power and position of educational processes. In at least two places he locates education as a basic right that serves as the condition for the possibility of other rights, including the right to truth:

> The oppressed have a direct material interest in knowledge of [power$_2$] relations that the oppressors do not. Is this why there is a constant tendency for those in power in times of (or in revenge for) crisis to repeat the sin against Socrates and education generally? The real importance of the explanatory critical derivation of values from facts and practices from theories is that it can be generalized to cover the failures to satisfy other axiological needs, necessities and interests besides truth, including *those which are the necessary conditions for truth*, such as basic health, *education*, and ergonic efficiency.
> (Bhaskar, 1993, p. 262; emphasis added)

So it is that all our global crises can be understood as crises of education. As Wilber (1995) argues in several places, the crises of the biosphere are in fact crises of education and decision-making. Until enough of humanity ascends to higher levels of worldcentric consciousness, capacity, and responsibility, even transformations of the legal system will not be enough to stave off ecological disaster, as citizens must not only know the letter of the law, but also understand why it should be considered as reasonable. In the US, the 2008 economic crisis has involved the best graduates from our most prestigious schools, our greatest test takers, and our academic over-achievers, who leveraged Ivy League success to land (ridiculously) high-paying jobs in the financial sector. Their greed and incompetence speaks eloquently to the failure of our educational system. But the economic crisis was also a crisis of capacity and decision-making, as the sheer complexity of the global economy has begun to outstrip the analytical tools used to understand it. Of course, our political crises are multi-fold and entrenched, but they are also all at root educational. The emergence of a 'post-truth' democracy coincides directly with the dominance of the RHCT educational reforms alluded to above. Just as unique technologically wrought spaces open possibilities for truly deliberative forms of democracy, they are occupied by a generation of minds warped by inadequate and oppressive schooling, who are unable to reflectively participate in democratic discourse. Terror and fundamentalism are the result of massive and perverse educational initiatives—terrorists of all stripes are educated into a life of murder and hold beliefs that are divorced from regulation by anything like the ideal of rationality implied by the four-part judgment form. And finally, our collective spiritual and personal crises appear in the common sense adoption of an abstract individualist materialism and a kind of crass and flagrant nihilism; these emerge from the very fabric and content of our schooling and socialization patterns. An education revolution is necessary for survival (ecology), security (terror and fundamentalism), liberation (economics), sanity (spirituality and personality), and democracy (politics).

It is for these reasons that I have chosen to focus on the revolutionary implications of the encounter between IT and DCR, and have located education as the focus of praxis aimed at realizing the possibilities of these emancipatory metatheories. In DCR terms, the next step is to begin the metacritically informed articulation of concrete utopian alternatives and to thus clarify the directions in which preferable futures lie. It is in working toward this end that a truly fruitful merger of DCR and IT might begin (Despain & Stein, this volume).

Notes

1 Parts of this chapter were published in my book, *Education in a Time between Worlds: Essays on the Future of Schools, Technology, and Society* (2019). I would like to thank Hans Despain for his comments and insights on a prior draft of this chapter. I would also like to thank Ali Akalin and Clint Fuhs for their help in tracking down some of the Wilber quotes. Finally, I would like to thank the editors of this volume for encouraging me to write this.
2 I am adopting the *lingua-Bhaskarian* and apologize for what at times will certainly be heavily jargoned text. There is simply not space to define all the DCR terms of art I need to use to make my point here. I am also choosing to work closely with this vocabulary because in the context of the encounter between DCR and IT, it is those working in DCR who appear to need the most convincing as to the fruitfulness of the encounter. So I am speaking in a language intended to convince this group more so than those who work in IT, who are keener on the endeavour of synthesis, yet need help in speaking outside their native tongue. Interestingly, a predilection for giving the benefit of the doubt is the way of IT, which is prone to go hunting for some way in which 'everyone is partly right', as opposed to looking for how 'everyone is partly wrong', which is the way of DCR; both stances imply the other and both get us to an integrative metatheory and metacritique—only one sees the glass half full, while the other sees it half empty.
3 The term 'Anthropocene' entered the Oxford English Dictionary remarkably late, in June 2014. That is 15 years after it is agreed to have been first coined; see Angus (2015); Purey (2015).
4 Between 1900 and 1999 the US consumed 4,500 million tons of cement; between 2011 and 2013, the Chinese consumed 6,500 million tons of cement; see Harvey (2016). Harvey points out that the real issue is not that they did it or by how much, but rather: '*why* did the Chinese pour so much concrete?' The answer is that it was a classic macro-economic crisis of overproduction and unemployment. The Chinese massively debt-financed internal investments in infrastructure and urban construction, mainly as a way to buy their own concrete and employ their own labour after losing 70 million jobs and whole markets for building materials during the 2007 US monetary crisis. Harvey's (2016) work in geography and in revitalizing Marxian theories of the production of space through uneven geographical development are essential in understanding the dynamics of present and future human-biosphere relationships.
5 For this very reason Jason Moore asks whether a better name for our current geological epoch would be the *Capitalocene* (see Moores's (2016) *Capitalism and the Web of Life*).
6 Moore (2016) is at pains to drive home this essential point about the co-constitution of society and nature. His notion of *double internality*—nature-in-society and society-in-nature—addresses this. As we will see with Wilber's quadrants, the differentiation of

society from nature, or mind from brain, has its analytical usefulness. But heuristic *differentiations*, such as the quadrants, must not be reified into hard-and-fast *dissociations*. We differentiate only so we can better re-integrate at a higher level of synthesis and insight. Society and Nature are not two and yet they are not one; we need concepts that capture their inter-animation and co-evolution.

7 See David Harvey (1978) *Limits to Capital*. Capitalism tends to solve its problems by spreading out or putting things someplace else in space, the so-called 'spatial fix'. This worked when there were frontiers. We are probably nearing the end of spatial fixes.

8 It should be noted that I do not address Bhaskar's 'spiritual turn' in this chapter, making no mention of his philosophy of metaReality and the manner in which it expands upon the DCR framework. The relations between Wilber and Bhaskar get even more complex when one brings in their views on non-duality, postmodern religiosity, spiritual awakening, and the continued relevance of the great religious traditions. I believe Bhaskar's work on metaReality is an important and good addition to DCR; I do not address it here simply due to limitations of space. It should be mentioned that the concept of 'dispositional realism' that emerges as part of the philosophy of metaReality has important implications for my argument here. Dispositional realism argues that potentials are *real*, even if they remain unactualized. This allows us to say that although the present state of humanity is one of incapacity and unactualized potential, humanity is nevertheless also, in just as real a way, a species in which every member is a non-dual, virtuous being undertaking transformed transformative praxis for the sake of all being (i.e., every human is potentially a Buddha or Avatar of the Divine, which is a classic statement from the religious traditions, cf. *The Lotus Sutra*, or synoptic accounts from Wilber and Huxley).

9 Throughout this chapter I will use the terms 'human development', 'developmental psychology', and 'developmental studies', and refer to 'developmentalists' etc. all in reference to a broad field of research concerned with the development of individual capacities for thought, action, and emotion (not to be confused with developmental studies in the sense of international development, economic development, etc.). For an overview of this field see Wilber (1999), Miller (2009).

10 As we will see in the penultimate section below, the *naturalness* and seeming inevitability of learning and development, which is a presupposition of much of the developmental tradition, points to the contradictory nature of educational systems in contemporary societies, where children struggle to learn and where learning often does not take place at all. As Habermas (1973) explains, drawing explicitly on a DECD inspired by Piaget and Kohlberg, and foreshadowing his definition of ideology:

> It is my conjecture that the fundamental mechanism for social evolution in general is to be found in an automatic inability not to learn. Not *learning*, but *not-learning* is the phenomenon that calls for explanation ... Therein lies the rationality of man. Only against this background does the overpowering irrationality of the history of the species become visible.
>
> *(p. 15; italics in the original)*

According to this view, the hegemonic ideologies of late-capitalism function as *impediments or barriers to learning*; they counteract the natural dialectical growth of the self and society, holding us in place, blinding our eyes to the truth of our condition.

11 As Norrie (2010, p. 135) notes, Bhaskar is well aware of the fact that the judgment form is, in a certain sense, an *idealization*. Aware of the gap between the actual and the ideal, Bhaskar's (1993, p. 285) response is to suggest their *constellational* unity—the ideal and the actual co-exist and stand in complex co-relation, which is one of the tensions that propels and gives directionality to geo-history. This is all well and good, but is beside the point I am making here. The issue here is not the relation between the ideal and the actual, but rather what capacities are actually needed to grasp the form of this specific ideal. That is, there may never be a pure instance of judgment (as defined by the four-fold judgment form)—it is an idealization—and yet to be moved toward this ideal it must be possible

to see it as distinct from the actual. As will be explained, the capacity to even recognize something like the four-fold judgment form is quite an achievement, let alone the capacity to reflectively correct one's words and behaviour in light of it.

12 I am not taking up the question of *why* these capacities are presented in this way: there is no space here for a metacritique$_2$ type exploration of the historical, socio-cultural, and political reasons behind the occurrence of the cognitive maturity fallacy. Academic insularity has been compounded by the politically Leftist nature of DCR. As I discuss in the body of the text, the Left takes as taboo any discussion of politically significant differences in individual capacity, which are taken as anti-democratic, and often rightly so, given the use by the Right of reductive (and racist) genetic arguments about innate intelligence (e.g., Herrnstein & Murray, 1994). This inarticulacy on the Left concerning individual differences in reasoning capacity and personality structure has contributed to the ineffectualness of many contemporary Leftist political movements, especially in educational reform, a point I will return to in the final section below.

13 One essential ontological difference between the two models that is not discussed here is Wilber's thoroughgoing *panpsychism*. That is, for Wilber, consciousness does not only (or suddenly) appear in highly organized forms of matter—popping out of the top, or being 'secreted' from matter only at the pinnacle of terrestrial evolution. Rather, consciousness (in some form) goes *all the way down*, and thus the unique qualities of human consciousness are taken as expressing not only the development of matter, but also the evolution of consciousness itself. There is not space here to go into the complexities of this view (which requires an essential distinction between *sentience* and *sapience*; see Brandom, 1994), nor is there space to explore the degree to which Bhaskar's ontology allows for this possibility (I think it does).

14 Some of the issues here concern the role of enactment and constructivism in developmental epistemologies, as well as the implications of the co-evolution of ontologies and epistemologies. The importation of DECD impacts some of the central elements of DCR, especially the relations and distinctions between the ontic/ontological and the transitive/intransitive dimensions.

15 Importantly, none of this talk about the absence of capacities in individuals should be taken to mean that true freedom is not a latent and native potential for all individuals, or that certain politically relevant capacities are simply not available to certain individuals. See footnote 8 above on Bhaskar's notion of *dispositional realism*. Barring severe and tragic forms of disability, the field of developmental studies provides no reason to consider any individual uneducable or to believe that certain capacities are beyond anyone's reach. We may not all have it in us to become Einsteins and Gandhis, but essential capacities constituting, for example, totalizing depth praxis should be understood as potentially available to all, *given the presence of the right educational environments and the absence of the wrong ones*.

16 For a big picture on the election of Trump and the related 'culture war' being fought over the right to shape the meta-narrative of the future see Jordan Greenhall's (2017) *Situational Assessment 2017: Trump Edition*.

17 Cambridge Analytica appears to be merely the most public face of a 'global election management agency' that serves as a Big Data psychometric backend used by elites to manipulate the social and news media feeds of everyday people. This dangerous and almost invisible hijacking of teacherly authority is reshaping the culture and worldviews of millions worldwide (see Grassegger & Krogerus, 2017). Whereas prior modes of media were centralized and focused on creating a single story or narrative for everyone to buy into (e.g., Public Radio; *The New York Times*), the new decentralized modes are focused on multiplying narratives and the disintegration of mutual understanding (e.g., Facebook; Twittter). With a kind of epistemic centrifugal force culture is pushed outward and apart, as identity and personality politics splinter the public sphere into a solipsistic hall of mirrors. Once divided the people are then easily conquered; the vulnerabilities of subgroups allow then to be manipulated into consolidation and alignment along polarized party lines during the ideological (and advertising) push of an election season.

18 The psychometrics produced by Cambridge Analytica are built around the OCEAN scale of personality traits. As for the content that is ultimately delivered, it is important not to underestimate the truncation of communication in accounting for the regression below the four-fold judgment form in public culture. Short-duration streaming video, sentence length or image- and word-based 'memes', and the Tweet—for some these have usurped reasoned argumentation as a warrant for teacherly authority.

References

Angus, I. (2015). When did the Anthropocene begin ... And why does it matter? *Monthly Review*, 67(4). Available at https://monthlyreview.org/2015/09/01/when-did-the-anthropocene-beginand-why-does-it-matter/ (Accessed 23 February 2022).
Apple, M.W. (2001). *Educating the 'Right' Way: Markets, Standards, God, and Inequality*. Routledge.
Apple, M.W. (2013). *Can Education Change Society?* Routledge.
Apple, M.W., & Bean, J.A. (eds) (1995). *Democratic Schools*. Association for Supervision and Curriculum Development.
Bhaskar, R. (1971). *On the Possibility of Naturalism*. Routledge.
Bhaskar, R. (1986). *Scientific Realism and Human Emancipation*. Verso.
Bhaskar, R. (1993). *Dialectic: The Pulse of Freedom*. Verso.
Blumenthal, D. (1993). *Facing the Abusing God: A Theology of Protest*. Westminster John Knox Press.
Brandom, R. (1994). *Making It Explicit*. Harvard University Press.
Despain, H., & Stein, S. (2022). Getting theory into public culture: Collaborations and interventions where metatheorists meet. In N. Hedlund and S. Esbjörn-Hargens (eds), *Big Picture Perspectives for Planetary Flourishing*. Routledge.
Dewey, J. (1916). *Democracy and Education*. The Macmillan Company.
Dewey, J. (1930). From absolutism to experimentalism. In *The Later Works of John Dewey* (Vol. 5). SIU Press.
Fanon, F. (1961). *The Wretched of the Earth*. Grove Press.
Fischer, K.W. (1980). A theory of cognitive development: The control and construction of hierarchies of skills. *Psychological Review*, 87(6), 477–531.
Fischer, K.W., & Biddle, T. (2006). Dynamic development of psychological structures in action and thought. In W. Damon & R.M. Lerner (eds), *Handbook of Child Psychology: Theoretical Models of Human Development* (Vol. 1). John Wiley & Sons.
Grassegger, H., & Krogerus, M. (2017). *The Data That Turned the World Upside Down*. Available at https://motherboard.vice.com/en_us/article/how-our-likes-helped-trump-win (Accessed 23 February 2022).
Greenhall, J. (2017). *Situational Assessment 2017: Trump Edition*. Available at https://medium.com/rally-point-journal/situational-assessment-2017-trump-edition-d189d24fc046 (Accessed 23 February 2022).
Habermas, J. (1967). *On the Logic of the Social Sciences*. MIT Press.
Habermas, J. (1971). *Knowledge and Human Interests*. Beacon Press.
Habermas, J. (1973). *Legitimation Crisis*. Beacon Press.
Habermas, J. (1984). *The Theory of Communicative Action: Reason and the Rationalization of Society*, transl. T. McCarthy (Vol. 1). Beacon Press.
Habermas, J. (1987). *The Theory of Communicative Action*, Vol. 2: *Lifeworld and System, a Critique of Functionalist Reason*. Beacon Press.
Habermas, J. (2003). *The Future of Human Nature*. Polity Press.
Harvey, D. (1978). *Limits to Capital*. Verso.
Harvey, D. (2016). *Ways of the World*. Oxford University Press.

Herrnstein, R.J., & Murray, C. (1994). *The Bell Curve: The Reshaping of American Life by Difference in Intelligence*. Free Press.

Kitchener, K. S., & King, P. M. (1990). The reflective judgment model: Ten years of research. In M. L. Commons, C. Armon, L. Kohlberg, F. A. Richards, T. A. Grotzer, & J. D. Sinnott (eds), *Adult Development* (Vol. 2, pp. 62–78). Praeger.

Kohlberg, L. (1981). *Essays on Moral Development*, Vol. 1: *The Philosophy of Moral Development*. Harper & Row.

Moore, J. (2016). *Capitalism in the Web of Life*. Verso.

Norrie, A. (2010). *Dialectic and Difference*. Routledge.

Piaget, J. (1928). *Judgment and Reasoning in the Child*. Littlefield and Adams.

Piaget, J. (1932). *The Moral Judgment of the Child*. Routledge and Kegan Paul.

Piaget, J. (1971a). *Biology and Knowledge*. The University of Chicago Press.

Piaget, J. (1971b). *The Insights and Illusions of Philosophy*. The World Publishing Company.

Piaget, J. (1972). *The Principles of Genetic Epistemology*, transl. W. Mays. Routledge and Kegan Paul.

Piaget, J. (1977). *The Essential Piaget: An Interpretive Reference Guide*, ed. H.E. Gruber & J.J. Voneche. Basic Books.

Piketty, T. (2014). *Capital in the 21st Century*. Harvard University Press.

Purey, J. (2015). *After Nature: A Politics for the Anthropocene*. Harvard University Press.

Ravitch, D. (2013). *Reign of Error: The Hoax of the Privatization Movement and the Danger to America's Public Schools*. Knopf.

Sahlberg, P. (2012). *Finnish Lessons: What Can the World Learn from Educational Change in Finland*. Teachers College Press.

Shonkoff, J., & Phillips, D. (2010). *From Neurons to Neighborhoods: The Science of Early Childhood Development*. National Academy Press.

Smith, L. (2002). Piaget's model. In U. Goswami (ed.), *The Wiley-Blackwell Handbook of Childhood Cognitive Development*. Blackwell.

Smith, L., & Voneche, J.J. (eds) (2006). *Norms in Human Development*. Cambridge University Press.

Stein, Z. (2010). On the difference between designing children and raising them: Ethics and the use of educationally oriented biotechnologies. *Mind, Brain, and Education*, 4(2), 53–67.

Stein, Z. (2013). Ethics and the new education: Psychometrics, biotechnology, and the future of human capital. Paper presented at the Integral Theory Conference, San Francisco, 15 August.

Stein, Z. (2016). *Social Justice and Educational Testing: John Rawls, the History of Testing, and the Future of Education*. Routledge.

Stein, Z. (2019). *Education in a Time between Worlds: Essays on the Future of Schools, Technology, and Society*. Integral Publishing House.

Van Geert, P. (1993). *Dynamic Systems of Development*. Harvester-Wheatsheaf.

Wallerstein, I. (1995). *After Liberalism*. The New Press.

Whitehead, A.N. (1978). *Process and Reality*. Macmillan Publishing Company.

Wilber, K. (1980). *The Atman Project*. Shambhala Publications, Inc.

Wilber, K. (1995). *Sex, Ecology, Spirituality: The Spirit of Evolution*. Shambhala Publications, Inc.

Wilber, K. (1999). *Integral Psychology*. Shambhala Publications, Inc.

Wilber, K. (2003). Excerpt D. Available at www.kenwilber.com/Writings/PDF/excerptD_KOSMOS_2004.pdf (Accessed 14 March 2022).

Wilber, K. (2006). *Integral Spirituality: A Startling New Role for Religion in the Modern and Postmodern World*. Integral Books.

PART 3
Education

6
METATHEORY
The Ontological Turn in Mathematics Education Research

Iskra Nunez

Introduction

At the onset of the new millennium, the mathematics education research (MER) community effectively succeeded at transposing questions of existence with a plurality of epistemic approaches.[1] By this time, MER was considered a relatively young but developing academic field,[2] in part due to contributions to the already existing plurality of epistemic approaches employed within it.[3] What the MER community struggled with, however, was succinctly captured with their explicit call for a metatheory.[4] This call was not a mere invitation for future research; it was an injunction to action. That is, this academic community needed its members to think, and think ingeniously, about the nature of and the methods for MER, a serious issue that has kept the MER community engaged for years. The challenge today for the MER community still concerns the lack of metatheoretical coordinates by which to understand mathematics education as a research field in its own right. The purpose of this chapter is to continue to address MER's explicit need for a metatheory with an exploration of a metatheory for and of MER by focusing on critical realism and integral theory. A problem with MER's plurality of epistemic approaches, and pluralism in general, is not that there are too many metatheories, nor the incommensurability of their competing paradigms; rather, it is that pluralism lacks the advantage of ontological realist metatheoretical coordinates on which to base knowledge and its applications.

1 Unpacking the Metatheoretical Coordinates of Critical Realism and Integral Theory

In this chapter, I take a basic critical realist metatheoretical vision of reality and science, and I then use integral theory as a common heuristic for inclusion.[5] Critical realism is a philosophy of science that is increasingly being employed in the social sciences,[6] and it is arguably the least implicit framework of most natural science that makes genuine discoveries. Integral theory is an increasingly recognized approach to integrating multiple theoretical perspectives.

Roy Bhaskar, the chief creator of the philosophy of critical realism, deepened his theses across three identifiable phases: basic, dialectical, and the philosophy of metaReality.[7] Ken Wilber, the chief creator of integral theory, also developed his theses across what may also be described as a three-phase outline: endo, ecto, and in praxis.[8] Basic critical realism emerged around 1975 as a critique of pre-existing philosophies. Integral theory emerged around the same time in 1977 as a way to systematically tackle the increasing complexity of daily life with the help of insights from various disciplines. Critical realism identified that other philosophies had omitted ontology from their conceptualization of reality and set out to revendicate it.[9] Integral theory identified that there was partial truth, however miniscule, in all schools of thought being considered, and it set out to include more of reality to assess, deal with, and potentially interrelate multi-theoretical awareness into a binding resolution of problems.[10] A comprehensive historical analysis of critical realism and integral theory is beyond the exploratory scope of this chapter.[11] For this chapter, however, it suffices to view critical realism as above all a metatheory of the deepening of ontology and, in turn, to view integral theory as primarily a metatheory of the systematic inclusion of epistemologies.

In exploring these metatheoretical coordinates of critical realism and integral theory for and of MER, this chapter begins with explicit ontological, epistemological, and methodological metatheorems (or arguments) about the world. These grounding metatheorems do not arbitrarily arise from obscurity. What this realist point of departure means is that metatheorems are argued for, and arrived at, by the processes of immanent critique and transcendental argumentation from the premise of intentional practice. In the process of immanent critique, we deploy a philosophical approach that allows us to take the argument of an opposing theory and show that it is internally inconsistent. In the process of transcendental argumentation, we deploy an examination into the necessary conditions of possibility for some human activity as conceptualized in our experience.[12] In the next section, I review the ontological, epistemological, and methodological metatheorems of basic critical realism; I shall draw upon them and dialectical logic to offer an omissive critique of integral theory.[13]

Ontological Metatheorems

The ontological metatheorems of critical realism begin with a duplex argument for (1) an inexorable and irreducible nature of real entities in the world (ontology) absolutely or relatively independent of our knowledge (epistemology), where (2) epistemology is included as part of ontology. The conflation of ontology and epistemology into epistemology is argued to be fallacious. This error is known as the epistemic fallacy. The conflation of ontology and discourse into discourse is argued to be fallacious. This error is known as the linguistic fallacy.[14]

From this (1)/(2) argument follows a third metatheorem, the critical realist multi-stratified and differentiated view of the world as consisting of three overlapping domains: the real, the actual, and the empirical. The all-encompassing domain of the real contains multi-generative mechanisms that power all existing things and also act at least partly independently of the flux of conditions that enable their identification. Generative mechanisms tend to be out of phase with the patterns of events and experiences that constitute the domain of the actual. The domain of the empirical consists of experiences.

It follows that a fourth metatheorem of critical realism involves the distinction between open and closed systems. From this view, the world is an open system but is susceptible under certain conditions to closure. This distinction between open and closed systems implies that the generative mechanisms of the world—at the level of the real and identified under experimental conditions (that is, artificially closed systems)—endure and act independently of those conditions and so cannot be empirical regularities or patterns of events. The degree to which reality may be an open system is debatable among critical realists.[15] To better illustrate this critical realist conception of an open and differentiated/multi-stratified world, I will contrast it now with its integral-theoretical counterpart.

Denegation of Non-Identity

Integral theory conceives that there is no reality apart from the worldviews depicted with the four perspectives (or dimensions) of the AQAL model. From this integral-theoretical approach, there is no world; there are only perspectives or consciousness-being. The AQAL model is a hallmark of the integral-theoretical approach and consists of five basic elements—all-quadrants, all-levels, all-lines, all-states, and all-types—denoting the foundational (repeating) patterns of an integral-theoretical conceived reality.[16] Because integral theory founds its knowledge claims on constructivism,[17] it is easy to begin to understand its idea of perspectives (or dimensions) by building the all-quadrant element of the AQAL model along two foundational axes. The first axis separates the interior and exterior perspectives, that is, the view from the inside and the view from the outside. The second axis separates the collective and the individual perspectives, that is, the plural view of a group of people from the singular view of an individual. Then setting the first axis (interior/exterior) orthogonal to the second one (individual/collective) will produce a conceptual coordinate system of perspectives (also called dimensions) denoted as the upper-left quadrant (ULQ), lower-left quadrant (LLQ), upper-right quadrant (URQ), and lower-right quadrant (LRQ). From a critical realist vantage point, however, neither the first axis (interior/exterior) nor the second axis (individual/collective) is acceptable; both tend to encourage an atomistic view that reproduces rather than overcomes the dualisms of collectivism (or holism)/individualism, structure/agency, naturalism/anti-naturalism, mind/body, reasons/causes, and facts/values.[18] Bracketing these objections *pro tem*, it is here that critical realism differs radically from integral theory. This is because critical realism acknowledges the not deny, omit, or neglect the existence of the world; rather, it mounts a strong philosophical defence for the existence of the world, arguing for the absolute or relative independence of the real entities of scientific research (ontology) from our knowledge about them (epistemology).

Integral theory, as a guiding framework, delivers a double punch. It combines intuition with forceful neutrality.[19] The logic of intuition makes an argument appear compelling because it seems obvious. If the argument for greater facilitation of multi-disciplinary knowledge with the practical potential to advance an ever-greater comprehensiveness across different schools of thought seems pretty obvious to you, then it must be almost rationally irrefutable. If this argument cannot be refuted, then it must be generally accepted and should increase your chances of success with every application. This is why integral theory appeals universally. What begins as logic in intuition can end as triumphalism.[20] As a guiding framework, integral theory also purports to achieve neutrality, which makes it seem detached from ideologies or fashions.

If integral theory's logic of intuition and neutrality is self-evident, then where do you begin? What is its point of departure? By way of response, this metatheory tells you that neither being (ontology) nor knowledge (epistemology) should concern you because Ken Wilber, chief creator of integral theory, thought such a dismissal of ontology/epistemology to be correct, as he writes:

> It is the refusal to ground ontology in epistemology or epistemology in ontology that sets Integral Theory apart from postmodernism and Critical Realism, respectively. Instead of, say, epistemology being grounded in ontology, there is instead a 'mutual resonance' that does—or does not—occur between these dimensions of being, and their enactive mutuality thus either 'meshes' (and the holon is carried forward by evolution) or fails to mesh (and the holon becomes extinct in the very next moment).
>
> *(Wilber, 2013)*

What do you do when someone denies the distinction between ontology and epistemology?[21] To reiterate the integral-theoretical position, Esbjörn-Hargens (2006), a leading scholar of integral theory, also explains how it 'assigns no ontological or epistemological priority to any of these (AQAL's) elements because they co-arise and "tetra-mesh" simultaneously' (p. 82). As with the emperor's new clothes, you either see it or you do not. The trouble is, if you cannot see it—that is, if you find that, for example, the 'mutual resonance' which takes responsibility for 'tetra-meshing' the existence or utter extinction of the 'holon' is not self-evident, but rather unsatisfying or utterly absurd—then you soon realize the necessity for transcendental argumentation.[22] What I find interesting about Wilber's and Esbjörn-Hargens' quotations is not simply that the epistemic fallacy is argued for, and arrived at, by a logic of intuition with forceful neutrality, before assigning priority to anything else; although effectively they do just that, they also display a keen awareness of their irrealist point of departure. Thus, we see an ironic (postmodernist) self-distancing from ontology/epistemology, which in turn generates an awareness of (committing) the epistemic fallacy, albeit without being expressed with such a precise term. Therefore, I claim that because integral theory (deliberately) commits the epistemic fallacy, it follows that it fails to sustain the ideas of difference and structure.

The reduction of the domain of the real to the actual is argued to be fallacious, following critical realism. This error is known as actualism.[23] Integral theory exemplifies actualism; as Wilber (2005) explains, discovering 'the profound patterns that connect is a major accomplishment of the Integral Approach' (p. 22). A problem with integral theory's actualism, and actualism in general, is that generative mechanisms at the level of the real are identified as the invariant regularities of repeating patterns of events at the level of the actual, implying a flat world—that is, the reduction of the real to the actual, in which there is only one level of the world composed of the most basic, invariant patterns of reality—and deterministically assuming that this level will remain constant. Thus, Wilber's critique of the 'flatland' of the 'myth of the given' functions to mask a flatland of his own![24]

To reiterate, the signature concept of integral theory is the AQAL model precisely because it helps us illustrate the idea of actualism with its five basic elements (all-quadrants, all-levels, all-lines, all-states, and all-types). These five elements constitute, as Esbjörn-Hargens (2010b) explains, the 'most basic repeating patterns of reality' (p. 35). The integral-theoretical approach provides us then with an undifferentiated (in the ontology/epistemology dismissal), unstructured (in recognizing repeating patterns at a single level in connecting perspectives in lieu of generative mechanisms at different levels of reality), and thus flat conception of reality. In this manner, we see that integral theory arguably commits a second fallacy; that is actualism.

Denegation of Negativity

Moreover, because integral theory cannot sustain difference and stunts structure in the world, this implies that it fails to conceptualize non-identity. A world without non-identity is a world without difference. A world without difference is a world without negativity, a world without absence. A world without negativity is a purely present and positive world. In this manner, the AQAL model also helps us exemplify the idea of ontological monovalence: the failure to distinguish negativity in the world in favour of a purely positive, undifferentiated/unstructured account of reality.[25] And that is how integral theory arguably commits a third fallacy; that is, ontological monovalence.

Denegation of Totality

Another problem with integral theory's atomism, and atomism in general, is that the whole totality is then reduced to its constitutive parts, called atoms, as the smallest, irreducible representatives of aspects of reality. Although critical realism and integral theory share concepts of totality and interrelatedness, their respective notions differ radically. Totality in the critical realist tradition, and in the most basic sense, references open, stratified systems or structures of internal relations that include its own holes, lacks, or absences. Integral theory denotes the whole totality of reality with the AQAL model, which is itself composed of four irreducible parts, denoted as perspectives (or domains). Leading integral-theory scholar Esbjörn-Hargens (2007) explains that by 'drawing on at least four distinctions ... you are staying in contact with a manageable amount of irreducible aspects of reality ... *the goal is not to be totalistic*' (p. 80; my emphasis). Then integral theory employs pattern recognition among the four domains of AQAL to fit them together into a more integral view that is itself a reduction by atomicity.

Instead of pattern recognition, I want to suggest that it is possible to understand the interconnectedness of the four AQAL domains through an understanding of their respective Achilles' heels.[26] Using critical realism, let us proceed sequentially to the first quadrant of the AQAL model by identifying the Achilles' heel of (individual/interior) ULQ. Integral theory denotes and associates this dimension grammatically with 'I' (the first-person pronoun) because it represents the AQAL perspective of subjective knowledge. Its point of vulnerability is that on which the Achilles' heel critique of hermeneutics fastens precisely because it is the realm associated with individual interpretation and experience, and it cannot sustain knowledge outside itself; that is, it fails to account for a dimension of knowledge outside narratives, interpretative knowledge, and experiences.

The second quadrant is (collective/interior) LLQ, the AQAL perspective of intersubjective knowledge. Integral theory denotes and associates this dimension grammatically with 'you/we' (plural pronouns). The vulnerability of LLQ is precisely that on which the Achilles' heel critique of transcendental idealism, the founding philosophy of the traditionally recognized forms of constructivism, fastens because it fails to posit the independence, or at least the prior existence and causal efficacy, of objects of scientific research; that is, in a dimension of our knowledge about the world that is properly ontological or intransitive, relatively independent of our theories and discourses about the world in the epistemological or transitive dimension. Because there are no worldly grounds for testing or choosing among the plurality of rival theories, transcendental idealism, including constructivism (social or otherwise), tends to lead towards relativism.

The identification of the Achilles' heel of (individual/exterior) URQ follows. Integral theory denotes and associates this dimension grammatically with 'it' (the third-person singular pronoun) because it is the AQAL perspective of objective knowledge. Its point of vulnerability is that on which the Achilles' heel critique of pragmatism fastens. In other words, pragmatism posits correctly the possibility of ontology independently of epistemology. We see, however, a reductionist tendency in which the dimension of objective knowledge tends to be misconstrued in terms of the identification of (repeating) patterns or regularities of events, behaviours, and/or functions of the brain (identified in closed systems).

We conclude this dialectical phenomenology with the identification of the Achilles' heel of (collective/exterior) LRQ.[27] Integral theory denotes and associates this dimension grammatically with 'its' (the possessive form of 'it') because it is the AQAL perspective of interobjective knowledge. Its point of vulnerability is that on which the Achilles' heel critique of postmodernism fastens. Without omitting or denying the possibility of ontology, in the dimension that encourages a worldview of structures (or systems), it often misconstrues them in terms of the collectivist account of individual activity in groups or the individual activity of groups (that is, the error of collectivism). Thus, it tends to reproduce the dichotomy of collectivism (or holism)/individualism. It is important to reiterate that the inclusion of four perspectives (ULQ, LLQ, URQ, and LRQ) does not occur here via a simple concatenation of four different perspectives or by pattern recognition. Rather, an inclusive understanding is possible because we are able to provide more explanatory power with the systematic identification of their respective Achilles' heels.

Denegation of Transformative Agency

If integral theory denies the transcendental necessities of non-identity and negativity, and if it under-theorizes totality, then does it help you to conceptualize change in the world? Guided by Parmenidean ontological monovalence, Plato analyses change in terms of differences in the history of philosophy. Parallel to this example, I now want to show that integral theory also transposes the concept of change, but not with difference, rather with the idea of an overt awareness of exclusion caused by its inability to sustain the negative (or absence) in reality. The following quotation by Esbjörn-Hargens exemplifies this point:

> By drawing on at least four distinctions within each element [of the AQAL model] you provide yourself with an even number of check-points to ensure that you are staying in contact with a manageable amount of irreducible aspects of reality ... The point here is not that the inclusion of more aspects is necessarily better. In other words, the goal is not to be totalistic ... *The point is less about including everything and more about being aware of what you are not including.*
>
> (Esbjörn-Hargens, 2007, p. 80; my emphasis)

To show that the above quotation cannot sustain its theory in practice, consider the following example: let us suppose that you are an active citizen living under Athenian democracy in classical Greek times. Informed by the AQAL model, you understand that the point of this regime is not that the inclusion of women and slaves in politics is necessarily better for democratic life. In fact, you think that the point of democracy is less about including them in democratic engagement and more about merely being aware that they are not being included; that is, it is enough to be aware of their deliberate exclusion from this political aspect of reality, perhaps because women and slaves are deemed to be unworthy by the advocates of this regime and their non-totalistic view of democracy. How is the AQAL model connected to this thought experiment? They both share a non-totalistic view of reality. History provides a record of the deliberate exclusion of disenfranchised individuals and the Athenian democratic collapse.[28] The point being made is that what begins as an under-theorization of totality can end as fragments. Thus, the integral-theoretical analysis of change as a mere recognition of exclusion results in an underdevelopment of this concept, and thus it cannot sustain the idea of the transformative capacity for agency. In contrast, a critical realist view of being (ontology) is bound to non-being (absence) as the dialectic of transformative agency; to change is a process of absenting absences, lacks, omissions, and constraints on freedoms.[29] Integral theory helps you to conceptualize change in the world with selected inclusion and a mere recognition of exclusion. Critical realism, in contrast, takes absence as the pivotal core of the nature of change.[30]

Critical realism differs further from integral theory in that it holds the ontologically least restrictive viewpoint available while remaining open to revisions and criticisms. This vision is possible to the extent to which it includes two features: (1) the insights of other multi-theoretical perspectives, while avoiding their disadvantages, which is also a distinctive feature in integral theory; and (2) the causal levels of reality relevant to the nature of the problem being studied and the possible interactions (and also determinations) among them, which is an absent feature in integral theory. These twin features have been referred to as critical realism's double-inclusiveness.[31] Before turning to the epistemological metatheorems, which are concerned with the nature of knowledge, I summarize the main findings of this section with an (irrealist) ensemble of some omissive errors of integral theory. Following dialectical logic, the arrow symbol (→ or ↓) means entails, implies, or towards.

(Irrealist) Ensemble of Some Omissive Errors of Integral Theory

1M Non-Identity: logic of intuition with forceful neutrality → ontology/epistemology dismissal → epistemic fallacy → triumphalism. A view of repeating patterns at a single level of reality in connecting worldviews in lieu of generative mechanisms at different levels of reality → lack of difference and stunted structure → flat reality → actualism.

↓

2E Negativity: transposition of change with awareness of exclusion → underdevelopment of absence/change → lack of negativity → purely positive world → ontological monovalence. AQAL's double-foundational axes (interior/exterior orthogonal to individual/collective) tend to encourage dualisms: collectivism (holism)/individualism, structure/agency, naturalism/anti-naturalism, mind/body, reasons/causes, and facts/values.

↓

3L Totality: AQAL is separated into four indivisible domains (or perspectives) → reduction of totality to its constitutive domains or parts → employs pattern-recognition to fit together domains of AQAL → non-totalistic goal of analysis → atomism.

Achilles' heel of (individual/interior) ULQ is akin to that of hermeneutics →
Achilles' heel of (collective/interior) LLQ is akin to that of constructivism →
Achilles' heel of (individual/exterior) URQ is akin to that of pragmatism →
Achilles' heel of (collective/exterior) LRQ is akin to that of postmodernism.

↓

4D Transformative Agency: under-development of absence/change as a selected inclusion and a mere recognition of exclusion → unsustainable concept of transformative capacity for agency.

Epistemological Metatheorems

Critical realism may provide the epistemologically least weak position. This is because the goal in scientific practice is to move from established phenomena, for instance, in regularities, the patterns of events, language, and behaviours, to their causal explanation in terms of underlying mechanisms or structures, and in doing so, it seeks to avoid the partial positions of rival theories.[32] Integral theory seeks to avoid partiality with its integral methodological pluralism (IMP) by revealing and including all the partial insights possible of multiple perspectives.[33] A problem with IMP's pragmatic principles, and pragmatism in general, is when researchers commit the fallacy of pragmatism; that is, when research is carried out without reference to ontology and epistemology,[34] which is precisely the integral-theoretical point of departure. Therefore, integral theory arguably commits another fallacy (that is, the fallacy of pragmatism). Although critical realism founds its knowledge claims and applications on reality, and integral theory founds its knowledge claims on constructivism and their applications within pragmatism, they both share a commitment to non-partiality as a common heuristic.

Methodological Metatheorems

Critical realism may provide a methodologically capable stance to move beyond reductionisms. At this point, it is important to differentiate between metaphysical pluralism and ontological pluralism. Metaphysical pluralism holds that there is more than one reality; ontological pluralism sees that reality as structured and differentiated. Metaphysically, critical realism is a (stratified) monism.[35] In other words, it conceives that there is but one reality, which nevertheless has a plural, differentiated, and stratified ontology. Integral theory is a post-metaphysical methodology used to integrate epistemologies.[36] It is arguably metaphysically atomistic. Methodologically, integral theory argues for transcending reductionist positions via an AQAL model. In contrast, in critical realism, the notion of ontological pluralism corresponds to the designation of a laminated system; that is, a model of applied explanations corresponding to the irreducibly relevant causal mechanisms at different levels of reality and a conceptualization of how these layered mechanisms might interact to produce phenomena.[37] Methodologically, ontological pluralism may be seen as a way of transcending reductionist positions via a laminated system precisely because it proposes that different levels of analysis, corresponding to a differentiated reality, are necessary and conceived as dynamic and interacting.[38]

2 Traditional Applications of AQAL versus Dialectical Critique of Metatheories

I now turn to reviewing some of the traditional applications of ULQ, LLQ, URQ, and LRQ to the fields of mathematics education and pedagogy. The purpose of this review is to appreciate the difference between applying the AQAL matrix without critical realism and the methodological advantages of such ontological pluralism obtained through an application of integral theory's AQAL model to integrate it along with the four metatheoretical positions found in MER's philosophical precursors; that is, hermeneutics, constructivist (social or otherwise), postmodernist, and pragmatist, drawn from the introduction.

Mathematics Education: A Quadrivium Vision of Perfect Numbers (without Critical Realism)

Elliot Benjamin (2006) provided a salient tetra or quadrant (also called a quadrivium) analysis applied to number theory, as mathematics education subject and as a research discipline in its own right, highlighting the various branches of mathematical inquiry. To show this, Benjamin offered a quadrivium view of perfect numbers. A perfect number may be defined as any counting number (1, 2, 3, 4, and so on) that equals the sum of its proper divisors. The number 6 is the first perfect number because its proper divisors are 1, 2, and 3, which together add up to 6; that is, $1 + 2 + 3 = 6$. The purpose of finding perfect numbers is to introduce young pupils to explorations of number patterns by using a quadrivium perspective to find the first five perfect numbers. In other words, ULQ involves an interior-individual process of creating and testing patterns through the practice of multiplication and division skills; URQ involves an interior-exterior process of monitoring behaviours and knowledge among peers themselves while working in small groups; LLQ involves a collective-interior process of sharing the outcomes of this investigation with the entire class; and, lastly, LRQ involves a collective-exterior process of engaging with technological means. At this LRQ stage, the use of a calculator or computer facilitates continued testing of the hypothesis to identify perfect number patterns. For example, when numbers become large, a calculator may be used to show that the fifth perfect number is 33,550,336. With this example, Benjamin illustrated an application of AQAL, and he demonstrated how he himself teaches a pure mathematics topic as an enrichment math activity engaged in a pure mathematics subject and as a research discipline in its own right.

Pedagogy: A Quadrivium Vision of Knowledge for Teaching (without Critical Realism)

Renert (2011) used the AQAL matrix to design a novel pedagogy of living mathematics education (PLME). Of the four dimensions of PLME, three roughly correspond to Lee Shulman's (1986) triad categorization of content, pedagogy, and curriculum knowledge applied to mathematics pedagogy. Mathematics content knowledge as objective knowledge corresponds to the PLME exterior-singular dimension (URQ). Mathematical pedagogical content knowledge as subjective knowledge corresponds to the PLME interior-singular dimension (ULQ). Mathematics curriculum knowledge as intersubjective knowledge corresponds to the PLME interior-plural dimension (LLQ). As part of the PLME exterior-plural dimension (LRQ), Renert added an additional dimension of interobjective knowledge that deals with the broader social system as the origin of resources for teaching. In this manner, Renert argued that PLME should be seen as an evolving disposition of these four dimensions for healing the teaching profession and the world (cf. Mark Edward's argument in the companion volume to this work). Arguably, a PLME metatheory holds a strong constructivist perspective.

A Critical Realist Vision of Metatheories to Explain MER as a Research Field

We see that the need for a metatheory has been addressed before in both educational studies and in MER.[39] If MER constitutes a subset of the field of education, then one may begin to address the need for a metatheory by adopting such a rationale. Exploration of the need is therefore an ontologically, epistemologically, and methodologically salient task that, if successfully executed, would place the range of epistemic approaches within the mathematics educational community, including integral theory, within a broader metatheory.

To understand how MER evolved as a research field, we need to understand how each particular metatheory among its philosophical precursors has evolved, and in turn, we need to ask the following question: what has been left out of this particular metatheory? Hermeneutics begins as an interpretative metatheory unable to account for knowledge outside itself, including the ULQ of integral theory. Then the emergence of constructivism may be seen as a patch[40] that covers the incompleteness of hermeneutics with a new perspective that effectively omits ontology (including the LLQ of integral theory) and preserves the old perspective (including the ULQ of integral theory), which cannot account for ontology. In turn, the emergence of pragmatism may be seen as a patch to cover the incompleteness of constructivism with a new perspective that includes the possibility of ontology (including the URQ of integral theory) but confuses the nature of ontology with the identifiable patterns found in experimental conditions, and in this manner, it comes to privilege the utility of finding patterns (as if closure always holds) over debates about what this perspective itself is unable to conceive of (an open stratified/differentiated world). In addition, the emergence of postmodernism may be seen as a patch that covers the incompleteness of pragmatism with a new perspective (including the LRQ of integral theory) that, while preserving the possibility of ontology found within the old perspective (including the URQ of integral theory), remains unable to theorize ontology in practice; that is, postmodernism lacks a conceptual detachment from reality, and in this manner, it resorts to encouraging a view of the world as a complex of clusters or networks of concepts in the form of purely discursive ontological realities.

Diachronically, the logical progression of MER's philosophical precursors may be understood as follows: seventeenth century, hermeneutics → eighteenth century, transcendental idealism (founding philosophy of the traditionally recognized forms of constructivism) → nineteenth century, pragmatism → twentieth century, postmodernism → twenty-first century, the ontological turn.

More generally, I propose that the necessity to employ multiple metatheories (including in MER) may be understood in four moments of evolution through history. Each moment in the analysis of this evolution may be seen as proceeding sequentially by identifying Achilles' heels in its metatheoretical precursor, from its first moment in seventeenth century hermeneutics (as the metatheory that cannot sustain a dimension of knowledge outside the appeal to inward narratives and experiences, to its second moment in eighteenth century transcendental idealism (as it omits to theorize worldly grounds for choosing among rival metatheories), to its third moment in nineteenth-century pragmatism (as it posits correctly the possibility of ontological knowledge independently of our theories, but it tends to favour utility over theory), and including but not limited to its fourth moment in twentieth century postmodernism (which, without omitting or denying ontological knowledge, tends to promote a view of the world as exhausted by concepts). Therefore, the idea of absence or incompleteness as a mechanism that drives developmental change in metatheories diachronically through four moments in history effectively helps us to explain the development and expansion of MER as a research field in its own right.

Conclusion: A Metatheory of and for Twenty-First-Century Mathematics Education Research

In this chapter, I have reviewed the persistent challenges and the role of metatheory in mathematics education studies with reference to two metatheories: critical realism and integral theory. I have argued that critical realism may hold the ontologically least restrictive viewpoint available, the epistemologically least weak position, and a methodologically capable stance by which to begin to overcome reductionism. To exemplify critical realist metatheoretical coordinates in practice, I have explained how integral theory (1M) (self-consciously) commits the epistemic fallacy, together with the fallacies of (2E) actualism and ontological monovalence, including (3L) atomism, and in its (4D) unsustainable transformative agency. This critique has shown that the trouble with integral theory is not, as Hampson (2007) argues, a lack of sufficient coherence or rigour,[41] nor that it represents, as Rutzou (2012) argues, a venomous chalice.[42] Rather, it is the banality of the integral-theoretical approach that is terrifyingly normal, to use Arendtian terms. And like so many other unoriginal metatheories, integral theory is strictly non-dialectical, a fact that has been illustrated in learning about a passage through the MELD dialectic.[43] Because integral theory fails at every moment in the passage from (1M) non-identity/structure, to (2E) negativity, to (3L) totality, to (4D) transformative agency of the critical realist dialectic, it is thus strictly non-dialectical. If, as Hampson concludes, the way to remedy the omissive absences of integral theory is through dialectical logic,[44] this should be taken, indeed, as I have illustrated, through this critical realist dialectical logic. Therefore, I have included the AQAL tetra-domains as part of a dialectical phenomenology that can be used to explain the development and expansion of MER as a research field and for the purpose of meeting MER's initial call for a twenty-first-century metatheory. In this manner, I have provided an exploration of a metatheory of and for MER with the wholehearted desire to encourage this community to begin to question the taken-for-granted or implicit ontological realities that inform the plurality of their theories.

Acknowledgements

I am happy and grateful that Routledge has agreed to publish a companion volume based on the dialogue between critical realism and integral theory. I am very grateful to the editors for this opportunity. I owe an enormous debt to Mervyn Hartwig for his stimulating comments, questions, and revisions to an earlier version. With love, this chapter is dedicated to him.

Notes

1 Whereas the transposition of existence and method into a hermeneutic approach studied what being mathematically educated actually meant for the new era, for example in Anderson (2002, p. 20), the transposition of existence and method into a linguistic approach argued for mathematical thinking qua multi-semiotic communicating, see for example Morgan (2006) and Sfard's (2008).
2 Dorier (2008) provides a historical account of MER's development, scope, and its legitimacy.
3 In Lerman's (2006, p. 8) analysis of the plurality of epistemic approaches employed in MER, we can find at least four of the most predominant philosophies that were firmly in place by the end of the last century: hermeneutics, constructivism (social or otherwise), postmodernism, and pragmatism. These four constitute MER's metatheoretical precursors to a large extent. Lerman's significance was not only the detailed delineation of MER's plurality; he also began to suspect that its very existence is problematic.
4 Bikner-Ahsbahs and Prediger (2006, p. 56) initially expressed the open need for a metatheory, inviting mathematics education researchers to inquire into new theories, methods, paradigms, or strategies capable of addressing MER's research values.
5 To clarify the relationship between a metatheory and a theory, we consider that in MER, Schoenfeld (2002) aligns perfectly with Edwards' (2008) view of integral metatheory, where they argue that the role of metatheory is to formulate questions regarding the aim of a theory, its logical structure, and the range of evaluating criteria to assess its

adequacy. In this chapter, however, we may take the metatheoretical vantage point of critical realism taken from Bhaskar and Danermark (2006) in perceiving no absolute differentiation among the theoretical, metatheoretical, and philosophical stances, as they are essentially referring to or describing the same reality, the same world, at different levels of abstraction.

6 Some examples of (dialectical) critical realist applications include Norrie's (2010) investigations of the philosophical underpinnings of justice, as well as my own work (see Nunez, 2013, 2014, 2015a, 2015b, 2016), all with the guiding premise of emancipatory intentionality.

7 This chapter mainly limits itself to basic critical realism. Within basic critical realism, there are three main groups of theory: transcendental realism, a philosophy of science (see Bhaskar, 2008/1975); critical naturalism, a philosophy of social science (see Bhaskar, 2007/1979); and the theory of explanatory critique, a philosophical theory of value (see Bhaskar, 2009/1986). The concept of explanatory critique is the means by which critical realists aim to resolve the dichotomy between facts and values. The notion of explanatory critique may be illustrated succinctly in three simple stages: (1) commitment to critiquing false or inadequate beliefs; (2) critique of action that is grounded in false beliefs; and (3) removal of the causes of false beliefs. For more on the second phase of dialectical critical realism, see Bhaskar (2008/1993), and for more on the third phase of the philosophy of metaReality, see Bhaskar (2012/2002).

8 The initial endo-phase of integral theory may be understood as an internal voyage or what Ken Wilber, its chief proponent, saw as a vision or perspective from within, mainly concerned with reductionisms; for example, see Wilber (1995, p. 115) and his notion of flatland in Wilber (2000, pp. 70–73). The second ecto-phase took Wilber's integral theory externally in a quest for an all-encompassing, indeed integral, paradigm capable of combining and connecting knowledge from a variety of scientific, philosophical, and even mystical-spiritual fields of study (see Wilber, 2006, p. 1); and the third phase of in praxis may be understood as the new beginning, a dawn in vision referring to an integral era in which we see its applications in action (Wilber, 2010, p. 431). The development of the application of integral theory remains an ongoing project. See Marshall (2016) for a succinct history and critical realist critique of integral theory.

9 See Bhaskar with Hartwig (2010) and Collier (1994) for introductions.

10 Esbjörn-Hargens and Wilber (2006, p. 529).

11 There is, however, work that contributes to re-enchanting the existing communication between critical realists and integral theorists; in particular, it is important to differentiate between Wilber's writings and others in the integral community. See, for example, the contributions of Gary Hampson (2007), Paul Marshall (2012, 2016), and Tim Rutzou (2012). In this volume and its predecessor, *Metatheory for the Twenty-First Century: Critical Realism and Integral Theory in Dialogue* (2016), see, for example, Bruce Alderman, Tom Murray, Paul Marshall, and Leigh Price.

12 Bhaskar (2007/1979, p. 8).

13 See Hartwig (2007b, pp. 105–108). An omissive critique involves transcendental argument. It is a type of metacritique$_1$, which takes the inner logic of an opposing argument and identifies the absences, lacks, or omissions of transcendentally necessary categories, and in doing so, brings out the interrelatedness of the contradictions or compromised formations needed to sustain faulty argumentation in practice. The nature of this chapter's argument is also dialectical; that is, it follows Roy Bhaskar's (2008/1993) logic of MELD. Here, dialectical logic is understood to be a passage through the transcendentally necessary categories of 1M: non-identity; 2E: negativity; 3L: totality; and 4D: transformative agency.

14 See Bhaskar (2008/1993, p. 104) for more on the linguistic fallacy, and for more on the epistemic fallacy see Bhaskar (2008/1975, p. 28).

15 See Mearman (2006).

16 See Esbjörn-Hargens (2010b).

17 Marshall (2016) highlights further differences between weak and strong constructivism.

18 See Hartwig (2007b, pp. 91–96) for succinct introductions to the main dualisms in social theory and their resolution via critical naturalism in tabular form.
19 Wilber (2005, p. 36).
20 See Hartwig (2007a, pp. 62–64). Triumphalism, along with centrism and endism, is an error of irrealism. It refers to the overweening appeal of power to control, to know, to have, and so on. Triumphalism entails (→) endism, a view of the future in which social change has plateaued or halted, and it is entrained by centrism, a view that takes human beings as the purposeful centre of their universe. The logical progression is as follows: centrism → triumphalism → endism.
21 These integral theorists, like many researchers, do not naturally begin by differentiating between ontology and epistemology. In some cases, investigators tend to avoid asking questions about presuppositions, and others even deny reality, a common strategy of containment indicating an implicit metatheoretical stance. Bhaskar (2007/1979, p. 192) coined the term 'natural attitude' to denote a stance in which one does not differentiate between ontology and epistemology because ontology becomes important when what is declared to pass for alethic knowledge is unsatisfying.
22 The necessity of implementing transcendental argumentation refers to the ontological metatheorems of critical realism.
23 See Bhaskar's (2008/1975) concept of actualism in Chapter 2.
24 See Wilber's (2000, pp. 70–73) notion of 'flatland' as an umbrella term for reductionism.
25 Bhaskar (2008/1993, p. 5).
26 This idea of an Achilles' heel critique is advantageous because this is not any arbitrarily weak point; it is the point at which the theory's proponents deem it strongest. See Bhaskar (2008/1993, p. 340).
27 A sequence of Achilles' heel critiques is denoted as dialectical phenomenology; see Nunez (2015a, 2016) for examples.
28 A similar argument can be made if we substitute women and slaves for historically marginalized communities—such as members of the LGBT+, #MeToo, or Black Lives Matter movements—living in today's democracies, say, in the time of Trump. It would be patently ridiculous to argue along the lines of integral theory when the analytic point is more about merely being aware that these communities are being excluded, rather than including them in society via an actual fight for human rights. These examples illustrate why the integral-theoretical transposition of change via a simple awareness of exclusion fails in reality.
29 Lotz-Sisitka (2015, pp. 318–339).
30 Norrie (2010, pp. 3–15).
31 Bhaskar and Danermark (2006, p. 281).
32 Bhaskar (2008/1975, 2010).
33 See Esbjörn-Hargens and Wilber (2006) and Martin (2008) for an overview of IMP. In brief, IMP is guided by three pragmatic principles: non-exclusion, enfoldment, and enactment. Non-exclusion refers to the acceptance of knowledge claims previously approved by their respective paradigm and scientific community, enfoldment refers to the recognition that some methodologies are more comprehensive than others, and enactment refers to the claim that a variety of inquiries will reveal diverse phenomena.
34 Scott (2000, p. 2).
35 Bhaskar (2009/1986, p. 101 f.).
36 Esbjörn-Hargens (2006, p. 79).
37 See Chapter 4 of Nunez (2014) for examples of *laminated systems* in education and other scientific fields, including the work of Leigh Price in Volume 2.
38 Bhaskar (2010, p. 5).
39 In education, see Aldridge et al. (1992); in MER, see Bikner-Ahsbahs and Prediger (2006); and in integral theory, see Wallis (2010).
40 See Nunez (2015a) for a more complete analysis of MER via a dialectical phenomenology of the metatheories that constitute it generally, including the traditionally recognized

forms of theories of activity, and ethnomathematics. See Nunez (2013, p. 48; 2016) for examples of patching.
41 Hampson (2007, p. 110).
42 Rutzou (2012, p. 215).
43 Nunez (2014, p. 9).
44 Hampson (2007, p. 147). In fact, integral theory is perfectly consistent with its own internal logic of irrealism, its knowledge claims founded on constructivism with applications rooted in pragmatism.

References

Aldridge, J., Kuby, P., & Strevy, D. (1992). Developing a metatheory of education. *Psychological Reports*, 70(3), 683–687.

Anderson, J. (2002). Being mathematically educated in the twenty-first century: What should it mean? In L. Haggarty (ed.), *Teaching Mathematics in Secondary Schools: A Reader*. The Open University.

Benjamin, E. (2006). Integral mathematics: An AQAL approach. *Journal of Integral Theory and Practice*, 1(4), 65–90.

Bhaskar, R. (2007). Theorising ontology. In C. Lawson, J.S. Latsis, & N.M.O. Martins (eds), *Contributions to Social Ontology*. Routledge.

Bhaskar, R. (2007/1979). *The Possibility of Naturalism: A Philosophical Critique of the Contemporary Human Sciences* (eBook edn). Routledge.

Bhaskar, R. (2008/1975). *A Realist Theory of Science* (eBook edn). Routledge.

Bhaskar, R. (2008/1993). *Dialectic: The Pulse of Freedom* (eBook edn). Routledge.

Bhaskar, R. (2009/1986). *Scientific Realism and Human Emancipation* (eBook edn). Routledge.

Bhaskar, R. (2010). Contexts of interdisciplinarity: Interdisciplinarity and climate change. In C. Frank, K.G. Høyer, P. Naess, J. Parker, & R. Bhaskar (eds), *Interdisciplinarity and Climate Change: Transforming Knowledge and Practice for Our Global Future*. Routledge.

Bhaskar, R. (2012/2002). *Reflections on MetaReality: Transcendence, Emancipation, and Everyday Life*. Routledge.

Bhaskar, R., & Danermark, B. (2006). Meta-theory, interdisciplinarity and disability research: A critical realist perspective. *Scandinavian Journal of Disability Research*, 8(4), 278–297.

Bhaskar, R., with Hartwig, M. (2010). *The Formation of Critical Realism: A Personal Perspective*. Routledge.

Bhaskar, R., Esbjörn-Hargens, S., Hedlund, N., & Hartwig, M. (eds) (2016). *Metatheory for the Twenty-First Century: Critical Realism and Integral Theory in Dialogue*. London: Routledge.

Bikner-Ahsbahs, A., & Prediger, S. (2006). Diversity of theories in mathematics education: How can we deal with it? *ZDM*, 38(1), 52–57.

Collier, A. (1994). *Critical Realism: An Introduction to Roy Bhaskar's Philosophy*. Verso.

Dorier, J. (2008). The development of mathematics education as an academic field. In M. Menghini, F. Furinghetti, L. Giacardi, & F. Arzarello (eds), *The First Century of the International Commission on Mathematical Instruction (1908–2008): Reflecting and Shaping the World of Mathematics Education*. Istituto della Enciclopedia Italiana. Available at https://archive-ouverte.unige.ch/unige:16853 (Accessed 7 July 2020).

Edwards, M. (2008). Evaluating integral metatheory. *Journal of Integral Theory and Practice*, 3(4), 61–83.

Esbjörn-Hargens, S. (2006). Integral research: A multi-method approach to investigating phenomena. *Constructivism in the Human Sciences*, 11(1), 79–107.

Esbjörn-Hargens, S. (2007). Integral teacher, integral students, integral classroom: Applying integral theory to education. *AQAL: Journal of Integral Theory and Practice*, 2(2), 72–103.

Esbjörn-Hargens, S. (2010a). An analysis of climate change: Integral pluralism and the enactment of multiple objects. *Journal of Integral Theory and Practice*, 5(1), 143–174.

Esbjörn-Hargens, S. (2010b). An overview of integral theory: An all-inclusive framework for the twenty-first century. In S. Esbjörn-Hargens (ed.), *Integral Theory in Action: Applied, Theoretical, and Constructive Perspectives on the AQAL Model*. SUNY Press.

Esbjörn-Hargens, S., & Wilber, K. (2006). Toward a comprehensive integration of science and religion: A post-metaphysical approach. In P. Clayton & Z. Simpson (eds), *The Oxford Handbook of Religion and Science*. Oxford University Press.

Hampson, G.P. (2007). Integral re-views postmodernism: The way out is through. *Integral Review*, 4, 108–173.

Hartwig, M. (2007a). Centrism → triumphalism → endism. In M. Hartwig (ed.), *Dictionary of Critical Realism*. Routledge.

Hartwig, M. (2007b). Critical naturalism. In M. Hartwig (ed.), *Dictionary of Critical Realism*. Routledge.

Hartwig, M. (2007c). Critique. In M. Hartwig (ed.), *Dictionary of Critical Realism*. Routledge.

Lerman, S. (2006). Theories of mathematics education: Is plurality a problem? *ZDM*, 38(1), 8–13.

Lotz-Sisitka, H. (2015). Absenting absence: Expanding zones of proximal development in environmental learning processes. In L. Price & H. Lotz-Sisitka (eds), *Critical Realism, Environmental Learning and Social-Ecological Change*. Routledge.

Marshall, P. (2012). The meeting of two integrative metatheories. *Journal of Critical Realism*, 11(2), 188–214.

Marshall, P. (2016). *A Complex Integral Realist Perspective* (eBook edn). Routledge. https://doi.org/10.4324/9781315753485

Martin, J.A. (2008). Integral research as a practical mixed-methods framework. *Journal of Integral Theory and Practice*, 3(2), 155–164.

Mearman, A. (2006). Critical realism in economics and open-systems ontology: A critique. *Review of Social Economy*, 64(1), 47–75.

Morgan, C. (2006). What does social semiotics have to offer mathematics education research? *Educational Studies in Mathematics*, 61, 219–245. https://doi.org/10.1007/s10649-006-5477-x

Norrie, A.W. (2010). *Dialectic and Difference: Dialectical Critical Realism and the Grounds of Justice*. Routledge.

Nunez, I. (2013). Transcending the dualisms of activity theory. *Journal of Critical Realism*, 12(2), 141–165.

Nunez, I. (2014). *Critical Realist Activity Theory: An Engagement with Critical Realism and Cultural-Historical Activity Theory*. Routledge.

Nunez, I. (2015a). Philosophical underlabouring for mathematics education. *Journal of Critical Realism*, 4(2), 181–204.

Nunez, I. (2015b). A dialogical relationship with cultural-historical activity theory: A realist perspective. In D. Scott & E. Hargreaves (eds), *The Sage Handbook of Learning*. SAGE Publications.

Nunez, I. (2016). Theoretical incompleteness: A driving mechanism of evolution in mathematics education research. *The Philosophy of Mathematics Education Journal*, 31, Special Issue: 'The Philosophy of Mathematics Education at ICME 13'. Available at https://socialsciences.exeter.ac.uk/education/research/centres/stem/publications/pmej/pome31/index.html (Accessed 7 July 2020).

Renert, M.E. (2011). *Living Mathematics Education*. Doctoral Dissertation, The University of British Columbia. Available at http://hdl.handle.net/2429/36911 (Accessed 24 August 2013).

Rutzou, T. (2012). Integral theory: A poisoned chalice? *Journal of Critical Realism*, 11(2), 215–224.

Schoenfeld, A.H. (2002). Research methods in (mathematics) education. In L.D. English (ed.), *Handbook of Research in Mathematics Teaching and Learning*. Lawrence Erlbaum Associates.

Scott, D. (2002). *Realism and Educational Research: New Perspectives and Possibilities*. Routledge.

Sfard, A. (2008). *Thinking as Communicating: Human Development, the Growth of Discourses, and Mathematizing*. Cambridge University Press.

Shulman, L.S. (1986). Those who understand: Knowledge growth in teaching. *Educational Researcher*, 15(2), 4–14.

Wallis, S.E. (2010). Toward a science of metatheory. *Integral Review*, 6(3), 73–120.

Wilber, K. (1995). *Sex, Ecology, Spirituality: The Spirit of Evolution*. Shambhala Publications, Inc.

Wilber, K. (1996). *Eye to Eye: The Quest for the New Paradigm*. Shambhala Publications, Inc.

Wilber, K. (2000). *Integral Psychology: Consciousness, Spirit, Psychology, Therapy*. Shambhala Publications, Inc.

Wilber, K. (2005). Introduction to integral theory and practice: IOS basic and the AQAL map. *AQAL: Journal of Integral Theory and Practice*, 1(1), 1–32.

Wilber, K. (2010). Afterword: The dawn of an integral age. In S. Esbjörn-Hargens (ed.), *Integral Theory in Action: Applied, Theoretical, and Constructive Perspectives on the AQAL Model*. SUNY Press.

Wilber, K. (2013). Response to critical realism in defense of integral theory. *Integral Life*. Available at http://integrallife.com/integral-post/response-critical-realism-defense-integral-theory?page=0,4 (Accessed 24 June 2013).

7
COALESCING AND POTENTIALIZING INTEGRATIVE HIGHER EDUCATION

Complex Thought, Critical Realism, Integral Theory, and a Meta-Matrix

Gary Hampson and Matthew Rich-Tolsma

Introduction

The accelerating severity and complexity of the socio-political crisis and its relationship to biospherical devastation urgently calls for new ways of thinking and acting commensurate with the nature and scale of this unprecedented situation. Such thinking needs to be underlaid by apposite theory and philosophy—panoramic in vision, rigorous in detail, complex in character. Education—in the very broadest sense—forms an integral part of this endeavour.

The current chapter advances this understanding in three ways:[1]

1   Positioning Edgar Morin's complex thought (CT), Roy Bhaskar's critical realism (CR), and Ken Wilber's integral theory (IT) as meta-approaches independently contributing to the overarching endeavour.
2   Bringing these three meta-approaches together in a way which points to 'the whole' cluster 'being greater than the sum' of their independent usage; this includes identifying key transversal conceptual areas.
3   Deepening such transversalities through advancing a metatheory matrix of the underlying structures of higher education.

Section 1 sets the stage by contextualizing the complex crises in education that we are currently facing. Section 2 then outlines the three meta-approaches—both in themselves and with respect to (higher) education.[2] In section 3 we explore three transversal threads of interconnection. In section 4, an indication of their potential—and that of integrative higher education theory in general—is explored through the furthering of a 'meta-matrix'—a theoretical framework comprising a three-by-three array of the meta-themes of educational content, educational process and educational system run through the meta-lenses of identity, relationality,

DOI: 10.4324/9781003140313-11

and contextuality (Hampson, 2011). We conclude by summarizing pertinent coalescences of connection with specific regard to prospective vectors of research and praxis.

1   Context: A Complex Crisis

The growth in our knowledge and understanding about the world that has emerged since the enlightenment has led us to encounter a never before imagined level of disorganization and complexity in the course of scientific endeavour (Weaver, 1948), which has led to a substantial reassessment of the scientific process as a principal means of knowledge production (Kuhn, 1972; Feyerabend, 1975; Bhaskar, 1978; Du Preez, 1980). At the same time the growing connectivity defined both by technology and a shared Earth identity (Morin, 1998) have contributed to a growing awareness of the wicked problems that humanity now faces. Wicked problems (a term originally coined by Rittel and Webber (1973)) may be understood in terms of a wide range of defining characteristics (Rittel & Webber, 1973; Ritchey, 2011; Conklin, 2001; Roberts, 2000; cf. the concept of 'social messes' in Horn (2001)), but most essentially they can be understood as ill-defined problems with unknown problem resolutions. Some wicked problems which humankind is presently facing include climate change, global systemic violence, unwise technological development, unaccountable structures of social control, the nexus of hegemonically biased media, endemic forms of poverty, and the sixth mass extinction. We would contend that prevalent contemporary pedagogical practice (what might be termed the 'schooling paradigm') is inherently incapable of addressing these sorts of complex challenges, because it is essentially rooted in a late-modernist worldview.

Worldviews play an essential role in individual and social transformation especially in the context of complex challenges (Hedlund-De Witt, 2013). This obviously has profound implications for the field of education. When viewed in this light the process of learning may be understood as a dialectic process of consciousness transformation (Freire, 1970; Mezirow, 1985, 1991, 1997, 1998, 2000) which manifests as a developmental embrace of increasingly complex understandings of reality (Cook-Greuter, 2000; Dawson, 2000; Fischer, 1980). For this reason, we have elsewhere (Hampson & Rich-Tolsma, 2015) identified transformative learning as the process which facilitates the transformative emergence from the late-modernist into a reconstructive postmodernist worldview as well as being one of the chief results of this transformation.

Hampson (2011) identifies the prevalence of late modernism—along with its key underlying structure of 'modern atomism'—as a dominant worldview systemically prevalent in the field of education. This worldview is characterized as overly economistic, technicist, and reductionistic; it seeks to understand the world in linear and mechanistic ways and relies on a contracted form of rational empiricism as the basis for uncovering truth. Wilber describes this sort of reductionism in the right-hand quadrants as 'flatland' (Wilber, 1996, p. 389) and states that it is particularly indicative of (orange) rational consciousness (Wilber, 2000). Bhaskar (1978) understands this worldview also in terms of positivist science which he identifies as committing the epistemic fallacy (Bhaskar, 1978; Collier, 1994) and committing two category errors: the 'derealization of reality' and the 'desocialization of science' (Bhaskar, 1986, p. 171).

The schooling paradigm has both military and economic origins; in this sense politics and education have always been intertwined. The original aim of school was to create malleable citizens who could serve as soldiers or as an unquestioning source of labour in service of the central goal of economic growth (Cremin, 1970; Hern, 2003; Gatto, 2001). One metatheoretical framing of the late-modernist worldview which thus seems highly appropriate in terms of education is that of Reductive Human Capital Theory (RHCT). It is in this vein that Stein (2013, p. 6) points out that:

> RHCT is, by definition, incapable of dealing with complexity, agency, or dialectal and communicative reason. This is because, using Bhaskar's terminology, RHCT is *ontologically monovalent*—a form of thought committed to reducing the ontological complexity of education as much as possible, concerned only with the control and prediction of closed systems.

In terms of curriculum development this has led to the growing prevalence of a social efficiency curriculum paradigm (Schiro, 2007) which views curriculum as a product rather than a process (Kelly, 2004) and in which teachers are viewed as technicians who 'deliver' a 'teacher-proof' curriculum. Behaviour modification is therefore at the centre of this approach which seeks to actively rob learners of their agency and freedom in an attempt to process human capital as efficiently as possible. In fact, Kelly (2004, p. 71) points out that,

> to adopt this kind of industrial model for education is to assume that it is legitimate to mould human beings, to modify their behaviour, according to certain clear-cut intentions without making any allowance for their own individual wishes, desires or interests.

In keeping with the RHCT theme this paradigm emphasizes three core factors: (1) the concept of learning as being equivalent to change in human behaviour; (2) the creation and sequencing of learning experiences (in contrast, for instance, to a possibly more emergent approach); and (3) accountability to clients for whom educators work, in most cases the state, which is driven by economic interests (Schiro, 2007). In the classroom this translates into a narrative relationship in which teachers become narrating subjects and learners become static objects who are expected to simply retain petrified pieces of information that possess no apparent relevance to their lives (Freire, 1997). Likewise, testing becomes dislocated from any genuinely meaningful measure of growth; instead efficiency has effectively trumped justice as a guiding principle (Stein, 2013). In this paradigm, testing is used as a way of sifting human capital to more efficiently channel 'manpower'; accordingly, new technologies which support mass-produced, high-stakes administration of assessment have overtaken and—in most cases—completely replaced testing approaches that are more deeply rooted in the science of learning.

2 The Meta-Approaches and Their Educational Discourses

Morin's Complex Thought

Morin was born in Paris in 1921, making him more than two decades older that the founders of the other two meta-approaches, and the only one whose work has been directly influenced by World War II (Morin, 1946; Montuori, 2008). Morin, a sociologist by training, was originally an active member of the French Communist Party, but was subsequently expelled in 1951. At the time of his retirement, Morin was Emeritus Director of the National Center of Scientific Research and co-founder and Director of the prestigious Edgar Morin Centre of the School for Advanced Studies in the Social Sciences, both in Paris. He is presently involved in the creation of the Multiversidad Mundo Real Edgar Morin[3] in Mexico. His writing has a continental flavour, in some ways reminiscent of his contemporary French philosophers such as Derrida (Montuori, 2004): it tends to be somewhat poetic, playful, humble, and self-reflexive. He also has an ongoing propensity to collaborate creatively with artists—something rather rare in the social sciences (Montuori, 2004). His work uniquely integrates such discourses as complex systems science, poststructuralism, and neo-Marxism into an encyclopedic, transformative whole—one imbued with both humour and curiosity. Morin's (1992, 2008) writing has been driven by the search for a method that would enable understanding of the complexity of humanity. This quest forms the basis for the development of Earth-citizenship, and concomitant ethics for the human genre (Morin, 1992, 1999, 2004, 2008). It is facilitated through taking action against knowledge-mutilating principles—such as disjunction, closed specialization, undue reduction, and false rationality—in favour of pertinent knowledge (Morin, 1999). Morin also adopts a dialogic principle in his work; this entails bringing ideas (both complimentary and contradictory) into relationship with one another in order to better identify and understand the complex nature of reality (Morin, 1992; Dobuzinskis, 2004; Montuori, 2004). Morin's dialogic emphasis stems from his Hegelian roots (Montuori, 2004, 2008; Doduzinskis, 2004). It differs from Hegel's dialectic, however, in that it does not offer any guaranteed synthetic resolution (Montuori, 2004). All the above can be identified as CT—an approach not without its challenges (Morin, 2006).[4] Ontological features of CT include the foregrounding of open systems, feedback loops and a holographic geometry. Phenomenological reality is understood as emerging and evolving in complex systems through a process of recursive organization—*self-eco-re-organizing systems*. Epistemological features of CT stem from an understanding of the organization of knowledge and its history—leading Morin to be oriented by transdisciplinarity. Through this, the global, multi-dimensional, complex and contextual are addressed; there is an integration regarding the role of the knower; and its meta-paradigmatic character enables the questioning of disciplinary assumptions. Transdisciplinary is identified by Morin as mostly inquiry-driven, and a degree of creative eclecticism is allowed. Human beings are identified as *homo complexus* (with all the dualities that entails), whilst due recognition is given to the difference between signifiers and signifieds, coupled with the resultant care required when attempting to speak about ontology.

Complex Thought and (Higher) Education

Morin is the only one of the founders of the three meta-approaches that has written extensively on education. The most thorough discussion occurs in the UNESCO-sponsored book *Seven Complex Lessons in Education for the Future* (Morin, 1999). Its key points can be summarized as follows:

- *Lucid veracity in education* ('Detecting error and illusion')—Morin points out that we humans have psychological and cultural propensities which make us vulnerable to error and illusion. Apropos, part of education's job should be to directly address such topics as rationality and rational uncertainty (including due self-vigilance). The situation is made worse by adherence to *blinding paradigms* such as the Cartesian dissociation of objective and subjective knowledge. Furthermore, ideas should be understood as mediating, but distinct from, reality: the only ideas we should trust are ideas that include the idea that the real resists the idea. Education should therefore facilitate the competence of construct-aware lucidity.
- *Pertinence in education* ('Principles of pertinent knowledge')—Morin argues that the dominant thrust of education is toward the disjuncture of *closed specialization, reductionism,* and *false rationality*: knowledge becomes dislocated and petrified. Such a template obscures attempts at aptly addressing the global, the multi-dimensional, the complex, and the contextual. 'We should teach methods of grasping mutual relations and reciprocal influences between parts and the whole in a complex world' (p. 1).
- *Complex human identity in education* ('Teaching the human condition')—Morin notes that human beings possess—at the least—physical, biological, cultural, social, and historical dimensions: we are *homo complexus*. Education should therefore directly address our complex nature. The disciplinary structure of knowledge, on the other hand, disintegrates—even mutilates—this complexity. Transdisciplinarities are therefore called for (Morin, 2008).
- *Planetary consciousness in education* ('Earth identity')—Morin argues that education needs to prioritize addressing the planetary nature of our present and future situation—we all share the same fate. Such a perspective would address both the beneficial and destructive effects of the rapidly accelerating geo-political inter-connectivity of the Earth since the sixteenth century. This includes address of the contemporary ecological crisis.
- *Uncertainty in education* ('Confronting uncertainty')—Morin indicates that whilst modern science has revealed many certainties, it has also provided us

with at least a similar amount of uncertainties—in the physical, biological, and social sciences. Given this, he argues that these uncertainties should play an essential part of education. There should be a prioritization of the teaching of complex systems and strategic principles for aptly addressing chance, chaos, and uncertainty.

- *Understanding in education* ('Understanding each other')—Morin indicates that a key purpose of education should be the development of understanding rather than the mere acquisition of information. He identifies communication as operating both inter-objectively and inter-subjectively, and that understanding is both the means and ends of communication. As a first step, education is required to identify and overcome obstacles to understanding, including egocentrism, ethnocentrism, and reductionism. He states that, 'if we learn to understand before condemning, we will be on the way to humanizing human relations' (p. 52), and that such ethics of understanding are developed through comprehensive thinking, continuous introspection, and open heartedness.
- *Ethics in education* ('Ethics for the human genre')—Last but not least, Morin addresses the interrelationship between human individual, society, and species with respect to critical awareness and action (*anthropo-ethics*). In this, he sees education as playing a core role. He posits that 'moral lessons' are insufficient for engendering the ethical sense required for true human expression and that instead it is necessary to cultivate a deep understanding of what it means to deeply embody individual autonomy, participate in community, and be aware of the responsibilities inherent in belonging to the human species. This ethical awareness helps to prepare us for the move towards the ethical-political imperative of realizing our Earth citizenship by way of democracy and fulfilment of humanity as a planetary community.

There is some reference made to Morin in discourse addressing complexity approaches to education (e.g., Mennin, 2010), but these should be distinguished from literature which shows a more thorough integration of Morin's ideas. Although Morin draws inspiration from complex adaptive systems research, his work has a far richer character than a narrow interpretation of this field: the move is from complex systems to a complexity paradigm (Morin, 1982). CT brings together a range of seemingly disparate perspectives united by a deep yet subtle spiritual impulse (Montuori, 2004). As a result, he is able to overcome many of the pitfalls of other complexity approaches, such as those identified by Brown (2010). Much of the educational literature arising from CT addresses *critical education* (e.g., Alhadeff-Jones, 2010). This suggests more direct links to critical education than is found in the other two meta-approaches examined. Morin's approach has also had significant impact upon the practice of academic research, both from the perspectives of complexity (Alhadeff-Jones, 2009) and transdisciplinarity (Del Re, 2008; Del Mello, 2008). Morin's dialogic approach, along with his epistemological and ontological position, necessitates an explicitly transdisciplinary engagement with knowledge (see e.g., Morin, 2008).

Bhaskar's Critical Realism

Roy Bhaskar first began to develop a new philosophy of science whilst working towards a PhD in Economics exploring the relevance of economic theory for under-developed countries at Oxford University. His approached developed over three decades of independent scholarship; prior to his recent death, his position was as 'World Scholar' at the Institute of Education, University of London. The discursive point of departure for Bhaskar's work is therefore that of the philosophy of science, specifically in relation to the British analytical school (Hartwig, 2008). A key purpose has been to create a viable alternative to positivism, a paradigm which has dominated scientific discourse in the modern era (Bhaskar, 1978). In so doing, Bhaskar has established himself as one of the most significant realist thinkers in the last 35 years (Baehr, 1990).[5] CR has continued to grow in influence.[6] It nonetheless remains on the periphery of philosophical discourse (Shipway, 2002): its radicality is seen not to easily connect with any 'epistemic point of view that has contemporary standing' (Corson, 1991a, p. 189). In terms of style and tone, Bhaskar's writing tends to be dense and critical; the prevalence of new terms and acronyms leads to a comparison with Hegel's writing (N. Hedlund, 2012). Ontologically, CR involves a transcendental realism—a realism which has ontological depth, one which hierarchically nests the domain of the empirical within that of the actual which itself is nested within the real (Bhaskar, 1978). Other key ontological features include the emergent character of ontological strata,[7] and a clear differentiation between intransitive and transitive dimensions[8] (Bhaskar, 1978). Additionally, dialectical thought indicates the primacy of ontological absence (Shipway, 2002; Bhaskar, 2008). Bhaskar distinguishes between open and closed systems, and also introduces the notion of the laminated system in which it is impossible to refer to one level of the system without reference to others (see e.g., Bhaskar et al., 2010). One example of such a laminated system is the four planar social being.[9] Bhaskar argues for an emergent or evolutionary model of reality by recognizing seven evolving levels of human agency and collectivity—seven scalar social-being[10] (Bhaskar in Bhaskar et al., 2010)—and seven stadia of the ontological-axiological chain of being[11] (Bhaskar, 2002a, 2008, 2012). Epistemologically, CR views science as a social activity about real things: a process in which transitive knowledge is generated in reference to intransitive mechanisms (Bhaskar, 1978). Additionally, Bhaskar posits that truth may be conceptualized as comprising concepts of *referential detachment*[12] and *alethic truth*,[13] as well as a concept which he refers to as the *judgment form*[14] (Bhaskar, 2008). The attempt to reduce ontology to epistemology is identified as the *epistemic fallacy* (Bhaskar, 1978; Collier, 1994). Other concerns include the attempt to reduce the real to the actual (*actualism*) and the attempt to account for ontology solely with regard to the positive, rather than acknowledging absence (*ontological monovalence*) (Bhaskar, 2008). Methodologically, the notion of *explanatory critique* problematizes the imaginary that facts can be absolutely differentiated from values; whereas *immanent critique* is a philosophical method which reveals internal contradictions within a philosophical or sociological system by employing its own logic.[15] Alongside these critical approaches, the notions of induction and deduction are transcended by *retroduction*, 'the move from a manifest phenomenon to an idea of a generative mechanism, which if it were real would account for the phenomenon in question' (N. Hedlund, 2012, p. 9). In terms of the disciplinary orientation of epistemology, CR valorises inter- and transdisciplinarity.

Critical Realism and (Higher) Education

Although Bhaskar himself had not written much on the field of education explicitly, before his death he was involved in editing a book series on critical realist education.[16] Of particular note in the CR literature on higher education is Ronald Barnett's (2012) *Imagining the University*. Barnett uses CR to dismantle prevalent conceptions of the university, and instead proposes that we imagine feasible utopias of the university built upon imaginative ideas and an optimistic, sensitive understanding of the deep structures underlying the institutions of higher learning. As a philosophy of science, CR has direct implications for research—see e.g., Scott (2005) regarding the relevance of CR to empirical educational research.[17] Corson (1990a, 1990b, 1991a, 1991b, 1997, 1998, 1999a, 1999b) provides a wide-ranging critique of particular philosophical approaches in education (most notably Dewey, Popper, and Quine). Additionally, Archer (1979) has provided important foundational work in the application of CR to the macroscopic investigation of how educational systems come into being. CR is most frequently encountered as an alternative knowledge paradigm being used as the basis for educational inquiry. It is used as the ontological (transcendental realist), epistemological (critical relativist), and methodological (explanatory critique) approach for specific research inquiries in the field of education (McGray, 2012; Soetaert, 2008; Loveday, 2009; Shipway, 2002).[18] It is interesting to note that of the four theses identified, two deal with the organizational aspect of higher education (in the broadest possible sense): Loveday (2009) explores cross-functional collaboration at community colleges, while Soetaert (2008) offers a CR-based analysis of strategic change in higher education. Shipway's (2002) thesis[19] stands out as the only doctoral thesis (to our knowledge) that deals exclusively with the implications of CR for education in a more holistic sense. Shipway expands upon the role of CR as an antidote to many of the problems facing educational research. He also provides an in-depth and wide-ranging exploration of the implications of CR for curriculum development as a test case for the application of CR in the philosophy of education. Shipway also examines the relevance of CR's emancipatory mission to the field of education. This is a theme which has subsequently been picked up by McGray (2012), whose doctoral research explores a CR approach to the topics of capacity building and citizenship education in light of global hegemony. The implication of the emancipatory and ethical aspects of CR are thus far reaching, indicating the emergent social-change agenda with broad implications in the educational field.[20] The value of CR for the development of curriculum is further expanded by Wheelahan's (2012) sociological arguments for the central value of academic knowledge in curricula. Additional applications in the literature along these lines include critical realist engagement with instructional design and technology (Evans, 2011), assessment (Dobson & Dale, In Press), the emancipatory capacity of science education (Zembylas, 2006), emancipation with respect to learning disabilities (Warner, 1993), and the education of Indigenous populations (Sarra, 2012).

Wilber's Integral Theory

Wilber is an autodidactic American philosopher with a background in transpersonal psychology and Buddhism. He is sometimes announced as one of the most popular, and most translated, of contemporary American philosophers. His writing often has something of an extraverted style. Whilst his writings prior to 1997[21] can be understood in relation to creating and contributing to IT, IT as such emerged explicitly in Wilber (1997). This emergence was enabled by his magnum opus, *Sex, Ecology, Spiritualty* (1995) which bears something of the scope of Tarnas' earlier *Passion of the Western Mind* (1993). Evolution is identified with respect to Eros, a universal or *kosmic* driver, whilst Eros is located with respect to the contrasting forces of *Agape* (descend-and-include), *Phobos* (ascend-and-exclude), and *Thanatos* (descend-and-exclude) (Wilber, 1995). Wilber also forwards Koestler's notion of *holon*, a concept which indicates that all things are simultaneously wholes and parts. Additionally, Wilber brings together the insights of other integral theorists including Sri Aurobindo and Jean Gebser. Regarding ontology and epistemology, Wilber argues that they are 'two mutually enactive and co-existing dimensions interactively resonating in the living Kosmos' (Wilber, 2013). Modernist reductionism is concomitantly critiqued as a 'flatland' ontology. IT ontology (see Esbjörn-Hargens, 2010) and epistemology (see Fuhs, n.d.) are understood through his AQAL model (Wilber, 1996, 1997, 2000a, 2000b, 2007a).[22] Methodologically, IT indicates the legitimacy of an integral methodological pluralism which uses first- and third-person (i.e. interior and exterior) views of each of its four quadrants to render eight distinct perspectival zones, each of which is resonant with a particular type of methodology—ranging from phenomenology to systems theory (Wilber, 2007a).

Integral Theory and (Higher) Education

Although Wilber has not written much on education, he has indicated that it is one of the most crucial areas of application for IT (Wilber, 2000, 2008). Following Wilber's explicit identification of IT in 1997, a few educational articles have mentioned Wilber in passing (Miller, 1999), but the focus on education (including higher education) with respect to IT has developed in a more focused way following Esbjörn-Hargens (2005). Two volumes on Integral Education were published in 2010—Esbjörn-Hargens, Reams, and Gunnlaugson (2010a) and Dea (2010a)—the former solely addressing higher education (in the broadest sense), including reference to non-Wilberian forms of Integral Education (e.g., Ferrer et al., 2010; Ryan, 2010). Themes identified from the literature are exemplified by the following:

- *Contexts, history, and theoretical identification*—Hampson (2010), Molz and Hampson (2010), Esbjörn-Hargens, Reams, and Gunnlaugson (2010b), Murray (2009).
- *General educational considerations*—Esbjörn-Hargens (2005, 2010), Toroyson (2010), Steckler and Torbert (2010), Reams (2010a).
- *Curriculum design, course development, and institutional renewal*—Renert and Davis (2010), Kreisberg (2010), Stack (2010), O'Fallon (2010a), Wheal (2000), Lloyd and Wallace (2004), Zierer (2011), Schmidt (2010); specifically including *spirituality*—Iannone and Obenauf (1999), Astin (2010); and *ecological sustainability*—Conway (2012), Renert and Davis (2012), Akiyami, Li, and Onuki (2012).
- *Pedagogy/andragogy*, including the significance of: *interior perspectives*—Martineau and Reams (2010), Gruber (2010); *dialogue*—Gunnlaugson (2010), Reams (2010b), Bronson and Gangadean (2010); and *experiential embodiment*—Wieler (2010), O'Fallon (2010b), Dea (2010b, 2010c).
- *Assessment*—Klein (2012), Davis (2010a, 2010b), Dawson and Stein (2011).
- *Case studies* such as regarding health care education—Kreisberg (2010), Pesut (2012).

3 Connecting the Three: Three Transversal Lenses

Having provided an overview of the territory of each meta-approach and its relationship to education, we are now in a position to transversally explore connections between them. The following provides an indicative reading of key transversal areas of higher education by looking through the lenses of philosophy of knowledge, andragogy/heutagogy, and normativity.

Philosophy of Knowledge

With regards to the philosophy of knowledge (implicating both research and 'curriculum'), the three meta-approaches share a common feature which can be understood as *knowledge as involving sufficient panorama*. Following an overview regarding such panorama, we look at two examples: transdisciplinarity and spirituality.

Panorama

A pertinent feature common to the three meta-approaches regarding approach to knowledge is interest in addressing what might roughly be called *the whole*, or more precisely to be signified by a semantic ecosystem[23] involving the terms unity, whole, system, organization, cosmos, planet (CT); totalities, constellation, system, cosmic envelope, unitary ground state of metaReality, non-duality (CR); holarchy, tetra-arising, Kosmos, Being, Spirit, Isness, The One, The All (IT). This differs from the dominant de facto approach to knowledge in higher education which carries the iterative mark of modern atomism (Hampson, 2010), as indicated, for instance, by the dominant prioritization of disciplines and sub-disciplines over the interdisciplinary and transdisciplinary. The *differentiation* of this whole can be identified in its diverse complexity via concepts not only such as physical, biological, psychological, cultural, and societal (CT), but also through discernments including mechanisms, events, experiences, domains, dimensions, strata (CR); and perspectives, holons, types, states, levels, lines, and quadrants (IT). Relationships among these aspects—and between these aspects and the whole—can be further elaborated by using such understandings as complexity, recursion, feedback loops (CT); dialectics, lamination (CR); intersubjectivity, interobjectivity, translation, and transformation (IT). Particular emphases include the notion of higher education as assisting we humans in becoming increasingly conscious of the evolution of consciousness and its complex (e.g., non-linear) character (see e.g., Midgley, 2002). Such metatheoretical lenses frame the complex 'nature of nature' (Morin, 1992) (including human nature) in ways which are often at variance with mainstream higher education approaches. Of specific note, the significance of transitive interiority (how things are relatively experienced on the 'inside' by both individuals and groups/cultures) is highlighted by all three meta-approaches.[24]

Transdisciplinarity

Both the valorisation of transitive interiority and that of frames addressing apt coherences of academic approaches (epistemologies, methodologies, etc.) are enabled by the notion of transdisciplinarity[25] (a notion which has implications for both research and curriculum).[26] Explicitly mediating between the 'two cultures' (Snow, 1998) of the humanities and natural science, transdisciplinarity (in contrast to disciplinary atomization) can more adequately address such complex issues as the human-induced ecological crisis (including global warming, radical biodiversity loss, systemic pollution, and resource depletion). It is also synergistic with the field of higher education, given that education is a particularly complex *open* system (Corson, 1998), one in which CR understandings regarding the causal efficacy of reasons can become a valuable part of sound educational research; and given transdisciplinarity's ability to aptly inquire into the character of particular educational traditions. A particular interpretation of transdisciplinarity is articulated by Nicolescu (2002). This involves relations between ontology and epistemology, multi-dimensionality, transculturalism, ethics, spirituality, and creativity; whilst transdisciplinarity as the 'mode 2 knowledge production' of Gibbons et al. (1994) is characterized by complexity, hybridity, non-linearity, reflexivity, and heterogeneity. From a slightly different angle, CT identifies transdisciplinarity's 'core conditions' as including: its inquiry-driven orientation, a reflexivity regarding meta-paradigmatic assumptions, a sense of the whole regarding the organization of knowledge, the prioritization of contextualization, and the explicit inclusion of the knower (Montuori, 2008). Transdisciplinarity involves at least two levels: whilst at specific levels there is an understanding regarding theoretical and methodological *plurality*, at the metatheoretical level there is a sense of *coherence* or unity. Together these combine as unity-through-complexity. The strong transdisciplinary orientation of the three approaches is concomitant with an interest in providing an appropriate balance regarding the status of the humanities *vis-à-vis* natural science, and the spectrum there between. Explicit in this interest is a serious contestability toward logical positivism and/or its over application. CR offers an alternative philosophy of science to its singular imaginary; IT aptly constrains it—or at least postpositivism—into one quadrant (honouring other modalities of legitimacy for the other three quadrants). Similarly, what might be termed a fundamentalist approach to relativism is also contested by all three approaches. Instead, relativism is relativized, and context-dependency is implicated as dependent on context: the transitive dimension of constructivism has its place (the left-hand quadrants of psychological and cultural realities) but should not *unduly* interfere with other domains.[27] This has implications for the humanities and for poststructuralism.

Spirituality

In contrast to the default imaginaries of both secular modernity and traditional religiosity, an integrative theory of higher education oriented by the three meta-approaches would also have to take spirituality into account. The identification of spirituality is amply articulated through IT (see e.g., Wilber, 2007), and also through Bhaskar's (2012) address of metaReality. IT frames emergence in spiritual terms and locates mystical and meditative traditions as inquiring into and regenerating the perennial philosophy (Wilber, 2000a). Whilst spirituality is less explicated in CT, Montuori (2004) nonetheless identifies a subtle spiritual impulse inherent in Morin's complex worldview as underpinning the totality of his work. Whist spirituality is discussed within higher education discourse (e.g., Shahajahan, 2010; Rockafeller, 2006), its import is still largely underenacted—perhaps thwarted by disciplinary Balkanization (constrained within the sub-discipline of comparative religion): the baby of trans-rational Spirit is still mostly thrown out with the bathwater of sub-rational mythic religion.

Andragogy/Heutagogy

Due to increasing levels of transformative agency and self-reflexivity associated with emerging ontological depth, developmental understanding foreshadows the movement from pedagogy via andragogy (Knowles, 1984, 1990) to heutagogy (Hase & Kenyon, 2000).

Democracy and Dialogue

Through the axiology of freedom, CR valorises, *inter alia*, equality of individual worth regardless of individual potential (Shipway, 2002). The collective extension of this can be understood as leading to CR's and CT's emphasis on democratic processes (Collier, 1994; Shipway, 2002). Such understandings have implications for the way in which higher education is conducted (e.g., inclusive decision making and ownership of the learning process). The democratic impulse of CT and CR synergizes with CT's prioritization of learning through dialogue. It similarly resonates with IT's address of the development of collective interiors through dialogue and developmentally appropriate communication (Gunnlaugson, 2010; Reams, 2010b; Bronson & Gangadean, 2010). The teacher's role is consequently less one regarding the transmission of knowledge and more one regarding the nurturing of meaning, and the facilitation of understanding and emancipation away from illusory (less real) imaginaries. Concomitantly, learners are seen less as objectified knowledge receptacles and more as developing subjects with context-specific histories and trajectories.

Facilitating Interior States

A particular andragogical strategy is the facilitation of particular states of consciousness—both in terms of embodying the dimensions encompassed by the AQAL conceptual map (e.g., Dea, 2010b; Wieler, 2010; O'Fallon, 2010b) as well as with respect to sensory and experiential engagement (Gruber, 2010; Dea, 2010c). The importance of engaging individual interiors through meditative practice (Martineau & Reams, 2010) is also valorised. These andragogical sensibilities oriented by individual interior (e.g., contemplative) and collective interior (e.g., dialogical) emphases sit in contrast to conventional expectations in higher education with respect to the more technicist ('transmission of information') andragogies implied by mainstream course structures. The meta-approaches further indicate that such interior dimensions—as well as exterior ones—can be aptly understood with reference to postformal developmental levels. Cook-Greuter (2003), for example, describes how the integral nature of the emergence of the self-identify developmental line impacts upon dimensions of being, doing, and thinking. Such framings can substantively assist in foregrounding learner-centred (Schiro, 2007) and process-oriented (Kelly, 2004) andragogies (and associated *currere*) in addition to those regarding 'dialogical action' (Freire, 1997). Despite such possibilities, explicit incorporation into university courses both of positive adult development and forms of complex reasoning beyond (Piagetian) formal operations remain a neglected potential.

Normativity[28]

Education is inherently a normative project: facilitating a movement from state A to state B where B is understood in some way as more or better educated, on the understanding that such advancement in education is seen as normatively good. Values are consequently infused throughout. The three meta-approaches offer an ecosystem of normativities regarding higher education. We focus on two indicative lenses: planetary ethics and emancipation.

Widening Ethics to the Planetary

A reading of the broad landscape of ethics from a developmental perspective is offered by IT. This includes the notion of widening spheres of responsibility and care arising with greater developmental depth—for example, from egocentric through nationcentric and worldcentric to kosmocentric. CR's notion of the individual's self-structuration of being (stadia of the axiological-ontological chain) and of the hierarchy of levels of scale (or span) at which social phenomena can be studied (the seven scalar social being) offers an analogous, although not identical, picture. Apt concern for the health of all levels can be identified as facilitated by Basic Moral Intuition—'protecting and promoting the greatest depth for the greatest span' (Wilber, 2000b, p. 510). Within such a framing, CT indicates the critical pertinence of addressing the *worldcentric* level arising from humankind's unique individual↔society↔species feedback loop (Morin, 1999), and its concomitant identification of human as planetary citizen. Such a prioritization would have radical implications for such fields as neoclassical economics, which, through such imaginaries as *homo economicus*, is based on assumptions—and thence de facto encouragement (Morin, 1999)—of egocentric self-interest and national interest rather than planetary interest. Recent trends regarding the 'pragmatization' of course priorities toward such fields as business and technology can also be questioned with respect to such spheres of responsibility: how much are such moves on behalf of the planet as a whole?

Emancipation

Of particular pertinence for higher education is the aim of emancipation (Morin, 1999; Montuori, 2008; Alhadeff-Jones, 2010; Bhaskar, 2008, 2012)—both social and spiritual, and as interpreted through different developmental levels.[29] CT is associated with critical theory (Montuori, 2004; Alhadeff-Jones, 2010) and its interest in *social* emancipation. This is perhaps no surprise given Morin's early involvement in the ideals of communism. Bhaskar's socialist heritage—indeed, the 'critical' of critical realism—also has a resonance with CT in this respect. In terms of the critical nature of the fate of humanity and many other species caused by human-made changes to the planet, Morin's work is very direct in its address, whilst CR provides a robust philosophy of science for such concerns. Additionally, vectors toward *spiritual* emancipation or Enlightenment are emphasized in CR's metaReality and in IT. Emancipation could be understood as resulting from the natural, evolutionary process of holonic emergence arising from the tensions of Eros↔Agape, and Agency↔Communion (tensions which are resolved in the non-dual heart) (Wilber, 2000a). This can be identified as a dialectical process involving the transformative manoeuvre of absenting absence. In the case of higher education, this can be interpreted as helping move stakeholders from unwanted/unneeded sources of determination to wanted/needed ones (Bhaskar, 1986; Collier, 1994; Shipway, 2002). The potential of emancipation as a key purpose of higher education has significance not only for such normativity to be explicitly integrated in social science, education, and the humanities (perhaps in reference to the classical philosophical question pertaining to The Good) but also indicates the pertinence of highlighting the critical context of natural science and technology: the consequences of scientific discovery and technological application are not socially or ecologically innocent; neither are funding priorities. From a different angle, the various ways in which the three meta-approaches address postformal developmental levels[30] also imbue higher education with an uncommon sense of directionality and purpose. In general, contra to a business-as-usual paradigm with respect to the purposes of higher education, the three meta-approaches surely beckon a radical reorientation, one sitting more in reference to such aims as human potential, social well-being and biospherical resilience (Hampson, 2011, 2012).

4 The Meta-Matrix: Potentializing Higher Education Theory through Deep Transversalization

In the previous section we explored a layer of transversalization across the meta-approaches. In the current section we deepen this further by exploring structural transversalizations.

Following the meta-matrix we will identify questions for further theorization and research.

A Meta-Matrix for Higher Education Theory

The matrix consists of a three-by-three array comprising: (1) content of education, (2) processes of education, and (3) systems of education—run through the lenses of (a) identity (micro/intra-connectivity), (b) relationality (meso/horizontal connectivity), and (c) contextuality (macro/superordinate connectivity).

A common critical context is provided for each matrix cell, namely that the valorised directions sit in contrast to modern atomism[31]—the atomistic mindset of modernism which, in the system under consideration, overprivileges nodes whilst undervaluing the relationships (at various levels) between them (Hampson, 2011). Another term for this is 'non-integrative'. This manoeuvre of binary construction is to help sharpen the focus of complex integration for current purposes.

Content of Education

We first look at educational content with respect to identity, relationality, and contextuality.

Content Identity

Non-integrative 'content' of education privileges such features as simplicity and 'small' scales, effecting standardization and closed system (technicist) sensibilities. Items able to be handled 'technically' such as data, information and knowledge-as-units-of-content are legitimized in preference to larger, more complex or nebulous items such as knowledge-as-capacity (Montuori, 1998), understanding (Maturana & Varela, 1987), and wisdom (Midgley, 1991; Beckett, 1995; Baltes, 2000; Sternberg, 2000; Kramer, 2003; Carr & Skinner, 2009). A corresponding approach to languaging can also be identified in this regard insofar as bureaucratic discourse assumes a literalist (Lum, 2004) or representational paradigm regarding relations between signifier and signified. An intensification of this technicist sensibility has led curriculum theorist Pinar (2007) to bemoan the character and requirement of 'curriculum guides to be covered as if they were so many ... income tax regulations and procedures' (Pinar, 2007, p. 10).

This situation regarding content of education can be contrasted to complex integrative approaches which involve substantive *intra*-relationalities. These may surface through myriad vectors. The following three—dialectics, dynamism, and polysemy—are indicative:

Dialectics (also see Hampson, 2018) may manifest with regard to content of education in such understandings as:

- knowing forms an intimate, complex union with not knowing
- knowing simultaneously involves (intransitive) discovery and (transitive) construction
- knowing involves both exterior and interior aspects
- holistic knowing involves both knowing and feeling
- creative knowing involves both 'knowing how' and 'knowing how to imagine'
- understanding involves both knowledge and intuition
- wisdom involves both knowing and caring.

Dynamism. Viewing material as a complex adaptive (i.e. open) system (Olssen, 2008) empowers processes responsive to context: a dialogic or 'living' curriculum can be identified as *currere* (Horn, 1999; Pinar, 2004). Consequently, a due theoretical direction for programmes would be to find a dynamic balance between centripetal agency and centrifugal creativity—'a modest rigidity with a structured flexibility' (Doll, 2008, p. 202).

Polysemy. Complex-integrative content can be identified as polysemous (Ricoeur, 2004/1969; Nerlich & Clarke, 2003): knowledge is complex (Allen & Torrens, 2005). With respect to the relationship between unequivocal and polysemous terms, a dimension of 'technicizability' could be identified—where one end could be connoted by Polanyi's (1962) category of *logical unspecifiability*; from a critical perspective attendant to technicism, this would be the undervalued end, one involving such concepts as wisdom, love (Nava, 2001), creativity (Craft et al., 2001; Fasko, 2001; Ozolins, 2007; Villaverde, 1999), archetype (Jung et al., 1981; Neville, 1989; Mayes, 1999), soul (Kessler, 2000) and, indeed, God (Hart, 1998; Alexander & McLaughlin, 2003). Although not easily formularized, are these not some of the most valuable things that could be associated with education? Inherent fuzziness in educational material problematizes the expectation that everything can be bureaucratically explicated.

Content Relationality

Non-integrative curricula involve substantive fragmentation and modularization. Indeed, essential arelationality can be seen at all scales of conceptual material from knowledge (Soucek, 1994; Kincheloe & Steinberg, 1998) through courses/programmes (Bagno et al., 2000) to disciplines and faculties (Dillon, 2007; Morin, 2008). Jardine (2006) identifies significant negative consequences of this paradigm:

> the disassembling of curriculum into disparate disciplines is all too akin to the ecologically disastrous and life-threatening disassembling of our Earth. And these foretell of a disintegration of spirit and character, a certain loss of a sense of where we are, a sense of the wholeness of our lives.
>
> (p. 172)

In addition to such atemporal considerations, modern atomism also involves temporal arelationality: insufficient recursive feedback loops are envisaged.

In contrast, complex-integrative sensibilities substantiate relationalities among educational material—whether at the scale of knowledge, courses/programmes, disciplines or faculties. Such connectivities of 'thinking the world together' (Palmer, 1998, p. 61) may be seen to operate through such metaphors as dialogue (Gangadean, 2008), balance, harmony, organism (Griffin, 1993), and ecology (Griffin, 1993). Regarding the scale of knowledge, Schumacher's (1977) 'four fields of knowledge' and the subsequent arising of Wilber's four quadrants (1997) exemplify schemas which identify connectivities between different types of knowledge. With respect to the scale of disciplines and faculties, transdisciplinarity can be identified as a central signifier.

Content Contextuality

Non-integrative curricula involve 'decontextualized bits of information' (Kincheloe & Steinberg, 1998, p. 5). Links to pertinent theory, greater purpose, history, possible futures, institutional culture, values, or ideology are minimized; big-picture psychological, social, and environmental concerns are marginalized (Orr, 1991a; Giroux, 2000); courses in education dealing with broad contexts are 'either eliminated or technicized' (Giroux, 2000, p. 56).

In contrast, trans-atomistic perspectives on educational material include salient contextualizations (Haggis, 2008). Salience implies 'pertinent knowledge' (Morin, 1999) in which normativity is implicated (Van Goor et al., 2004). Perhaps such knowledge might variously involve consideration of the following directions (as richly interpreted):

- Philosophy—what?
- Purpose—why?
- Power—for whom?

- Participation—by whom?
- Place—where?
- Period—when?
- Process—how?
- Price—how much?
- Presence—how deep?
- Pattern—what coherence?

Salient contexts of educational material include address of social ethics and metaphysics. Contexts of social ethics might take the form of 'troubling knowledge'—a type that can be 'disruptive, discomforting, problematizing' (Pinar, 2007, p. 64); whilst examples of metaphysics as context include the 'new metaphysics' of post-disciplinary curricula (Ford, 2002, p. 75), and the context of Gaia (Lovelock, 2000; Okoro, 2003), *anima mundi* or 'world soul' (Lewin, 1991), including that through cosmosophy (Siena, 2005). An approach that includes both social ethics and new metaphysics is Guattari's ecosophy (Guattari, 2000; Peters, 2002; also see Naess, 1989). Involving Bateson's (1987) 'ecology of mind' as a key point of departure, Guattari's nuanced integrative schema draws together considerations of three ecological registers of biosphere, society, and psyche, respectively, identifying parallels and differences among them (see Hampson, 2012).

Processes of Education

We now use the lenses of identity, relationality, and contextuality as we turn our attention to the multifaceted processes involved in education: the facilitation of learning or 'occasioning' (Davis, 2004).

Process Identity

Modernistically, identities of educators and educatees tend toward forms of independence and standardization. There is a sense of interchangeability with regard both to students and to teachers; the self-managing (Peters et al., 2000) 'individualized person is a number in the mass' (Conroy, 2004, p. 6), an ahistorical *tabula rasa* (Wood, 1992). Teachers become 'paid functionar[ies]' (Hansen, 2004, p. 121), deprofessionalized (Kincheloe & Steinberg, 1999) 'factory workers' (Pinar, 2004, p. 5), 'managers of inert knowledge, distributors of pre-selected skills' (Abbs, 2003, p. 56).

In contrast, from the trans-atomistic perspective that we are *homo complexus* (Morin, 1999)—perhaps through such transformative metaphors as human as dolphin (Hampson, 2005)—the student becomes a 'text of complexity' (Berry, 1999, p. 340). Meanwhile, the complexity of the teacher can be envisaged through an assemblage of archetypes including teacher as:

- gardener (Baptist, 2002; Tubbs, 2005)
- poet (Conroy, 2004)

- trickster (Jung & Francis, 2003; Garrison, 2009)
- friend and mentor (Forbes, 1996)
- 'The time-honoured image of an older, prepared, and sympathetic human being serving as a guide to a young and hopeful being' (Hansen, 2004, p. 121)
- wise (Arlin, 1999)
- 'Discloser, reflector and inverter' (Conroy, 2004, p. 9)
- 'Releaser, a midwife, aiming to give birth to existential acts of learning and spiritual engagement in the student' (Abbs, 2003, p. 15), a 'cultural guardian and initiator into the symbolic life … connector … water diviner' (Abbs, 2003, p. 17).

Process Relationality

Atomistically, andragogical processes between educatee and educator are conceived through a technicist lens involving standardized procedures whereby qualities of relationship are minimized. Beyond undue metaphors of economic trade (Bunge, 1999), fragmentation between educator and educatee might even take on that of siege, whereby 'both the old and the young become understood only in their worst aspects' (Jardine, 2006, p. 197).

In terms of complex integrative educational approaches, the necessarily communicative (Habermas, 1987) richness of andraogogical practice and relation as a whole (Day, 1999; Beckett & Hager, 2002) is perhaps Buber's valorisation of I-Thou relations (Buber, 1970; Hendley, 1978), a key aspect of which is the foregrounding of the second-person over the third-person perspective. Such an orientation facilitates the authentic pedagogy (Tubbs, 2005) of 'real interactions with real people' (Burwood, 2006, p. 128); even a pedagogy of love (Cho, 2005).

With respect to teaching, Davis (2004) offers the following interrelated set: teaching as drawing out, drawing in, instructing, training, facilitating, empowering, occasioning, and conversing. Does not such an ecology indicate that teaching is inherently a craft (Watkins & Mortimore, 1999) or art in the broadest sense—a fluid performance (Burwood, 2006; Stillwaggon, 2008)?

From the perspective of learning, similar depth can be identified. One expression of this is that offered by the dialectics of learning—as exemplified below through four vectors, namely, those of determinacy, orientation, character and orderliness, specifically the counter-hegemonic identification of: (1) learning becomes 'an uncertain adventure' (Morin, 1999); (2) learning is an organic process which requires a certain ebb and flow, periods of fallow as well as fertility or activity (Ferrer et al., 2006)—for a variety of time scales; (3) the dialectical principle of silence as complementing the active 'noise' of learning; and (4) 'learning through crisis' (Pinar, 2007, p. 65) or even—somewhat strikingly—learning through wounding (Cajete, 1994).

Process Contextuality

Atomistically, contextualizations of educational occasions are minimized. If learning contexts are identified, they are imagined as (insubstantive) containers of content which do not influence content per se (Griffiths & Guile, 1999; Edwards & Miller, 2007). Otherwise, contexts—such as philosophy (Carr, 2004), theory (Bane, 1994), ideology (Giroux, 1981), institutional culture (Postman & Weingartner, 1971; Gatto, 1992; Tyack & Tobin, 1994), and architecture (Orr, 1991a)—are under-regarded.

Trans-atomistically, salient contexts of the process of education (Giroux & McLaren, 1994; Young & Lucas, 1999; Edwards & Miller, 2007) include those regarding socio-cultural locations—whilst noting that such identifications might involve context-dependencies or hindrances to transferability among different contexts (Ireson et al., 1999; Watkins & Mortimore, 1999). One can envisage cultural locations from macro (global) through meso (regional/national/sub-cultural) considerations to the micro cultures of particular social localities; and one can envisage sociological locations including educational institutions (divided into sectors), workplaces, and society in general. For instance, regarding meso-cultural considerations—including 'culturally appropriate pedagogy' (Nguyena et al., 2006, p. 2) or 'culturally relevant pedagogy' (Ladson-Billings, 1995, p. 160)—attention might focus across sub-cultures within a nation or across nations within a world region.

Systems of Education

We now turn our attention to identity, relationality, and contextuality in relation to education systems.

System Identity

From a modern atomistic perspective there is in the first instance a tendency not to regard the system as a whole. Where the system is regarded as a whole, this tends to be framed through default technicist discourse (Kincheloe & Steinberg, 1999; Hoffer, 2000) whereby the denumberability of all significant educational items is assumed (Kerr, 2002; Kenan, 2003): quantifiability takes precedence over matters harder to quantify (Delanty, 2003; MacLure, 2006). Additionally, atomism prioritizes 'short frequencies' of time, locality, and meaning over more panoramic considerations regarding the long-term, eco-social issues and/or semantic depth. A corresponding linguistic paradigm one might identify as 'literalism' or 'prosaicism' is implicated (Van Niekerk, 1998; Lum, 2004), in which a technicist approach to educational languaging is assumed.

In contrast, complex integrative education systems would involve richer, more complex conceptualizations than those identified above. This may involve the articulation of pluralities, complexities, and/or aesthetic understandings. Regarding pluralities with respect to the university, for instance, Marginson explicates orientations beyond the economic as including

> the University as site of political conflict and resolution; the University as privileged site for the workings of the scientific imagination; the University

as community of scholars; the University as the fountainhead of culture and civilisation; the University as the arena of cultural diversity and global linkages; [and] the University as producer of common public goods.

(Marginson, 2004, p. 162)

A further general orientation of rich identity is generated through aesthetic perspectives (Schiller and Snell, 1954; Egan, 1997; Berchman, 2002), for which 'philosophy of education is accordingly the art of understanding, developing and formulating the art of education in relation to its own times' (Kemp, 2006, p. 175). The resultant 'poetics' of education (Bonnett, 1996) would rely on an 'aesthetic intelligence which perceives holistically' (Abbs, 1989, p. 177).

System Relationality

Regarding an indicative vector with respect to due identification of relationality within a complex integrative education system, the following is exemplary. Morin identifies that education systems actually include the physical, biological, and noetic so that such considerations as human bodies, institutional architecture, school cultures, administrative cultures, college ground ecologies, and a sense of place are addressed. An integrative vision would that of '"symbiosophy", the wisdom of living together' (Morin, 1999, p. 63).

This contrasts with the more fragmented imaginaries promoted by late modernism.

System Contextuality

From a modern atomistic perspective there can be a tendency toward acontextuality when addressing an education system as a whole. This may be affected by 'naturalized' narratives which imply that contextualizations are not required. Such a technicist mindset focuses on questions of 'what works', despite the fact that, as Biesta indicates, 'an exclusive emphasis on "what works" will simply not work' (Biesta, 2007, p. 22)!

In contrast, identifications of education system(s) beyond modern atomism saliently contextualize. Pertinent in this regard are questions of purpose (Orr, 1991b; Freire, 2004; Mezirow et al., 2000; Aronowitz, 2001; Gouthro, 2002; Giroux, 2003; Noddings, 2003; Biesta, 2007; Dewey, 2007; Gupta, 2008). The valorisation of such big-picture ethical inquiry forms part of trans-atomistic (eco-logical) understanding. One might say in summary that complex integrative contextualization goes beyond default contexts of economic instrumentalism toward concern for the long-term well-being of individuals, society, and biosphere. These three domains can be pragmatically identified as forming a Venn diagram with intersecting domains suitable for application regarding both curricula and research (see Hampson, 2014b).

Conclusion and Research Vectors

Complex-integrative higher education theory and praxis is fitting for adequately addressing the value-laden multi-dimensionality of the contemporary global crisis. The meta-approaches of Morin's complex thought, Bhaskar's critical realism, and Wilber's integral theory—as well as the meta-matrix furthered above—offer considerable wealth of insight toward this endeavour, both by themselves and when considered in conjunction.

The following research and action vectors are indicative[32] of those additionally necessary to inform a more detailed integrative higher education theory. The vectors are grouped as follows: contexts, ecosystem of education, and orientation.

Inquiring into Contexts

Integrative higher education theory involves both discursive and material contexts.[33]

Discursive Contexts

What is the ecosystem of discourses which informs, could inform, or should inform higher education? Are there any discourses which could benefit from being prioritized? What of higher education in futures studies? Or higher education as a form of social innovation? What types of conceptual insights for higher education arise—both actually and potentially—from the three meta-approaches (separately and jointly) discussed in this chapter? What enables apt hermeneutic coherence? Additionally, what influential non-academic discourses might be pertinent? And thence what relations between the academic and non-academic? Following on from this: What terms should be used (and in which discursive/developmental contexts)? What reflexive explication (if any) should be given regarding relations between signifiers and signifieds? What degree and type of semantic clustering could be aptly employed in order to facilitate collective meaning? Many such questions are underaddressed; rather, the technicist languaging of late modernism is often allowed to further colonize the academy. Has the contemporary institutional decline of the humanities with its ability to reflect—through the philosophy of science, the philosophy of art, the philosophy of higher education—contributed to such colonization?

Material Contexts

What macro-contexts would be useful to address? Regarding cross-cultural and temporal (historical/contemporary) lenses: How significant might some forms of Indigenous knowledge be for ecological resilience? Do we need to prioritize a kind of deep socio-cultural psychoanalysis and subsequent radical re-alignment or collective healing? What are the most pertinent critical contexts of the contemporary situation? What emphases of purpose (and concomitant process and structures) should be therefore empowered by higher education? How significant is it that humanity is conducting the sixth mass extinction event of the planet? How significant is the possibility of severe radiation poisoning? Or the unintended consequences of twenty-first-century technologies? Or radical human-induced climate change?

Inquiring into the Education Ecosystem

From an integrative perspective, the whole (eco)system of education needs to be addressed. The following windows are indicative.

Informal Education

What apt forms of learning occasion can be identified? What connections should there be between formal higher education and the learning that occurs in non-institutional environments—including that with peers (e.g., through social media)? How could the formal and informal be cohered? What role for technology? This is currently a topic which has much traction. There is, for instance, much to be gained by variously integrating gaming into educational occasions. But given its fashionable character, prudence would additionally try to ensure that the possible benefits of structural changes arising from such manoeuvres do not get hijacked by the forces of modernist economism—saving money, dumbing down.

Pre-Tertiary Education

What due relationship should there be between higher education and primary and secondary education from a reconstructive postmodern viewpoint? To what extent and in what ways do the age-regimented categories foster fragmented silos? Why is it that children's creativity generally diminishes rapidly as soon as they begin schooling regardless of what age this occurs at? Is there any relationship between this and the difficulty that some PhD candidates have in finding their unique creative voice? Should specialization happen so early in secondary school (e.g., do art and science really not 'belong together')? Should 13-year-olds get a taste of a university experience? Conversely, might schooling benefit from postgraduates re-experiencing school with a view to offering informed policy-related feedback?

Architecture

How much and in what way does aesthetic sensibility influence learning? What ecological impact does a higher educational institution have? What relations might there be between outer architecture and the 'inner architecture' of course structures and institutional subcultures? Do square boxes condition square minds? Is biophilia thwarted by 'indoor-ist' education? What food do university canteens serve, and what relationships might such food have with health, democracy, science, art?

Administration

What relations should the administration of higher education ideally have to faculty? What is possible, what is desirable? The two often seem divorced from each other—each with their own culture and languaging with subsequent prospects of non-generativity: A necessary state of affairs? Or a result of undue modernist fragmentation of work roles? What effect on administration and faculty has the increasing bureaucratic culture of accountability had? To what extent have the due academic freedoms of faculty been thwarted?

Evaluation

What would be apt forms of evaluation and assessment for a fully integrative higher education? How key a role might integral theory play in the assessment of integrative higher education, such as with respect to (1) its honouring of first, second, and third perspectives, (2) its address of postformal developmental levels, and (3) its acknowledgement of types, for example types of intelligence (see Gardner, 2011), types of assessment, types of learning and individual preferences therein? What key roles might critical realism offer integrative higher education assessment such as (1) in its ability to incisively critique the current dominant assessment paradigm, or via (2) the concept of explanatory critique? And how might complex theory contribute to the aforesaid assessment—for instance, in explicating that particular types of evaluations form undesired consequences (feedback loops) with respect to relations between the academy and society, or in its recognition that, holographically, paradigms are embedded (albeit in an elaborately fractal way (Davis, 2006)) in the very fabric of educational systems 'all the way down' and thus the system needs to take heed of the understanding that students respond to what they holistically experience in addition to that which they are formally told?

Inquiring into Orientation

Overarchingly, an apt educational philosophy of knowledge and action would include due embrace of such attractors as dialogical consciousness, reflexivity, transdisciplinarity, spirituality, and our organic substrate. An apt worldview descriptor is that of reconstructive postmodernism (Griffin, 2002). Consequential inquiries include: How fully might dialogical consciousness be enabled to permeate higher education? How can reflexivity be aptly enacted?[34] What would enable the divergent voices of the various disciplines to be sufficiently honoured whilst simultaneously maintaining (a possibly evolving) transdisciplinarity frame? What ways might contemporary spiritual directions (or higher reason) inform the purpose, fabric, and process of higher education? What is the significance of human biology to higher education? What apt connections can we identify between our organic nature and that of the planet[35]? And how can reconstructive postmodernism be appropriately relayed and advanced?

At a more concrete level, how might the ethical orientation of I-Thou (Buber, 1970) inform both the andragogy of educational occasions and the collegiality of educational institutions? What apt forms of learning occasions can be identified? How might Davis's (2004) Inventions of Teaching inform apt educational processes in higher educational learning occasions? What place has dialogue (Bohm, 2013)? Presencing (Scharmer, 2000)? And how might the university foster authentic interpersonal dialogue and development among and between faculty and students? Can the university of the future nurture and enact an adequate feeling of community—university as an affective community of scholars, staff, and students (see Hampson, 2010b)?

In general, we hope that seriousness is given to the quest to put 'higher' (back) into higher education, and the *uni*-verse[36] (back) into the university—for the sake of life on this precious planet.[37]

Notes

1 To attempt to provide an adequate reading of the interrelationships between Edgar Morin's complex thought (CT), Roy Bhaskar's critical realism (CR), and Ken Wilber's integral theory (IT) feels like a daunting task. To then draw out implications and potentials for higher education—through substantively furthering the development of integrative higher education theory—adds a further dimension of challenge. To do all of this in the short space of a single chapter seems a mission impossible. And yet—from what perspective is such an impossibility imagined? It would presumably include the perceived necessity of sufficient detail and precision; indeed, academic writing and the analytical mind are predicated on this requirement. But if allowance is made for layered expression (perhaps analogous to layered ontology and layered epistemology), then it might be that we could move from the necessity of the binary of *either-precision-or-vagueness* toward the allowance of a more nuanced articulation of being *clear* at one level of resolution about when certain types or degrees of *vagueness* might be appropriate at another level. This chapter is exploratory, initiatory, indicatory: preparatory work toward a panoramic form of integrative higher education theory. A little fuzzy logic therefore feels apt in trying to form a short singular narrative (albeit with centrifugal but pertinent lines of flight) pointing to the panorama of horizons offered by these three meta-approaches. Indeed, the Incompleteness Theorems of early twentieth-century mathematician Kurt Gödel can be understood as indicating that (most) systems can either achieve self-consistency or comprehensiveness but not both. So perhaps such inclusion of 'soft semantics' in the current instance are inevitable, even desirable. We should surely also owe our allegiance here to a rich interpretation of the scholarship of integration (Boyer, 1990) and its prospective interest in meshing, metaphor, and meaning. A certain degree of clustering will therefore be enacted, one which minimizes contestabilities between the three meta-approaches in favour of highlighting similarities.
2 Whilst some of the literature explicitly refers to higher education, much addresses education in general (inclusive of higher education). We have included both. A particular limitation is that whilst much of Morin's work is in French and Spanish, the paper is bounded by Anglophone research. This limitation is ameliorated both by English-language versions of Morin's key works such as *Method* (1992) and *Seven Complex Lessons in Education for the Future* (1999) as well as by useful English-language overviews of Morin such as those given by Montuori (2004, 2008).
3 Among other courses, this university offers a range of qualifications (from Diploma to PhD level) addressing various aspects of the application of complex thought in the field of education.

4 These challenges include: a realization of the limits of conventional logic; irreducible disorder in complex relationship with organizational order; the intricacy of biological and social phenomena; the notion of clear distinctions (e.g., between an object and its environment, or between an observed phenomenon and the observer) as not necessarily offering a criterion of sound reasoning and methodological appropriateness; and the role of the observer in his or her own observation (Morin, 2006).
5 His work has passed through three phases (Hartwig, 2012; N. Hedlund, 2012): (1) (basic) CR, which focuses on transcendental realism in the natural sciences, and critical naturalism in the social sciences (Bhaskar, 1978, 1979, 1986); (2) dialectical CR, which brings CR into a rich relationship with dialectics—notably the philosophies of Hegel and Marx (Bhaskar, 1994, 2008); and signals the beginning of Bhaskar's 'spiritual turn'(Hartwig, 2012) with the introduction to transcendental dialectical CR (Bhaskar, 2000); and (3) the philosophy of metaReality (Bhaskar, 2002a, 2002b, 2002c, 2012), including the deepening of the aforesaid spiritual turn toward such notions as an infrastructural 'absolute reality' or 'ground state' (Bhaskar, 2012). For convenience, our chapter identifies all three phases under the umbrella term 'CR'. This should not be confused with other approaches that have identified themselves as critical realist including theological critical realism. A thorough discussion of the various uses of the term 'critical realism' can be found in Shipway (2002).
6 The CR movement has become increasingly fragmented in recent years as CR's Marxist proponents have responded with distress to Bhaskar's metaphysical turn (Shipway, 2002).
7 CR argues that nature is stratified. This implies that there is a basic hierarchy of being with some ontological strata being more basic than others. This effectively describes the way in which being emerges through a hierarchical process of evolutionary complexity and is—in some ways—similar to the holarchical principals developed by Koestler (1967) and later developed by Wilber (1995). For example, the actions of living creatures are governed by the laws of the natural (inorganic world)—animals are constrained by the laws of physics and chemistry—however these laws are not sufficient to explain their workings; because living organisms are also subject to the laws of biological systems. Thus, anything belonging to a higher stratum is necessarily governed by more than one set of laws as—to borrow Wilber's (1995) terminology—each successive stratum transcends and includes the ones which precede it. We can thus observe a movement towards greater complexity moving, in broad strokes, from the physiosphere (the world of material beings), to the biosphere (the world of living beings), to the world of rational beings (Collier, 1994).
8 The intransitive refers to underlying mechanisms which form the ultimate objects of scientific inquiry, whilst the transitive refers to the relativistic, subjective, and intersubjective aspects of science.
9 Bhaskar (in Bhaskar et al., 2010, p. 9) writes,

> This specifies that every social event occurs in at least four dimensions, that of material transactions with nature; that of social interactions between humans; that of social structure proper; and that of the stratification of the embodied personality. These four planes constitute, of course, a necessarily laminated system of their own in so far as reference to any one level or dimension will also necessarily involve reference to the others.

10 These are identified by Bhaskar (in Bhaskar et al., 2010, p. 9) as:

> (i) the sub-individual psychological level; (ii) the individual or biographical level; (iii) the micro-level studied, for example, by ethnomethodologists and others; (iv) the meso-level at which we are concerned with the relations between functional roles such as capitalist and worker or MP and citizen; (v) the macro-level orientated to the understanding of the functioning of whole societies or their regions, such as the Norwegian economy; (vi) the mega-level of the analysis of whole traditions and civilizations; and (vii) the planetary (or cosmological) level concerned with the planet (or cosmos) as a whole.

Coalescing and Potentializing Integrative Higher Education   195

11 The first four stadia (identified during transcendental dialectical critical realism) are: (1) first moment (1M) deals with 'being as such and as structured non-identity; (2) second edge (2E) deals with being as process or 'becoming'; (3) third level (3L) deals with being as totality; (4) fourth dimension (4D) deals with intentional transformative agency, transformative praxis; the last three (identified in the *Philosophy of MetaReality*) are: (5) fifth aspect (5A) deals with being as incorporating reflexivity (and spirituality); (6) sixth realm (6R) deals with being as re-enchantment; (7) seventh zone (7R) deals with being as non-duality (or as involving essential unity) and therefore exists as the ground state of all being (7 Z/A).
12 Referential detachment is 'the ontological dislocation of referent from the act of reference' (Bhaskar, 2008, p. 131).
13 Alethic truth refers to the truth of things which exists independently of propositions. Propositional truth presupposes alethic truth.
14 The judgment form is the basis of judgmental rationality and is the formal method that can be used to distinguish between the veracity of competing theories. This form is built of the stratified nature of truth and involves examining theories in terms of expressive veracity, fiduciariness, descriptive veracity, and evidential proof (Bhaskar, 2008, p. 221).
15 The self-reflexive application of this critique undoubtedly contributes to the robustness of CR theory.
16 Entitled *New Studies in Critical Realism and Education*, which is pulling together a number of the leading advocates for critical realism in the field.
17 Scott argues that it is essential that empirical research is underpinned by a metatheory which gives it a clear epistemological and ontological orientation, one which acknowledges real objects of inquiry (which scientific exploration logically necessitates) whilst not committing one to the spurious belief that only one interpretation of knowledge is possible (or ultimate). CR is, in his opinion, the most appropriate metatheory to address these concerns. Furthermore, he redresses the unconstructive dualisms that exist between structure and agency in research. This has implications for research into the field of higher education as well as research as an educational activity.
18 It is often referred to as the 'theoretical' approach or perspective (e.g., by McGray and Soetaert) or as a 'philosophical' approach or orientation (e.g., by Loveday).
19 Unfortunately Shipway's research was completed ahead of the development of PMR.
20 Extending beyond curriculum and organizational critiques to include andragogy, and foreseeably other aspects such as assessment.
21 Wilber's work is often understood as being divided into five phases (Helfrich, 2007): Phase I (1972–1978)—'recaptured goodness', or the Romantic Jungian (Wilber, 1977, 1979); Phase II (1978–1983)—'growth to goodness'(Wilber, 1980, 1981, 1983); Phase III (1983–1993)—holonic (Wilber, 1983, 1986, 1991); Phase IV (1993–2000)—holarchic, or AQAL (Wilber, 1995, 1996, 1997, 1999, 2000a, 2000b); and Phase V (2000–)—Integral Post-Metaphysics (Wilber, 2007a, 2007b).
22 AQAL stands for 'all quadrants, all levels, all lines, all states, and all types'. Quadrants are identified as four 'tetra-arising' perspectives of reality rendered from two essential distinctions, namely, individual-collective and interior-exterior. Levels describe the evolutionary way in which development emerges in stages. Regarding human individuals, for example, these include postformal levels of complexity, indicating psychological development beyond Piagetian formal operations (including transpersonal psychology). The understanding is that each level offers a different type of true-but-partial view, and that more advanced levels 'transcend and include' (in Hegelian terms, *sublate*) preceding ones. Lines describe different types of developmental phenomena such as emotional development and cultural worldview (Esbjörn-Hargens, 2009), whilst states describe transitory shifts of consciousness. Gross states include waking (gross), dreaming (subtle), and deep sleep (causal) (Wilber, 2007a), whilst other states form in response to internal or external stimuli (e.g., hormonal states, altered states). Other examples might include weather states. Last but not least, types are identified as relatively durable structures or characteristic formations identified within each quadrant (e.g., personality types, governance types).

23 Within which the terms interrelate complexly—involving intersections, parallels, divergences, and contestabilities.
24 CT identifies psychological and cultural dimensions; CR clearly differentiates intransitive and transitive dimensions; whilst interior perspectives (both individual and collective) are central to Wilber's framework. Of corresponding note is a critique of monolithic positivist orientations, and uncohered relativist positions: CT identifies both of these in terms of the fragmentation and mutilation of knowledge (Morin, 1992, 1999); CR identifies them as classic sites of the epistemic and ontic fallacies (Bhaskar, 1978); and IT addresses them as quadrant reductionisms (Wilber, 2007a).
25 CR emphasizes the term *interdisciplinarity*. Whilst CR enables linking between disciplines, it more greatly offers an overarching philosophy of science or 'underlabouring' framework which accords with the notion of transdisciplinarity (notwithstanding the recursive notion that philosophy is a discipline—although some disciplines such as philosophy and education can be identified as having considerable transdisciplinary character). Elsewhere, IT regards itself as *postdisciplinary* in that it can be used in conjunction with 'transdisciplinarity' or any discipline. That may be so; however, transdisciplinarities are also used in conjunction with disciplines; and, as with all transdisciplinarities, IT provides an overarching orientation.
26 The term 'transdisciplinarity' was first used by Piaget, Morin, and Jantsch in the early 1970s (Hampson, 2010). Integrative scholar Julie Thompson Klein (2004) defines it as 'a common system of axioms for a set of disciplines' (p. 515). She notes that it can include comprehensive paradigms such as Marxism, broad interdisciplinary fields such as cultural studies, and even synoptic disciplines such as philosophy.
27 Noting that apt 'interference' includes such manoeuvres as indicated by post-positivism.
28 In terms of the relationship between normativity and description, their intertwined nature is highlighted by Morin, and given an explicit concept—'explanatory critique'—by Bhaskar.
29 IT does not tend to use the term *emancipation*. This is perhaps due to the fact that Wilber's thought finds its lineage in Hindu and Buddhist philosophy (the perennial philosophy) and contemporary transpersonal psychology, whereas Bhaskar and Morin share neo-Marxist roots.
30 A large number of detailed adult development frameworks now exist which provide a detailed understanding of the unfolding of development across multiple lines, including: cognitive (e.g., Commons et al., 1984; Kegan, 1982; Kegan, 1994); psycho-spiritual (Aurobindo, 1975); psycho-social (Erikson, 1978); moral (Kohlberg, 1984; Gilligan, 1993); values and worldview (Graves, 2005; Beck & Cowan, 1996; and Gebser, 1991); self-identity (Loveinger, 1976; Cook-Greuter, 2003); and perspectives on axiological-ontological depth (Bhaskar, 2012). Building on Loveinger (1976) and Cook-Greuter's (2003) research into the development of self-identity, Fisher et al. (2002); Rooke & Torbert 2005)—later followed by Joiner & Joseph (2007)—worked towards refining the articulation of action logics. These frameworks—especially when read in conjunction with, for instance, Kegan's work on 'orders of consciousness'—provide valuable insight into the mode of operation at different levels of development.
31 The interpretation of atomism that acts as the section's point of departure is that of Post (1975); his interpretation can be identified as modern. He indicates that (modern) atomism's preference is toward the standardization of units, and that it follows a paradigm of simplicity such that only one singular—specifically, the hierarchically lowest—ontological level is legitimated as explanatory. Post also summarizes the main problem with atomism as being its insistence on the lack of interdependence among the postulated units. From a critical perspective, modern atomism operates as the dominant underlying paradigm in education. That which is beyond this hegemony can be identified in relation to a cluster of signifiers including 'complex integrative', 'postconventional', 'metatheoretical', 'trans-atomistic', 'post-atomistic', 'integrally pluralistic', 'postformally integral' and 'eco-logical'.
32 Though not comprehensive.

33 From an integrative perspective, context can be identified as a form of content.
34 For example, in the current context: What pertinent questions might be asked? Could the above list benefit from modification? Given Arlin's (1975) address of 'problem-finding' as a postformal manoeuvre, such questions should remain present throughout research engagement (as continuously generative but without becoming debilitating through 'ongoing revision fatigue').
35 There are, of course, a host of (other) specific topics, including many explicitly arising from the three meta-approaches discussed here. Unfortunately, space does not permit further discussion.
36 'One turn' of knowledge: the poetics of complexity-within-unity.
37 In the above, of course, there is a (serious) playing with the term 'higher' by allowing it not only to refer to tertiary education but also to indicate that there is something significant—perhaps partly lost, partly not yet achieved—regarding the relationship between the mainstream university system and postformal psychological developmental levels (i.e. those 'higher' than formal operations). For instance, an education dominantly oriented by instrumental concerns regarding a student's individual career—as defaultly interpreted through the contemporary late modernist worldview which insufficiently prioritizes planetary well-being and long-term futures—is one which is (to say the least) not oriented by its potential. In contrast, an authentically higher education would place at its heart such concerns as planetary well-being and regard for the forthcoming seven generations (Clarkson et al., 1992), rather than the short-term interests of ego-based or nation-based competition set in the ultimately lose-lose game of mainstream economics. Similarly, there is also a (serious) playing with the term 'uni-verse'. The connection here is that modernism has in a significant way lost its way regarding the pertinent implications of 'universe', namely that this whole phenomenological reality is all one verse or 'turn': it is of a piece, and that if we propagate dominant systems which do not take this to heart it is hard to imagine that we will not suffer from a severe counter-adjustment (also see Hampson, 2018). In Winton's (2010) Pattern Dynamics, this 'swing-back' ecological pattern is signified as enantiodromia. Universal knowledge is not facilitated by the modern university's insistence on hyper-fragmentation with insufficient regard for the multi-layered intra-connectivity of the universe. Last but not least: what, reflexively, might we make of the authors' manoeuvres of '(serious) play'? From where does the modernist notion of work as the antithesis of play come from? Is this conceptualization congruent with the various individual and societal malaises of the contemporary predicament? Is this what we still want? Would not an integrative (reconstructive postmodern) worldview soften, readjust, or radically transversalize such a configuration? Moreover: Are we not all already inside a kosmic play anyway?

References

Abbs, P. (1989). *A is for Aesthetic: Essays on Creative and Aesthetic Education*. The Falmer Press.
Abbs, P. (2003). *Against the Flow: Education, The Arts and Postmodern Culture*. RoutledgeFalmer.
Akiyami, T., Li, J., & Onuki, M. (2012). Integral leadership education for sustainable development. *Journal of Integral Theory and Practice*, 7(3), 55–69.
Alexander, H., & McLaughlin, T.H. (2003). Education in religion and spirituality. In N. Blake, P. Smeyers, R.D. Smith, & P. Standish (eds), *The Blackwell Guide to the Philosophy of Education*. Blackwell.
Alhadeff-Jones, M. (2009). Revisiting educational research through Morin's paradigm of complexity: A response to Ton Jörg's programmatic view. *Complicity: An International Journal of Complexity and Education*, 6(1), 61–70.
Alhadeff-Jones, M. (2010). Challenging the limits of critique in education through Morin's paradigm of complexity. *Studies in Philosophy and Education*, 29, 477–490.
Allen, P.M., & Torrens, P.M. (2005). Knowledge and complexity. *Futures*, 37(7), 581–584.

Archer, M.S. (1979). *Social Origins of Educational Systems*. SAGE Publications.
Arlin, P. (1975). Piagetian operations in problem finding. *Developmental Psychology*, 13(3), 297–298.
Arlin, P. (1999). The wise teacher: A developmental model of teaching. *Theory into Practice*, 38(1), 12–17.
Aronowitz, S. (2001). Preface. In H.A. Giroux (ed.), *Theory and Resistance in Education: Towards a Pedagogy for the Opposition*. Bergin & Garvey.
Astin, A., & Reams, J. (2010). Spirituality and integral thought in higher education. In S. Esbjörn-Hargens et al. (eds), *Integral Education: New Directions for Higher Learning*. SUNY Press.
Aurobindo, S. (1975). *The Life Divine* (Sri Aurobindo Birth Centenary Library, Vols 18–19). Sri Aurobindo Ashram Trust.
Baehr, P. (1990). Review article: Critical realism, cautionary realism. *Sociological Review*, 38(4), 765–777.
Bagno, E., et al. (2000). From fragmented knowledge to a knowledge structure: Linking the domains of mechanics and electromagnetism. *American Journal of Physics*, 68(1), 16–26.
Baltes, P.B.S., & Ursula, M. (2000). Wisdom: A metaheuristic (pragmatic) to orchestrate mind and virtue toward excellence. *American Psychologist*, 55(1), 122–136.
Bane, M.C. (1994). *An Analysis of Educational Reforms in Mali, 1962–1992*. Doctoral Dissertation, University of Kansas.
Baptist, K.W. (2002). The garden as metaphor for curriculum. *Teacher Education Quarterly*, 29(4), 19–37.
Barnett, R. (2012). *Imagining the University*. Routledge.
Barr, R.B., & Tagg, J. (1995). From teaching to learning: A new paradigm for undergraduate education. *Change*, 27(6), 12–25.
Bateson, G. (1987). *Steps to an Ecology of Mind: Collected Essays in Anthropology, Psychiatry, Evolution, and Epistemology*. Jason Aronson.
Beck, D., & Cowan, C. (1996). *Spiral Dynamics: Mastering Values, Leadership and Change*. Wiley-Blackwell.
Berchman, R.M. (2002). Aesthetics as a philosophical ethos: Plotinus and Foucault. In R.B. Harris (ed.), *Neoplatonism and Contemporary Thought*. SUNY Press.
Berry, K.S. (1999). Destabilizing educational thought and practice: Post-formal pedagogy. In S. Steinberg, J.L. Kincheloe, & P.H. Hinchey (eds), *The Post-Formal Reader: Cognition and Education*. Falmer Press.
Bhaskar, R. (1978). *A Realist Theory of Science* (2nd edn). Harvester Press.
Bhaskar, R. (1979). *The Possibility of Naturalism: A Philosophical Critique of the Contemporary Human Sciences*. Harvester Press.
Bhaskar, R. (1986). *Scientific Realism and Human Emancipation*. Verso.
Bhaskar, R. (1994). *Plato, Etc: The Problems of Philosophy and Their Resolutions*. Verso.
Bhaskar, R. (2002a). *From Science to Emancipation: Alienation and Enlightenment*. SAGE Publications.
Bhaskar, R. (2002b). *Reflections on Meta-Reality: Transcendence, Emancipation and Everyday Life*. SAGE Publications.
Bhaskar, R. (2008). *Dialectic: The Pulse of Freedom*. Verso.
Bhaskar, R. (2012). *The Philosophy of MetaReality: Creativity, Love and Freedom* (2nd edn). Routledge.
Bhaskar, R., Frank, C., Høyer, K.G., Naess, P., & Parker, J. (2010). *Interdisciplinarity and Climate Change: Transforming Knowledge and Practice for Our Global Future*. Routledge.
Biesta, G.J.J. (2007). Why 'what works' won't work: Evidence-based practice and the democratic deficit in educational research. *Educational Theory*, 57(1), 1–22.

Bohm, D. (2013). *On Dialogue*. Routledge.
Bonnett, M. (1996). 'New' era values and the teacher-pupil relationship as a form of the poetic. *British Journal of Educational Studies*, 44(1), 27–41.
Boyer, E.L. (1990). *Scholarship Reconsidered: Priorities of the Professoriate*. Carnegie Foundation for the Advancement of Teaching.
Bronson, M., & Gangadean, A. (2010). Encountering the (w)hole: Integral Education as deep dialogue and cultural medicine. In S. Esbjörn-Hargens et al. (eds), *Integral Education: New Directions for Higher Learning*. SUNY Press.
Brown, B.C. (2010). *Complexity Leadership*. Unpublished manuscript.
Brown, G. et al. (1997). *Assessing Student Learning in Higher Education*. Routledge.
Buber, M. (1970). *I and Thou*. Touchstone.
Bunge, M. (1999). *Social Science under Debate: A Philosophical Perspective*. University of Toronto Press.
Burwood, S. (2006). Imitation, indwelling and the embodied self. *Educational Philosophy and Theory*, 39(2), 118–134.
Cajete, G. (1994). *Look to the Mountain: An Ecology of Indigenous Education*. Kivaki Press.
Carr, D., & Skinner, D. (2009). The cultural roots of professional wisdom: Towards a broader view of teacher expertise. *Educational Philosophy and Theory*, 41(2), 141–154.
Carr, W. (2004). Philosophy and education. *Journal of Philosophy of Education*, 38(1), 55–73.
Cho, D. (2005). Lessons of love: Psychoanalysis and teacher-student love. *Educational Theory*, 55(1), 79–96.
Clarkson, L., Morrissette, V., & Regallet, G. (1992). *Our Responsibility to the Seventh Generation: Indigenous Peoples and Sustainable Development*. International Institute for Sustainable Development.
Collier, A. (1994). *Critical Realism: An Introduction to Roy Bhaskar's Philosophy*. Verso.
Commons, M.L., Richards, F.A., & Armon, C. (eds) (1984). *Beyond Formal Operations: Late Adolescent and Adult Cognitive Development*. Praeger.
Conklin, J. (2001). *Wicked Problems and Social Complexity*. CogNexus Institute.
Conroy, J.C. (2004). *Betwixt & Between: The Liminal Imagination, Education and Democracy*. Peter Lang.
Conway, M. (2012). Sustainable futures: What higher education has to offer. *Social Alternatives*, 31(4), 35–40.
Cook-Greuter, S.R. (2000). Mature ego development: A gateway to ego-transcendence. *Journal of Adult Development*, 7(4), 227–240.
Corson, D.J. (1990a). Old and new conceptions of discovery in education. *Educational Philosophy and Theory*, 22(2), 26–49.
Corson, D.J. (1990b). Applying the stages of a social epistemology to school policy-making. *British Journal of Educational Studies*, 38(3), 259–276.
Corson, D.J. (1991a). Educational research and Bhaskar's conception of discovery. *Educational Theory*, 41(2), 189–198.
Corson, D.J. (1991b). Bhaskar's critical realism and educational knowledge. *British Journal of Sociology of Education*, 12(2), 223–241.
Corson, D.J. (1995). *Discourse and Power in Educational Organizations*. Hampton Press.
Corson, D.J. (1998). *Changing Education for Diversity*. Open University Press.
Corson, D.J. (1999a). Critical realism: Post-Popper realism and the real world. In J. Pratt & J. Swann (eds), *Improving Education: Realist Approaches to Method and Research*. Cassell.
Corson, D.J. (1999b). Using critical realism in policy-making at school level. In J. Pratt & J. Swann (eds), *Improving Education: Realist Approaches to Method and Research*. Cassell.
Craft, A., et al. (eds) (2001). *Creativity in Education*. Continuum.
Cremin, L. (1970). *American Education: The Colonial Experience, 1607–1783*. Harper & Row.

Davis, B. (2004). *Inventions of Teaching: A Genealogy*. Lawrence Erlbaum Associates.
Davis, B., & Sumara, D. (2006). *Complexity and Education: Inquiries into Learning, Teaching, and Research*. Lawrence Erlbaum Associates.
Davis, N.T. (2010a). Matching educational intentions with assessment: Using an integral map. In S. Esbjörn-Hargens et al. (eds), *Integral Education: New Directions for Higher Learning*. SUNY Press.
Davis, N.T. (2010b). Learning from assessment: A story of a journey towards Integral Education. In W. Dea (ed.), *Igniting Brilliance: Integral Education for the 21st Century*. Integral Publishers.
Dawson, T. (2000). Moral reasoning and evaluative reasoning about the good life. *Journal of Applied Measurement*, 1, 372–397.
Dawson, T., & Stein, Z. (2011). *Virtuous Cycles of Learning: Redesigning Testing During the Digital Revolution*. Available at https://dts.lectica.org/PDF/2012_0929_virtuous_cycles.pdf (Accessed 15 May 2013).
Day, J. (1999). The primacy of relationship: A meditation on education, faith and the dialogical self. In J. Beckett & C. Conroy (eds), *Catholic Education: Inside/Out Outside/In*. Lindisfarne.
Dea, W. (ed.) (2010a). *Igniting Brilliance: Integral Education for the 21st Century*. Integral Publishers.
Dea, W. (2010b). An overview of embodying with awareness. In W. Dea (ed.), *Igniting Brilliance: Integral Education for the 21st Century*. Integral Publishers.
Dea, W. (2010c). Cultivating integral awareness in the classroom. In W. Dea (ed.), *Igniting Brilliance: Integral Education for the 21st Century*. Integral Publishers.
Del Mello, M. (2008). Towards an all-embracing optimism in the realm of being and doing. In B. Nicolescu (ed.), *Transdisciplinarity: Theory and Practice*. Hampton Press.
Del Re, G. (2008). Transdisciplinarity and the plight of education. In B. Nicolescu (ed.), *Transdisciplinarity: Theory and Practice*. Hampton Press.
Delanty, G. (2003). Ideologies of the knowledge society and the cultural contradictions of higher education. *Policy Futures in Education*, 1(1), 71–82.
Dewey, J. (2007). *Democracy and Education: An Introduction to the Philosophy of Education*. NuVision.
Dillon, P. (2007). A pedagogy of connection and boundary crossings: Methodological and epistemological transactions in working across and between disciplines. *Proceedings of the Creativity or Conformity? Building Cultures of Creativity in Higher Education Conference*, Cardiff, 8–10 January.
Dobson, S., & Dale, E. (2021). *A Critical Realist Approach to Pupil Assessment: Global Challenges and Dilemmas*. Routledge.
Dobuzinskis, L. (2004). Where is Morin's road to complexity going? *World Futures*, 60(4), 433–455.
Doll, W.E. (2008). Complexity and the culture of curriculum. *Educational Philosophy and Theory*, 40(1), 190–212.
Du Preez, W.P. (1980). *The Politics of Identity: Ideology and the Human Image*. St. Martin's Press.
Edwards, R., & Miller, K. (2007). Putting the context into learning. *Pedagogy, Culture & Society*, 15(3), 263–274.
Egan, K. (1997). The arts as the basics of education. *Childhood Education*, 73(6), 34–38.
Erikson, E. (ed.) (1978). *Adulthood*. W.W. Norton & Company.
Esbjörn-Hargens, S. (2005). Integral Education by design: How integral theory informs teaching, learning, and curriculum in a graduate program. *ReVision*, 28(3), 21–29.
Esbjörn-Hargens, S. (2009). *An Overview of Integral Theory: An All-Inclusive Framework for the Twenty-First Century*. Integral Institute.

Esbjörn-Hargens, S. (2010a). Integral theory in service of enacting Integral Education: Illustrations from an online graduate program. In S. Esbjörn-Hargens et al. (eds), *Integral Education: New Directions for Higher Learning*. SUNY Press.

Esbjörn-Hargens, S. (2010b). An ontology of climate change: Integral pluralism and the enactment of multiple objects. *Journal of Integral Theory and Practice*, 5(1), 143–174.

Esbjörn-Hargens, S., Reams, J., & Gunnlaugson, O. (2010a). *Integral Education: New Directions for Higher Learning*. SUNY Press.

Esbjörn-Hargens, S., Reams, J., & Gunnlaugson, O. (2010b). The emergence and characteristics of Integral Education: An introduction. In S. Esbjörn-Hargens et al. (eds), *Integral Education: New Directions for Higher Learning*. SUNY Press.

Evans, M.A. (2011). A critical-realist response to the postmodern agenda in instructional design and technology: A way forward. *Education Technology Research and Development*, 59, 799–815.

Fasko, D. (2001). Education and creativity. *Creativity Research Journal*, 13(3), 317–327.

Ferrer, J. et al. (2006). The four seasons of Integral Education: A participatory proposal. *ReVision*, 29(2), 11–23.

Ferrer, J., Romero, M., & Albareda, R. (2010). Integral transformative education: A participatory proposal. In S. Esbjörn-Hargens et al. (eds), *Integral Education: New Directions for Higher Learning*. SUNY Press.

Feyerabend, P. (1975). *Against Method: Outline of an Anarchistic Theory of Knowledge*. NLB Humanities Press.

Fielding, M. (2007). On the necessity of radical state education: Democracy and the common school. *Journal of Philosophy of Education*, 41(4), 539–557.

Fischer, K. (1980). A theory of cognitive development: The control and construction of hierarchies of skill. *Psychological Review*, 87, 477–531.

Fisher, D., Rooke, D., & Torbert, W.R. (2003). *Personal and Organizational Transformations: Through Action Inquiry*. Edge/Work.

Forbes, S.H. (1996). Values in holistic education. *Proceedings of the Third Annual Conference on 'Education, Spirituality and the Whole Child'*, London, 28 June.

Ford, M.P. (2002). *Beyond the Modern University: Toward a Constructive Postmodern University*. Praeger.

Freire, P. (1997). *Pedagogy of the Oppressed*. Continuum Books.

Freire, P. (2004). *Pedagogy of Hope: Reliving Pedagogy of the Oppressed*. Continuum.

Gangadean, A. (2008). *Meditations of Global First Philosophy: Quest for the Missing Grammar of Logos*. SUNY Press.

Gardner, H. (2011). *Frames of Mind: The Theory of Multiple Intelligences*. Basic Books.

Garrison, J. (2009). Teacher as prophetic trickster. *Educational Theory*, 59(1), 67–83.

Gatto, J.T. (1992). *Dumbing Us Down: The Hidden Curriculum of Compulsory Schooling*. New Society.

Gatto, J.T. (2000). *The Underground History of American Education: A Schoolteacher's Intimate Investigation into the Problem of Modern Schooling*. Oxford Village Press.

Gebser, J. (1991). *The Ever-Present Origin*. Ohio University Press.

Gibbons, M., Limoges, C., Nowotny, H., Schwartzman, S., Scott, P., & Trow, M. (1994). *The New Production of Knowledge: The Dynamics of Science and Research in Contemporary Societies*. SAGE Publications.

Gilligan, C. (1993). *In a Different Voice*. Harvard University Press.

Giroux, H.A. (1981). *Ideology, Culture and the Process of Schooling*. Falmer Press.

Giroux, H.A. (2000). *Impure Acts: Practical Politics of Cultural Studies*. Routledge.

Giroux, H.A. (2003). Selling out higher education. *Policy Futures in Education*, 1(1), 179–200.

Giroux, H.A., & McLaren, P. (eds) (1994). *Between Borders: Pedagogy and the Politics of Cultural Studies*. Routledge.

Gouthro, P.A. (2002). Education for sale: At what cost? Lifelong learning and the marketplace. *International Journal of Lifelong Education*, 21(4), 334–346.

Graves, C., Cowan, C., & Todorovic, N. (2005). *The Never Ending Quest: Dr. Clare W. Graves Explores Human Nature*. ECLET Publishing.

Griffin, D.R. (1993). Whitehead's deeply ecological worldview. In M.E. Tucker & J.A. Grim (eds), *Worldviews and Ecology*. Associated University Presses.

Griffin, D.R. (2002). Introduction to SUNY Series in Constructive Postmodern Thought. In C. Keller & A. Daniell (eds), *Process and Difference: Between Cosmological and Poststructuralist Postmodernisms*. SUNY Press.

Griffiths, T., & Guile, D. (1999). Pedagogy in work-based contexts. In P. Mortimore (ed.), *Understanding Pedagogy and Its Impact On Learning*. SAGE Publications.

Gruber, J. (2010). Botany in all dimensions: The flowering of integral science. In W. Dea (ed.), *Igniting Brilliance: Integral Education for the 21st Century*. Integral Publishers.

Guattari, F. (2000). *The Three Ecologies*. Continuum.

Gunnlaugson, O. (2010). Presencing the optimal we: Evoking collective intelligence in the classroom. In W. Dea (ed.), *Igniting Brilliance: Integral Education for the 21st Century*. Integral Publishers.

Gupta, A. (2008). Education: From telos to technique? *Educational Philosophy and Theory*, 40(2), 266–276.

Habermas, J. (1987). *The Theory of Communicative Action*, Vol. 2: *Lifeworld and System: A Critique of Functionalist Reason*. Polity Press.

Haggis, T. (2008). Knowledge must be contextual: Some possible implications of complexity and dynamic systems theories for educational research. *Educational Philosophy and Theory*, 40(1), 158–176.

Hampson, G.P. (2005). Human: Machine, ape or dolphin? *Journal of Futures Studies*, 9(4), 29–44.

Hampson, G.P. (2007). Integral re-views postmodernism: The way out is through. *Integral Review*, 4, 108–173.

Hampson, G.P. (2010a). Facilitating eco-logical futures through postformal poetic ecosophy. *Futures*, 42(10), 1064–1072.

Hampson, G.P. (2010b). Western-Islamic and Native American genealogies of Integral Education. In S. Esbjörn-Hargens et al. (eds), *Integral Education: New Directions for Higher Learning*. SUNY Press.

Hampson, G.P. (2011). *Regenerating Integral Theory and Education Postconventional Explorations*. PhD Thesis, Southern Cross University.

Hampson, G.P. (2012). Eco-logical education for the long emergency. *Futures*, 44(1), 71–80.

Hampson, G.P. (2014a). *Leadership in Transforming the Modern Worldview: Exploring Postformal Integration*. Palacky University Press.

Hampson, G.P. (2014b). Toward transformative higher education: Weaving understanding together for humanity and biosphere. In G.P. Hampson & M. Rich-Tolsma (eds), *Leading Transformative Higher Education*. Palacky University Press.

Hampson, G.P. (2018). The Taijitu, Western dialectics and brain hemisphere function: A dialogue facilitated by the scholarship of complex integration. In A.K. Giri (ed.), *Social Theory and Asian Dialogues: Cultivating Planetary Conversations*. Madras Institute of Development Studies.

Hampson, G.P., & Rich-Tolsma, M. (2015). Transformative learning for climate change engagement: Regenerating perspectives, principles, and practice. *Integral Review*, 11(3), 171–190.

Hansen, D.T. (2004). A poetics of teaching. *Educational Theory*, 54(2), 119–142.

Hart, K. (1998). Jacques Derrida: The God effect. In P. Blond (ed.), *Post-Secular Philosophy: Between Philosophy and Theology*. Routledge.

Hartwig, M. (2008). Introduction. In R. Bhaskar, *A Realist Theory of Science*. Routledge.

Hartwig, M. (2012). Introduction. In R. Bhaskar, *The Philosophy of MetaReality: Creativity Love and Freedom*. Routledge.

Hase, S., & Kenyon, C. (2000). *From Andragogy to Heutagogy*. ultiBASE.

Hedlund, N. (2012). Critical realism: A synoptic overview and resource guide for integral scholars. Resource Paper, December. Available at: https://foundation.metaintegral.org/sites/default/files/Critical%20Realism_4-12-2013.pdf (Accessed 3 May 2022).

Hedlund-de Witt, A. (2013). *Worldviews and the Transformation to Sustainable Societies: An Exploration of the Cultural and Psychological Dimensions of Our Global Environmental Challenges*. PhD Thesis, Vrije Universiteit.

Helfrich, P. (2007). *Ken Wilber's Model of Human Development: An Overview (v.5.0)*. Available at www.paulhelfrich.com/library/Helfrich_P_The_Five_Phases_of_Wilber.pdf (Accessed 15 May 2013).

Hendley, B. (1978). Martin Buber on the teacher/student relationship: A critical appraisal. *Journal of Philosophy of Education*, 12(1), 141–148.

Hern, M. (2003). *Field Day: Getting Society Out of School*. New Star Books.

Hoffer, T.B. (2000). Accountability in education. In M.T. Hallinan (ed.), *Handbook of the Sociology of Education*. Springer.

Horn, R. (1999). The dissociative nature of educational change. In S.R. Steinberg, J.L. Kincheloe, & P.H. Hinchey (eds), *The Post-Formal Reader: Cognition and Education*. Routledge.

Horn, R. (2001). Knowledge mapping for complex social messes. A presentation at the David and Lucile Packard Foundation, Los Altos, 16 July.

Iannone, R.V., & Obenauf, P.A. (1999). Toward spirituality in curriculum and teaching. *Education*, 119(4), 737.

Ireson, J. et al. (1999). The common strands of pedagogy and their implications. In P. Mortimore (ed.), *Understanding Pedagogy and Its Impact on Learning*. SAGE Publications.

Jardine, D.W., Frieson, S., & Clifford, P. (eds) (2006). *Curriculum in Abundance*. Lawrence Erlbaum Associates.

Joiner, W.B., & Joseph, S.A. (2007). *Leadership Agility: Five Levels of Mastery for Anticipating and Initiating Change*. Jossey-Bass.

Jung, C.G., & Francis, R. (2003). *Four Archetypes: Mother, Rebirth, Spirit, Trickster*. Routledge.

Jung, C.G. et al. (1981). *The Archetypes and the Collective Unconscious, Collected Works of C.G. Jung* (Vol. 9, Part 1). Princeton University Press.

Kegan, R. (1982). *The Evolving Self*. Harvard University Press.

Kegan, R. (1994). *In Over Our Heads: The Mental Demands of Modern Life*. Harvard University Press.

Kelly, A.V. (2004). *The Curriculum: Theory and Practice* (5th edn). SAGE Publications.

Kemp, P. (2006). Mimesis in Educational Hermeneutics. *Educational Philosophy and Theory*, 38(2), 171–184.

Kenan, S. (2003). *Education under the Impact of Mechanistic and Positivistic Worldviews: The Case of Turkish Socio-Educational Transformations (1923–1940)*. Doctor of Education Dissertation, Columbia University Teachers College.

Kerr, L.A. (2002). *The Plight/Flight of Secondary Teachers: Educational Reform in Ontario*. Masters Dissertation, University of Toronto.

Kessler, R. (2000). *The Soul of Education: Helping Students Find Connection, Compassion, and Character at School*. Association for Supervision and Curriculum Development.

Kincheloe, J.L., & Steinberg, S.R. (1998). Students as researchers: Critical visions, emancipatory insights. In S.R. Steinberg & J.L. Kincheloe (eds), *Students as Researchers: Creating Classrooms that Matter*. Falmer Press.

Klein, J.T. (2004). Prospects for transdisciplinarity. *Futures: The Journal of Policy, Planning and Futures Studies*, 36(4), 515–526.

Klein, S.R. (2010). Integral theory and e-portfolio development: A model for professional development. *Journal of Integral Theory and Practice*, 7(1), 81–93.

Knowles, M.S. (1984). *Andragogy in Action*. Jossey-Bass.

Knowles, M.S. (1990). *The Adult Learner: A Neglected Species* (4th edn). Gulf.
Koestler, A. (1967). *The Ghost in the Machine*. Arkana.
Kohlberg, L. (1984). *Essays on Moral Development*, Vol. 2: *The Psychology of Moral Development*. Harper & Row.
Kramer, D. (2003). The ontogeny of wisdom in its variations. In J. Demick & C. Andreoletti (eds), *Handbook of Adult Development*. Kluwer Academic.
Kreisberg, J. (2010). Integral Education, integral transformation, and the teaching of mind-body medicine. In S. Esbjörn-Hargens et al. (eds), *Integral Education: New Directions for Higher Learning*. SUNY Press.
Kuhn, T. (1962). *The Structure of Scientific Revolutions*. The University of Chicago Press.
Ladson-Billings, G. (1995). But that's just good teaching! The case for culturally relevant pedagogy. *Theory into Practice*, 34(3), 159–165.
Li, H.I. (2005). Rethinking civic education in the age of biotechnology. *Educational Theory*, 55(1), 23–44.
Lloyd, D., & Wallace, J. (2004). Imaging the future of science education: The case for making futures studies explicit in student learning. *Studies in Science Education*, 40, 139–178.
Loevinger, J. (1976). *Ego Development*. Jossey-Bass.
Loveday, J.E. (2009). *Working Together for Student Success: Cross-Functional Collaboration at Community Colleges*. PhD Thesis, Oregon State University.
Lovelock, J. (2000). *Gaia: A New Look at Life on Earth*. Oxford University Press.
Lum, G. (2004) On the non-discursive nature of competence. *Educational Philosophy and Theory*, 36(5), 485–496.
MacLure, M. (2006). The bone in the throat: Some uncertain thoughts on baroque method. *International Journal of Qualitative Studies in Education*, 19(6), 729–745.
Marginson, S. (2004). University futures. *Policy Futures in Education*, 2(2), 159–174.
Martin, J.R. (1987). Reforming teacher education, rethinking liberal education. *Teachers College Record*, 88(3), 406–410.
Martineau, M., & Reams, J. (2010a). What does it take to be an integral educator? In W. Dea (ed.), *Igniting Brilliance: Integral Education for the 21st Century*. Integral Publishers.
Mason-Martineau, M., & Reams, J. (2010b). On the value and importance of personal development. In W. Dea (ed.), *Igniting Brilliance: Integral Education for the 21st Century*. Integral Publishers.
Maturana, H.R., & Varela, F.J. (1987). *Tree of Knowledge: The Biological Roots of Human Understanding*. Shambhala Publications, Inc.
Mayes, C. (1999). Reflecting on the archetypes of teaching. *Teaching Education*, 10(2), 3–16.
McGray, R.G. (2012). *Capacity Building for Citizenship Education: Global Hegemony and the New 'Ethics of Civilization'*. PhD Thesis, University of Alberta.
Mennin, S. (2010). Self-organization, integration and curriculum in the complex world of medical education. *Medical Education*, 44, 20–30.
Mezirow, J. et al. (2000). *Learning as Transformation: Critical Perspectives on a Theory in Progress*. Jossey-Bass.
Midgley, M. (1991). *Wisdom, Information and Wonder: What Is Knowledge For?* Routledge.
Midgley, M. (2002). *Evolution as a Religion: Strange Hopes and Stranger Fears*. Routledge.
Miller, J.P. (1986). Atomism, pragmatism, holism. *Journal of Curriculum and Supervision*, 1(3), 175–196.
Miller, R. (1999). Holistic education for an emerging culture. In S. Glazer (ed.), *The Heart of Learning: Spirituality in Education*. Jeremy P. Tarcher/Putnam.
Molz, M., & Hampson, G.P. (2010). Elements of the underacknowledged history of Integral Education. In S. Esbjörn-Hargens et al. (eds), *Integral Education: New Directions for Higher Learning*. SUNY Press.

Montuori, A. (2004). Edgar Morin: A partial introduction. *World Futures*, 60(5), 349–355.
Montuori, A. (2008). Foreword. In E. Morin. *On Complexity*. Hampton Press.
Morin, E. (1946). *L'An zéro de l'Allemagne*. Editions de la Cité Universelle.
Morin, E. (1982). *Science avec conscience*. Fayard.
Morin, E. (1992). *Method: Towards a Study of Humankind*, Vol. 1: *The Nature of Nature*. Peter Lang.
Morin, E. (1999). *Seven Complex Lessons in Education for the Future*. UNESCO.
Morin, E. (2007). Restricted complexity, general complexity. In C. Gershenson, D. Aerts, & B. Edmonds (eds), *Worldviews, Science and Us, Philosophy and Complexity*. World Scientific.
Morin, E. (2008a). *On Complexity*. Hampton Press.
Morin, E. (2008b). The reform of thought, transdisciplinarity, and the reform of the university. In B. Nicolescu (ed.), *Transdisciplinarity Theory and Practice*. Hampton Press.
Murray, T. (2009). What is the integral in Integral Education? From progressive pedagogy to integral pedagogy. *Integral Review*, 5(1), 96–134.
Naess, A. (1989). *Ecology, Community and Lifestyle: Outline of an Ecosophy*. Cambridge University Press.
Nava, R.G. (2001). *Holistic Education: Pedagogy of Universal Love*. Foundation for Educational Renewal.
Nerlich, B., & Clarke, D.D. (2003). Polysemy and flexibility: Introduction and overview. In B. Nerlich, Z. Todd, V. Herman, & D.D. Clarke (eds), *Polysemy: Flexible Patterns of Meaning in Mind and Language*. Mouton de Gruyter.
Neville, B. (1989). *Educating Psyche*. Collins Dove.
Nicolescu, B. (2002). *Manifesto of Transdisciplinarity*. SUNY Press.
Nicolescu, B. (ed.) (2008). *Transdisciplinarity: Theory and Practice*. Hampton Press.
Noddings, N. (2003). *Caring: A Feminine Approach to Ethics and Moral Education*. University of California Press.
O'Fallon, T. (2010a). Grounding integral theory in the field of experience. In S. Esbjörn-Hargens et al. (eds), *Integral Education: New Directions for Higher Learning*. SUNY Press.
O'Fallon, T. (2010b). Integral curriculum and program development in a technical world. In W. Dea (ed.), *Igniting Brilliance: Integral Education for the 21st Century*. Integral Publishers.
Okoro, J.I. (2004). *The Earth as a Living Superorganism: From the Scientific Gaia (Hypothesis) to the Metaphysics of Nature*. Peter Lang.
Olssen, M. (2008). Foucault as complexity theorist: Overcoming the problems of classical philosophical analysis. *Educational Philosophy and Theory*, 40(1), 96–117.
Orr, D.W. (1991a). *Earth in Mind: On Education, Environment, and the Human Prospect*. Island Press.
Orr, D.W. (1991b). What is education for? *Context: A Quarterly of Humane Sustainable Culture*, 27 (The Learning Revolution). Available at: www.context.org/ICLIB/IC27/Orr.htm (Accessed 3 December 2009).
Ozolins, J.J. (2007). Creativity, education and the subversion of the state. *Proceedings of the Philosophy of Education Society of Australasia Conference*, Wellington, 6–9 December.
Palmer, P.J. (1998). *The Courage to Teach: Exploring the Inner Landscape of a Teacher's Life*. Jossey Bass.
Pesut, D.J. (2012). Transforming inquiry and action in interdisciplinary health professions education: A blueprint for action. *Interdisciplinary Studies Journal*, 1(4), 53–63.
Peters, M. (2002). Anti-Globalization and Guattari's The Three Ecologies, *Globalization*, 2(1). Available at: http://globalization.icaap.org/content/v2.1/02_peters.html (Accessed 3 December 2009).

Peters, M. et al. (2000). Managerialism and educational policy in a global context: Foucault, neoliberalism, and the doctrine of self-management. In N.C. Burbules & C.A. Torres (eds), *Globalization and Education: Critical Perspectives*. Routledge.

Pinar, W.F. (ed.) (1975). *Curriculum Theorizing: The Reconceptualists*. McCuthan.

Pinar, W.F. (2004). *What Is Curriculum Theory?* Lawrence Erlbaum Associates.

Pinar, W.F. (2007). *Intellectual Advancement through Disciplinarity: Verticality and Horizontality in Curriculum Studies*. Sense.

Polanyi, M. (1962). *Personal Knowledge: Towards a Post-Critical Philosophy*. Routledge.

Post, H. (1975). The problem of atomism. *The British Journal for the Philosophy of Science*, 26(1), 19–26.

Postman, N., & Weingartner, C. (1971). *Teaching as a Subversive Activity*. Penguin.

Radford, M. (2008). Complexity and truth in educational research. *Educational Philosophy and Theory*, 40(1), 144–157.

Reams, J. (2010a). What can integral do for education? In W. Dea (ed.), *Igniting Brilliance: Integral Education for the 21st Century*. Integral Publishers.

Reams, J. (2010b). Classroom conversation: How to move beyond debate and discussion and create dialogue. In W. Dea (ed.), *Igniting Brilliance: Integral Education for the 21st Century*. Integral Publishers.

Renert, M., & Davis, B. (2010). An open way of being: Integral reconceptualization of mathematics for teaching. In S. Esbjörn-Hargens et al. (eds), *Integral Education: New Directions for Higher Learning*. SUNY Press.

Renert, M., & Davis, B. (2012). Ecological sustainability and mathematics education: Integrally connected. *Journal of Integral Theory and Practice*, 7(1), 94–104.

Ricoeur, P. (2004/1969). *Conflict of Interpretations*. Continuum.

Ritchey, T. (2011). *Wicked Problems—Social Messes: Decision Support Modelling with Morphological Analysis*. Springer.

Rittel, H., & Webber, M. (1973). Dilemmas in a general theory of planning. *Policy Sciences*, 4, 155–169.

Roberts, N.C. (2000). Wicked problems and network approaches to resolution. *The International Public Management Review*, 1(1). Available at https://journals.sfu.ca/ipmr/index.php/ipmr/article/view/175/175 (Accessed 23 February 2022).

Rockefeller, S.C. (2006). Meditation, social change, and undergraduate education. *Teachers College Record*, 108(9), 1775–1786.

Rooke, D., & Torbert, W.R. (2005). Seven transformations in leadership. *Harvard Business Review*, April. Available at https://hbr.org/2005/04/seven-transformations-of-leadership (Accessed 23 February 2022).

Ryan, J. (2010). The complete yoga: The lineage of Integral Education. In S. Esbjörn-Hargens et al. (eds), *Integral Education: New Directions for Higher Learning*. SUNY Press.

Sarra, C. (2012). *Strong and Smart—Towards a Pedagogy for Emancipation Education for First Peoples*. Routledge.

Scharmer, C.O. (2000). Presencing: Learning from the future as it emerges on the tacit dimension of leading revolutionary change. Presented at the Conference on Knowledge and Innovation, Helsinki School of Economics, 25–26 May.

Schiller, F., & Snell, R. (1954). *On the Aesthetic Education of Man*. Yale University Press.

Schiro, M. (2007). *Curriculum Theory: Conflicting Visions and Enduring Concerns*. SAGE Publications.

Schmidt, M.E. (2010). Educating the essential self: The AQAL model in socially conscious curricula. *Journal of Integral Theory and Practice*, 7(1), 67–80.

Schumacher, E.F. (1977). *A Guide for the Perplexed*. Perennial.

Scott, D. (2005). Critical realism and empirical research methods in education. *Journal of Philosophy of Education*, 39(4), 633–646.

Seddon, T. (1994). *Context and Beyond: Reframing the Theory and Practice of Education*. Falmer Press.
Shahajahan, R.A. (2010). Toward a spiritual praxis: The role of spirituality among faculty the colour teaching for social justice. *The Review of Higher Education*, 33(4), 473–512.
Shipway, B. (2002). *Implications of a Critical Realist Perspective in Education*. PhD Thesis, Southern Cross University.
Siena, D. (2005). Cosmosophy. *World Futures: The Journal of General Evolution*, 61, 409–440.
Snow, C.P. (1998). *The Two Cultures*. Cambridge University Press.
Soetaert, E.D. (2008). *Strategic Change in Higher Education: A Critical Realist Analysis*. PhD Thesis, University of Alberta.
Soucek, V. (1994). Flexible education and new standards of communicative competence. In J. Kenway (ed.), *Economising Education: The Post-Fordist Directions*. Deakin University Press.
Stack, S. (2010). Expanding our vision in the teaching and design of university science—Coming to know our students. In S. Esbjörn-Hargens et al. (eds), *Integral Education: New Directions for Higher Learning*. SUNY Press.
Steckler, E., & Torbert, W.R. (2010). A 'developmental action inquiry' approach to teaching first-, second-, and third-person action research methods. In S. Esbjörn-Hargens et al. (eds), *Integral Education: New Directions for Higher Learning*. SUNY Press.
Stein, Z. (2013). Ethics and the new education: Psychometrics, biotechnology, and the future of human capital. *Journal of Integral Theory and Practice*, 8(3–4), 146–163.
Sternberg, R.J. (2000). Intelligence and wisdom. In R.J. Sternberg (ed.), *Handbook of Intelligence*. Cambridge University Press.
Stillwaggon, J. (2008). Performing for the students: Teaching identity and the pedagogical relationship. *Journal of Philosophy of Education*, 42(1), 67–83.
Toroyson, R. (2010). Teaching integratively: Five dimensions of transformation. In S. Esbjörn-Hargens et al. (eds). *Integral Education: New Directions for Higher Learning*. SUNY Press.
Tubbs, N. (2005). Philosophy of the teacher. Chapter Five: The spiritual teacher. *Journal of Philosophy of Education*, 39(2), 288–298.
Tyack, D., & Tobin, W. (1994). The 'grammar' of schooling: Why has it been so hard to change? *American Educational Research Journal*, 31(3), 453–479.
Van Goor, R. et al. (2004). Beyond foundations: Signs of a new normativity in philosophy of education. *Educational Theory*, 54(2), 173–192.
Van Niekerk, M.P. (1998). *Transforming Education: The Role of Epistemology*. Doctor of Education Dissertation, University of South Africa.
Villaverde, L.E. (1999). Creativity: Creativity, art, and aesthetics unraveled through post-formalism: An exploration of perception, experience, and pedagogy. In S. Steinberg, J.L. Kincheloe, & P.H. Hinchey (eds), *The Post-Formal Reader: Cognition and Education*. Falmer Press.
Warner, M.M. (1993). Objectivity and emancipation in learning disabilities: Holism from the perspective of critical realism. *Journal of Learning Disabilities*, 26(5), 311–325.
Watkins, C., & Mortimore, P. (1999). Pedagogy: What do we know? In P. Mortimore (ed.), *Understanding Pedagogy and Its Impact on Learning*. SAGE Publications.
Weaver, W. (1948). Science and complexity. *American Scientist*, 36(4), 536–544.
Wheelahan, L. (2012). *Why Knowledge Matters in Curriculum: A Social Realist Argument*. Routledge.
Wieler, C. (2010). Embodying Integral Education in five dimensions. In S. Esbjörn-Hargens et al. (eds), *Integral Education: New Directions for Higher Learning*. SUNY Press.
Wilber, K. (1977). *The Spectrum of Consciousness*. The Theosophical Publishing House.

Wilber, K. (1979). *No Boundary: Eastern and Western Approaches to Personal Growth*. Center Publications.

Wilber, K. (1980). *The Atman Project: A Transpersonal View of Human Development*. The Theosophical Publishing House.

Wilber, K. (1981). *Up from Eden: A Transpersonal View of Human Evolution*. Anchor/Doubleday.

Wilber, K. (1983a). *A Sociable God: A Brief Introduction to a Transcendental Sociology*. McGraw-Hill.

Wilber, K. (1983b). *Eye to Eye: The Quest for the New Paradigm*. Anchor/Doubleday.

Wilber, K. (1991). *Grace and Grit: Spirituality and Healing in the Life of Treya Killam Wilber*. Shambhala Publications, Inc.

Wilber, K. (1995). *Sex, Ecology, Spirituality: The Spirit of Evolution* (Rev. edn). Shambhala Publications, Inc.

Wilber, K. (1996). *A Brief History of Everything*. Shambhala Publications, Inc.

Wilber, K. (1997a). *The Eye of Spirit: An Integral Vision for a World Gone Slightly Mad*. Shambhala Publications, Inc.

Wilber, K. (1997b). An integral theory of consciousness. *Journal of Consciousness Studies*, 4(1), 71–92.

Wilber, K. (1999). *One Taste: The Journals of Ken Wilber*. Shambhala Publications, Inc.

Wilber, K. (2000a). *Sex, Ecology, Spirituality: The Spirit of Evolution* (Rev. edn). Shambhala Publications, Inc.

Wilber, K. (2000b). *A Theory of Everything: An Integral Vision for Business, Politics, Science and Spirituality*. Shambhala Publications, Inc.

Wilber, K. (2000c). *Integral Psychology: Consciousness, Spirit, Psychology, Therapy*. Shambhala Publications, Inc.

Wilber, K. (2007a). *Integral Spirituality: A Startling New Role for Religion in the Modern and Postmodern World*. Shambhala Publications, Inc.

Wilber, K. (2007b). *The Integral Vision*. Shambhala Publications, Inc.

Wilber, K. (2013). Response to critical realism in defence of integral theory. *Integral Post*. Available at www.integrallife.com/integral-post/response-critical-realism-defense-integral-theory?page=0,4 (Accessed 6 May 2016).

Willmott, R. (1999). School effectiveness research: An ideological commitment? *Journal of Philosophy of Education*, 33(2), 253–268.

Winton, T. (2010). Developing and integral sustainability pattern language. *Journal of Integral Theory and Practice*, 5(1), 1–26.

Wood, N. (1992). Tabula rasa, social environmentalism, and the 'English paradigm'. *Journal of the History of Ideas*, 53(4), 647–668.

Young, M., & Lucas, N. (1999). Pedagogy in further education: New contexts, new theories and new possibilities. In P. Mortimore (ed.), *Understanding Pedagogy and Its Impact on Learning*. SAGE Publications.

Zembylas, M. (2006). Science education as emancipatory: The case of Roy Bhaskar's philosophy of meta-Reality. *Educational Philosophy and Theory*, 38(5), 665–676.

Zierer, K. (2011). Pedagogical eclecticism. *The Journal of Educational Thought*, 45(1), 3–19.

8

GETTING THEORY INTO PUBLIC CULTURE

Collaborations and Interventions Where Metatheorists Meet

Zachary Stein and Hans Despain

Introduction

What follows is a window into one of the first collaborative projects to emerge from the meetings of metatheorists documented in this book and its predecessor volume. The authors initially spoke in 2011 at the first symposium on the interface of critical realism and integral theory. The symposium had us meeting as strangers in San Francisco only to discover we lived merely a couple of towns apart in Western Massachusetts. With this proximity and potential collaboration as an incentive, we each thoroughly engaged the metatheory of the other. Zak read Bhaskar thoroughly and worked out a series of papers that integrated dialectical critical realism into his thinking regarding human development, education, and metatheory in general (Stein, 2016, 2019). Hans engaged integral theory extensively, especially Wilber's pioneering early work in transpersonal psychology. He was especially impressed by the use of developmental psychology and ideas regarding the potential for self-actualization contained within it. This lead to an exchange and public debate in the pages of the *Journal of Critical Realism*, where IT was defended and argued to offer DCR important insights regarding the dynamics of human development (Despain, 2013c, 2014). We began to meet regularly—'beer summits', they might be called—and found each and every conversation returning to diagnostic critique of the existing educational system and concrete utopian theorizing about what preferable educational systems could look like.

Our conversations also revolved around the seeming ineffectualness of academic publishing and the *perceived* irrelevance of metatheory to the lives and work of everyday people in the educational system. We decided therefore to write a series of popular statements—specifically, Op-Eds which have been published in several major newspapers (*Worcester Telegram & Gazette*, *Connecticut Post*, *Springfield Republican*, and *Post-Keynesian Forum*)—that would explain our ideas about

DOI: 10.4324/9781003140313-12

education in ways that would be understood and engaging to non-specialists. This was decided not so much because it would impact discourse in the public sphere, for this is a complex and complicated process. Rather, our attention to popular writings was understood by us both as a way to work towards a certain discipline in our writing and collaborations. We are seeking the simplicity on the other side of our complex metatheoretical diagnostics. Seeking to get theory into public culture. These were our first fumbling attempts.

We share the view that metatheory is radically important and relevant to political discourse. However, it is little understood and much neglected. Thus, our humble efforts at popular discourse are an attempt to summarize and simplify our academic work to a popular audience in the hope and belief that this effort brings the insights of integral theory and dialectical critical realism from our academic work to a wider and more political audience.

This chapter begins with an overview of the metatheoretical insights and principles that grew out of our conversations and into the public-facing writings. Then we present four of the Op-Eds, each of which was submitted to a New England area newspaper. Three of these were published. These are presented without commentary as artifacts of our collaboration. At the end of the chapter we provide some final reflections on the pieces and how they served as a vehicle for our metatheoretical partnership

1 An Educational Theory in the Making

Central to our project is Bhaskar's (1986, pp. 181–211; 1993, pp. 258–270) practice of *explanatory critique*, which is the use of scientific knowledge in general and social science in particular to diagnose false needs and differentiate them from *real* needs. The existential condition of living under a regime of false needs is a dysfunction of social being, a 'throwness' of being into the demi-real—that is, the lived illusions that are false but nonetheless causally efficacious. Socially sanctioned demi-realties function as *unjustifiable* constraints and limits on the development of individuals, resulting in alienation from both the realities of nature and the self. Explanatory critique is thus doubly critical: it demonstrates falsity of a belief *and* an ethical critique of the institutional conditions that perpetuate it through practice. Explanatory critique involves identifying where social scientific research reveals the falsity of widely accepted beliefs, identifying the causal role of social structures in explaining why these beliefs are widely accepted and issuing an ethical critique and call for engaged and critical action.

Bhaskar contends that when a social scientific theory confirms (1) that some widely held belief is false and (2) a prevailing social structure or institutional form is an important causal factor in sustaining the prevalence of this false belief, then (3) a negative normative valuation can be made against the prevailing social structure or institutional form. In this sense, explanatory critique pushes against 'Hume's law', which argues that 'ought' is logically independent from 'is', or that there is a strict dichotomy between 'facts' and 'values'. Bhaskar contends that scientific knowledge can reveal human values.

We agree and argue that this way of thinking should be at the forefront of educational theorizing. Explanatory critique does not end in thought. If (1) a widely held belief is shown to be false, and (2) a prevailing institutional form is an important causal factor in sustaining this false belief, wherefore (3) a negative normative valuation is made against the prevailing institutional form, and a soundly established theory confirms (4) that a certain activity may contribute to transferring or deposing the institutional form, then (5) a positive normative valuation can sanction that activity and *emancipatory* activity and change can ensue to remove the institutional form that is generating false beliefs, false needs, and prohibiting the process of self-actualization.

Our approaches hinge on the fact that contemporary educational configurations are radically open to explanatory critique. Stein's book *Social Justice and Educational Measurement* (2016) demonstrates that a fundamentally flawed approach to standardized testing and 'accountability' have emerged historically as the hegemonic force in educational reform. The results are both unjust and unethical, resulting in forms of schooling that undermine learning and healthy personal development. Stein demands and describes the forms of institutional change, political action, and educational activity that would constitute a standardized testing infrastructure that is ethical and facilitates healthy personal development. Stein (2019) deepens and expands this argument in his book *Education in a Time between Worlds*, where he argues that schools as we have known them are obsolete and require redesign from the ground up. As global economic and ecological crises deepen, and our global civilization enters the epochal crisis of the capitalist world system, schools must be replaced by a decentralized network of educational hubs. In the context of a global pandemic the *fragility* of large centralized school systems has been revealed. This has been shown alongside overwhelming evidence for the *resiliency* of digital educational platforms. The tide was already shifting towards using digital technologies as the basic foundation for new forms of education, and now the tide has turned. The near-term results of this change could be disastrous, as the very foundations of enculturation and learning shift perilously close to chaos. But there is an outside chance that we stand at the threshold of the most profound transformation of human education in history. Offering an integral redux of Ivan Illich's (1972) *Deschooling Society*, Stein suggests that technological, scientific, and cultural trends are ripe for the rethinking of the very concept of schooling.

In a series of articles, Despain (2011, 2013c, 2016) argues that the contemporary aims of higher education are built from the belief that college is primarily job training. This is false. Despain's argument is twofold. First he offers an empirical immanent critique: there are not enough well-paying jobs to incorporate all college graduates (let alone college dropouts) in the labour market. Tens of millions of college graduates (and those with 'some' college but no degree) will spend a lifetime paying off student loans working jobs that pay well below $50,000 USD annually. Second, American institutions of higher education were never intended to be institutions of job training. The curriculum is not well designed for vocational aims. Despain argues that the primary aim has historically been, and should continue to be, the attainment of personal knowledge and social self-awareness. Society downgrades higher education to job preparation at great peril to culture and democracy.

We both follow the great critical theorist of education Michael Apple (2001, 2004, 2013) in arguing that institutions of education are *contradictory* by nature. This means that educational systems hold both an *emancipatory* potential for helping to facilitate a process of self-actualization and an *oppressive* potential for generating blockages to personal development. We believe that institutions of education hold social power and means of increasing personal knowledge and understanding. Institutions of education have the potential to increase social consciousness and self-awareness and to facilitate the process of individual self-actualization. At the same time, as articulated above, institutions of education also function as organizations of social indoctrination, thus constraining and blocking self-actualization, thereby generating false beliefs and false needs. Education is simultaneously a process of social indoctrination and the foundation of self-understanding and wisdom. The social indoctrination aspect of schools means that they do not necessarily counteract the homogenous culture of modernity which is based on mass consumption, mass advertising, mass media, industrial management, and market-oriented modes of thought (Marcuse, 1964). Instead, schooling tends to encourage and reinforce an orientation towards mass consumption. The 'cultural industry' of modern capitalism promotes a personal development of docility and passivity in both the thoughts and actions of individuals (Adorno & Horkheimer, 1944, p. 95); it *creates false social needs* and a homogenous or 'one-dimensional' world of thought and behaviour (Marcuse, 1964, p. 5).

When we internalize socially created needs of mass culture, these needs not only dominate our desires and mind, but we feel them in our bodies. We feel the craving for the latest fashions and fads in our whole being. We get a bodily satisfaction from the images on screens and from the food and drinks we consume. Every time we satisfy these emotional, physical, and socially generated needs we reaffirm and reproduce the system and the technocrats who control it. Our participation in the cultural industry convinces us that it 'is a good way of life'—much better than before—and as a good way of life, it militates against qualitative change. Thus emerges a pattern of *one-dimensional thought and behavior*' (Marcuse, 1964, p. 12, emphasis in original). The cultural industry of modern capitalism is based on 'mass production', 'mass consumption', 'mass media', and one-dimensional being that claims the entire individual. 'In the process, the "inner" dimension of the mind in which opposition to the status quo can take root is whittled down' (Marcuse, 1964, p. 10). We are alienated from our own sense of possibility, and the typical individual fails to realize we could choose otherwise (Despain, 2011). False needs and false beliefs are generated by demi-reality (Bhaskar, 2002).

Our position holds tensions and affinities with the modern enlightenment idea that scientific knowledge informs human emancipation. Following Bacon, Descartes, and Voltaire, scientific knowledge helped to eliminate the causal sources of constraints generated from social processes and cognitive errors inherited from the past. This sense of modern 'enlightenment, understood in the widest sense as the advance of thought, has always aimed at liberating human beings from fear and installing them as [self-]masters. Yet the wholly enlightened earth radiates under the sign of disaster triumphant' (Adorno & Horkheimer, 1944, p. 1). According to Adorno and Horkheimer (1944, p. 94), modernity has generated a homogenous mass culture 'infecting everything with sameness'.

Fully embracing the sophisticated and rather theoretically esoteric models of integral theory and critical realism, and informed by the Frankfurt School's critique of the cultural industry, Zak and Hans discussed in our meetings the pedagogical necessity and urgency of helping a wide audience understand that the ideas and beliefs they hold concerning social being are false, or demi-real. We believed that we could develop explanatory critiques that would be interesting, inspiring, and accessible to a wide audience. In addition to our theoretical work and interest, we shared a desire to make the emancipatory work of Wilber and Bhaskar immediately accessible. Thus, we focused on prioritizing the aspects of our thoughts that could be organized into short pieces with high accessibility.

2 Getting Theory into Public Culture

Below find a series of four public-facing writings that seek to operationalize some of the metatheoretical ideas presented above. The first three were published and the fourth one was submitted but never published.

'College Is Not Just about Jobs'

Worcester Telegram & Gazette, 12 August 2014

Students will be returning to campus in a few weeks and college towns will be bustling. The frenetic energy that marks the beginning of a new school year will mask the recent decline in college enrolments. Why are fewer young people choosing to go to college?

It is perfectly simple. All indications are that the job prospects for the class of 2015 will be weak. There are bright employment opportunities for nurses and physicians, post-secondary educators, and accountants and auditors. Likewise, engineer, economic, finance, management, and education majors should do fine in the next several years. Nevertheless, unemployment for those under 25 is nearly 14 percent, and 11 percent for those aged 20–24.

The biggest problems for future graduates are not business pessimism, an unwillingness to hire, or the recession levels of unemployment. The main problems are structural shifts in labour markets; there simply are not enough high-skilled, well-paying, college degree jobs for the number of students graduating from college.

43 percent of science majors graduating in the years 2009–2011 are employed in positions that do not require a college degree; most of these jobs pay less than $30,000 per year. Economists call this 'underemployment'. For social science majors, 48 percent are underemployed. 52 percent of liberal arts majors and 50 percent of business majors are underemployed.

For decades it has been 'normal' for 30 percent or more of college graduates to be underemployed. However, time was when the majority of these jobs, for example mechanics, electricians, dental hygienist, and other skilled trades, paid well and were career-oriented or 'good' non-college jobs, filled by college graduates.

Theorists Jaison R. Abel, Richard Deitz, and Yaqin Su demonstrate in the Federal Reserve's *Current Issues in Economics and Finance* things have changed. In the 1990s, more than 40 percent of college graduates were underemployed. However, 50 percent of these underemployed recent-college-graduates had 'good' non-college jobs, and only 16 percent were in low-paying non-career-oriented positions. Today, nearly 45 percent of college graduates are underemployed, with more than 20 percent of them in low-paying positions, and only a dismal 36 percent in 'good' non-college jobs. Worse still nearly 1 out of 5 recent college graduates can only find part-time work.

These numbers are the result of structural labour market shifts that have nothing to do with curriculum or what individual professors or colleges are teaching. There are simply not enough good jobs. Neither for those with or without a college degree. It is simple arithmetic. Only 23 percent of jobs pay above $50,000, while more than 30 percent of the American population graduates with a four-year college degree. 50 percent of jobs pay less $25,000 per year.

These dismal job prospects go a long way in explaining the recent decline in college enrollments. Compounding the problem is the trillion-dollar student loan industry. College is simply too expensive for individual households, often without any hope for a 'good' job.

Many commentators conclude that these data suggest we need to decrease college enrollment. For example Ohio economist Richard Vedder and his colleagues conclude, 'All of this calls into question the wisdom of the "college for all"'. According to Vedder 'the underemployed college graduate is an expensive luxury we can ill afford as a nation'. The problem for Vedder is not merely underemployment, but 'overinvestment' in higher education.

We draw nearly the opposite conclusion.

The very idea that one could 'overinvest' in higher education shows a profound misunderstanding of what higher education is for (and an almost willing ignorance of who it is that actually foots the bill: the students who take on often crushing levels of debt). College is not, nor has it ever been, merely about getting a job.

Higher education in the United States has a heroic tradition of educating for social integration (including one's career) but also civic engagement (such as informed voting) and personal development. This tradition stretches from Thomas Jefferson through John Dewey to today, and values a well-educated enlightened citizenry, for its own sake, and for the health of our democracy—not merely for the functioning of our economy. This is a tradition that is something we cannot afford to neglect. It is only through active engagement in democratic processes and public debate that we reach a true understanding of the social ills that plague our society and find solutions that can be politically institutionalized.

Psychologists have for years been insisting on the cognitive and emotional impacts of higher education, specifically how college contributes to the creation of reflective civic engagement, empathy, and healthy lifestyle choices. These essential components of responsible citizenship are threatened by simplistic economic ideas about what higher education is for.

When the economy is underperforming, this leads to reactionary argumentation, like Vedder's, 'due to the lack of jobs—not everyone deserves college education'. Universities and colleges, likewise, often mistakenly overemphasis the job training aspects of their mission at the expense of undermining the civic, cognitive, and socio-emotional responsibilities of higher education.

During the presidential campaign of 2008, President Obama expressed a desire for providing a college education to everyone, so to achieve some level of economic success. This latter aim is clearly illusionary. The time has come to transcend the economic rhetoric about education and see education anew as a force for the health of our democracy and individual personal development.

We must move beyond the illusory calculations of the 'return on investment' in a college degree driving the (unconscionably profitable and predatory) student loan industry. No other industrialized nation has burdened its young adults with such debt; they have instead invested in them and in the long-term future of their societies. Education is the only way toward enlightened public debate, which remains our best hope for addressing the profound social ills that face our country: a lack of good jobs, household and business indebtedness to mega-sized corporate banks, trillion-dollar indebtedness of college graduates, and a far too cozy relationship between Wall Street and Washington.

US Meritocracy Is an Illusion

Worcester Telegram & Gazette, 14 January 2015

There is a strong belief that educational success leads to financial pay-offs. The idea is that the smartest and most hard working are the ones who receive the greatest financial rewards. Data illustrates that on average, the more education, the higher one's pay. Salary appears to be related to educational attainment and merit. These 'averages' can be misleading in very surprising ways.

As Thomas Piketty points out in his recent high-profile book, *Capital in the Twenty-First Century*, education cannot explain the difference between high earners and the *super* high earners. In other words, those making between $100,000 and $200,000 a year and those making above $1 million a year have nearly identical educational attainments, and while the former have seen wage stagnation, the latter have experienced an explosion in compensation.

Similarly, there has been a significant divergence between median income earners and the poorest 10 percent. This has very little to do with educational attainment or skill deficiencies and far more to do with the (dis)function of contemporary labour markets, the erosion of unionization, and management strategies of businesses to keep wages low.

The 'impressive' November jobs report showed 321,000 new jobs and a 5.8 percent rate of unemployment. Meanwhile wages remain remarkably sluggish. Worst still, *the most elevated unemployment has been for workers with a college degree.* Also glaring and historically unprecedented is the fact that 53 percent of recent college graduates are either unemployed, employed part-time, or working in an industry that does not require a college degree. Data by the National Bureau of Economic Research (NBER) shows that the real annual income of American college graduates has decreased since the year 2000.

Labour markets are egregiously unfriendly to recent college graduates and other workers. The decline in income is not due to the lack of ability or knowledge possessed by Americans, but is instead caused by very weak domestic labour markets, as well as drastically lower wages and salaries in countries such as India and China. Without policies to protect American wages and salaries, the income of American households will tend to stagnate or fall, regardless of the level of education.

Educational attainment is not the main factor that explains the distribution of wealth in our society.

Throughout most of US history there has been a very strong link between 'productivity' and wages: when worker productivity rose, wages increased. Since 1973 this strong link broke. Productivity in the US is unambiguously increasing. The economy in terms of real GDP, or actual goods and services produced, has more than doubled since 1970. However, it is only the richest 10 percent of Americans that have benefited from this increase in productivity. According to NBER economists, 90 percent of American households have seen their real income fall since 1975. The problem here is not a lack of education; in fact the increases in productivity can be attributed to an educated and highly skilled workforce. Rather the problem is one of distribution and the lack of economic justice. Our policies are failing to protect American workers, wages, and salaries.

It is a mistake to vilify American schools for the state of the economy. Instead we must look toward the outsourcing of jobs and the weakened bargaining position of American workers, along with their declining wages and salaries. We contend that the explanation for our current crisis lies in how financial markets are now functioning and the related concentration of economic wealth and power. As emphasized by Piketty, there has been a massive shift from wages and salaries (aka labour income) to income from interest payments, dividends, rents, and profits (aka capital income, which is at a 70-year high). If it were not for the 1940s, when wage income was purposefully suppressed for the war-effort, capital income would be the highest in US history. The improved position of capital income has occurred at the same time that the bargaining position of workers has worsened.

As Harvard economists Claudia Goldin and Lawrence Katz have argued in their book, *The Race between Education and Technology*, wage inequality in the United States has been due to a failure to sufficiently invest in higher education. According to Goldin and Katz, too many people have failed to obtain a college education, in part because of limited access, weak and dated curriculum, and high tuition. We strongly endorse the insight that broader access to college and increased public investment in higher education are necessary for economic growth and social health. Nevertheless, we cannot 'school' our way out of bad economic policies.

We do not have an educational policy problem; we have an economic labour policy problem. Regardless of education levels, outsourcing jobs and the bargaining position of American workers will worsen unless policy is in place to protect low-educated *and* highly educated American workers alike.

Show Me the Money: Wage Stagnation Creates the Illusion of a Skills Gap

Worcester Telegram & Gazette, 21 March 2015

In recent years there has been a growing concern regarding the workplace skills of American college graduates. Numerous reports have complained that employers are having a difficult time finding graduates with the right skills. The Bureau of Labor Statistics reports confirm that employers are taking longer to fill vacancies.

Harvard economists Claudia Goldin and Lawrence Katz have claimed that starting in 1970 education began to 'lose the race' with technology, skills acquired in college no longer keep pace with changes in the labour market's demand. They argue that we need to renovate college curricula to better keep pace with technological change, calling for more college for more people on the grounds that it is good for the economy and leads to higher incomes for individuals.

This is an important argument, and we agree with much of it, but it falls prey to the classic American tendency of 'blaming the schools' for economic failures. There is important evidence suggesting that reports of college graduates' lack of job skills are exaggerated and misleading. Nearly all the evidence suggesting that college graduates lack job skills come from employer surveys and consulting firms. There are good reasons to have scepticism toward these surveys and their simplistic interpretation that the schools are failing.

Firms have reduced their recruiting efforts. Many firms that have in the past relied on recruiting agencies to oversee hiring are now trying to save money by doing their own recruiting, which is far less efficient. Some firms have reduced ranks within their human resource departments. Moreover, it can be difficult to hire and retain workers when there are problems within organizational cultures. If applicants get a sense of unpleasant bosses or a hostile workplace, they will decline offers, and employers will experience this as an inability to fill vacancies. Recent surveys of work culture suggest that toxic levels of stress are common and they are degrading the quality of working environments across a wide range of sectors.

However, the number one reason for the increase in vacancy times and the apparent inability of businesses to find the 'right' person is the current trend toward decreasing payrolls. In other words, businesses are hiring but at significantly lower salaries and benefits, so many applicants are simply turning down offers. There is very strong evidence to support this. The Economic Policy Institute has recently released a report documenting 35 years of wage and salary stagnation. Reports from the Federal Reserve and Pew Research Center document the difficulties college graduates have in finding 'acceptable' paying jobs.

If the problem were that employers are not finding the proper skills, economists would expect to see an increase in wages and salaries to attract those skills. The evidence suggests exactly the opposite; wages and salaries for new hires are stagnant and low. Thus, firms are enduring longer vacancies because their offers are too low. Vacancies are not due to a lack of workers with the right job skills, exactly the opposite. The average worker and job candidate has more education than their current job requires. The average wages and salaries for new hires have been falling. We contend that changes to college curricula toward a greater focus on 'job skills' would do little to impact these trends.

Employers are taking advantage of our most recent economic downturn, and the related overabundance of highly skilled unemployed, to significantly lower their payrolls. American workers are not undereducated, but overeducated. Employers have a large supply of very talented, highly skilled, and well-educated job applicants. They thus make very low offers. It takes more time for companies to fill job vacancies when salaries are low.

Educational reform fails without corresponding job policy.

Tax policy and labour law should encourage full-time employment and discourage internships and part-time work. Low-wage workers are entitled to an increase in minimum wage, which establishes a real living wage. Moreover, the long-term prospects of both higher education and the economy require that we expand the federal subsidization of higher education and reduce the loan dependency of students.

The illusion of a 'skills gap' has us ignoring job policy, and clamoring instead to make job skills the sole focus of what college is about.

DeVos is Shadow Projection of the Left in Education Reform

Unpublished, June 2017

President Trump's most controversial cabinet pick was Department of Education Secretary Betsy DeVos. The main complaints were her complete lack of experience, her ignorance of education, and her antipathy toward public schools. In her confirmation hearing she demonstrated a painful witlessness of the Department of Education and its programs.

She was narrowly confirmed 51 to 50 with no Democratic support.

The concerns of DeVos' critics were confirmed with the 13 percent slash in the proposed 2018 budget for the Department of Education.

Democrat Rep. Rosa DeLauro of New York declared DeVos' budget proposal to be 'cruel', 'inhumane', and 'heartless'. Even the Republican Chairman, Senator Roy Blunt of Missouri, expressed concern about her priorities, and explained 'this is a difficult budget to defend'.

The budget cut in half the work-study program and proposed deep cuts in student financial aid services which help lower-middle and middle class students to afford college. In all more than 30 programs will have funding reductions or face elimination.

DeVos' 'cruelty', 'heartlessness', inexperience, ignorance, and antipathy toward public schools make her easy to loathe.

However, the attack on public education did not start with Betsy DeVos or Donald J. Trump's pronouncement that public schools are 'a disaster, a complete disaster'. The campaign against public schools has been bipartisan and often led by the Democrats.

For several decades Democrats and Republicans have in a bipartisan effort embraced an education 'reform' agenda that has been 'cruel' and 'heartless' for American children and public schools. No one has analyzed this bipartisanship more accurately than Michael Apple of the University of Wisconsin.

Several forces have come together to unite liberals, libertarians, and conservatives in an alliance to dismantle the American tradition of common schools and public education. The result has been an 'authoritarian populism' that despises public schools, abhors its teachers, has undermined creativity and learning, and cruelly and heartlessly abandoned America's most vulnerable and disadvantaged children.

There are four major elements to this political alliance of 'cruelty' and 'heartlessness' toward public education, each of which DeVos well represents. The first and dominant element that unites the alliance is a group of business and economic elites who are intent to marketize and privatize all social institutions. They are certain that markets best solve all social problems. This group of elites has strong support for privatized choice plans and vouchers for private secular and religious schools.

The second element is fiscal and cultural conservatives who promote an American cultural education and demand high standards, discipline, and historical knowledge of the American experience. Increasingly the cultural aspect of this thrust includes a Christian religious bias.

The third element is working-class and middle-class groups who have a severe mistrust of the state and believe government involvement makes institutions dysfunctional. These groups have suffered the greatest losses regarding unemployment and lost pay from global competition and the financial crisis.

The fourth element is the new professional middle class of technocrats who are deeply committed to technical and managerial solutions to educational dilemmas. They emphasize accountability, efficiency, and business management techniques.

Betsy DeVos' primary focus has been the privatization of public schools using the language of 'choice'. However, she well represents each element, by promoting federal dollars for private Christian schools, a strong mistrust of the state, and her support for business management techniques to lead educational administration.

These four elements have become a political alliance that has successfully pushed for school 'reform' that is a market-orientated authoritarian populism that has implemented a national curricula, national standards, common-core, and ubiquitous standardized testing and assessment.

An important contradiction of this authoritarian populist alliance is that it demands a diminished role of the state with a turn toward private for-profit and non-profit educational firms *and simultaneously* demands an increased role of the state for the regulation of national curricula, national standards, common-core, and standardized testing.

The primary contradiction is that private companies such as Kaplan, Harcourt, McGraw-Hill, Riverside Publishing, and Pearson, driven by profits, prevent and corrupt educational aims. These companies account for more than 90 percent of all exams administered at the state level. In addition they produce the majority of textbooks, data management, professional development programmes, online classes, and teacher certification. Privatization has failed to achieve No Child Left Behind, but has succeeded regarding No Profit Left Behind.

The profit motive can inspire innovation and spur economic growth; it can also corrupt organizations. Not every institution should be marketized.

Most people understand that marketizing human organs for transplant patients or marketizing sex leads to perverted incentives and corruption of these activities. Education is another sector in which the profit motive generates perversion and corruption.

There are challenges in public education, but privatization is a defective response, not a solution. The profit motive perverts and corrupts educational aims.

The profit motive in education encourages schools to employ illicit educational methods. Virtual instruction, such as Rocketship Schools, pay instructors $12–$18 per hour to instruct 130 children on computers. Charter schools have decreased the pay of teachers while simultaneously increasing the pay of administrators. For-profit universities, such as Phoenix and DeVry, have made a mockery of higher education by employing predatory recruitment techniques and leaving millions of students with heavy debt burdens, poor education, and weak job prospects.

Most people agree public education is in crisis. The authoritarian populist alliance places blame for the perceived crisis on public schools, poor parenting, bad teaching, and unions. Authoritarian populism assumes the goal of education is job skills.

There is an alternative view that education is about personal development; an understanding of history, civics, and the natural world; the development of creativity and an appreciation of the arts and humanities; and developing a love of learning. Policy geared toward job skills and economic markets undermines the other educational goals.

There are many well-intentioned people who embrace part or all of authoritarian populist school reform. This does not make these people bad, but they are misguided. This movement is well funded by corporate think tanks and has spent hundreds of millions of dollars in political lobbying. At stake are billions of dollars of profits. The bank roles funding the authoritarian populist alliance are billionaires, like Betsy DeVos and Bill Gates, who have their own children in elite private schools that pay their teachers well and treat them with admiration and respect.

When teachers are able to focus on creativity, personal development, and a varied curriculum that is relevant to the student demographic they service—rather than being forced to teach to a test, achieve arbitrary assessment measures, and a common core—children excel and enjoy learning. When teachers are treated with admiration and respect instead of a culture of assessment intimidation, the school environment for children is more nurturing and conducive to learning.

3 Crisis Tendencies in Higher Education: What Is College for Anyway?[1]

The popular press gives the impression that greater investment in and access to higher education will reduce income inequality (Kraushaar, 2014; Colvin, 2014). Top level government officials express the same sentiment. Secretary of Education Arne Duncan (2013) contends: 'In today's ... globally competitive economy ... some postsecondary schooling is essential. As President Obama has said, "Education is no longer just a pathway to opportunity and success. It's a prerequisite for success"'.

We take exception with this line of reasoning. It misidentifies the most important purposes of education, is based on a misunderstanding of the scientific notion of causation, and results in ill-prescribed policy.

There is now overwhelming evidence that schooling does not diminish income inequality (Piketty, 2014). Since 1970, enrolment in and graduation from four-year colleges and universities have increased, while income inequality has widened. Bowles and Gintis (2011/1976) argue schooling does not add to or subtract from income inequality, because the mechanisms of inequality are institutionally economic. We strongly endorse this position.

4 The Nature of the Crisis: The Illusion of Return on Investment in College

US Census reports (2002, 2011), contend roughly $1.8 million difference in lifetime earnings between college graduates and those with no college. Unfortunately, these figures are highly misleading. Our own calculations demonstrate a range of $40,000 to $320,000 return from college versus high school graduates for the lifetime earnings of the 'typical' student. There is a range because educational 'returns' depend on: (1) major chosen, and (2) the specific institution of higher education attended (Despain, 2011). This 'return range' is trending downward.

Five years into 'recovery' and unemployment for workers under 25 is 14.3 percent (BLS, 2014, Table A-10). One out of every five college graduates working can find only part-time work (Wessel, 2014); 45 percent of 2009–2011 college graduates are working in jobs requiring no college. Underemployment of college graduates is not unusual, 30 percent is the historical average (Abel et al., 2014). However, college graduates are no longer finding 'good' non-college jobs. Jobs not requiring college, but that otherwise pay well and are career-orientated (e.g., mechanics, electricians, dental hygienist, and other skilled trades) are becoming increasingly rare (Abel et al., 2014).

In the 1990s, approximately 40 percent of college graduates were underemployed; 50 percent of these underemployed recent college graduates had 'good' non-college jobs, 16 percent were in low-paying non-career-oriented positions. Today, nearly 45 percent of college graduates are underemployed, with more than 20 percent in low-paying positions, and a dismal 36 percent in 'good' non-college jobs (Abel et al., 2014).

Another serious problem facing recent and future college graduates is unemployment. Economists contend the BLS figures fail to account for 'missing workers' (EPI, 2014). Shierholz et al. (2014) argue calculating in 'missing workers' increases unemployment for workers under 25 to above 18 percent.

When these underemployment and unemployment problems are seen alongside the ubiquity of loan-based financing of higher education, the unsustainability of the situation becomes clear. Under current law, dismal job prospects, and high levels of borrowing, we are predicting 20–30 percent of current college students will fail to pay off their schools loans. The injustice of the student loan industry is now well documented (e.g., Collinge, 2010; Tabbi, 2012). An entire generation has been shackled in education-debt bondage.

It is not just students enduring the process of financialization. Universities are directly confronting financialization with their use of a broad array of financial instruments to fill the financial gap left by cuts in state and federal appropriations. Financialization has now infiltrated university governance (Eaton et al., 2014; Hudson, 2014). Since 2002, colleges and universities have taken on crushing amounts of debt; interest payments 'have nearly doubled from $6 billion in 2002 to $11 billion in 2012' (Eaton et al., 2014). Financialization, neoliberal management, and austerity are creating an almost dystopian educational environment (Giroux, 2014).

5 Responses to the Crisis: Gatekeepers and Liberators

Many commentators conclude that these data suggest a need to decrease college enrolment. Ohio economist Richard Vedder and colleagues (2013) conclude, 'All of this calls into question the wisdom of "college for all"'. Vedder continues, 'the underemployed college graduate is an expensive luxury we can ill afford as a nation'. The problem for Vedder is not merely underemployment, but higher education 'overinvestment'. This obtuse line of argument is as follows: (1) the purpose of higher education is preparation for job entrance; (2) the economy doesn't produce enough jobs requiring college degrees, therefore; (3) most people have no reason to go to college.

Following Vedder's logic, the future of higher education would be radically truncated, especially if trends toward automation and de-skilling of labour continue. If college is a bad investment, and fewer individuals can go, who are the few that attend? The government shouldn't foot the bill because scholarships don't pay off, leaving only the wealthy who can afford the 'luxury' of college. And it would be these few individuals who then occupy those few jobs that require higher education—the most complex and powerful positions in society. A deeply troubling policy position.

We draw nearly the opposite conclusion.

Vedder's idea that we could 'overinvest' in higher education shows a profound misunderstanding of what higher education is for. College is not, nor has it ever been, merely about getting a job.

US higher education has a heroic tradition of educating for social integration (including one's career) but also civic engagement (such as informed voting) and personal development. This tradition stretches from Jefferson through Dewey to critical pedagogy (Giroux, 2003), and values a well-educated enlightened citizenry, for its own sake, and for the health of our democracy—not merely for the functioning of our economy (Apple, 2013). It is only through active engagement in democratic processes and public debate that we reach a true understanding of social ills. The American democratic tradition should not be truncated (Apple & Beane, 2007).

Psychologists insist on the cognitive and emotional impacts of higher education (Harre, 1989), specifically how college contributes to the creation of reflective civic engagement, empathy, and healthy lifestyle choices (Pascarella & Terenzini, 2005; Noddings, 2003). These essential components of responsible citizenship are threatened by simplistic economic ideas of higher education.

When the economy is underperforming, reactionary arguments like Vedder's come to predominate. Universities and colleges, likewise, often mistakenly overemphasis the job training aspects of their mission at the expense of undermining the civic, cognitive, and socio-emotional responsibilities of higher education (Giroux, 2014).

The illusory logic of the 'return on investment' from college must be rejected—and with it the unconscionably predatory student loan industry this logic supports. No other industrialized nation burdens young adults with such education-loan induced peonage; instead education is socially supported and with it society and social reciprocity. Education is the only way toward enlightened public debate, which remains our best hope for addressing profound social ills: a lack of good jobs, household and business indebtedness, radically undemocratic workplaces, and a far too cozy relationship between Wall Street and Washington.

6 Policy Implications: Set the Students Free!

Today's workers are more educated, more skilled, and work more hours—with no increase in real income. American schools are producing more educated workers than the American workplace can absorb. Crushing levels of student loan debt force the hand of recent graduates toward underemployment, discouraging the risk-taking and entrepreneurship that could potentially contribute to changing the character of the job market. Seeing this outcome, many students are simply choosing not to go to college, evidenced by the recent decline in college enrolment (Fain, 2014).

We suggest a sevenfold response to the current crisis in higher education. Educational reform fails without (1) a corresponding progressive job policy

(Bowles &Gintis, 2011/1976), which should promote ecological sustainability (Despain, 2012) and extend democracy in the workplace (Wolff, 2012; Despain, 2013c). Students and recent graduates will continue to be exploited as peons until there are (2) laws that encourage full-time employment and discourage internships and part-time work (Perlin, 2012). All workers are entitled to (3) a large increase in minimum wage, which establishes a real living wage (Pollin, 2012). Likewise, everyone stands to benefit from (4) tax policies that increase the share of national income going to labour and decreases the share of national income going to capital (Galbraith, 2014). The long-term prospects of both higher education and the economy require that we (5) create conditions for education-debt forgiveness (Graeber, 2011; McArble, 2011; studentloanjustice. org). Teachers and students will continue to be alienated and oppressed until we (6) democratize educational institutions (Apple & Beane, 2007). And, finally, we must simply (7) expand federal subsidization of higher education and diminish the loan dependency of students, recognizing that spending on education creates more jobs than any other spending (Pollin & Garrett-Peltier, 2011). All of this depends upon new economic literacy concerning federal deficits (Wray, 2012), fiscal responsibility (Kregel, 2010), and proper monetary management (Galbraith, 2014; Kregel, 2014). The problem for the above proposal isn't a lack of money, but how the money is spent.

Final Reflections: The Importance of Metatheory for Public Discourse

In the pages of the *Journal of Critical Realism*, Timothy Rutzou (2012, 2014) questioned the compatibility of integral theory with critical realism. To some extent the debate between Roy Bhaskar and Ken Wilber can offer some support to Rutzou's argument. Although Hans Despain (2013c, 2015) directly debated Rutzou's position, the ongoing collaboration between Stein and Despain demonstrates the fruitfulness of the IT and CR engagement.

Although in our popularly orientated articles (and even in our more academic collaboration) we do not specifically unfold the metatheories that inform our thinking and writing, we believe it is our metatheoretical orientation that has made our collaboration so successful. We have shared many hours in conversation, sketching notes and drinking beer. The metatheories of IT and CR are erudite and relatively complicated to the layperson.

Our association begins with the belief that whatever the tensions are between integral theory and critical realism they primarily complement each other at a metatheoretical level. Despain (2013c, 2015) elaborates on this view in his debate with Rutzou; Despain's position is in agreement with positions articulated by Stein (2016), Marshall (2016), Esbjorn-Hargens (2016) and Hedlund (2016). In addition, both CR and IT are normative projects, (dialectical) critical realism toward emancipation from oppressive institutional conditions of the social order, and integral theory toward overcoming immature ego-orientated modes of consciousness and realizing transpersonal transcendence. We immediately recognized that integral theory tends to be weak on conceptualizing social structure, while critical realism is weak on the psychology of consciousness and personal (especially transpersonal) development.

Critical realism attempts to illustrate social being with the four-planar social being, as articulated in Bhaskar's (1993) *Dialectic: The Pulse of Freedom*. In this model there are four positive planes, two ([a] and [d]) constitute the biosphere, [a] is the plane of material transaction of human being with nature (critical realism emphasizes especially the production process and labour relations on this plane), [d] is the plane of the subjectivity of human beings inter-/intra subjective (or personal) actions. [a] and [d] are heavily mediated, before the existence of any particular human being by planes [b] and [c]. Planes [b] and [c] constitute the 'social cube', and it is made quite clear in critical realism these planes cannot be conflated. Conflation leads to theoretical and logical contradictions. Thus, keeping them distinct and an emphasis on the social structure generates very insightful results. In other words, agency and structure have ontological uniqueness. Plane [b] is the plane of inter-/intra subjective actions. Plane [c] is the plane of social relations. Planes [a] and [b] are the site of (oppressive) social power relations, what Bhasker calls power$_2$ relations, and structures and mechanisms in plane [c] may not be visible, as is arguably the case in capitalism due to reification, fetishism, and alienation. In others words, Bhaskar develops a model of social being whereby inter-/intra actions of human beings (plane [b]) generate rationalizations and false beliefs about the social relations (plane [c]) which reproduce oppressive structures (in part) by the voluntary actions of those directly oppressed (see Esbjörn-Hargens, 2016, pp. 106–107 for an insightful comparison between Bhaskar's social cube and Wilber's four quadrants).

Integral theory also offers models of human development whereby human beings can be stunted from full development, or fail to fully achieve self-actualization and transpersonal awareness. Moreover, human beings can have false beliefs and rationalizations of their stunted development. Wilber (1980, 1977) develops a stage theory and levels of consciousness model, what he calls 'the complete life cycle'. Wilber's life cycle model follows psychological theories of development quite closely by contending the infant/child develops from the instinctual, impulsive and 'id-ish' modes of 'subconsciousness' to egotistic, conceptual, and syntaxical levels of consciousness.

The development from instinctual to syntaxical levels of consciousness constitutes late ego persona or relative mature identity within what is considered 'normality' given the social institutional order. The fictional or mythical illustration of this development is 'the Hero' and 'also the story of the ego, for the ego *is* the Hero' (Wilber, 1996/1980, p. 5).

For Wilber the Hero and ego story is the 'outward arc' development, the development from subconsciousness to self-consciousness and social 'normality'. But this is only half of the Wilberian evolution of consciousness. Beyond social normality is a potential for 'superconsciousness'. The path to superconsciousness is the path of mystical return and the 'psychology of eternity', which is an internal story of the Atman Project and constitutes the inward arc.

The life cycle model as developed by Wilber delivers an important insight. A subconsciousness has a completely different conception of the self than does the self-consciousness. The late ego has a strong understanding of their social identity, rules, norms, and practices, the subconsciousness strongly identifies with their impulses and bodily instincts. Likewise, the superconsciousness begins to shed significant aspects of their social identity and becomes increasingly motivated by compassion, love, and gratefulness. The superconsciousness can further develop the capacity for transpersonal identity with the eternal archetypal-divine. For the superconsciousness, social normality begins to appear as, and is experienced to be, radically *abnormal* and *oppressive*.

In our philosophical beer summits we recognized that from critical realism and integral theory we had two theoretical positions that helped to explain how the motives of students in school were mistakenly understood to be about getting work skills and good jobs, i.e. the financial return on the college 'investment'. The idea that college is primarily about the 'return on investment' is a demi-reality because although it is causally efficacious, it is also significantly false.

The warrant of truth of the 'return on investment' position is that with a college degree a person tends to do better in the labour market than a person without a degree. However, it is false for numerous reasons, which include the fact that more than 30 percent of college graduates work jobs that do not require a college degree. Nearly 50 percent of recent college graduates (those graduating within the last six years), either do not have jobs, are only employed part-time although they desire full-time work, or have a job that does not require a college degree. Moreover, nearly 30 percent of college graduates have a negative return on their college educational investment, i.e. they pay more for college than they make up in the labour markets post-graduation. The demi-reality of the 'return on investment' model of schooling further reveals two aims of real education, one from a Wilberian perspective and the other from a Bhaskarian perspective. From a Wilberian perspective college education should help facilitate personal development of the 'inward arc' and, toward superconsciousness, the fulfilment of self-actualization and transpersonal identity with the psychology of eternity. From a Bhaskarian perspective college education should help reveal and make coherent hidden social structures or plane [c] of Bhaskar's social cube. These two aims increase understanding and enhance the meaningfulness of life, but do *not* necessarily increase the financial return of education. Indeed, an increase in self and social awareness may be antithetical to a 'return on investment' motive of education and pecuniary motives in life.

We enthusiastically understood we have two complementary theoretical and metatheoretical bodies of knowledge that are capable of explaining why the majority of students, parents, educators, and administrators had a false conception of higher education. The social structure of especially weak labour markets and brutal work conditions has everyone anxious about obtaining work skills, knowledge, and a good job. On the other hand, we also understood that the mass consumption, mass advertising, and impoverished knowledge of the potential of superconsciousness and the inward arc has human beings in Western society double down on 'normality' and ego development stunting their ability to develop toward superconsciousness.

But these (meta-)theoretical insights are difficult, esoteric, and rationalized away by ego consciousness to make them a poor vehicle for articulating our explanatory critiques to a large audience. Thus, we decided to attempt to bring our economic, educational, psychological, philosophical, and metatheoretical insights forward in a more exoteric way. We identify the circumstances and results of frustration, anxiety, and anger, for example the illusion of meritocracy, i.e. people get into Ivy League universities based on personal accomplishment, and provide an explanatory critique without any explanation of the metatheoretical positions that help clarify our critiques to us personally.

Our readers have been impressed with our uniqueness of thought. They often believe that we are really good statisticians and are better able to scrutinize quantitative data. Frankly, neither of us is particularly strong in the specifics of statistics and statistical modelling. Instead, our metatheoretical positions have us view reality differently, and understand that conventional wisdom is often false. This insight has us look at the quantitative work of others differently.

For example, the US Census Bureau with true experts and quantitative data generated a report that claimed a college graduate makes $1.8 million USD more in a life of work than non-college graduates. The Census Bureau's 'college graduates' included college graduates and graduate degree holders such as JDs, MDs, PhDs, and master's degree holders. The non-college graduates included high school graduates *and* high school dropouts. We did two quite simple things to re-analyze the data: first, we excluded anyone with any degree beyond bachelor's level and excluded high school dropouts. This allowed us to compare specifically 'college degree' holders to specifically 'high school' degree holders. This change reduced the difference between bachelor's degree holders and high school degree holders in a 35-year lifetime of work to $800,000 USD. Second, we excluded the richest 5 percent. We called this the Billy Madison effect. In the movie Billy Madison, Billy will inherit his father's business on the condition he finishes high school. These network effects are well known. Many wealthy children simply need to graduate high school or college to get their job. So regardless of the degree obtained, if a person is in the richest 5 percent we excluded them from the analysis. This reduced the difference in a lifetime of work between bachelor's degree holders and high school degree holders to a dismal $123,000 USD, a difference of $67 USD per week. This figure of $67 a week is the average: some will be above, some below. Thus, the significant numbers are as follows: approximately 30 percent of students are wasting their time in college if the goal is simply a 'return on investment'.

Finally, we contend college is not a waste of time if we have a better conception of what 'college is really for'. We believe as an entry point that college is about becoming aware of and developing capacities for superconsciousness development, and becoming aware of the hidden structures, false beliefs, and oppressive power$_2$ relations that prohibit it.

With emphasis, it was our metatheoretical insights about social structures and personal development that informed us that the $1.8 million USD number seemed far too large. In other words, if this number were correct perhaps college really would be about job skills and return on investment. Rejecting this latter claim, we borrowed the data from the Census Bureau and reshaped it to reveal the hidden facts within.

We would like to conclude this chapter with some collaborative and metatheoretical inspiration. Theory and metatheory matter. In fact, it is the radically unique position of critical realism and integral theory that have us looking at reality different from conventional wisdom. In particular, we know all people, including ourselves, act on false or illusionary beliefs and are socialized and must navigate oppressive social circumstances that prohibit superconsciousness development and self-actualization. Thus, of course reading and studying thinkers such as Roy Bhaskar and Ken Wilber are worth the effort even when it is not necessarily rewarded within academia and the mainstream literary order. Hold faith in your intuition about the truthfulness and necessity of metatheory. Second, collaboration with others is essential. Our personal collaboration reinforces and inspires us as individuals. For this reason alone the integral theory/critical realism symposiums organized by Sean Esbjörn-Hargens and Nicholas Hedlund in 2011 and 2013 in San Francisco have had a profound impact on our lives and work.

Note

1 Note this was not an Op-Ed, but was published in the *Post-Keynesian Economics Forum*, 12 August 2014.

References

Abel, J.R., Deitz, R., & Su, Y. (2014). Are recent college graduates finding good jobs? *Current Issues in Economics and Finance, Federal Reserve Bank of New York*, 20(1). Available at www.newyorkfed.org/research/current_issues/ci20-1.pdf (Accessed 23 February 2022).
Apple, M.W. (2001). *Educating the 'Right' Way: Markets, Standards, God, and Inequality*. Routledge.
Apple, M.W. (2004). *Ideology and Curriculum*. Routledge.
Apple, M.W. (2013). *Can Education Change Society?* Routledge.
Apple, M.W., & Beane, J.A. (2007). *Democratic Schools: Lessons in Powerful Education* (2nd edn). Heinemann.
Bhaskar, R. (1986). *Scientific Realism and Human Emancipation*. Verso.
Bhaskar, R. (1993). *Dialectic: The Pulse of Freedom*. Verso.
Bhaskar, R. (2002). *Meta-Reality: The Philosophy of Meta-Reality*, Vol. 1: *Creativity, Love and Freedom*. SAGE Publications.
Bowles, S., & Gintis, H. (2011/1976). *Schooling in Capitalist America: Educational Reform and the Contradictions of Economic Life*. Haymarket Books.
Bureau of Labor Statistics (2014). The employment situation—July 2014. News Release, 1 August. Available at www.bls.gov/news.release/archives/empsit_08012014.pdf (Accessed 14 March 2022).
Collinge, A. (2010). *The Student Loan Scam: The Most Oppressive Debt in US History and How We Can Fight Back*. Beacon Press.
Despain, H.G. (2011). College does pay—For some. *Worcester Telegram/Gazette*, 26 July. Available at www.telegram.com/article/20110726/NEWS/107269874/1020 (Accessed 23 February 2022).

Despain, H.G. (2012). Pragmatic employment policy. *Post-Keynesian Economics Forum*, 16 November. Available at http://pke-forum.com/2012/11/16/pragmatic-employment-policy/ (Accessed 23 February 2022).

Despain, H.G. (2013a). Few jobs for class of 2013. *Worcester Telegram-Gazette*, 16 May. Available at www.telegram.com/story/news/local/north/2013/05/16/few-jobs-for-class-2013/46933962007/ (Accessed 14 March 2022).

Despain, H.G. (2013b). The salubrious chalice? *The Journal of Critical Realism*, 12(4), 507–517.

Despain, H.G. (2013c). It's the system stupid: Structural crises and the need for alternatives to capitalism. *Monthly Review*, 65(6), 39–44. Available at http://monthlyreview.org/2013/11/01/its-the-system-stupid/ (Accessed 23 February 2022).

Despain, H.G. (2014). Integral theory and the search for earthly emancipation: On the possibility of emancipatory and ethical personal development. *The Journal of Critical Realism*, 13(2), 183–188.

Despain, H.G. (2015). Wanted: Jobs for 2015 graduates. *Worcester Telegram-Gazette*, 21 June. Available at www.telegram.com/story/opinion/columns/guest/2015/06/21/wanted-jobs-for-2015-graduates/34107237007/ (Accessed 14 March 2022).

Despain, H.G. (2016). *Homo debitor*: Money and debt as power$_2$ relation. *The Journal of Critical Realism*, 16(4), 402–415.

Duncan, A. (2013). Remarks of US Secretary of Education Arne Duncan to the Congressional Caucus Hispanic Institute. 2013 Public Policy Conference: Education, Economy and Workforce Plenary: A Stronger America, 30 September. Available at www.ed.gov/news/speeches/remarks-us-secretary-education-arne-duncan-congressional-caucus-hispanic-institute (Accessed 23 February 2022).

Eaton, C. et al. (2014). *Borrowing against the Future: The Hidden Costs of Financing US Higher Education*. The Center for Culture, Organizations, and Politics (CCOP), UC Berkeley Institute for Research on Labor and Employment.

Esbjorn-Hargens, S. (2016). Developing a complex integral realism for global response: Three meta-frameworks for knowledge integration and coordinated action. In R. Bhaskar, S. Esbjorn-Hargens, N. Hedlund, & M. Hartwig (eds), *Metatheory for the Twenty-First Century: Critical Realism and Integral Theory in Dialogue*. Routledge.

Fain, P. (2014). Nearing the bottom. *Inside Higher Ed*, 15 May. Available at www.insidehighered.com/news/2014/05/15/new-data-show-slowing-national-enrollment-decline (Accessed 23 February 2022).

Galbraith, J.K. (2014). *The End of Normal: The Great Crisis and the Future of Growth*. Simon & Schuster.

Giroux, H.A. (2014). *Neoliberalism's War on Higher Education*. Haymarket Books.

Graeber, D. (2011). *Debt: The First 5000 Years*. MelvilleHouse.

Hedlund, N. (2016). Rethinking the intellectual resources for addressing complex twenty-first-century challenges: Towards a critical realist integral theory. In R. Bhaskar, S. Esbjorn-Hargens, N. Hedlund, & M. Hartwig (eds), *Metatheory for the Twenty-First Century: Critical Realism and Integral Theory in Dialogue*. Routledge.

Illich, I. (1972). *Deschooling Society*. Harper & Row.

Kraushaar, J. (2014). The proven way to income inequality: Education. *The Atlantic*, 7 January. Available at www.theatlantic.com/education/archive/2014/01/the-proven-way-to-fight-income-inequality-education/282875/ (Accessed 14 March 2022).

Kregel, J.A. (2010). Fiscal responsibility: What exactly does it mean? Levy Economics Institute of Bard College, Working Paper No. 602. Available at www.levyinstitute.org/pubs/wp_602.pdf (Accessed 23 February 2022).

Kregel, J.A. (2014). *Minsky and Dynamic Macroprudential Regulation*. Levy Economics Institute of Bard College, Public Policy Brief No. 131. Available at www.levyinstitute.org/publications/minsky-and-dynamic-macroprudential-regulation (Accessed 23 February 2022).

Marcuse, H. (1964). *One-Dimensional Man*. Beacon Press.

Marshall, P. (2016). Towards a complex integral realism. In R. Bhaskar, S. Esbjorn-Hargens, N. Hedlund, & M. Hartwig (eds), *Metatheory for the Twenty-First Century: Critical Realism and Integral Theory in Dialogue*. Routledge.

McArble, M. (2011). Debt jubilee? Start with student loans. *The Atlantic*, 6 October. Available at www.theatlantic.com/business/archive/2011/10/debt-jubilee-start-with-student-loans/246307/ (Accessed 23 February 2022).

Pascarella, E.T., & Terenzini, P.T. (2005). *How College Affects Students: A Third Decade of Research*. Jossey-Bass.

Perlin, R. (2012). *Intern Nation: How to Earn Nothing and Learn Little in the Brave New Economy*. Verso.

Piketty, T. (2014). *Capital in the Twenty-First Century*. Harvard University Press.

Pollin, R. (2012). *Back to Full Employment*. MIT Press.

Pollin, R., & Garrett-Peltier, H. (2011). *The US Employment Effects of Military and Domestic Spending Priorities: 2011 Update*. December. Political Economy Research Institute, University of Massachusetts.

Randall, W.L. (2012). *Modern Money Theory: A Primer on Macroeconomics for Sovereign Monetary Systems*. Palgrave Macmillan.

Shierholz, H., Davis, A., & Kimball, W. (2014). *The Class of 2014: The Weak Economy Is Idling Too Many Young Graduates*. Report, 1 May. Economic Policy Institute.

Stein, Z. (2016). Beyond nature and humanity: Reflections on the emergence and purposes of metatheories. In R. Bhaskar, S. Esbjorn-Hargens, N. Hedlund, & M. Hartwig (eds), *Metatheory for the Twenty-First Century: Critical Realism and Integral Theory in Dialogue*. Routledge.

Stein, Z. (2016). *Social Justice and Educational Measurement: John Rawls, the History of Testing, and the Future of Education*. Routledge.

Stein, Z. (2019). *Education in a Time between Worlds: Essays on the Future of Schools, Technology, and Society*. Bright Alliance.

US Census Bureau (2011). *Education and Synthetic Work-Life Earnings Estimates*. American Community Survey Reports, September. Available at www.census.gov/prod/2011pubs/acs-14.pdf (Accessed 23 February 2022).

Vedder, R., Denhart, C., & Robe, J. (2013). Why are recent college graduates underemployed? University enrollments and labor-market realities. Policy Paper from the Center of College Affordability and Productivity, January. Available at http://centerforcollegeaffordability.org/uploads/Underemployed%20Report%202.pdf (Accessed 23 February 2022).

Wilber, K. (1977). *Spectrum of Consciousness*. Theosophical Publishing House.

Wilber, K. (1996/1980). *The Atman Project*. Shambhala Publications, Inc.

AFTER WORDS[1]

The Spirit of Evolution and Envelopment[2]

Frédéric Vandenberghe

> The integral knowledge admits the valid truths of all views of existence, valid in their own field, but it seeks to get rid of their limitations and negations and to harmonise and reconcile the partial truths in a larger truth which fulfills all the many sides of our being in the one omnipresent Existence.
>
> Sri Aurobindo (2006, pp. 692–693)

It is not only the Spirit that evolves. People evolve and change too. Roy Bhaskar started off as an anti-positivist philosopher of science (CR), became subsequently a grand dialectician in the analytical tradition (DCR) and, eventually, in a rather risky but courageous move, he also turned into an integral world philosopher (PMR).[3] The question for anyone who followed his trajectory is not so much to understand how this acorn grew into a sturdy oak, but to decide for oneself whether one should take the whole tree on board or rather stay with the roots (CR), the trunk (DCR), or the foliage (PMR). Kenneth Earl Wilber was originally a romantic developmental psychologist with a rather strong interest in Eastern mysticism. Later, he expanded his evolutionary model of transpersonal developmental psychology into a quadrilateral model of the development of the Kosmos, understood as the integration of the physio-, bio-, noo- and theospheres. The model, known as AQAL ('all quadrants, all levels'), includes behavioural, intentional, cultural, and social aspects into an encyclopedic evolutionary scheme that offers the key to the universe.

While both started to publish at about the same time in the mid-1970s and became leading figures of philosophical movements on the academic fringe, they did so from opposing and complementary sides of the geographical and geopolitical spectrum: UK versus USA, Oxford versus Lincoln (Nebraska), New Left versus New Age, Verso versus Shambhala, or, as Marshall (2012, p. 206) says in a thoughtful comparison between CR and IT, 'social emancipation vs self-realization'. From his early critique of standard economics, Bhaskar's impetus has always been political and subversive. Notwithstanding his spiritual turn, he would remain an unconventional socialist at heart till the very end. His philosophy of metaReality can even be considered a prefiguration of a joyful communism in which the personal development of each and every one would go hand in hand with the societal development of all in a free, democratic, agapic community.

Ken Wilber for his part has little sympathy for Marxism or socialism.[4] His heart is elsewhere and so are his intellectual investments. He's not so much interested in social action and political change as in silent meditation, personal transformation, and self-development. He's not concerned with social structures, but with evolving spirals. To the extent that Eastern mysticism blends the quest for the Divine with a search for a higher Self, developmental psychology is a perfect outlet for his cosmic yearnings. As a psychologist steeped in spiritual practices, he wants to work out transpersonal psychology into an integral theory of holons (a term coined by Arthur Koestler).[5] What he knows best is Western developmental psychology, dynamic systems theory and Oriental mysticism. Unlike Bhaskar, he never quotes Lukács, Gramsci, or Althusser. His main references are Plotinus (who travelled in India), Sri Aurobindo and Whitehead on the philosophical axis, Piaget, Habermas, and Gebser on the developmental one. While his knowledge of Eastern spirituality is truly exceptional, his knowledge of the Western canon is often superficial and based on second hand readings (e.g., Lovejoy, Taylor, etc.). Whereas Bhaskar's texts are characteristically dense and his style is often forbidding (not to say, as his critics, 'appalling'), without any concession to the reader, Wilber writes above all for a non-academic public. His texts are clear and limpid; at times, they shade off into self-help literature. Unlike Bhaskar, he does not complexify, but simplify. That is his strength, but also his weakness.

The different structures of sensibility and engagement of the British philosopher and the American psychologist explain, in part, the divergences and convergences in form, content, and style that one can encounter in the book. Hans Despain, Iskra Nunez, Neil Hockey, and Leigh Price basically come from CR. If they engage the dialogue with IT, they characteristically do so from the vantage point of dialectical critical realism and not, as I had expected, that of the philosophy of metaReality. They are obviously receptive to spirituality, but that, one may surmise, is a precondition for engaging with IT in the first place. Even when they invoke the evolution of the Spirit, one can still sense the pulse of emancipatory politics beating through their texts. Their style is dialectical and, however constructive or reconstructive their approach, they are involved in critique.

Zachary Stein, Kevin Bowman, Gary Hampson, Matthew Rich-Tolsma, Otto Laske, and Bruce Alderman come from IT. In Wilber's writings, they have found a 'big picture theory'. They espouse his holarchic developmental approach with its hierarchical rainbow (orange, green, turquoise, etc.) and feel part of a spiritual avant-garde. They find CR attractive, share its militant anti-positivism and its wholesale rejection of 'flatland' conceptions of reality. They want to supplement IT with a more robust ontology and think that CR might offer it. Their incorporation of CR is rather limited, however. They use it in the same way as they use systems theory—to rethink the natural sciences and, to a much lesser degree, the social sciences. They, thus, naturally concentrate on the Lower-Right quadrant and seek to syncretize constructivist epistemologies with realist ontologies. Although they are concerned with the environment and the imminent collapse of the ecosystem, as indicated by the reference to the Anthropocene in the very title of the book, they do not blame capitalism as such and do not show strong sympathy for 'radicals' (Bowman, for instance, puts Occupy Wall Street in the same basket of 'less developed extremes' as the Tea Party). They rather seem to believe that the ecological crisis is the outcome of a 'fractured worldview' and an 'industrial ontology' and that education will solve the issue. Their style is synthetic, their endeavour is encyclopedic, their approach classificatory.

1 Metatheory[1, 2, 3]

This is the follow-up volume of a protracted dialogue between hardline critical realists and softline integral theorists. Interestingly, both volumes are presented as contributions to metatheory: *Metatheory for the Twenty-First Century* and *Metatheory for the Anthropocene*. In spite of the title, the foreword (Walsh, 2016), and introduction to the first volume (Hedlund et al., 2016), the question remains: What is metatheory? As the prefix indicates, metatheory is theory about, above, or beyond theory. In an attempt to bring some clarity in an obscure issue, I will suggest it is so in a triple sense: as an overarching worldview (metatheory$_1$), as a mapping device (metatheory$_2$) and as a propaedeutic to substantive theorizing (metatheory$_3$).[6]

As an overarching worldview, metatheory$_1$ is an integral set of 'orienting generalizations' (Wilber, 1995, p. 5) for the systematization and organization of existing theories into a single overarching framework. As such, metatheory is an organizing device—a 'red thread' as Marx once said about his historical materialism—that runs through and connects a string of existing theories into a higher-level theory that transcends all and integrates each of them.

Thanks to its general drift, it is capable of infusing different theories, traditions, disciplines, paradigms, etc. with a deeper sense of unity and direction. Kant's system of transcendental deductions, Hegel's dialectics, and Comte's law of three stages offer historical examples of complex systematics that sort out and file away encyclopedic knowledge. Nowadays, Morin's complexity theory, Wilber's integral theory, and Bhaskar's critical realism are primary instances of totalizing frameworks for the Anthropocene.[7] Taken together, they have the potential to arrange a whole range of theories into a complex, transdisciplinary, encyclopedic, developmental, non-reductionist, dialectic metatheory of being, becoming, and nothingness—hence, a 'theory of everything' (Wilber, 2000a).

As a mapping device, metatheory$_2$ provides a topological analysis (*analysis situs*) of the underlying principles of vision and division that generate the multiplicity of theories within an existing field of research. Understood as a kind of a 'generative grammar of theory', it takes the form of a systematic analysis of the philosophical presuppositions (the ontological, epistemological, and axiological premises) that structure a given field and make the reduction of the multiplicity of theories to a couple of basic positions and oppositions possible.

In philosophy, the basic oppositions that fracture the field are rationalism versus empiricism, idealism versus materialism, realism versus nominalism, holism versus atomism (or 'heapism', as Wilber (2000a, p. 53) occasionally calls it). These traditional oppositions, which unite the opponents in their common struggle, reappear in transfigured form in the sciences. In sociology, for instance, the philosophical positions are condensed into an opposition between agency and structure; in geography, between space and place; in psychology, between the mind and the brain. Once one has identified the main axes, factors, or vectors that traverse the field and carved up the space into sectors, quadrants or hori-zones, one can then continue the taxonomic approach and assign the various schools, paradigms, and authors to their respective quarters (e.g., Wilber, 1996, p. 77; 2000a, p. 51). Single names (e.g., Piaget, Freud, Parsons) or substantives (e.g., ecofeminism, hermeneutics, positivism) become, thus, 'epistemic subjects' who represent the different approaches in person and in substance.

Metatheory is not only mapping device. Its real function is to act as a propaedeutic to substantive theory construction. By making one conscious of the philosophical principles of vision and division that articulate a field, metatheory$_3$ allows us to test the architecture of existing theories, check the solidity of their foundations and the cogency of their conceptual articulations. As a 'holistic indexing system' (Wilber, 2000a, pp. 108–112), AQAL does not only sort out extant theories into discrete categories ('pigeonholing'), it also enjoins the analyst to integrate a whole range of existing theories ('pigeonwholing' as it were) into a non-reductionist, multi-dimensional, interdisciplinary, developmental, dynamic, holistic framework.

By forcing one to ponder the philosophical dimensions of any scientific theory—not just of one's opponents ('cynical' use of metatheory, according to Bourdieu, 1997), but also one's own ('clinical' use)—it also serves as an aid to develop a synthetic theory that is in continuous dialogue with the other contenders of the field. This synthetic drift is, of course, one of the hallmarks of integral philosophy. The adjective 'integral' does not only express reverence for the philosophy of Aurobindo and the Mother, but also a reference to the transdisciplinarity of its multi-tracking approach.

The relation between metatheory and theory is not one of mere subsumption of the particular under the general. Theories intervene at a lower level of generality and have to craft their own concepts and their own articulations. Let's take my own field, social theory, as an example: The general injunction to explore the different aspects of reality in an integral fashion corresponds to a demand to develop a multi-level and multi-dimensional theory of society that reduces neither structure to agency (or vice versa) nor action to instrumental-strategic action (Alexander,

1981–1982). How the different social theories take that injunction into account and how they articulate their main concepts (system, structure, autopoiesis in the case of Luhmann; field, habitus and practice for Bourdieu or system; lifeworld and action for Habermas) is up to them. Metatheory only tells them to develop the concepts in such a way that they cover the whole spectre of possibilities without reduction or conflation.

2 Metacritique[1, 2]

Integral theory and critical realism are both metatheories. Proposing a systematic representation of the world, they are sophisticated mapping devices that highlight the interrelations between the parts and the wholes that make up the universe, as well as the theories that try to capture them. At their best, they function like a GPS that helps us to find where we stand, tells us what to look for, and indicates to us where to go (both in the theoretical universe and the cosmos at large).

What distinguishes IT from CR is metacritique. Hans Despain (2013, p. 509) has aptly summarized the difference in the following terms: 'Integral theory is a metatheory, dialectical critical realism is a metacritique of the real contradictions'. If metatheory is theory about theory in the triple sense we've outlined above, metacritique is, literally, critique of critique (as in Hamann's and Herder's critiques of Kant's *Critique of Pure Reason*), critique that comes after or on top of critique and points to a possible transcendence of the antinomies. In CR, metacritique comes essentially as a two-pronged critique of theories and metatheories (like Popper's positivism or Rorty's postmodernism) that ties conceptual criticism via *Ideologiekritik* to social critique. In Bhaskar's conceptual universe, metacritique comes in two forms (Bhaskar, 1993, pp. 354–365): metacritique$_1$ isolates an absence in a text, theory, or practice, indicating an incompleteness, inconsistency, or tension that is not contingent, but of a systematic nature. The pinpointing of a 'T/P inconsistency' within positivism, which denies in theory both the causality of freedom scientific experiments presuppose (von Wright) and the communication among scientists (Habermas) it practices, is an example of the first type of metacritique.

Wilber also practices immanent conceptual critique, but unlike his British-Indian colleague, he does not proceed to social analysis and social critique. Inspired by Apel's and Habermas's systematic tracing of 'performative contradictions', time and again he looks for tensions in the theories of his contenders and slams them for saying one thing (e.g., 'everything is relative', 'there are no hierarchies'), while doing something else (e.g., affirming the superiority of one's own theory, introducing a hierarchy that denies hierarchy). Usually, the drift of his argument goes in the direction of a more encompassing theory that resolves the tension through transcendence and inclusion of the lower-level theory. Following through the enfolding spiral, the *telos* of the affirmative negations is an integral theory that ideally includes everything into the Spirit and excludes nothing from the Universe.

While Wilber's theory is evolutionary, in spite of its occasional invocations of Hegel, it is hardly dialectical, however. More driven by the pull of identity than the push of difference, it lacks the negativity and the causality of absences. In Bhaskarese, this *horror vacui* implies 'ontological monovalence' (Bhaskar, 1993, p. 40), understood as denial of the negativity in Being. With its neo-Platonic dialectic ascending from the many to the One and descending from the One to the many, it spiritualizes the whole of existence and dissolves difference and contradiction in the process of transcendence. The imposition of a teleological, univocal, and monovalent narrative on the multiplicity papers over the real contradictions in life and suggests that cultivation of the Self can overcome domination, alienation, and reification. Wilber's non-engagement with Marxism may be related to the 'mystical shell' of his spiritual dialectics and explain why he abstains from social analysis and from social critique, which brings us to metacritique$_2$.

In Bhaskar, theoretical metacritique is immediately followed by social critique. If metacritique$_1$ identifies the omission of a concept or category in a theory as a symptom of a systematic error in the theoretical construction, metacritique$_2$ traces this error back to its historical roots and to the underlying structures of oppression and domination in society. Thus, radicalizing Horkheimer's classic critique of so-called 'traditional theory' (Horkheimer, 1988/1937), Bhaskar explains the theory/practice inconsistency of positivism through a reconceptualization of the latter as an ideology of science that obfuscates the possibility of practice (Bhaskar, 1986, pp. 151–218), an inconsistency that can only be overcome in practice through a radical transformation of society. In their respective chapters, both Despain and Price make creative use of the subscript$_2$ to tie immanent conceptual to practical social critique. For them, as for Bhaskar, metacritique$_2$ operates as a bridge between the theory under scrutiny and the practices that help to reproduce it. Like in critical theory, from Marx to Adorno and Bourdieu, the reflexive analysis of the structural powers of 'generalized master–slave relations' that weigh on the mind of the social actors and block their correct perception and conceptualization of reality, is a preamble to the resolution of theoretical gaps in and through transformative social practices. Nothing forecloses to trace back social transformative practices to their existential ground. That is what the later passage from transformative to 'transformed transformative practice' (Bhaskar, 1993, pp. 119–120) was all about. It is one of the moves that connect DCR to the philosophy of metaReality. It is at this point where IT and CR can meet, making CR more developmental, existential, and internal, but, conversely, also making IT more social, political, and external, gearing into the outer world. Not only transfiguring it, but also actively transforming it.

3 Radical Constructivism

Whether they originally come from CR or IT, the authors of this volume (and its companion) all seem to agree that CR is definitely stronger on ontology and that it can help to upgrade IT's credentials and make it more robust, by moving away from Wilber's constructivist epistemology (see Marshall, 2012a; Hedlund, 2016). I concur, but at the same time I think that the development of critical realism, from basic (first-wave CR) via dialectical critical realism (second wave CR) to the philosophy of metaReality (third wave CR), has not only deepened, but to a certain extent also weakened Bhaskar's strong ontological stand. I do not mean that to detract from Bhaskar's main achievements, but to indicate some problems with the canonical distinction between the intransitive (ID) and the transitive dimensions (TD) of knowledge. As one moves from the philosophy of the natural sciences to the philosophy of social science and, from there, to the philosophy of metaReality, the categorical distinction starts to blur. The hard and fast 'ID/TD'-distinction of transcendental realism morphs into the 'quasi-intransitivity' of critical naturalism and then, eventually, evaporates into the 'in/transitivity' of non-duality.[8] Through an insistence on the productivity of culture, language, and consciousness, I will bring CR closer to IT. The position I'll defend is not that of integral realism, however, but of a realist hermeneutics (Vandenberghe, 2014).

But let us first look at the debate between Wilber and Bhaskar in the *Journal of Integral Theory and Practice* (Bhaskar, 2012; Wilber, 2012; and the follow-up essay in Wilber, 2013; see also Alderman in Volume 2).[9] The main point of contention concerns the relation between epistemology and ontology. Can ontology 'subsist' without epistemology, as Bhaskar claims? Or are ontology and epistemology interdependent, co-created, and uni-dual, as Wilber argues? The whole discussion concentrates on the philosophy of the natural sciences and the ontology of nature. The social world as such is not really taken into account, lest it reappears within science as a context of determination that affects the truth. There are occasional references to dialectics and spirituality, but the fact that Wilber considers the philosophy of metaReality a form of 'cheating' (Wilber, 2012, p. 46)—i.e. smuggling consciousness into the CR edifice—is indicative that the argument is about basic (or first-wave) critical realism, as set out in *A Realist Theory of Science* (Bhaskar, 1978).

First-wave critical realism is an anti-positivist war machine and a defence of science. A realist theory of science is really a theory for science. It does not privilege the philosophical theories of science, but fastens on the ordinary practices of scientists and brings them to conceptual clarity. Against positivist philosophies that conceive of science as an ongoing application of regression analysis and of causality as a mental correlation between contingent events, Bhaskar insists that science is 'abductive' and inventive (rather than deductive and falsificationist, as in Popper-Hempel's DN-model). It consists in imagining hypothetical complex generative mechanisms whose existence, if demonstrated by sense extending technologies, would explain the correlation between events not as contingent but as necessary.

Bhaskar leaves no doubt that the theoretical invention of hypothetical causal mechanisms is a *conditio sine qua non* of science; yet at the same time he strongly denies that theories 'produce', 'perform', or 'enact' the mechanisms they postulate. To that effect, he introduces the distinction between the 'transitive' and 'intransitive' dimension of knowledge (Bhaskar, 1979, pp. 26–27), the former pertaining to the historically variable theories—the succession of 'paradigms'—that try to capture the real; the latter referring to the reality that exists independently of those theories, yet that they presuppose as their reference, ground, and condition of possibility.

For critical realism, this distinction between the epistemic/transitive and the ontological/intransitive is essential. It is enough to even suggest that the transitive might in one way or another induce the intransitive and immediately the red card of 'epistemic fallacy' (Bhaskar, 1979, p. 36) will be shown.[10] Hence, it comes as no surprise that when Wilber contests that the object can exist independently of consciousness, and *a fortiori* of the knowledge we have of it, critical realists charge him of deliberately fusing and confusing the TD and the ID. The only way to avoid the epistemic fallacy, according to Bhaskar (2013, p. 40), is to 'allow that the object exists independently of consciousness'.

Wilber resists, though, and assails basic critical realism from a similar vantage point as the philosophy of metaReality. Accessing higher levels of consciousness that reveal a higher truth and a higher reality, he looks down on CR as a philosophy of the 'demi-real'. It is not that IT refuses ontology altogether; rather it proposes a non-dual ontology that considers the ID and TD, ontology and epistemology, being and consciousness as two aspects of a single 'in/transitive' or 'epistemontological' reality. The first and most basic tenet of IT leaves no doubt about it: 'Reality as a whole is not composed of things or processes, but of holons' (Wilber, 2005, p. 43)—all the way up and all the way down. Every part is part of a whole, which is in turn part of a larger whole, and so forth *ad infinitum*. Thus, like the extremes, the part and whole touch each other and commingle: from every part, one can ascend to the whole, which is in the part, which is in the whole (to paraphrase Morin's (1986, pp. 101–102) 'principle of hologrammatics'). Through consciousness, every part is merologically connected to something larger and more encompassing that includes and transcends it. The Spirit is everywhere. Wilber insists that all beings, all entities in the universe have an interior and, therefore, a consciousness or, at least, a proto-consciousness. All things, including material things, have an interior that connects them to the Spirit. He not only defends a 'panpsychism' in the Schellingian tradition of Western Vedanta, which is kind of fine—the Spirit dwells in the material world and, we, humans, are only the conscious tip of the evolving universe—but also argues that ontology cannot be separated from epistemology: 'IT is panpsychic—epistemology and ontology/consciousness and being cannot be torn asunder' (Wilber, 2013, p. 44).[11]

This is the case, according to Wilber, because our conception of reality is actually constitutive of reality. It 'co-creates' and 'co-constructs', 'performs' and 'enacts' reality, precisely as 'reality' (please note the quotation marks). Although this may sound like radical anti-realism, a closer look reveals, however, that his 'enactivism' is more akin to a form of 'actualism': 'the intransitive object is dissolved into actualized relations and perspectives' (Rutzou, 2012, p. 217). The real is not necessarily denied in its existence, but it is reduced to an actuality ('reality') and identified with a series of contingent events (events as experienced by some sentient, protoconscious or conscious entity) that can neither be grasped from without, nor exist without a perspective or interior that co-creates and co-constitutes it in the act of cognition. The real is not only known, but necessarily 'enacted' and 'performed' by contingent acts of knowledge.

Wilber cannot think of reality without an observer, without someone or something who conceives of the world and apprehends it. Note, however, that if Wilber commits both the epistemic and the actualist fallacies, he does not commit the anthropic fallacy. Drawing on Maturana and Varela's radical constructivism, he argues that non-human, living animals (like frogs) construct their own world from their own point of view.[12] To understand what they see, one must observe what they cannot see, to wit their point of view on the world that is also a point of view in the world and of the world. Following Whitehead's process philosophy, Wilber takes the freedom to extend biological phenomenology to physics and argues that what holds for living beings also holds for non-living organic beings (e.g., atoms and molecules) who, allegedly, 'pre-hend' in their own way their own reality. What holds for frogs and atoms also holds for humans. They also can only apprehend the world from their own point of view.

The radical constructivism of system theorists, like Von Foerster, Maturana, and Varela, but also Morin and Luhmann, should not be confounded with the philosophical deconstruction of a Derrida or the social construction of sociologists and social psychologists (Le Moigne, 1999), though, as we will see below, Wilber willingly fuses the two. It is actually much more radical and constitutes in my opinion the most serious challenge to realism. Through a scientific analysis of how organisms (not only frogs, but also humans, and among humans, scientists) observe and necessarily constitute their environment from a certain perspective, second-order cybernetics introduces an observer into the observing system—'observing systems', to use the wonderfully reflexive title of Von Foerster. Through a recursive loop, it shows that there is and can be no object without a subject, no environment without a system, no world without a worldview that constitutes it.

From the point of view of radical constructivism, realism is the philosophy of a science that protects its foundations, but that is unwilling to consider its foundations as a result of its own epistemic operations (Fuchs, 2001). On a first level of observation, constructivism confirms the transcendental presuppositions of realism, but—and here comes the rub—as presuppositions of the sciences. Without them, the sciences could not operate. What appears obvious and necessary to the sciences appears, however, to an observer of the second order as pretty contingent. For sure, the world is as it is, but for the constructivist who observes the realist who observes the scientist, this self-same world that is always already presupposed by them can only appear as it is from a certain perspective, namely that of the scientist, which is different from that of common sense, which is different from that of the artist, the religionist, or the extraterrestrial visitor. From this perspective, the presuppositions of observations are not seen as the consequence of its very observations, but held as an invariant and necessary presupposition. Without a transcendental observer of all observers, realism is, at best, a contingent attempt to reduce contingency, and, at worst, a lack of reflexivity that transforms its own weakness into strength.

4 Social Constructivism

As a developmentalist, Wilber is committed to the evolution of the Spirit to ever higher levels of enfolding. What interests him is tracking the unfolding of the levels of consciousness through history, both onto- and phylogenetically, both in individuals and collectives. When one changes levels, going from, say, 'preop' to 'conop' and 'formop' (Piaget) or—moving now from individuals to whole collectives—from mythic to rational and beyond (Wilber), the worldview changes. And with the worldview, the Kosmos changes as well: The Kosmos looks different at each of these stages because the Kosmos *is* different at each of these stages' (Wilber, 2006, p. 72). 'Different worldviews create different worlds, enact different worlds, they aren't just the same world seen differently' (p. 52) 'And at each stage of development the world looks different because the world *is* different—and there is the great postmodern revelation' (p. 58).

The emphasis on the verb leaves no doubt about it—Wilber is no realist at all.[13] He does not assent to an ontology that is relatively independent from epistemology, but in typical postmodern mode, melds the two together in some kind of 'epistemontology'. For someone who approaches reality from a non-dual perspective, that could hardly be otherwise. In the same way as epistemology cannot be separated from ontology, the object cannot be separated from the subject or the transitive from the intransitive. The transitive is in the intransitive, and vice versa. It is in/transitive.

Changes of levels are akin to paradigm changes (Wilber, 2000a, pp. 158–160). Like Thomas Kuhn, Wilber assumes that when the worldview changes, the world changes as well. It is not the same world seen from a different perspective; it is a different world altogether that emerges. What we call 'worldview' is not a view on the world, the selfsame world that is analyzed and experienced differently at different levels by differently situated observers, as realists would claim, but a view or vision of the world and a perspective on it that constitutes a world by enacting a certain version of it as the world, as pragmatists, constructivists, and perspectivists like Whitehead, Latour, and Viveiros de Castro would claim.[14] What we as observers of the world (of the others) call a worldview (perspective of the observer) is experienced by those who perform it (perspective of the participant) as the world itself.

Phenomenologically speaking, Wilber is, of course, correct, but for a realist the question is not so much how the world is experienced or observed by the participant, but how the world that is analyzed by the sciences really *is*, independently from the theories, the paradigms, the worldview from which it is observed. Rigorously speaking, Wilber is talking about the lifeworld—the *Lebenswelt*, to be understood by phenomenologists—not about the world as such. When he extends the experience of the world from a certain worldview to the world as such, he commits the fallacy of actualism (i.e. reduction of the real to the actual, of laws to constant conjunctions of events and experiences). And, worse, when he confuses the worldview with the world, when he induces the world from the worldview, substituting surreptitiously the 'world' for the world (without quote marks), he commits the epistemic fallacy as well.

Nick Hedlund (2016), who also reads IT through the lens of CR, summarizes Wilber's ontology in the following terms:

> For Wilber, and IT at large, ontology is enactively or *empirically contingent* (i.e., a product or 'co-creation' of the knowing-consciousness or experience of sentient beings/holons), *developmentally stratified* (i.e., according to species and psychological levels of consciousness), and therefore *pluralistic* (i.e., there are multiple ontologies and many worlds that may or may not referentially overlap). In short, IT champions an irrealist *ontology of the phenomenal*, which is in marked contrast to that of CR (for whom it wouldn't really be considered an ontology at all).
>
> (p. 189)

As always, though, the tables can be turned. With Michael Schwartz (2016), we can argue that CR's emphasis on the real has led to a correlative neglect of actuality and of experiences. The critique of actualism has led CR to abandon the lived experience (*Erlebnis*) to hermeneutics, pragmatism, and phenomenology. This is unfortunate. Rather than dispensing of those rival approaches, CR should try to reclaim them and offer, when possible, realist interpretations of them.[15] As actualism is constellationally contained within realism, this can easily be done. From this perspective, one could say that IT is philosophically wrong when it muddles the world and the lifeworld, but that it is right when it leads science back to the natural experience of the world and, thus, to the lifeworld. As far as I am concerned, it should even be more phenomenological and go back with Husserl and Heidegger 'to the things themselves' as they are given in ordinary experience. This shift from scientific experiments with nature to experiences of nature allows one not only to interpret and make sense of pseudo-ontological statements about multiple worlds, but also to see that in spite of everything CR remains transcendentally tied to its origins in the philosophy of science. Even if it offers a radical critique of positivist science, it still shares a certain scientism with its opponents. Science is not only presupposed by it, but it is also reaffirmed with the double result that the ontology of science is generalized ('ontologized' as it were) and that non- and pre-scientific experiences of nature are devalued. Indeed, it is only with the philosophy of metaReality that a poetics of nature can be envisaged.

5 The Constitution of Society

In this collection of essays, integralists and realists encounter each other as fellow metatheorists. In her superb contribution to the volume, Iskra Nunez has found the right formula for the common endeavour: the exploration takes 'a basic critical realist metatheoretical vision of reality and science', and then uses 'integral theory as a common heuristic for inclusion'. This formula is synthetic, not syncretic, and indicates the direction of a fruitful dialogue with IT (see also Hedlund,

2016). Like a fusion of differing perspectives of the right and left eye that allow depth perception ('stereopsis'), the blending of CR's depth ontology with IT's epistemic pluralism can be expected to deepen our philosophical understanding and to broaden our perspective on the world. I concur, but I also think that Wilber's more hermeneutical position can be used to open up CR from within and disconnect it from the materialism to which realists remain committed, not just politically, but also theoretically and metatheoretically. I am no longer entirely convinced by the twinning of CR and Marxism. To untie the knot, I will suggest that nothing excludes that CR adopts a more idealist and constructivist approach in the social sciences. My suggestion is not only that a hermeneutic analysis of the social and historical world is compatible with CR. Rather I want to introduce hermeneutics as an idealist version of critical realism.

When Bhaskar analyzed the ontological presuppositions of the natural sciences through a transcendental investigation of scientific experiments, he did not tie his fate to any of the theories in physics, biology, or chemistry. In the social sciences, however, he was not that cautious and explicitly took sides. Against Durkheim and Weber, he opted for Marx and enthroned Marxism as the epitome of a critical naturalism. The question is now if this alliance can be partially undone and whether the pluralism that characterizes the social sciences can be reinstated.

To make my argument, let me state the obvious. Human beings are, by nature, cultural beings, endowed with transformative powers and reflexive capabilities. Thanks to culture, and above all, thanks to language, they live in a world (the lifeworld) that always already makes sense. It is against this inherited background of symbols and meanings, norms and rules, and expressions that actors can endow their action with meaning and intervene in the world to change it or to adapt to it. The social world is shot through with meanings, norms, and aesthetic expressions. Unlike the natural world, the social world is cultural and historical.[16] It is, literally, made by humans; yet culture, society, and history are also what make Man and transform a biological animal into a human 'species being' (Feuerbach's and Marx's *Gattungswesen*), endowed with reflexivity, capability, and creativity.

Thanks to these endowments, human beings are able to make history and society with will and consciousness, though not, as is well known, 'in conditions that they themselves have freely chosen' (*nicht aus freien Stücken*). The social, cultural and historical preconditions of agency are 'immediately encountered', 'given', not chosen, 'transmitted', not created (*unmittelbar vorgefundenen, gegebenen und überlieferten Umständen*) (Marx, 1988, p. 215). To the extent, however, that the preconditions of action that are transmitted have themselves to be produced and reproduced, changed or transformed to retain their causal power, they are not transcendental, but, as Habermas (1973, p. 240) says, 'quasi-transcendental' conditions of social action, social order, and social change.

Following Bhaskar, who emphasizes that the preconditions of action are themselves the result of action, and Margaret Archer (1988), who stresses that the conditions of action that the social sciences analyze are not produced by the social scientists, nor, strictly speaking, by the actors themselves who encounter them, but, rather, by their predecessors who made them by incorporating descriptions of the social world into their actions, we can now better understand why in the social sciences the transitive dimension of knowledge cannot be as rigorously separated from the intransitive dimensions as in the natural sciences.[17]

Though they act at different times, causes and consequences are intrinsically interconnected in the social world. What appears as a transcendental precondition of action is itself an inherited product; yet the product of the past that is a precondition of present action has itself to be acknowledged and activated by the agent to be active. Given that the knowledge of the social is somehow always implicated in the constitution of the social, the intransitive is not really intransitive, but 'quasi-intransitive'. As far as I am concerned, one might as well say 'quasi-transitive'. Rather than stressing the independent nature of the social, one might as well emphasize the dependency of the social on common sense and fully incorporate Wilber's enactivism into a hermeneutic sociology of transformative social action.

In the social world, the descriptions of the social world are reflexively and constitutively tied to its reproduction and transformation. This is true for the scientific descriptions, which 'circle in and out' of the sciences, and also, *a fortiori*, for the common sense descriptions and symbolic representations of the world that ordinary actors use in their everyday life. As scientific concepts slip over into common sense, the social sciences are complicit in the constitution of the social world they describe. In this sense, every competent actor may be said to be a social theorist. Consequently, as the transitive (social-cultural-historical) is in the intransitive, as the transitive constitutes the intransitive dimension (culture-society and history), the distinction between the transitive and the intransitive dimension of knowledge collapses.

Hermeneutics is more than a method of understanding. It is an ontological condition of life in society as such (Gadamer, 1999). It is only because the world is always already 'pre-interpreted, pre-understood, and pre-structured' by the background of a shared context of meaning that human action is possible. The world is disclosed to us as a meaningful one that always already makes sense. Yet, in another sense, the world is disclosed through us. As actors, we give meaning to the world. Between the actors and the world, cultural understandings always intervene as a mediating element that discloses the world as a properly human world that is shared by others.

6 Integral Sociology

In spite of everything, Wilber remains a developmental psychologist with mystical inklings. He's not a sociologist, and if he is one, he's definitely not a very good one, if I may say so. Unlike Bhaskar, who has done a serious effort to grapple with the classics of the discipline, was deeply involved in the social theory of the 1980s (remember structuration theory?) and is now being relaunched by prominent American sociologists (like Phil Gorski, Chris Smith, and George Steinmetz), Wilber is not well versed in sociology. His knowledge of sociological authors seems rather dated (Talcott Parsons, Gerhard Lenski, etc.), going back to his student days, and limited—with occasional references to cultural anthropology (Clifford Geertz, Mary Douglas) and religious sociology (Robert Bellah, Peter Berger, etc.).

Although he accepts the phenomenon of so-called 'emergence' in other fields (cf. Tenet 3, Wilber, 1995, pp. 53–56), apparently unaware of Durkheim's foundations of sociology, he refuses to grant relative autonomy to social facts and, thereby, implicitly negates the relative autonomy of sociology as a discipline too. For him, the individual and the social are only 'two aspects of the same thing, not two fundamentally different things (or levels)' (Wilber, 1995, p. 90). Going against the basic premises of a stratified social ontology, the social does not refer to a different stratum of reality that emerges out of the relations between individuals and groups, but rather to the interactions between individuals and groups themselves. In Wilber's conception, there seems to be hardly any room for social structure. Instead of a relational conception of the social sciences (Bhaskar, 1979, pp. 41–47), we get, at best, an interactionist view of society as individuals and groups acting together, and at worst, a positivist, cognitivist, and behaviourist view of society as embodied brains behaving together. In terms of the stratified conception of social reality and its celebrated distinction between the real (the totality of social relations), the actual (the totality of interactions), and the empirical (the correlations that are observed by 'brainspotters'), this amounts to a systematic reduction of the real to the actual and of the empirical to the observable.

To make things worse, he systematically seems to equate sociology with a positivist, empiricist and behaviourist approach of social externalities, with the result that it appears as a flat systems theory of the social world that has all the trappings of Comte's 'social physics':[18]

> The Lower-Right quadrant, in other words, represents all the exterior forms of *social* systems, forms that also can be *seen*, forms that are empirical and behavioral (everything on the Right half of the diagram is empirical, because it involves the exterior forms of holons; in this case, the social holon). This is why the study of human 'sociology' (especially in Anglo-Saxon countries) has usually been the study of the observable *behavior* of social systems (or 'social action systems').
>
> (Wilber, 1995, p. 128)

Indeed, in his encyclopedia of the sciences, both sociology and systems theory occupy the same space—the Lower-Right quadrant (Wilber, 1995, p. 127; 2006, p. 65; 2010, p. 43)—which makes one wonder not only how adequate his scheme is (it's an analytic device for pigeonholing that has serious trouble with intersections and complex cases), but also how he actually defines sociology and separates it from systems theory. Moreover, as he denounces positivism, but does otherwise not really question its relevance in the natural sciences, positivism is not overcome in the social sciences either. Sharp as ever, Mervyn Hartwig (2016) draws hard conclusions:

> In classic hermeneutical fashion (cf. e.g. Habermas, a key philosophical mentor), the whole right hand (RH) half of the four quadrants is ceded to

positivistically conceived science by Wilber—a move that pre-empts the possibility of a non-positivist naturalism or unification of the social and natural sciences.

In principle, nothing precludes, however, the development of a multi-dimensional conception of sociology as a discipline that is able to conceptualize and integrate social structure, culture and agency into a unique framework. The overall scheme of AQAL may be right. It is just that our psychologist has misidentified sociology. I think that is the case.[19] But before I get there and retranslate the Quad of integral development into the metatheoretical 'space of possibilities' of the social sciences (Vandenberghe, 2009), let me quickly remind the reader how the grid is actually constructed (Wilber, 1995, pp. 115–157, 197–198; 1996, pp. 63–95).

The basic idea behind the AQAL-model is simple: 'Spirit-in-action manifests as all four quadrants' (Wilber, 2006, p. 94). This single idea can, in turn, be decomposed in two affirmations, an analytical one and a developmental one, and two corresponding injunctions, a multi-dimensional and a multi-level one: (1) the Spirit manifests itself in all corners of the universe and these corners can be mapped according to two arch-polarities, namely the interior-exterior and the individual-collective. In order to develop a multi-dimensional, non-reductive analysis of reality, one must simultaneously track all its quadrants ('All Quadrants', see Wilber, 1997); (2) The Spirit evolves and is teleologically directed towards the attainment of higher levels of consciousness throughout the Kosmos. Those levels of consciousness have to be hierarchically ordered into developmental sequences at different levels of attainment ('All Levels', see Wilber, 2000b).

The analytic idea is that everything in the Kosmos is a holon in which the Spirit 'plays' out. Every thing, be it a material, corporeal, psychic, social, cultural, or spiritual thing, has both an interior and an exterior aspect, as well as an individual and collective one. These distinctions are not empirical ones, but to adapt Talcott Parsons's (1937, p. 757) 'analytical realism' to the case at hand, analytical ones.[20] This means that 'no holon simply exists *in* one of the four quadrants'; 'each holon *has* four aspects' (Wilber, 1995, p. 135). Each holon, whether a piece of clay, a bush in the garden, a chimpanzee or a bureaucrat behind his desk, has four quads and has, therefore, to be analyzed from multiple, complementary perspectives, though, obviously, not all holons have the same depth. A sentient being as a bureaucrat has more depth than his desk.

If we fill in the scheme, we arrive at the well-known diagrammatic representation of the integral quadrants (see Figure A.1), with the soul (*psyche*: individual and internal) in the Upper-Left Hand, culture (*pneuma*: collective and internal) in the Lower-Left Hand, the material body (*soma*: individual and external) in the Upper-Right Hand and society (*societas*: collective and external) in the Lower-Right Hand. Of the corresponding sciences, psychology (psycho-analysis *senso latu*) investigates intentional (conscious, unconscious, and supraconscious) states of the self at the individual level, whereas pneumatology (hermeneutics *senso strictu*) studies cultural worldviews and lifeworlds of communities at the collective level.

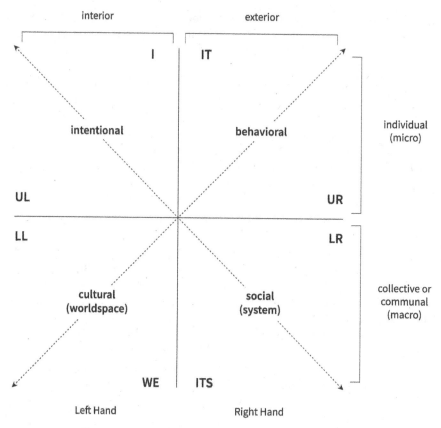

FIGURE A.1 Wilber's four quadrants

Both analyze interiors, seek depth, and are interpretative. Somatology studies the behaviour of brains and bodies at the individual level in behaviourist and cognitivist terms, while sociology, its collective counterpart, tries to explain collective behaviour in functionalist, structuralist, and systemic terms. Dealing with exterior behaviours, both are determinist and reductionist.

7 Revisiting the Quad: RAQAL

Assuming that any study of communities and collectives must be integral and integrative, we can now outline the contours of a multi-dimensional and multi-level sociology.[21] On the internal-external axis, it would be both anthropological and sociological, idealist and materialist, intersubjective and interobjective, culturalist and naturalist, emic and etic, interpretative and explanatory, quantitative and qualitative. It would ideally combine an external, structural, and systemic approach of the social world (etic perspective of the external observer) with an internal, interpretative and hermeneutic approach (emic perspective of the participant).

Working with a multi-dimensional concept of action (rational and non-rational action, symbolic and non-symbolic action) and a two-level conception of society (both as lifeworld and system), it would neither reduce action to strategic action (as in rational choice) nor culture to a system of codes (as in structuralism).[22]

On the individual-collective axis, it would be both micro and macro and avoid the errors of 'conflation' (Archer, 1988, 1995), be it the 'upwards' conflation of the action fraction or the 'downwards' conflation of the culture structure. It would not only fully acknowledge the phenomenon of 'emergence', but transcending the opposition between agency and structure, it would also fully take into account the mediating role of culture and satisfactorily work out the micro-macro linkages without reducing structure to agency or society to an assemblage of individuals and groups.[23]

To avoid the nominalist, actualist, and empiricist tendencies of IT, I would suggest the introduction of the realism-nominalism polarity as a supplementary dimension. This realist enhancement of the AQAL-model—its transformation from a bi-dimensional into a tri-dimensional RAQAL-model (sic)[24] that could be graphically represented as a cube—would have different advantages: it would avoid the 'disemergence' of the social and the flattening of sociology that corresponds to it; it would also fully acknowledge the pluralism within the social sciences (at least six zones).[25] Moreover, and more importantly perhaps, it would provide for a distinction between two versions of realism, a materialist-externalist one and an idealist/internalist one, and to fully acknowledge hermeneutics and structuralism as realist approaches to culture that complement CR's realist approach to structure. Indeed, the difference between hermeneutics and structuralism does not pertain to the third axis (realism-nominalism), nor to the second one (micro-macro), but to the first one (external-internal or etic-emic).

With the three dimensions in place and the full recognition of hermeneutics as a realist-internalist approach to culture, it would be possible to combine the strengths of CR's transformational model of social action with IT's more hermeneutic approach to cultural worldviews and lifeworlds. Assuming that it can be done and that one could indeed integrate the best of CR (its strong conception of structure as a system of relations, its dialectics between agency and structure, its transformational impetus) with the best of IT (its consistent defence of multi-dimensionality, its pluralist methodology, its hermeneutic insistence on culture structures, and its developmentalism), one would then have a reformulated CR that would maintain Marx's emancipatory interest of knowledge, but not his historical materialism.

Pushing CR in a more hermeneutic direction that takes the causal and transformative power of culture more seriously, going back to the authors who have influenced Wilber (Hegel, Dilthey, Heidegger, Gadamer, Habermas), one could then join the critique of domination and generalized master–slave relations with a hermeneutic reconstruction of what, for lack of a better world, one could call historical idealism. It would analyze the evolution of the Spirit and show how cultural change can put the individuals and collectives into action, potentially leading to the emergence of a fully 'morphogenic society' (Archer, 2013).

In this society, culture and personal existence are transformed at the same time.

8 Beyondism

The RAQAL-model and the tridimensional cube of the social sciences that corresponds to it is only an analytic and static device. By mapping out the articulations between the basic oppositions of philosophy (subject–object: nominalism–realism), anthropology (nature–culture: external–internal) and sociology (individual–society: agency–structure), it indicates the necessary constitutive elements that every social theory with general pretensions, at whatever level of analysis and whatever its paradigm, has to take into account and integrate in a coherent framework: intentional consciousness (UL quadrant: individualism–idealism), material things and bodies (UR quadrant: individualism–materialism), culture (LL quadrant: holism–idealism) and social structure (LR quadrant: holism–materialism). Theories that absent an element or that are built on a single quadrant will not pass the metacritical test of multi-dimensionality (Vandenberghe, 2009). That does not mean that all theories have to give equal weight to all the quadrants, but it means that, whatever one's starting point (the Upper-Left Hand for Wilber, Lower-Left for Bhaskar), one should be able, in principle, to engage all the quads in the field and learn from them, not to weaken them, but to strengthen one's own theory through dialogue.

Now that we have analyzed the analytic dimension of the AQAL-model ('All Quadrants'), we can take a look at its developmental aspect ('All Levels', as shorthand for 'all levels, all lines, all states, etc.' (Wilber, 2000b)—and given that IT has a strong Piagetian pedigree, also learn something from IT. Following Piaget's post-Hegelian, neo-Kantian approach to developmental psychology, Wilber's model is a dynamic, evolutionary, sequential, but non-linear one that distinguishes various 'levels' (or 'waves') of consciousness, stretching from matter to body to mind to soul to spirit, both at the individual and at the collective scale. Through the various levels pass various developmental 'lines' (or 'streams'—mainly the 'Big Three': cognitive, moral, and aesthetic, but also affective, motivational, interpersonal and spiritual lines). A given person can be at a high level of development in one line (e.g., cognitive development), medium in another (e.g., emotional intelligence), and at a lower level in still others (e.g., moral or interpersonal development). Moreover, a person at any level of development can experience an altered state of consciousness ('peak experience') and get access to the metaReal whatever his or her level of development may be.

Wilber adores hierarchies and developmental schemes. His books are full of them. What they all have in common, though, and what differentiates them from the more reputable developmental schemes one finds in Piaget, Maslow, Erickson, or Habermas, is their 'beyondism'. They all point to ever higher levels of consciousness beyond the personal, the rational, the real, etc. to the etheric heights and the mystical highs of the transpersonal, the suprarational, the metaReal, or in short: the Divine. This is, of course, in accordance with the great spiritual traditions of the East and the mystical traditions of the West. Underneath, above and beyond the world, there's another world that sustains it. It is the world of non-duality, which we can access through spiritual techniques (yoga, meditation, zazen, etc.), occultism (clairvoyance, telepathy, sex magic) or in peak experiences (ecstasy, trance, rapture). Sages, sadhus and other professional mystics can have continuous access to this world. It is the same world as ours, they say, but accessed from higher levels of consciousness and, therefore, transfigured: 'This is it'. Everything is the same; yet, everything has changed.

Beyond the ordinary and the mundane lie the extra-ordinary and the supramundane regions of consciousness beyond the Ego, but within the Self, that 'transpersonal psychology' investigates scientifically.[26] In accordance with the canons of developmental psychology, but subverting, uplifting, and transcending it, Wilber presents the staircase to heaven as a cosmic spiral that leads to the Divine. He distinguishes four more thresholds (Wilber, 1995, pp. 287–318): the psychic, subtle, causal, and non-dual levels of consciousness (which correspond, more or less, to Bhaskar's (2002) 5A (Fifth Aspect), 6R (Sixth Re-enchantement) and 7A (Seventh Awakening) in the Meldara Sequence of the Philosophy of metaReality).[27] One can ascend (from Many to One) or descend (from One to Many) the staircase, but eventually, one will realize that they are the same—that All is One and is One is Many.

In an extraordinary exegesis of the 'Triple Formula of the Supermind' (Aurobindo, 2006, p. 149), Wilber (echoing Shankara, Aurobindo, and a certain Sri Ramana Maharshi) summarizes the ultimate viewpoint of non-dual realization (I quote Wilber at length here, because I think it is worth pondering the depth and the beauty of India's perennial philosophy that traverses all of the Wilberiana):

> The world is illusory
> Brahman alone is real
> Brahman is the world.
>
> The first two lines represent pure causal-level awareness, or unmanifest absorption in pure or formless Spirit; line three represents the ultimate or nondual completion. The Godhead *completely transcends* all worlds and thus *completely includes* all worlds. It is the final within, leading to a final beyond—a beyond that, confined to absolutely *nothing*, embraces absolutely *everything*.
> (Wilber, 1995, p. 310, italics in original)

Wilber, a practicing Buddhist himself, considers this absolute emptiness as the font, the origin and the destination of everything that exists. It is at the same time the alpha and the omega point of existence. Subject and object, inside and outside, individual and collective, transitive and intransitive—all these dualist oppositions lose their ultimate meaning. In the state of non-duality, the knower, the knowledge, and the known are one. This is the realm of the in/transitive. Out of this non-dual realm, which precedes and transcends the four quadrants of existence as their absolute condition of possibility, everything emerges with joy. *Sat-cit-ānanda.* When one identifies in and with the Brahman, Consciousness-Existence-Bliss are one and the same. *Atman* (the Self) is *Brahman* (the supreme soul). 'You are not in the universe, the universe is in you' (Wilber, 2008, p. 22).

Those blissful experiences in which the higher Truth and the Divine can be directly seen, felt and intuited have been extensively analyzed, described and systematized by *rishis* (seers) over millennia. Their phenomenal analyses of the noumenal/numinous are consistent (experimental, replicable, and fallible), so consistent that Wilber does not hesitate to qualify them as 'contemplative sciences' (Wilber, 2000a, p. 77). And to bring his message home, he adds emphatically: 'There is absolutely nothing "metaphysical" about these systems: they are empirical phenomenological developmental psychology at its most rigorous and most comprehensive' (Wilber, 1995, p. 346).

As a fellow meditator (Vandenberghe, 2001), I do not have any qualms about that. With his masterful knowledge of the Eastern philosophical traditions (especially of India and Japan), his profound understanding of spiritual systems and practices, as well as his expertise in Western transpersonal psychology, Wilber is at his best when he plumbs the depths of the Divine. What I want to question, however, is the sequence of all his developmental schemes. As a card-carrying post-secular humanist, I cannot fully endorse the idea that the apex of human development is to be found in the religious realm. I also object to the idea that the highest stage of development coincides with the Enlightenment (*Samadhi*) the master himself has allegedly arrived at. That trick was already tried out by Hegel in the nineteenth century and up till today it is continued by gurus without scruples to sell their spiritual wares and attract devotees to their conferences, seminars, and workshops. Not that I reject spirituality as a matter of principle, but, as a good Habermasian, I think we should always try to reformulate the transcendent into secular language (Habermas, 2014). The fusion of the levels and lines of development (the cognitive, ethical, aesthetic, and religious) that characterizes spiritual experiences seems to indicate a confusion of the cognitive with the aesthetic and of the affective with the religious. Instead of waffling about the overcognitive, the supramental, and the meta-Rational, I suggest the mystical should be recognized, recoded and reformulated for what it is—not the highest level of noetics, but a form of high poetics.

Such an aesthetic understanding of the spiritual as poetics brings us back to politics and social critique. There's nothing wrong with mysticism, of course, but its truth should be accessible to all and should not be limited to a happy few who reached 'third-tier consciousness' (around 2 percent of the population, according to Wilber's guesses), who were so lucky to have visions and experience the Divine. This elitism and the misplaced avant-gardism that comes with it are untimely—they are neither of our age, nor do they announce a New Dawn. This aristocracy of the Spirit, which we find in most integral thinkers of the twentieth century (Aurobindo, Teilhard de Chardin, Scheler, Steiner) is hardly compatible with the humanist egalitarianism of Bhaskar, Habermas, or Morin for that matter. The denunciation of the 'mean green meme' (Wilber, 2000a, pp. 122–125) that we find in Spiral Dynamics and Wilber's more recent writings is not very promising. I think that as critical realists and progressive integralists we should resist it and insist all the more on our humanist, socialist and democratic convictions. Not because we are mean-spirited and vindictive, but because we are post-secular and progressive.

The point is not to oppose the New Left to the New Age—they are complementary—but to invert their priority. The point of departure and arrival of Wilber's reflections is always the same—the Self (Upper-Left Quadrant). Although his AQAL-model of integral unfolding can, in theory, be fully developed from any quad, in practice, as we have seen, he tends to neglect society and demean sociology (Lower-Right Quadrant). To finish this afterword, I will now try recuperating some of the developmental logic for sociology, metacritique, and emancipatory politics of the morphogenic society.

9 Politics of the Morphogenic Society

To apply AQAL as a systematic device for the investigation and diagnosis of the existing social order and the possibilities of social, cultural, and personal change, one has to recast it as a DRAQAL-model (sic)—with the D standing both for Dialectics and Development. The developmental model transforms the general analytics of the social world into a morphogenetic dialectics. To apply the scheme to contemporary societies and make it move, one has to move, I suggest, from dialogic metatheory to developmental metahistory. In accordance with Habermas' (1976) proposal to reconstruct historical materialism in such a way that collective processes of learning through discursive testing of validity claims would allow human societies to move steadily forwards to ever higher levels of cognitive, moral, and expressive consciousness, from the pre-conventional and the conventional to the post-conventional stage, we can make a distinction between the 'developmental logics' and the 'factual dynamics' of history. Developmental metahistory is the consequent exploration of possible futures—counterfactual futures that could be realized if their conditions of possibilities that are not satisfied now were to be imminently fulfilled.

To find out how the basic elements are configured and, thus, whether societies tend towards morphostasis or, rather, towards morphogenesis, one needs, basically, to introduce the temporal dimension of human development and interlink the elements of the space into an 'integral field' (Arnsperger, 2009, pp. 43–57, 72, 86). The idea behind the integral field is that individual consciousnesses, material bodies, cultures, and social structures are not contingently, but systematically related to each other in specific configurations that define a variety of social formations through the ages. Through an evolutionary sequence of morphogenetic cycles of human development, individuals, cultures, societies, and humanity as such can attain higher levels of consciousness, from the pre-personal and pre-modern (subconscious, instinctive, and mythical) via the personal and modern (self-conscious, rational, and scientific) to the transpersonal, the postconventional, and the post-postmodern (postmaterial, spiritual, integral). While the developmental logics of personal, cultural, and social unfolding point to the attainment of integral consciousness of universal 'Oneness' of all that exists, nothing guarantees that the end state of full-spectrum consciousness will be attained. Just as persons, cultures, and societies may be arrested in their development, humanity may fail to realize its potential, regress, and never reach its Pleroma.

In accordance with the principle of 'ecumenical secularism', which stipulates that encompassing doctrines have to be reformulated in terms that are acceptable to (post-)secular humanists, I would like to displace the cursor from the Upper-Left to the Lower-Right Quadrant, explore possible societal development beyond global capitalism and, thereby, politicize the whole AQAL-model. To avoid individualism and quietism, one should neither fold society into the individuals nor plunge them back into the Kosmos. One should rather place the individuals back into society, and society back into the hand of its members. Instead of focusing on individual consciousness, one should look at collective consciousness, social movements, and social change. In social movements, the movement goes from within to without, and then back. The plan is to change culture, society, and the subjects all at once.

A generalized morphogenesis does not require a spiritual transformation of the individuals, though it doesn't exclude it either. It presupposes conscious and conscientious subjects—'metareflexive individuals', to speak like Margaret Archer (2003)—who know that the good life is not individual, but social, the development of each being a condition for the development of all in a just, convivial, and democratic society. Social change does not exclude the turn within, nor a return to the Other, but it calls for a turn to alterity and a lived openness to the others.

This politicization of transpersonal psychology and its transformation into a convivial sociology involves a double movement—one that is critical (critique of capitalism: 'clearing the rubble') and a second one that is constructive (outline of the convivialist society: 'cutting the umbilical cord').

With a modicum of developmental psychology, evolutionary sociology, and reflexive philosophy of history, capitalism can be understood as a social formation that systematically arrests further development towards post-material, convivial, democratic societies (Arnsperger, 2005, 2009). With its mechanical linkages between the base and the superstructure, historical materialism is, perhaps, the philosophy of history that best captures the world-historical obstruction of capitalism. Going back to AQAL, but interpreting it now as a metahistorical field of becoming, we can characterize capitalism as a social formation that systematically reduces the human being to a sensing body with needs and interests that faces a (pseudo-)natural social environment which it tries to control instrumentally and to which it tries to adapt itself strategically to survive.

Folding back the quadrants of the metatheoretical space into one, the behavioural space of the psycho-somatic (UR), capitalism is the social system that suppresses the cultural meanings of existence that transcend self-interest and produces the *homo economicus* that its utilitarian vision of the world presupposes. It is true that capitalism ignores neither culture nor meaning. To the contrary, it knows all too well that the human being is more than a producer and a consumer of commodities, but by systematically interpreting human existence in the utilitarian language of a rational choice between preferences, it reduces all possible goods (things and ideas) to commodities that can be possessed and exchanged. By occupying the body and the mind, its non-culture of utilitarianism produces the subjects that produce the goods and live to consume them as commodities. Thus, it tends not only to occupy the whole space of experience, but also to arrest the development of persons, cultures, societies, and humanity as such to a higher level of 'conscientious consciousness', i.e. awareness, connectedness, and togetherness. With its insistence on private property, accumulation, work, competition, innovation, consumption, and continuous growth, capitalism is a self-perpetuating system of alienation that commodifies, instrumentalizes, and colonizes the spirit and the soul, as well as the mind and the body.

Capitalist industrialism is the real 'flatland' of modernity. It disenchants the world and alienates the subjects. But as always, alienation (*Entfremdung*) is dialectical. At the height of the metacrisis, when the subjects are cut off from nature, from their own body, from their fellows, from society—in short, from themselves (*Selbstentfremdung*, to speak like the young Marx (1964, pp. 510–522))—a countermovement may set in and we see all kinds of local initiatives emerging from the margins of society: producer and consumer cooperatives, mutualism, fair trade, parallel and complementary currencies, local exchange trading systems, and numerous mutual-aid associations; the digital sharing-economy (Linux, Wikipedia, etc.); *décroissance* and post-development; the 'slow food', 'slow town', and 'slow science' movements; the call for *buen vivir*, the affirmation of the rights of nature, and the admiration for Pachamama; alter-globalization, political ecology and radical democracy, the Indignados, Occupy Wall Street, Syriza, etc. What all these civic initiatives have in common is a desire for cultural change and social reconstruction. What they share is a post-capitalist worldview of collective eudaimonia in which individuals search for the good life not in isolation from others, in meditation as it were, but in communal projects that make sense and re-enchant society.

We call it 'convivialism'. Together with a platoon of francophone intellectuals (Morin among them), we have recently written a *Convivialist Manifesto*.[28] We conceive of convivialism as a new syncretic ideology fit for new times. It includes the best of liberalism, socialism, anarchism, and communism, but transcends their limitations in a post-developmental and post-capitalist design for a more joyous, solidary, and just society. Based on the principles of common humanity, common sociability, and common responsibility, it is a project that enables human beings simultaneously to compete and cooperate with one another, with a shared concern to safeguard the world. How can individuals live together with one another in relative peace, 'opposing themselves to each other, without massacring each other' (Mauss, 1950, p. 278)? That is the central question that convivial societies have to satisfactorily resolve in the twenty-first century if they are to survive the Anthropocene. The answer is a reflexive control of *hybris* at all levels. Control not in the sense of repression, but in the sense of self-conscious mastery of tensions and impulsions at all levels, to make them compatible with the whole, so that both individuals and collectives can thrive and flourish.

Convivialism is not a new theory, but a new *praxis*, i.e. a practice inspired by a new transideological worldview. It only makes the principles that subtend the cooperative practices of civil society explicit and manifest. In the same way as integral theories have to be completed by integral practices, the convivial practices of the lifeworld have to be complemented by a theory of civic communication, association, and cooperation. We may start with self-observation, self-transformation, and self-realization, but, one way or another, we have to go back to the community. As Wilber says in one of those rare passages where he talks about social practices:

> These waves of existence (from physical to emotional to mental to spiritual) need to be exercised—not just in self (boomeritis!)—but in culture as well. Exercising the waves in culture might mean getting involved in community service, working with the hospice movement, participating in local government, working with inner-city rehabilitation, providing services for homeless people.
>
> *(Wilber, 2000a, p. 138)*

We do not only have to go back to the community, but we have to continue the process of Enlightenment in social movements that consciously seek to change culture to change social practices and society. Returning for a last time to the domains of the AQAL-model—'spirit, nature, body, civics' (Wilber, 1995, p. 480)—we can now finally conclude and describe convivialism as the theory of the civic, civil, and civilized practices that reintegrate nature, the body, culture, and society in and through a societal-communal project of living the good life on Earth with and for others.

Notes

1 [*Sic*].
2 I thank the editors of the book for the invitation to write an afterword. No doubt they are doing me too much honour. I have accepted it as a final homage to Roy Bhaskar, whose fascination for India and its philosophical tradition I share. I have greatly profited from the comments, critiques, and suggestions of Mervyn Hartwig, Nick Hedlund, Michael Schwartz, Michel Bauwens, Sean Esbjörn-Hargens, and Tim Rutzou. They show not only how difficult it is to please everybody at the same time, but also how easy it is to come to a reasonable consensus concerning the essentials.
3 The use of multiple TLAs (three letter acronyms) has become standard practice in both CR (critical realism) and IT (integral theory). I apologize for continuing an ugly practice, but at this stage of the game I have to presuppose that the reader knows not only the theories, but also their jargon.
4 The younger generation of integralists or, in any case, those who have demonstrated an interest in CR, seem more drawn to emancipatory politics on the Left than its founder (who supported the Bush regime!). Following Molz (2016), we can distinguish an 'integral' and an 'emancipatory' function of metatheories without suggesting that the two cannot be found in the same person.
5 In systems theory, a holon refers to a part that is at the same time a self-contained whole and a dependent part. Embedded in a larger whole of which it is a part, it also contains subsystems that at a lower level are themselves wholes. Whether the analysis is bottom up or top down, one always encounters parts and wholes—'all the way up and all the way down'.

6 In terms of the introduction to *Metatheory for the Twenty-First Century* (Hedlund et al., 2016), my metatheorizing is definitely metatheory 2.0. Like Wilber & co., I am too much of a Habermasian to accept the one-man, monological metaphysical systems of the past. The distinction I make between various types of metatheory fuses the distinction between α and β and is therefore broadly consistent both with CR and IT. The real difference between CR and IT is not to be found at this level, but at the level of metacritique. If I had to introduce one supplementary type, I would say that thanks to the incorporation of axiological and political metacritique, CR moves beyond the epistemic confines of metatheory 2.0 and represents, therefore, metatheory 2.1. As such, it is a type of metatheory for the twenty-first century that retains the hope of the twentieth-century social movements in an age of political regression.

7 In contemporary systems theory, one finds a whole gamut of metatheories. If Edgar Morin is singled out, rather than, say, Niklas Luhmann, Mario Bunge, or Enrique Dussel, it is because he's an exemplary figure: a humanist, an ecologist, an encyclopedist and a public intellectual with ample moral capital and a fascinating life history. To properly appreciate his contributions, one must, however, be able to read French or Spanish. Otherwise, I'm afraid, it's like ringing a bell.

8 At the critical realism conference in New York in 2013, Bhaskar gently responded to my queries about the auto-deconstruction of the ID/TD-distinction saying that people had made too much of it and that it precluded neither hermeneutics in the social sciences nor non-duality in the philosophy of metaReality.

9 The debate between Wilber and Bhaskar is by proxy. Owing to their respective illnesses, they did not meet in person and, as Esbjörn-Hargens (2012, p. v) indicates in the introduction to the special issue of the *Journal of Integral Theory and Practice* dedicated to the debate, Wilber has most probably not read Bhaskar in depth or in a systematic way. What he knows about CR largely comes from Esbjörn-Hargens's (2010) 'ontological pluralism' (2010) and the synopses of CR by Marshall (2012a) and Hedlund (2013).

10 Remember: the epistemic fallacy 'consists in the view that statements about being can be reduced or analysed in terms of statements about knowledge; i.e. that ontological questions can always be transposed into epistemological terms' (Bhaskar, 1978, p. 36).

11 Compare with Sri Aurobindo (2006, p. 23): 'All phenomenal existence consists of an observing consciousness and an active objectivity'.

12 In a famous paper entitled 'What the frog's eye tells the frog's brain', Maturana and colleagues show that the world of the frog is constructed by its brain. Frogs do not move their eyes to follow prey. The frog only sees what moves and does not see what is stationary. 'He will starve to death surrounded by food if it is not moving. He will leap to capture any object the size of an insect or worm, providing it moves like one' (Lettvin et al., 1968, p. 234). This will lead the constructivist biology of cognition to question realism's basic assumption that there's a pre-given world that is not dependent on the structure of the organism of the observer.

13 Aware of the slippery slopes of social and cultural constructivism, he avoids the extremes. Here and there, one finds realist counterpoints in his writings—like this one:

> So just because these experiences have an interpretative component does not mean that they are merely cultural creations. When you watch the sun set, you will bring interpretations to that experience as well—perhaps romantic, perhaps rational, each with a cultural coloring, but that doesn't mean that the sun ceases to exist if your culture disappears. No, these are ontologically real events. They actually exist. They have real referents.
>
> *(Wilber, 1996, pp. 192–193)*

The following passage shows, however, that his realism is contextual and strategic: 'Due to the prevalence of extreme constructivist epistemologies, I often emphasize the objectively real components of many forms of knowing, since that is the partial, but important truth that is most often being unfortunately denied' (Wilber, 2000a, p. 156).

14 Looking for an 'ontology of climate change' (Esbjörn-Hargens, 2009), IT has discovered CR. In his pioneering text, Esbjörn-Hargens, the editor of the *Journal of Integral Theory and Practice* who has introduced Bhaskar to the practice community of integral theorists, has constructed ontology as a multiple object. He blends Whitehead's pragmatist ontology with the ANT of Latour, Law, and Mol—which is fine, because like Wilber and following Stengers, Latour is a Whiteheadian—with the 'enactivism' of Varela and Maturana, as well as the realism of Bhaskar and Carolan. I concede that any two perspectives can be integrated, but not three. Three seems just another case of 'voracious overassimilation' (Molz, 2016).

15 Like 'analytical Marxism', CR represents a dialectical stream within analytical philosophy. In an attempt to reconnect CR to continental philosophy, I have explored rapprochements between CR and non-analytical streams within philosophy. See Vandenberghe (2014, pp. 23–57 for hermeneutics, pp. 105–137 for pragmatism and pp. 251–261 for phenomenology).

16 The whole debate about the coming Anthropocene is not so much about the social or cultural construction of nature, but about 'its' destruction—it referring not to nature, but to the human species that alters the environment that sustains its existence. For a pioneering investigation of how a biological agent can become a geological force, see Chakrabarty (2009); for a terrible, but rather good preview of a world without us, see Danowski and de Castro (2016). Interestingly, Meillassoux (2006) also grounds the non-anthropocentric claims of his speculative realism on a world 'without us'—a world that precedes the arrival of the human being in history and is, therefore, allegedly, non-correlationist, anti-Kantian and post- (or better, perhaps, radically pre-) humanist.

17 In his dialectical phase, Bhaskar makes a distinction between existential and causal intransitivity. The distinction is a subtle one, but serves to explain why in the social sciences only existential intransitivity applies. To the extent that accounts of the social world reflexively produce the social world they describe, causal intransitivity does not obtain. However, once anything happens in history or in society as in nature, it is determined and determinate, and nothing can now alter it. It is, therefore, indeed existentially intransitive. I thank Mervyn Hartwig for this clarification, but as a hermeneutician, I am interested in the causal and existential transitivity of history and society. One implication of the hermeneutical circle is that we cannot know the past 'as it really was' (*wie es eigentlich gewesen ist*, to quote Ranke's well-known phrase), for the simple reason that every new interpretation allows us to uncover one more dimension of the same event.

18 The superficial characterization of August Comte's positivism one finds in the introduction to the companion volume (Hedlund et al., 2016)—rather than as the first and foremost integral sociologist who dabbled with an 'internal synthesis' well before Sorokin or Wilber—confirms the authors have constructed a straw man of sociology. The same observation holds for Wilber's reduction of Parsons to a cybernetician—as if the social system could be unconnected from the cultural system, whereas, in fact, his structural functionalism is the most accomplished example we have of an integral cultural sociology.

19 Interestingly, elsewhere, Wilber himself acknowledges that there's space for an interpretative sociology.

> Like psychology, sociology has, almost from its inception, divided in two huge camps, the interpretative (Left Hand) and the naturalistic or empirical (Right Hand). The one investigates culture or cultural meanings from within, in a sympathetic understanding. The other investigates the social system or social structures from without, in a very positivistic and empirical fashion.
>
> *(Wilber, 1996, p. 86)*

20 It may be of interest to note that, like Wilber, Parsons was attempting a synthesis of a neo-Kantian epistemology and a Whiteheadian process ontology.

21 The drive towards multi-dimensionality is in line with Jeffrey Alexander's (1981–1982) metatheoretical reconstruction of the theoretical logic of sociology, from Marx, Weber,

and Durkheim to Parsons. I've used it as well in my critique of reification theories, from Hegel and Marx via the Frankfurt School to Habermas (Vandenberghe, 2009).
22 Habermas' (1981) *Theory of Communicative Action* satisfies all the criteria and corresponds most closely to the ideal-type of an integral sociology that takes the internal-collective dimension seriously.
23 Formulated in this way, Bhaskar's critical naturalism, Margaret Archer's morphogenetic approach, and Bourdieu's genetic structuralism fit the bill.
24 The R of RAQAL stands for Revised and Realist, but can also be read as shorthand for Rationally Reconstructed Reflexive Relational Revised Realism.
25 To work out a full social theory, one would have to think through the three dimensions. A rapprochement of CR and IT would still leave out the whole field of micro-sociology (pragmatism, symbolic interactionism, phenomenology, ethnomethodology, etc.) which both of the macro-approaches have largely neglected so far.
26 Transpersonal psychology (not to be confounded with parapsychology) emerged in the 1960s from humanistic psychology and religious studies as the branch that studies states of consciousness beyond the conventional ego-boundaries. It studies those states and processes in which people experience a deeper sense of who they are, or a greater sense of connectedness with others, with nature, or the spiritual dimension. As an empirical, soteriological and applied investigation of altered states, it not only aims to investigate the highest potential of the Self, but also to contribute to the realization of unitive, spiritual, and transcendent states of consciousness. For a good overview of the contested field, see Strohl (1998).
27 Since 2000, Wilber has ceased referring to the transpersonal levels as psychic, subtle, causal, and non-dual. He has since adopted terms that help to distinguish between vertical stages and horizontal states.
28 The first *Convivialist Manifesto* was published in French in 2013; the second one in 2019. Initiated by Alain Caillé, the founder of the MAUSS (Mouvement Anti-Utilitaire dans les Sciences Sociales / Anti-Utilitarian Movement in the Social Sciences), both Manifestos were written as collective documents by prominent intellectuals from the alternative left. They are now also available in English (Convivialists, 2014 and Convivialist International, 2020) and were signed (among many others) by Roy Bhaskar, Margaret Archer and David Graeber.

References

Alexander, J.C. (1981–1982). *Theoretical Logic in Sociology* (4 vols). University of California Press.
Archer, M. (1988). *Agency and Culture: The Place of Culture in Social Theory*. Cambridge University Press.
Archer, M. (1995). *Realist Social Theory: The Morphogenetic Approach*. Cambridge University Press.
Archer, M. (2003). *Structure, Agency and the Internal Conversation*. Cambridge University Press.
Archer, M. (2013). Introduction: Social morphogenesis and the prospects of morphogenic society. In M. Archer (ed.), *Social Morphogenesis*. Springer.
Arnsperger, C. (2005). *Critique de l'existence capitaliste: Pour une éthique existentielle de l'économie*. Éditions du Cerf.
Arnsperger, C. (2009). *Éthique de l'existence post-capitaliste: Pour un militantisme existentiel*. Éditions du Cerf.
Aurobindo, S. (2006). *The Life Divine*. Aurobindo Ashram.
Bhaskar, R. (1978). *A Realist Theory of Science*. Harvester Press.
Bhaskar, R. (1986). *Scientific Realism and Human Emancipation*. Verso.

Bhaskar, R. (1993). *Dialectic: The Pulse of Freedom*. Verso.
Bhaskar, R. (2002). *The Philosophy of MetaReality*, Vol. 1: *Creativity, Love and Freedom*. SAGE Publications.
Bhaskar, R. (2012). Considerations on Ken Wilber's comments on critical realism. *Journal of Integral Theory and Practice*, 7(4), 39–42.
Bourdieu, P. (1997). *Les usages sociaux de la science: Pour une sociologie clinique du champ scientifique*. INRA.
Chakrabarty, D. (2009). The climate of history: Four theses. *Critical Inquiry*, 35, 197–222.
Convivialists (2014). *Convivialist Manifesto: Declaration of Interdependence*. Centre for Global Cooperation Research. Available at www.gcr21.org/publications/global-dialogues/2198-0403-gd-3/ (Accessed 23 February 2022).
Convivialist International (2020). Second Convivialist manifesto: For a post-neoliberal world. *Civic Sociology*, June, 1–14. Available at https://online.ucpress.edu/cs/article/1/1/12721/112920/THE-SECOND-CONVIVIALIST-MANIFESTO-Towards-a-Post (Accessed 23 February 2022).
Danowski, D., & Viveiros de Castro, E. (2016). *The Ends of the World*. Polity Press.
Despain, H. (2013). The salubrious chalice? *Journal of Critical Realism*, 12(4), 507–517.
Esbjörn-Hargens, S. (2010). An ontology of climate change: Integral pluralism and the enactment of environmental phenomena. *Journal of Integral Theory and Practice*, 5(1), 183–201.
Esbjörn-Hargens, S. (2012). Executive editor's introduction. *Journal of Integral Theory and Practice*, 7(4), v–vi.
Fuchs, S. (2001). *Against Essentialism: A Theory of Culture and Society*. The University of Chicago Press.
Gadamer, H.G. (1999). *Hermeneutik I: Wahrheit und Methode*. In *Gesammelte Werke* (Vol. 2). Mohr.
Habermas, J. (1973). *Erkenntnis und Interesse*. Suhrkamp.
Habermas, J. (1976). *Zur Rekonstruktion des historischen Materialismus*. Suhrkamp.
Habermas, J. (1981). *Theorie des kommunikativen Handels*. Suhrkamp.
Habermas, J. (2014). *Nachmetaphysisches Denken II: Aufsätze und Repliken*. Suhrkamp.
Hartwig, M. (ed.) (2007). *Dictionary of Critical Realism*. Routledge.
Hartwig, M. (2016). Why I'm a critical realist. In R. Bhaskar, S. Esbjörn-Hargens, N. Hedlund, & M. Hartwig (eds), *Metatheory for the 21st Century: Critical Realism and Integral Theory in Dialogue*. Routledge.
Hedlund, N. (2013). Critical realism. A synoptic overview and resource guide for integral scholars. Resource Paper, MetaIntegral Foundation.
Hedlund, N. (2016). Rethinking the intellectual resources for addressing complex 21st-century challenges: Towards a critical realist integral theory. In R. Bhaskar, S. Esbjörn-Hargens, N. Hedlund, & M. Hartwig (eds), *Metatheory for the 21st Century: Critical Realism and Integral Theory in Dialogue*. Routledge.
Hedlund, N., et al. (2016). On the deep need for integrative metatheory in the twenty-first century. In R. Bhaskar, S. Esbjörn-Hargens, H. Nicholas, & M. Hartwig (eds), *Metatheory for the 21st Century: Critical Realism and Integral Theory in Dialogue*. Routledge.
Horkheimer, M. (1988/1937). Traditionelle und kritische Theorie. In *Gesammelte Schriften*, Vol. 4: *Schriften 1938–1941*. Fisher Verlag.
Le Moigne, J.L. (1999). *Les épistémologies constructivistes*. PUF.
Lettvin, J.Y., Maturana, H.R., McCulloch, W.S., & Pitts, W.H. (1968). What the frog's eye tells the frog's brain? In W. Corning & M. Balaban (eds), *The Mind: Biological Approaches to its Function*. Wiley.
Marshall, P. (2012a). Toward an integral realism. Part 1: An overview of transcendental realist ontology. *Journal of Integral Theory and Practice*, 7(4), 1–34.

Marshall, P. (2012b). The meeting of two integrative metatheories. *Journal of Critical Realism*, 11(2), 188–214.

Marx, K. (1968). *Ökonomisch-philosophische Manuskripte aus dem Jahre 1844: Marx Engels Werke* (Vol. 40). Dietz Verlag.

Marx, K. (1988). *Der achtzehnte Brumaire des Louis Bonaparte (1852)/Marx-Engels Werke (MEW)* (Vol. 8). Dietz Verlag.

Mauss, M. (1950). Essai sur le don. In *Sociologie et anthropologie*. PUF.

Meillassoux, Q. (2006). *Après la finitude: Essai sur la nécessité de la contingence*. Éditions du Seuil.

Molz, M. (2016). Afterword. In R. Bhaskar, S. Esbjörn-Hargens, N. Hedlund, & M. Hartwig (eds), *Metatheory for the 21st Century: Critical Realism and Integral Theory in Dialogue*. Routledge.

Morin, E. (1986). *La méthode*, Vol. 3: *La connaissance de la connaissance*. Éditions du Seuil.

Parsons, T. (1937). *The Structure of Social Action*. McGraw-Hill.

Rutzou, T. (2012). Integral theory: A poisoned chalice? *Journal of Critical Realism*, 11(2), 215–224.

Rutzou, T. (2014). Integral theory and the search for the Holy Grail: On the possibility of metatheory. *Journal of Critical Realism*, 13(1), 77–83.

Schwartz, M. (2016). After integral gets real: On meta-critical chiasma of CR and IT. In R. Bhaskar, S. Esbjörn-Hargens, N. Hedlund, & M. Hartwig (eds), *Metatheory for the 21st Century: Critical Realism and Integral Theory in Dialogue*. Routledge.

Strohl, J. (1998). Transpersonalism: Ego meets soul. *Journal of Counseling & Development*, 76, 397–403.

Vandenberghe, F. (2002). Uncartesian meditations on the Buddhist phenomenology of the nostril and the dissolution of the ego. *Psychological Foundations, The Journal*, 4(1), 48–62.

Vandenberghe, F. (2009). *A Philosophical History of German Sociology: Alienation and Reification*. Routledge.

Vandenberghe, F. (2014). *What's Critical about Critical Realism? Essays in Reconstructive Social Theory*. Routledge.

Walsh, R. (2016). The potentials of metatheory. In R. Bhaskar, S. Esbjörn-Hargens, N. Hedlund, & M. Hartwig (eds), *Metatheory for the 21st Century: Critical Realism and Integral Theory in Dialogue*. Routledge.

Wilber, K. (1995/2000). *Sex, Ecology, Spirituality: The Spirit of Evolution*. Shambhala Publications, Inc.

Wilber, K. (1996). *A Brief History of Everything*. Shambhala Publications, Inc.

Wilber, K. (1997). An integral theory of consciousness. *Journal of Consciousness Studies*, 4(1), 71–92.

Wilber, K. (2000a). *A Theory of Everything: An Integral Vision for Business, Politics, Science, and Spirituality*. Shambhala Publications, Inc.

Wilber, K. (2000b). Waves, streams, states and self: Further considerations for an integral theory of consciousness. *Journal of Consciousness Studies*, 7(11–12), 145–176.

Wilber, K. (2006). *What We Are, That We See. Part 1: Response to Some Recent Criticism in Wild West Fashion*. Available at www.kenwilber.com/blog/show/46 (Accessed 23 February 2022).

Wilber, K. (2008). *The Pocket Ken Wilber*. Shambhala Publications, Inc.

Wilber, K. (2012). In defense of integral theory: A response to critical realism. *Journal of Integral Theory and Practice*, 7(4), 43–52.

Wilber, K. (2013). Critical realism revisited. Resource Paper, 1–3, May. MetaIntegral Foundation.

INDEX

Page numbers in *italics* refer to figures and page numbers in **bold** refer to tables.

absence 45n5
accumulation theory 67
actualism 155, 175, 241
Adorno, T.W. 120, 123, 213
After Capitalism: Economic Democracy in Action 41
Agape 177
agency 33, 38, 41, 98, 122; irreducibility of 136; levels of 175; preconditions of 242; stratification of 135; transformative 157–159, 180
agriculture 6
alethic resonance 8
alethic truth 21n11, 175, 194n13
alienation 33–34, 123, 253
all-quadrant, all-level (AQAL) model 30, *31*, 32, 41, 153–163, 181, 195n22, 234, 245–246, 248, 251–252
Almaas, A.H. 12
Alperovitz, Gar 41
'alternative facts' 142
America Beyond Capitalism: Reclaiming Our Wealth, Our Liberty and Our Democracy 41
analytical realism 245
analytical reasoning 114
anamnesis xxxvi
andragogy 180–181
Andrews, D. 90n68
anger 36
anima mundi 186
animism 77–78, **79**, 81

animistic-Biblical analogies 77–78, **79**, 86
Anthropocene: and capitalism 124; characteristics of 2; and education 122–125; emergence of 5–10; 'good' xxiv; origin of the term 8, 21n13, 123–124, 144n3
Anthropocene Working Group (AWG) 21n13
anthropocentrism 22n22
anthropo-ethics 174
anxiety 30, 36
Apple, Michael 212
'appreciative inquiry' 13
AQAL *see* all-quadrant, all-level (AQAL) model
Arab Spring 35
Archer, M.S. 176, 242, 252
archetypes 184
Aristotle xxxiv, xxxv, 14, 33, 43, 142
Asia Indigenous Peoples' Pact (AIPP) 76
Asian economies 66
Atman Project 34, 42, 44, 225
atomic bomb 5, 21n13; *see also* nuclear weapons
atomism 155, 170, 179, 183, 185, 188, 196n31
attentional support 116–117
Aufhebung 99, 102
Aurobindo, Sri xxxiv, 177
austerity 37, 222
Australia 76, 78–81

Index

autocratic leaders 66
automobiles xxv
'autonomous' individuals 44
autonomy 127, 139, 174
awakening xxxvii–xxxviii
awareness xxxv, 38; meta-linguistic 135; spiritual 34, 38; *see also* construct awareness
AWG *see* Anthropocene Working Group

Baldwin, J.M. 127, 128, 130
Baran, Paul 40
Barnett, Ronald 176
Basic Moral Intuition 182
Basseches, M. 100–103, 106
Bateson, G. 186
beauty xxxv, 11, 30
behaviourism 128
beliefs xxxvi, 210–212, 228
Bell, Daniel 123
Bello, Walden 91n72
benefits 37, 39
Benjamin, Elliot 160
Bhaskar, Roy xvii–xxii, xxxiii, xxxiv–xxxv, xxxvii–xxxviii, 29–32, 122–123, 152, 175–176, 224–226, 231–232, 237–238; on blockism 34–35; on capitalism 10; on causation 45n10; on cognitive development 97, *98*, 128; on developmental consistency 130; on dialectical life 127; on education 143; on eudaimonistic society 66, 122; on four moments of dialectic (MELD) 97–120, 163; on four-planar model of social being 31, *32*, 41, 44; on human judgment 131–132; on metacritique 44, 46n14, 235–236; on modernity 67; phases of work 194n5; on power$_2$ relations 33, 38, 42–44, 45n3, 46n14, 123, 135, 138–140, 143, 225, 227; on socioeconomic involution 34–35; on synchronic emergent power materialism (SEPM) 136–137; on UDR movement 99, 102, 103; on universal meaningfulness 43
Bible, the 78, 90n54
Big Data 142, 146n17
'Big History' 19
'billionaire boys club' 141
Billy Madison effect 227
biological reductionism 43
birds xxvi
Blair, Tony xx
blame, deflection of 53, **55**, 57, 61

blinding paradigms 173
blockism (blocked universalism) 34–36, 43, 44
Bodhisattva xxxviii
bodyego 43
boom and bust cycles 37
Borneo xxiv–xxvi
Bowman, K. 50, 53, 64
Brexit campaign 142
Brown, A. 51
Brown, B.C. 174
Buber, M. 187
Buddhism xxxiv, xxxvii–xxxviii, 177, 249

California 6
Cambridge Analytica 142, 146n17, 147n18
Campbell, J. 64
Campos, J. 66
capacity building 176
capital, approach to 50
Capital in the Twenty-First Century 215
capitalism xxxv, 6, 10, 21n16, 122–124, 252–253; alternatives to 37–38, 41–42, 44; corporate 30; crony 65; 'double movement' 36, 37; ecological and geographical limits of 122, 124–125, 145n7; injustices of 39; and learning 145n10; liberal-democratic 33; monopoly 37, 40, 44; and moral foundations 36; 'new culture' of 36; oligopolistic 40; and personal development 44; and power relations 30; and stagnation 37, 39, 40, 45n13, 46n15
Capitalocene 9–10, 144n5
carbon emissions 56, 65; *see also* greenhouse gas emissions
carbon pricing 65
carbon taxes 56, 57, 58, 65
Carson, Rachel xxv
category errors 13, 102, 103, 114, 116–117, 171
cats xxv–xxvi
CDF *see* constructive developmental framework
cement 124, 144n4
Centre for Critical Realism xvi, xxi
Centre for Orang Asli Concerns (COAC) 76
centrism 165n20
ceremony 75, 85
change: integral theory on 157–158; Plato on 157; social xx, xxi, 114, 165n20, 176, 242, 252; technological 34; *see also* climate change

child protection 79, 80–81
children: autonomy 139; Indigenous 79, 80–81, 86; in out-of-home care 80–81; *see also* child protection
China 36, 124
Christianity 82
Churchill, Ward 72
CINA (capitalism is no alternative) 37, 41, 44
citizenship education 176, 223
civic capital 60–62
civic engagement 223
class alliances 39
class formations 39
climate xxvii–xviii; *see also* climate change; climate justice; climate science
climate change: and automobiles xxv; consequences of 35–36; and global supply 35; multi-perspective approach xxvi–xxviii; myths of xxxi; as an opportunity xxx–xxxii; perception of risks xxx; and Precautionary Principle xxvi; as a religious discourse xxix; responsibility for xxix; urgency of action on 35–36
climate justice xxxii
climate science xxviii
closed systems xix–xx, 153, 175
co-creation 16
cognitive ability 138
cognitive behaviour *106*, 107
cognitive development 11–12; four eras of 97, *98*; as a social practice 97–120
cognitive interviews 97–99, 114–116
cognitive maturity fallacy 22n25, 126, 127, 131–136, 138, 146n12
cognitive profile 98
cognitive score 106–107
collaborative metapraxis 3, 10–17
colleges 211, 213–217, 221–223, 226–227
Collins, R. 13
colonization 76–78; *see also* decolonization
commercial relations 34
Commission of Inquiry into Child Protection in Queensland 80–81
communication xxi, 64, 174
communism 120, 182, 232, 253
community: agapic 232; going back to 254; participating in 174; planetary 174; sense of 74; *see also* community development; community learning
community development 74, 78, 80
community learning 84
competitiveness 56

complex crisis 170–172
complexity 112
complex systems 172, 174
complex thought (CT) xxiii, xxxviii, 169, 172–174; and higher education 173–174
conglomeration 40
consciousness: 'conscientious' 253; deeper states of 82; development of 33, 43, 97, 179; false 123; planetary 173; rational 170; structures of 22n23; and *telos* 33; transformation 170; Wilber on 146n13, 225–226
conservatives 51–52, **53**, **54**, 57–62
construct awareness 99
constructive developmental framework (CDF) 100, *109*, *111*, 116, 118
constructivism xxxvi, 16, 153, 156, 161; radical 236–239; social 240–241
consumption-driven economy 62
consumption patterns 35
contradictions 33, 45n5
contrasts 106
Conundrum xxv
convivalism 253–254
Cook-Greuter, S.R. 99, 181
corporate profits 56
corporations 39, 78; *see also* megacorporations
Corson, D.J. 176
cosmic development xxxiv
'cosmic envelope' metaphor xxi
cosmos xxxiii
cosmosophy 186
CPR thought forms 99, 103
CR *see* critical realism
creation story 19
creativity 184, 220
crime 30
criminal justice system 79
crisis: complex 170–172; 'Endless' 37; environmental 29–30, 40, 48; epistemic 16; existential 30–32; global 125, 143; identity 9, 125; legitimacy 125; mental health 36; as an opportunity 21n7; *see also* Financial Crisis of 2008–2009; metacrisis; quintuple crisis; Triple Crises
CR-IT dialogue 82–87
critical education 174
critical facilitators 117
critical realism (CR) xxi, xxiii, xxxiii, xxxvi, xxxviii–xxxix, 29, 31–32, 175–176; basic 164n7; directionality in 82–83; double-inclusiveness of 158; emergence of 14, 152; hermeneutic

and ontological generosity 13; and higher education 176–177; and integral theory (IT) 12, 14–16, 22n28, 151–163, 224–225, 235–238, 241–242; metatheoretical coordinates 151–160; *see also* dialectical critical realism (DCR)
critical thinking 107
critique 13; explanatory, 164n7, 175, 210–211; immanent 175, 235; *see also* metacritique
Critique of Pure Reason 98
Crutzen, Paul 6, 123
CT *see* complex thought
cultural capital 59, 60–62
cultural industry 212
cultural interactions 32
cultural risk assessment model xxix–xxx
culture wars 66
curricula 171, 176; and job training 211; non-integrative 185; post-disciplinary 186
custodial species 22n20

DDT xxiv–xxvi
DECD *see* diachronic emergent capacities developmentalism
decolonization 75, 83
deep ecology 22n22
demigods 7
demi-reality 7, 126, 210, 238
democracy 41, 143, 157, 180–181
Democracy at Work: A Cure for Capitalism 41
Denmark 48, 50, 64–66
depression 30, 36
depth praxis 83–84, 88n28, 122, 126, 132, 135, 138, 141, 146n15
deregulation 40, 56
Deschoooling Society 211
Despain, Hans 14, 61, 211, 224
development 66, 126–127; community 74, 78, 80; cosmic xxxiv; and dialectical critical realism (DCR) 126–127, 130; and human emancipation 127–130; emotional 12; individual 129, 130, 133, 136–138, 142; lines of 196n30, 248; moral 49; personal 30, 32, 35, 42–44, 212, 220, 223; psychological xxxiv, 128, 195n22; sustainable 52; Wilber on 42–44, 66, 128–129, 131, 136, 225; *see also* cognitive development; developmental process; developmental psychology; developmental stage theories; developmental studies; international development
developmental consistency 130, 131

developmental process 34, 132, 135
developmental psychology 16, 18, 43, 125–128, 145n9, 209, 231–232, 248–250
developmental stage theories 18
developmental studies 128, 138, 145n9, 146n15
Development and Change 74
DeVos, Betsy 218–221
Dewey, J. 139, 142–143
diachronic emergent capacities developmentalism (DECD) 126–127, 130, 136–141
Dialectic: The Pulse of Freedom xxi, 34, 122, 126, 127, 130, 132–136, 143, 225
dialectical critical realism (DCR) 45n5, 45n12, 71, 97–101, 107–108, 118–120, 127–128; and cognitive maturity fallacy 127, 132, 134–136; and integral theory (IT) 125–127, 138–144; and learning and development 126–127, 130
dialectical engagement 10, 12, 22n25
dialectical explanatory argument 73, 83
dialectical metatheory 22n25
dialectical schemata framework 100–103, 106
dialectical text analysis 114
dialectical thinking 18, 22n25, 34, 97, 99, 107–108, 111–112; absence of 114; phases of development 101–103; teaching of 113–120
dialectical thought forms (DTF) 100–120; definition 97–100; dialogue modes 116–117; table of **104–**105; transformational 102–103; uses of 106
dialogue: CR-IT 82–87; dialectical thought forms (DTF) 116–117; in education 180–181; internal 102, 119; willingness to 11
Diamond, Jared 32–33
directionality 33, 82–83
discrepancy index 106
dispositional realism 145n8, 146n 15
double internality 144n6
Dougherty, C. 66
Douglas, Mary xxix
Down Under 90n68
DRAQAL model 251
drug use 30
D'Souza, Radha 74
DTF *see* dialectical thought form

earthquakes 6
EASE (existing alternatives starting emancipation) 41, 44

ecological debt 21n16
'ecology of mind' 186
economic domination 34
economic hegemony 38
economic justice 216
economic literacy 38–39
economic policies: collective pathology 61–64; cooperation in 64–66; coordination of 57–61; healthy versus unhealthy 52–55, 61–64; outcomes 55–57, 62
economics 17, 39, 49; categorization of principles 50, **51**
economic security 37
ecosophy 186
ecumenical secularism 252
education 18, 122–144; in the Anthropocene 122–125; authoritarian modernization 141; as a basic right 143; coercive versus emancipatory 139–140; complexity approaches to 173–174; contradictory nature 127, 133, 141, 212; crisis of 143; critical 174; ecosystem of 191–192; and ethics 174; hijacking of 140; informal 191; oppressive forms of 141, 143, 212; pertinence in 173; philosophy of 142–143; planetary consciousness in 173; pre-tertiary 191; processes of 186–188; as a revolutionary catalyst 125; systems of 188–189; testing in 171–172, 211; uncertainty in 173–174; understanding in 174; *see also* colleges; educational content; educational reform; educational systems; educational theory; higher education
educational activism 125
educational content 183–186; contextuality 185–189; identity 183–184, 186–189; relationality 185, 187, 189
educational reform 137, 211, 223–224
educational relationships 139
educational systems 125–126, 133, 141, 145n10, 176, 192, 209, 212
educational technologies 142
educational theory 209–228
Education in a Time between Worlds 211
'edu-tainment' 142
efficiency dilemma xxv, 115
egalitarians xxx
egocentrism 133, 174, 182
Eisenstein, C. 2
electric cars xxv
emancipation 127–130; and higher education 182–183; social 182, 232; spiritual 182

emancipatory metatheory 18
emotional development 12
employment 36; *see also* jobs; underemployment; unemployment
Emptiness 76
enactment 116–117, 165n33
endism 165n20
'Endless Crisis' 37
Endless Crisis: How Monopoly-Finance Capital Produces Stagnation and Upheaval from USA to China, The 40
enfoldment 165n33
enlightenment xxxviii, 170, 182; cosmic 44; modern 212; personal 34; spiritual 34
Environmental and Energy Institute (ESSI) 65
environmental crisis 29–30, 40, 48
epistemic crisis 16
epistemic fallacy xviii, 114, 116, 119, 125, 145n8, 152, 154–155, 171, 175
epistemic-hermeneutic variability 16
epistemic humility 11
epistemic limits 107–113
epistemic reflexivity 12, 14
epistemic relativism 11, 16
epistemological metatheorems 159
epistemology xviii, 11, 16; and ontology 99, 102, 119, 152, 154, 165n21, 237–238, 240–241
Erikson, E. 42
eros xxxiv
Eros 38, 177, 182
errors 152, 173, 214; category 13, 102, 103, 114, 116–117, 171; of integral theory 158–158; *see also* epistemic fallacy
Esbjörn-Hargens, S. 154–157
ESSI *see* Environmental and Energy Institute
Eternity in Their Hearts 81
ethical participation 2
ethics: in education 174; social 186; widening the sphere of 182
ethnocentrism 136, 174
eudaimonistic society 2, 3, 20n4, 66, 122, 132
evil, problem of xxxiii, xxxiv
executive teams 114
existential absurdism 36
existential contradictions 33
existential crisis 30–32
existential intransitivity xxxvi
existential meaningfulness 36
explanatory critique 164n7, 175, 210–211

extinction of species 35
extremism 140

faith 81, 82; *see also* spirituality
false beliefs 210–212, 228
false consciousness 123
false needs 212
false rationality 173
fatalists xxx
Faux, Jeff 38
Financial Crisis of 2008–2009 37, 48, 56, 61–64, 66
financialization 37, 40, 222
financial satisfaction 36
financial sector 37–38, 56
fiscal policy 37
Fischer, K.W. 132
'flatland' 72, 87n4, 155, 170, 177
flexicurity 64
flextime 65
fluidity index 101, 106, 108, 111
Flynn Effect 49
force fields **114–115**, 116
fossil fuels xxv, xxvi
Foster, John Bellamy 40
four-planar model of social being 31, *32*, 41, 44
Fox News 38
fragmentation 3, 29, 45n2, 185
Frankfurt School 18, 213
freedom 122–123, 131; and education 139–140; and technological change 34
Freud, Sigmund 33, 36, 42
Freudianism 43
friendship 14–15
Fromm, Erich 36, 43
Fukuyama, Francis 33
fundamentalism 140, 143

Gaia 186
Gaianthropocene 9
gambling 36
game theory 55–61
Gebser, Jean 22n23, 177
geo-engineering xxv, xxvii, xxxi
geo-history 33, 122
geological substrate 6, 10
GERM *see* global education reform movement
Germany 65
Gilded Age 141
global crises 125, 143; *see also* crisis
global education reform movement (GERM) 141

globalization 49, 56, 62, 78
Global North 82, 87
global pandemic 211
Global South 82, 87
global supply 35
God 184
Gödel, Kurt 193n1
Goldin, Claudia 216, 217
Gore, Al xxix
Görtz, Daniel 17
government: distrust in 38; Ronald Reagan on 37; views on the role of 52; *see also* government bailouts
government bailouts 56
Great Acceleration 6, 7, 10, 21n13
Great Creator Spirit 81, 89n41
Great Depression 39
greenhouse gas emissions 49; *see also* carbon emissions
group authorship 16–17
Guattari, F. 186
Guiso, L. 60

Habermas, Jürgen 7, 49, 63, 131, 136–137, 145n10, 251
Hampson, G.P. 162–163, 170
happiness 36
Harvey, David 145n7
health insurance 39, 64
Hedlund, Nick 82–83, 87, 241
Hegel, Georg Wilhelm Friedrich xxi, xxxv, 33, 98, 175, 250; *Aufhebung* 99, 102
hermeneutic generosity 13
hermeneutics 161–162, 242, 243, 246–247
Heron, John 14
heutagogy 180–181
hierarchalists xxx
higher education 169–193, 197n37; administration of 192; aims of 211–212; architecture of 191; and critical realism (CR) 176–177; discursive contexts 190; evaluation and assessment for 192; and internal theory (IT) 177–178; material contexts 190–191; Meta-Matrix 183–189; orientation 192–193; *see also* colleges
Hirsch, Fred 36
Hochachka, Gail 71, 81–82, 86
holarchical approach 73
holistic law 75, 85
Holocene 6
holons 88n16, 154, 177, 179, 232, 238, 244, 245, 254n4
homo complexus 173, 186

homo economicus 182
hope 2, 74–76
Horkheimer, M. 213
Hulme, Mike xxvi–xxxii
human capital 56, 125, 171; *see also* reductive human capital theory (RHCT)
Hume's Law 210
humility xxxii
hyper-specialization xxiv, 3; *see also* over-specialization; specialization

ICS *see* International Commission on Stratigraphy
identity: crisis 9, 125; and educational content 183–184, 186–189; politics 146n17; shared 8–9
ideology, 'end of' 123
IDM 100, 113–117
Illich, Ivan 211
illusion 173
Imagining the University 176
immature/mature type fallacy 52–53, **54**, 57, 63, 66
IMP *see* integral methodological pluralism
imperialism 40
income inequality 221
Inconvenient Truth, An xxix
Indigenist scholars 72
Indigenous communities 17
Indigenous peoples 71–87
Indigenous research paradigms 72
Indigenous thinking 22n20
individual development 129, 130, 133, 136–138, 142
individualists xxx
inequality 36, 37, 40, 41, 48; income 221
infancy xxxvii
Inquiring Systems 119
institutional decentralization 64–65
institutions 32
Integral Ecology: Uniting Multiple Perspectives on the Natural World xxvi
Integral Educational practice 11
integral methodological pluralism (IMP) 63, 83, 159, 165n33
Integral Political Economy (IPE) 48–61, 63, 66–67
integral post-metaphysics 83
Integral Psychology 138
integral realism 14, 20n3, 237
integral sociology 243–246
integral theory (IT) xxiii, xxxiii–xxxiv, xxxviii–xxxix, 29, 30–31, 108–109, 177–178; and change 157–158; and

critical realism (CR) 12, 14–16, 22n28, 151–163, 224–225, 235–238, 241–242; and diachronic emergent capacities developmentalism (DECD) 136–138; and dialectical critical realism (DCR) 125–127, 138–144; directionality in 83; emergence of 152; hermeneutic and ontological generosity 13; and higher education 177–178; metatheoretical coordinates 151–160; and reality 153–156, 238–239; *see also* CR-IT dialogue
integral thinking 18, 99, 108–109, 119, 120
intelligence quotient (IQ) 49
'inter-being' 22n19
interdisciplinarity 196n25
inter-inner connectivity 32
interior states 181
internal workplace 114
International Centre for Critical Realism xxi
International Commission on Stratigraphy (ICS) 21n13
international development: 'depth participation' in 74; faith-inspired 81; and Indigenous peoples 71–87; urgent issues **73**
internet 63
interpersonal process 112
interpersonal relations xxxii
interpretation 116–117
intuition 154
involution 34–36, 42–44
'inward arc' 42, 44, 225–227
IPE *see* Integral Political Economy
irrealism 165n20
IT *see* integral theory
I-Thou relations 187, 193

Jantti, Markus 65
Japan 36
Jenkins, Philip 82
Jevons, William Stanley xxv
jobs: low-paid 37; security 39; seeking 64; skills 217–218; training 211–212, 215; *see also* employment; income inequality; labour markets; underemployment; unemployment; wages
judgmental rationality 11, 195n14
judgment form 131–133, 142, 143, 145–146n11, 147n18, 175

kairos 21n7
Kant, Immanuel 98, 142
Katz, Lawrence 216, 217

Kegan, R. 107–108
Kelly, A.V. 171
Kelly, S.M. 9
Kennedy, John E. xxxi
King, P.M. 132
kinship 75–76, 85
Kitchener, K.S. 132
knowing xxxvi
knowledge: 'fire of' 7; 'pertinent' 185; philosophy of 178–180; quadrivium vision of 161; scientific 212; and social transformation xx; 'troubling' 186
koan xxxvii
Koestler, A. 177
Kyoto Protocol 35, 66

labour force 41
labour markets 64, 65, 211, 213–217, 226
labour rights 36
laissez-faire economy 57, 65
Lake Wobegon effect 38
laminated systems 129, 159–160, 165n37, 175
land 75, 85
Lane, Robert E. 36
language 12
languaging 75, 85, 184, 188
Laske, Otto 22n25
law 75–76, 86; holistic 75, 85
Lawson, T. 50, 60
Learning for Liberation 75, 83
learning process 119, 128, 181
Lee, F.S. 55
Left, the 138, 140, 142, 146n12
legitimacy 125
leisure time 36, 39
liberals 51–52, **53**, **54**, 57–62
Limits to Capital 145n7
linguistic fallacy 152
LLQ 156–157, 159–161
logical unspecifiability 184
logic fields 12
logos 7, 12
long-run outcomes 55–57, 62
Lost History of Christianity, The 82
love 184
Loveday, J.E. 176
low-skilled workers 57, 59, 62
LRQ 156–157, 159–162

Magdoff, Fred 40
Magdoff, Harry 40
Maheshvarananda, Dada 41
malaria xxiv–xxv

Malaysia 76, 89n45
Marcuse, H. 34, 120
Marginson, S. 188
marital satisfaction 36
marketization 220
Marshall, Paul 82, 87
Marx, Karl xxxv, 33, 233
Marxism 40, 57, 72, 232, 235, 242; *see also* neo-Marxism
Maslow, A. 42–44
mass advertising 212
mass consumption 212
mass culture 212
mass media 212
mathematics education research (MER) 18, 151–163
McChesney, Robert W. 40
McGray, R.G. 176
meaningfulness 36, 42, 43; *see also* universalism
meaning-making 3–5, 9, 10, 16, 125; social–emotional 107, 108, *109*
media 38, 63; decentralized modes of 146n17; mass 212; *see also* social media
meditative practices 181
megacorporations 37
MELD (Bhaskar's four moments of dialectic) 97–120, 163
membership–cognition 43
memes 147n18
mental growth 112–113, 118
mental health: crisis 36; development 44; systems 36
MER *see* mathematics education research (MER)
meritocracy 215–217
metacrisis 2–5, 9–10, 15–16, 17
metacritique 44, 46n14, 46n15, 235–236
meta-linguistic awareness 135
meta-matrix 169
meta-memes 9
metamodernism 15, 23n34
metanarratives 9
metaphysical pluralism 159
metaphysics 4, 142, 186
metapraxis 2, 3, 4
metapraxis, collaborative 10–17
metaReality xxi, xxxviii, 145n8, 180, 232, 237
meta-reflexivity 134–135
metatheorizing 4, 10, 15–17, 19, 20n6
metatheory 233–235; dialectical 22n25; as a geological force 9; integrative xxiii–xxiv, 1, 3–5, 19; lack of 123; politically

emancipatory 122–123; and theory 163n5, 234–235
Metatheory for the Twenty-First Century: Critical Realism and Integral Theory in Dialogue 1, 3, 16, 233
meteorological fundamentalism xxvii
methodological metatheorems 159–160
Miliband, Ralph xx
modernism 170–171, 189, 190, 197n37
modernity xxxiii, xxxviii, 66–68, 180, 212–213, 253
Molz, Markus 16
monism 159
monocapitalism 7
Monthly Review 40–41, 44
Moore, Jason 9–10, 21n16, 144n5
moral development 49
moral foundations 36, 37
morality 43
Morin, Edgar xxiii, 10, 18, 169, 172–174, 180, 182, 189
morphogenic society 251–254
movements-in-thought 106–107
multicapitalism 7
multiple causation model 45n10
Murray, Henry 100
mutual learning 11
mutual understanding 11, 146n17
mythos 19

Nagarjuna xxxiv
Nash equilibrium 58–60
National Bureau of Economic Research (NBER) 216
nationalism 140
natural necessity 71
natural resources 35, 56
nature: alethic resonance with 8; 'cheap' 21n16; historical 124; and society 124–125, 137, 144–145n6; stratification of xix, 194n7; wild xxvii–xxviii
needs 73, 84; false 212; Maslow's hierarchy of 44
negation xxxv, 127, 129
negativity 155, 158
neo-integrative worldviews 72
neoliberalism 37, 40, 67
neo-Marxism 172
neuroticism 36
neutrality 154
New Labour xx
new realism xx
Nicolescu, B. 179
Nicomachean Ethics 14

Nielsen, P. 61
Nietzsche, Friedrich xxxii–xxxiii
nihilism xxxii–xxxiii
No Boundary xxxvii
non-duality xxxiii, xxxiv, xxxv, xxxviii, 77, 237, 249
non-exclusion 165n33
non-identity 33, 45n5, 153–155, 158
normativity 181
Norrie, Alan 71, 131, 145n11
novel experiences 117
nuclear weapons 124; *see also* atomic bomb

Obama, Barack 38, 215, 221
Occupy Movement 35, 38–39
Occupy Wall Street 64
On the Logic of the Social Sciences 136
On the Possibility of Naturalism 136
'one-dimensional man' 34, 212
ontogeny 34
ontological generosity 13
ontological metatheorems 152–153
ontological monovalence 155, 171, 175
ontological pluralism 159–160
ontological realism 11, 151
ontological truth 21n11
ontology 82–83, 85, 99; and epistemology 99, 102, 119, 152, 154, 165n21, 237–238, 240–241
open systems xx, 153, 175, 179
Out and Out 90n68
outsourcing 56, 62, 216
'outward arc' 42
overconsumption 35
over-specialization 29; *see also* hyper-specialization; specialization
Owens, David xxv

panorama 178–179
panpsychism 146n13, 238
PARE *see* participatory action research and evaluation
Parenti, Christian 9–10
participatory action research and evaluation (PARE) 77–81, 84, 86
Passion of the Western Mind 177
Patten, T. 21n7
Paulson, Graham 78
peace 32–33
pedagogy 161, 187–188; of living mathematics education (PLME) 161
Pedersen, O. 64
Perls, F. 43
pensions 39

perception xviii–xix
perfect numbers 160
personal data 142
personal development 30, 32, 35, 42–44, 212, 220, 223
personality 130, 147n18
phase shift 6
philia 14–15
Philippines 76
Philosophy of MetaReality: Creativity, Love and Freedom xxi
Phobos 177
phronesis 7
Piaget, J. 33, 42, 99, 126, 127, 128, 130, 132–133
Piketty, Thomas 215, 216
Pinar, W.F. 184
Pinker, Steven 32–33
planetary flourishing 2
Plato xxi, xxxiv, xxxv, xxxvi, 157
Plato Etc: The Problems of Philosophy and Their Resolution xxi
pleroma 43
Polanyi, K. 36
Polanyi, M. 184
political domination 34
political–economic discourse 48–68; healthy versus unhealthy 52–55
political–economic extremism 63
political–economic types 51–53, 63; *see also* conservatives; liberals, radicals
political economy 17, 30; as the generative mechanism of crisis 36–41; key components 50–55
political protest 35, 40–41
positivism xviii, xxxv, 180, 235, 236, 244
Possibility of Naturalism, The xx
postmodern greens xxx, xxxi
postmodernism xxxviii, 23n34, 157, 162, 192
'post-truth' democracy 143
poverty 36, 39, 44
power$_2$ relations 33, 38, 42–44, 45n3, 46n14, 123, 135, 138–140, 143, 225, 227
practical, the 14
pragmatism 156, 159, 161–162
Prasad, Monica 65
praxis xxiii, xxxii, xxxix, 34, 126; duality of 31, 45n4; *see also* depth praxis
Precautionary Principle xxvi
presidential debates 49
pre/trans fallacy xxxvii
price adjustments 37

private sector, 50, **51**
productivity 56, 216
projections 63
Prometheus, the myth of 6–7
psychological development xxxiv, 128, 195n22
psychological growth 126
psychological healing 12
psychotic breakdown 43
public sector, 50, **51**
purposefulness 42

quadrant analysis 156–157, 160
Queensland 80–81
quintuple crisis 17, 29–44; and corporate capitalism 30; and political economy 36–41; as a totality 29–30, 32, 35

Race between Education and Technology, The 216
racism xxvii
radical constructivism 236–239
radical relativism 11
radicals 51–52, **53**, **54**, 57, 62
radionuclides 5–6
Rank, Otto 44n1
RAQAL model 246–248
rationality 173
rational modernists xxx
rational-scientific myths 19
Reagan, Ronald 37
Real, the xix
realism: analytical 245; dispositional 145n8, 146n15; integral 14, 20n3, 237; 'new' xx; ontological 11, 151; and radical constructivism 239; transcendental 45n10, 164n7, 175, 237; *see also* critical realism (CR); dialectical critical realism (DCR)
Realist Theory of Science, A xx
reality xviii–xix, 159, 170; derealization of 171; evolutionary model of 175; and integral theory 153–156, 238–239; as an open system 153; partialization of 29, 44n1
Reclaiming Reality xx
reductionism 45n2, **54**, 115, 164n8, 170; biological 43; modernist 177; *see also* 'flatland'
reductive human capital theory (RHCT) 140–141, 143, 171
referential detachment 175, 195n12
reflexivity 83; epistemic 12, 14; forms of 135
relativism 156, 180; epistemic 11, 16; radical 11

religion 72
Renert, M.E. 161
renewable energy 65
research xxiv
resilience 82
retraining 56, 64–65
retroduction 106, 116, 176
RHCT *see* reductive human capital theory
Richardson, Don 81
Riesman D. 44
Right, the 138, 140, 141, 146n12
risk management xxvi
rocks xxxv
Rogers, C. 3
Root, H. 66
Ross, Andrew xxviii
Rousseau, J-J. xxxvi
rules xxx
Rutzou, Timothy 82, 87, 163, 224

Schmachtenberger, Daniel 7
Schoenfeld, A. H. 163n5
schooling paradigm 171
schools 140, 211, 218–221
Schwartz, Michael 241
Schweickart, David 41
science: credibility of xxviii; and critical realism 175; desocialization of 171; modern xxxii
Scientific Method xix
Scott, D. 176, 195n17
secularism 81, 252
secularization 36, 40
self, the 32; 'one dimensional' 43; socio-cultural 'normality' 43; Stratified Model of 134
self-actualization xxxv, 33, 43, 67, 211, 212
self-awareness 44, 45n12, 134, 212
self-consciousness 34, 133, 134, 225–226
self-efficacy 41
self-emancipation 71
self-enlightenment 45n12
self-esteem 67, 78
self-identity 181
self-monitoring 135
self-radicalization 71
self-reflection 135
self-reflexivity 9, 180
self-understanding 6, 8, 10, 125, 212
Sennett, Richard 36
sensemaking 3–5, 9, 10, 11, 15–16; cognitive 108, *109*; meta-level 16
SEPM *see* synchronic emergent power materialism
'seriousness' 14
Seven Complex Lessons in Education for the Future 173
Sex, Ecology, Spirituality xxxiv, 137, 177
shadow projections 63
Shipway, B. 176
short-run outcomes 55–57, 62
Shulman, Lee 161
Silent Spring xxvi
Skocpol, Theda 38
social bonds xxx
social change xx, xxi, 114, 165n20, 176, 242, 252
social conflict xxxv
social conscience logistics 76, 77, 84, 86, 87
social consciousness 34, 212
social constructivism 240–241
social efficiency 171
social emancipation 182, 232
social ethics 186
social indoctrination 212
social innovation 15, 23n33
social integration 223
social interaction xxx, 32
socialism xxxv
social justice 71, 122
Social Justice and Educational Measurement 211
social media 142, 146n17
'social messes' 170
social networks 63; *see also* social media
social oppression 34
social organization xxxii
social pathology 63
social practice 31, 97–120, 254
social psychology 18
social structures 32, 67
social transformation 18, 38, 170
social welfare 49
social world 22n18, 242–243
society: constitution of 241–243; eudaimonistic 2, 3, 20n4, 66, 122, 132; morphogenic 251–254; and nature 137, 124–125, 144–145n6
socio-cultural transformations 74–75
socio-political uprising 35
Soetaert, E.D. 176
South Korea 36
'spatial fix' 145n7
specialization xxiv, 173; *see also* hyper-specialization; over-specialization
'spectre of uselessness 36
Spectrum of Consciousness 137

spirit beings 18, 72, 77, **79**, 86; *see also* Spirits
Spirits 72–81; *see also* spirit beings
spiritual awareness 34, 38
spiritual experiences xxi
spiritual dimension 19
spiritual emancipation 182
spiritual enlightenment 34
spirituality 21n10, 175, 249–250; and higher education 180; Indigenous 72, 74–87; post-secular xxxiii, 81
standardized testing 211
state subsidies 65
Stein, Zachary 2, 7–9, 14, 171, 211, 224
strategic critical inquiry 78–80, 84
student loans 211, 214, 215, 218, 222–224
suicide 30, 36
superexploitation 40
sustainability xxv, 61–62, 67, 74
sustainable development 52
Sweezy, Paul 40
'symbiosophy' 189
synchronic emergent power materialism (SEPM) 126, 136–137
systems: complex 172, 174; educational 125–126, 133, 141, 145n10, 176, 192, 209, 212; laminated 129, 159–160, 165n37, 175; open versus closed xix–xx, 153, 175; *see also* system stability; systems thinking index
system stability **114–115**, 116
systems thinking index 107

Tarnas, R. 177
task process 112
taxes 39; carbon 56–58, 65; inadequate 56; on natural resources 56–58; progressive 57–59
teacherly authority 138–144; crisis of 142; hijacking of 142, 146n17, 147n18
teachers 186–187
teaching 187
Tea Party movement 64
Tebtebba 76
'technicizability' 184
technological change 34
telos xxxv, 33, 235
terrorism 30, 35, 42, 143
Thailand 76
Thanatos 177
Thatcher, Margaret 37
theism 72
thinking: constructive 107; critical 107; Indigenous 22n20; integral 18, 99, 108–109, 119, 120; *see also* dialectical thinking
TINA (there is no alternative) 37
TMSA *see* transformation model of social activity
totalitarianism 34
totality 158–159; denegation of 155–157; quintuple crisis as 29–30, 32, 35
Towards an Aboriginal Theology 78
traditional conservatives xxx, xxxi
tragic events 21n7
transcendental argumentation 154, 164n13
transcendental idealism 156
transcendental realism 45n10, 164n7, 175, 237
transdisciplinarity 29, 173, 174, 196n26; and higher education 179–180
transformational thinkers 19
transformation model of social activity (TMSA) 31, 45n5
transformative agency 157–159, 180
transformative learning 170
transpersonal psychology 257n25
trickle down effects 39
Triple Crises 48–49, 51; *see also* crisis; global crises
triumphalism 154, 165n20
Trump, Donald 142, 218, 219
trust 142
truth xxxv, 131, 134, 175; alethic 21n11, 175, 194n13; ontological 21n11; right to 143
Tyndall Centre for Climate Change Research xxvi

UDR movement 99, 102, 103, 117, 117
ULQ 156–157, 159–161
uncertainty 173–174
underemployment 214–215, 221–222
unemployment 36, 65, 213, 215–216, 222
unintended consequences xxiv–xxvi
unions 56, 64
United Nations: GEO-4 report 35; Intergovernmental Panel on Climate Change 35
universalism 43, 43
universalizability 131, 134
universities 222
upbringing 63
Up from Eden: A Transpersonal View of Evolution xxxvii
upward mobility 65
uroboros 43
URQ 156–156, 159–162

Index

values xxix, 49, 210
vantage point 60
violence 36
Visch De, J. 114
vocational schools 65
Voltaire xxxii
Vygotsky, L. 42

wages 39, 56–59, 215–218, 221
Warlpiri people 78
wars 30, 35, 42
Washington Consensus 37, 40, 67
water 6
wealth distribution 216
welfare benefits 64
well-being xxiv, xxxiv; blocks to development of 33; and spirit beings 77, 83
Westoby, Peter 74
Wheelahan, L. 176
Whitehead, A.N. xxi, xxxiv, 137
Why We Disagree about Climate Change xxvi
'wicked' problems xxiii, xxvi, xxxii–xxxiii, 170
Wilber, Ken xxiii, xxxiv–xxxv, xxxvii–xxxviii, 29–30, 48, 125–126, 145n8, 177–178, 224–226, 231–232, 237–241, 243–245, 248–251; on the 'compound individual' 137; on consciousness 146n13, 225–226; on crises of the biosphere 143; epistemic structures in the work of 107–113; on 'flatland' 72, 87n4, 155, 170, 177; on human development 42–44, 66, 128–129, 131, 136, 225; on human ontogeny 34; on involution 34; on 'metaphysical dogmatisms' 83; on ontology/epistemology 154; phases of work 195n21; on social practices 254; on *telos* 33
Wildavsky, Aaron xxix
wisdom 184, 212
Wladawsky-Berger, I. 73
Wolff, Rick 39, 41
Wordsworth, William xxxvi
worker productivity 39
working hours 39
work satisfaction 36
world soul 186
worldviews xxix, 9, 240; de-totalized 123; four perspectives of the AQAL model 153; mythic 83; neo-integrative 72, 85; and social transformation 170
worship 36

Yong, A. 77
Yunkaporta, Tyson 22n20

Zen xxxviii